Human Rights in the Media

This collection sets about untangling some of the knotty issues in the underexplored relationship between human rights and the media. We investigate how complex debates in political, judicial, academic and public life on the role and value of human rights are represented in the media, particularly, in print journalism. To focus the discussion, we concentrate on media representation of the controversial proposals in the United Kingdom to repeal the Human Rights Act 1998 and to replace it with a British Bill of Rights. The collection is underpinned by the observation that views on human rights and on the proposals to repeal and replace are polarised. On the one hand, human rights are presented as threatening and, therefore, utterly denigrated; on the other hand, human rights are idolised, and, therefore, uncritically celebrated. This is the 'fear and fetish' in our title. The media plays a decisive role in constructing this polarity through its representation of political and ideological viewpoints. In order to get to grips with the fear, the fetish and this complex interrelationship, the collection tackles key contemporary themes, amongst them: the proposed British Bill of Rights, Brexit, prisoner-voting, the demonisation of immigrants, press freedom, tabloid misreporting, trial by media and Magna Carta. The collection explores media representation, investigates media polarity and critiques the media's role.

Michelle Farrell is Senior Lecturer in Law at the University of Liverpool.

Eleanor Drywood is Senior Lecturer in Law at the University of Liverpool.

Edel Hughes is Senior Lecturer in Law at Middlesex University.

Routledge Research in Human Rights Law

Available titles in this series include:

Socio-Economic Rights in Emerging Free Markets
Comparative Insights from India and China
Surya Deva

Comparative Executive Clemency
The Prerogative of Mercy in the Commonwealth
Andrew Novak

Social and Economic Rights in Theory and Practice
A Critical Assessment
Helena Alviar Garcia, Karl Klare and Lucy A. Williams

Challenging Territoriality in Human Rights Law
Building Blocks for a Plural and Diverse Duty-Bearer Regime
Wouter Vandenhole

Care, Migration and Human Rights
Law and Practice
Siobhán Mullally

China's Human Rights Lawyers
Advocacy and Resistance
Eva Pils

Indigenous Peoples, Title to Territory, Rights and Resources
The Transformative Role of Free Prior and Informed Consent
Cathal M. Doyle

For more information about this series, please visit: www.routledge.com/Routledge-Research-in-Human-Rights-Law/book-series/HUMRIGHTSLAW

Human Rights in the Media

Fear and Fetish

Edited by Michelle Farrell, Eleanor Drywood and Edel Hughes

LONDON AND NEW YORK

First published 2019
by Routledge

2 Park Square, Milton Park, Abingdon, Oxfordshire OX14 4RN
52 Vanderbilt Avenue, New York, NY 10017

Routledge is an imprint of the Taylor & Francis Group, an informa business

First issued in paperback 2020

British Library Cataloguing-in-Publication Data
A catalogue record for this book is available from the British Library

Library of Congress Cataloging-in-Publication Data
Names: Farrell, Michelle, 1981– editor. | Drywood, Eleanor, editor. | Hughes, Edel, editor.
Title: Human rights in the media : fear and fetish / edited by Michelle Farrell, Eleanor Drywood, and Edel Hughes.
Description: Abingdon, Oxon [UK] ; New York, NY : Routledge, 2019. | Series: Routledge research in human rights law | Includes index.
Identifiers: LCCN 2018037794 | ISBN 9781138645813 (hbk)
Subjects: LCSH: Human rights—Press coverage—Great Britain. | Human rights—Great Britain. | Human rights in mass media. | European Court of Human Rights—Press coverage. | European Union—Great Britain. | Great Britain. Human Rights Act 1998.
Classification: LCC KD4080 .H8625 2019 | DDC 070.4/4934241085—dc23
LC record available at https://lccn.loc.gov/2018037794

ISBN: 978-1-138-64581-3 (hbk)
ISBN: 978-0-367-66252-3 (pbk)

Typeset in Galliard
by Apex CoVantage, LLC

Contents

Acknowledgements

This edited collection has its roots in a one-day seminar, 'Human Rights in the UK Media: Representation and Reality', held in September 2014 at the University of Liverpool. We would like to thank the Modern Law Review for funding the event. We are particularly grateful to the MLR as, at the time, they were supporting an unconventional and interdisciplinary idea. The seminar brought together a very fine set of papers and an engaged audience. We would like to thank all those who participated in the initial event. We are grateful also to the School of Law and Social Justice, University of Liverpool for financially supporting editorial and research assistance through its student intern scheme.

It was obvious to us that the relationship between human rights and the media was underexplored and so we set about the daunting task of finding a home for our work. Routledge greeted our proposal with enthusiasm. We are grateful to the reviewers for their useful comments and to Routledge for a smooth publishing process. In particular, we would like to thank Chloe James and Olivia Manley for their prompt and patient insight, understanding and professionalism.

Edited collections can be a real challenge. It is an immensely collaborative endeavour. We would like to pay particular tribute to our contributors. All have been incredibly patient, many have had to work under immense pressure and, as with any task of this size, we have all had to get on with things no matter what life throws at us. In the course of reaching the final draft of this collection, there have been births and deaths, promotions, moves, marriages and illnesses, all of the usual stuff. It would have been an even bigger challenge for us to complete this collection without the help of our amazing families, friends and colleagues. We would like to give special thanks to Stephanie Reynolds, Yvonne McDermott, Patrick Butchard, Robert Knox and Thomas Beaumont.

Our final acknowledgement is perhaps better described as a non-acknowledgement. On p.33 of this volume, we have reproduced the frontpage of *The Sun* newspaper from 27 May 2015, which naturally required that we, as editors, secured, and paid for, the appropriate licence (from News Syndication who administer licensing for *The Sun*). This presented us with a difficult dilemma. A city-wide boycott of *The Sun* newspaper has existed in Liverpool since its infamous 'The Truth' headline (19 April 1989) in the days following the Hillsborough disaster. This book is inextricably linked to the city of Liverpool, through its inceptive conference, two of its three editors and many of its contributors. In Liverpool, we do not buy The S*n, we do not support it financially, something that is so embedded into the city's conscience and identity that it is an absolute stance. We, therefore, felt uncomfortable deviating from this through a payment to News Syndication, even for the most worthwhile of causes (David Mead's forensic critique of a frontpage). For this reason, we approached News Syndication with a suggestion: that they accept *in lieu* of payment for the copyright a donation to a mutually agreeable charity. We received a fast and short reply: that they would only grant permission to use the image according to their standard terms, the payment of a £75+VAT fee. We are extremely grateful to our editors at Routledge for their sympathetic approach to the issue and for stepping in and paying the fee on our behalf (an imperfect, but liveable with, compromise), and to David Mead for his patience and understanding whilst we scratched our heads to find a solution. To *The Sun* (and News Syndication): please do better to heal the wounds of the city of Liverpool. To the 96: YNWA.

Contributors

Ekaterina Balabanova is Senior Lecturer in Political Communication at the University of Liverpool.

Eleanor Drywood is Senior Lecturer in Law at the University of Liverpool.

Michelle Farrell is Senior Lecturer in Law at the University of Liverpool.

Lieve Gies is Senior Lecturer in Media and Communication Studies, University of Leicester.

Michael Gordon is Professor of Constitutional Law at the University of Liverpool.

Harriet Gray is Lecturer in Law at the University of Liverpool.

Edel Hughes is Senior Lecturer in Law at Middlesex University.

Yvonne McDermott is Associate Professor in Legal Studies at Swansea University.

David Mead is Professor of UK Human Rights Law at the University of East Anglia.

Colin Murray is Reader in Law, Newcastle University.

Colm O'Cinnéide is Professor of Human Rights Law at University College London.

Stephanie Reynolds is Senior Lecturer in Law at the University of Liverpool.

Jacob Rowbottom is Associate Professor of Law at the University of Oxford.

Introduction

Eleanor Drywood, Michelle Farrell, Edel Hughes

Human rights law has a significant impact today, globally, and at the domestic level, on law, politics and life. Despite its extensive institutionalisation and its universal, transnational and domestic acceptance and presence, the value of human rights law is highly contested in politics and in practice. In academic scholarship, human rights law has long been – and continues to be – the subject of intense critical scrutiny. The origins and value of human rights law are extensively debated.[1]

The role of the media in the discussion of human rights law, in the critique of rights and in both the celebration and denigration of human rights law has, however, been largely neglected in scholarship.[2] Given the impact of human rights law

1 There is far too much contemporary critical scholarship on international human rights law to be exhaustive here. C Douzinas and C Gearty, *The Cambridge Companion to Human Rights Law* (Cambridge University Press, 2012) is a good place to start. That collection deals with contemporary challenges to human rights law and critical perspectives on human rights law. Samuel Moyn provides a rich discussion of the problems with trying to account both for a history of human rights and for the value of human rights. See S Moyn, *Not Enough: Human Rights in an Unequal World* (Harvard University Press, 2018); S Moyn, *The Uses of History* (Verso, 2014), S Moyn, *The Last Utopia: Human Rights in History* (The Belknapp Press of Harvard University Press, 2010). See also, S Marks, 'Four Human Rights Myths' in D Kinley, W Sadurski, K Walton (eds) *Human Rights: Old Problems, New Possibilities* (Edward Elgar Publishing, 2013). Marks examines the myth-busting work of a number of authors who challenge the intellectual framework of human rights.

2 This collection builds on a small but burgeoning scholarship on the media and human rights. Our collection builds particularly on the pioneering work of Ekaterina Balabanova, Lieve Gies, Susan Marks, David Mead and Eric Heinze. See E Balabanova, *The Media and Human Rights: The Cosmopolitan Promise* (Routledge, 2015); L Gies, *Mediating Human Rights: Media, Culture and Human Rights Law* (Routledge, 2015); D Mead, 'You couldn't make it up: Some narratives of the media's coverage of human rights' in K S Ziegler, E Wicks and H Loveday, *The UK and European Human Rights: A Strained Relationship?* (Hart, 2015). On the backlash against human rights by the government and the media, see S Marks, 'Backlash: the undeclared war against human rights' (2014) 4 European Human Rights Law Review 1361. On the media and public consciousness in relation to human rights, see E Heinze, 'The reality and hyper-reality of human rights: Public consciousness and the mass media' in R Dickinson et al., *Examining Critical Perspectives on Human Law* (Cambridge University Press, 2012).

and the ever-increasing visibility of human rights legal language in the media, it is crucial that we deepen our understanding of the links amongst the law of human rights, the media representation of human rights and the public perception of rights. It is crucial for an obvious reason: the media has an impact on constructing popular debate and it influences public opinion.

In the United Kingdom, the 1998 Human Rights Act and the European regional human rights system, comprising the European Convention on Human Rights and Fundamental Freedoms 1950 and the European Court of Human Rights, have been subject to intense and fractious political, legal and popular debate. The controversy over human rights in the UK stems largely from its relationship with the European Court. As the contributions in this collection will discuss, the Court in Strasbourg is accused of interfering with UK law and with the sovereignty of parliament due to human rights 'mission creep', judicial overreach and interference and influence on multiple issues in the areas of, amongst others, criminal justice, counter-terrorism and immigration. There has always been a certain amount of disquiet in the political institutions about the UK's involvement with this European human rights system. The enactment of the Human Rights Act in 1998, which gave further effect to the European Convention in UK law, really stoked the fire. The Conservative government has proposed to repeal the Human Rights Act and to replace it with a British Bill of Rights. These proposals are at the heart of the controversy. Withdrawal from the European human rights system has also been mooted, though without serious policy consideration, at least at the time of writing. Of course, the UK's decision to withdraw from the European Union has affected human rights-related plans. That said, the UK's relationship with the European Court and the overriding issue of UK sovereignty continue to capture the political and public mind-sets.

Views on human rights and on the proposals to repeal and replace are polarised. On the one hand, human rights are utterly denigrated; on the other hand, human rights are uncritically celebrated. The media plays a decisive role in constructing this polarity through its representation of political and ideological viewpoints and its, arguably, significant influence on public perception of rights. This is the 'fear and fetish' of our title.

This collection sets about untangling some of the knotty issues in the relationship between human rights and the media. We explore the interrelationships amongst the representation of rights in the media (particularly, in print journalism), public opinion on rights, and human rights law and practice. Our discussion is filtered through the media representation of controversial debates around the repeal of the Human Rights Act 1998 and the possible withdrawal from the European human rights system. The chapters in this collection aim to *explore media representation* of human rights law and issues. The collection is premised on the – of course, contestable – contention that ideological polarity exists in the media on the question of human rights. We try, therefore, to *understand this media polarity.* In addition, the collection is geared towards provoking discussion and debate on the ways in which the media reflects or neglects ongoing and significant academic and legal debates about the salience and value of human rights. As such, we *critique the media's role.*

This is certainly an interesting time to write about the media. In the United States, the current President, Donald Trump, responds to any media reportage he does not like by branding it 'fake news'. In the United Kingdom, the decision to withdraw from the European Union has led to chilling media attacks on the institutions of government: the Daily Mail's 'Enemies of the People' headline was greeted with horror.[3] It is unsettlingly obvious how much we need the media. It is also, sometimes, alarmingly obvious how influential the media is. For that reason, it deserves the kind of attention paid in this collection We want to pry open a space to interrogate the relationship between the media and human rights. We do not, however, want to fall into the trap of either demonising, or being overly protective, of the media. We have not aimed either to achieve some kind of artificial balance on our portrayal and examination of the media in relation to human rights law. Nor have we aimed at, or succeeded in, achieving any form of balance in our discussion of the role and the value of human rights law. The objective of this collection is to understand, explore and critique, whatever the implications may be for balance.

In the 'Headlines', the contributors set the scene, contextualise debates around the media and human rights and remind us of the UK's position within Europe, its politics and its legal frameworks. David Mead's opening contribution points to the skewed and partial approach often taken by the mainstream media to the reporting of human rights. He investigates how misreporting, and the misconception and misconstruction of reality, offer us 'slanted interpretations and an unbalanced diet'. In support of these criticisms, he deploys communications theory and content analysis to take us beyond what he calls a 'juriscentric' critique of human rights reporting in the media. Stephanie Reynolds tackles the unenviable task of making sense of the media's coverage of, and role in, 'Brexit' (or 'the UK's withdrawal from the European Union' to those who favour dry legal language over snazzy portmanteaux). Her careful and forensic analysis of the reporting of both pro-remain and pro-leave publications around the referendum leads her to conclude that a polarising 'them and us' narrative has stifled any meaningful scrutiny of either the benefits of EU membership, or indeed the pitfalls of its democratic deficiencies, in the UK media. This, she argues, is the result of a long-standing hostility in the media towards UK–EU relations and has profound implications, not only for the scrutiny of the Brexit process, but also for future relations with the entirely separate European Convention. Lieve Gies asks us to cast our eyes towards Europe, reflecting upon how UK human rights scepticism is viewed abroad. She argues that, whilst attempts to reform the European human rights system have been seen as a distinctly British preoccupation in certain quarters of the European press, there is a notable absence of robust defence of the Convention. She argues that there is a striking failure in the European press to engage fully with the strength of anti-human rights feeling in the UK, and the attendant threat to cosmopolitan rights ideals.

In the 'Features' section, critiques of the relationship between the media and human rights are developed in the context of a series of issues relevant to the

3 J Slack, 'Enemies of the People' *Daily Mail* (4 November 2016).

current debates (our selection of issues is, in no way, exhaustive): prisoner voting rights, immigration and the right to a fair trial. Colin Murray's contribution addresses the issue which has perhaps most tested the relationship between the UK state and Europe's human rights frameworks, that of prisoner voting. He asks us to situate newspaper campaigns for tougher sanctions within the criminal justice system – and their accompanying critique of the European Convention on Human Rights – within the wider context of the relationship between the UK media, politicians and think tanks. This, he argues, is essential to understanding how *Hirst,* a judgment which might have been relatively uncontroversial, has been transformed into a 'monstrous' example of judicial overreach in popular rhetoric. Eleanor Drywood and Harriet Gray consider treatment of immigrants in the UK press, arguing that, somewhat counter-intuitively, a human rights angle to stories actually exacerbates media demonisation of this group. They support this argument by pointing to the way in which the role of human rights claims in UK immigration law actually structurally favours negative reporting. They go on to argue that there is a wider failing of human rights to imbed at a grassroots level, which sheds further light on the hostility of the UK press towards immigrants. Yvonne McDermott offers a rigorous overview of reporting around cases that concern a right to fair trial in criminal law under the European Convention. She observes that press reaction to these cases varies considerably, concluding that the opportunity to cast criminal defendants as villains, thus invoking accusations that the ECHR is a villains' charter, best explains where the press chooses to target its attention. She notes the absence of meaningful engagement with more profound questions about criminal procedure, or, indeed deficiencies in the Strasbourg court's own fairness towards applicants.

The 'In-depth' contributions shift our focus to profound questions around the role of the media in a democratic society. Ekaterina Balabanova draws our attention to media–state relations in the context of human rights, asking us to consider whether this relationship is one of watchdog or lapdog. She uses theories developed within the field of media studies to help us unpack questions of balance, focus, selection and salience in human rights reporting. Her chapter ends with a reminder that internet-based communications are changing the face of all news reporting, human rights included. Jake Rowbottom's chapter looks at press freedom, itself a human right, and one that, unsurprisingly, newspapers have been less critical of. He highlights the double standards of a press that is, on the one hand, constantly critical of 'foreign', activist judges, and, on the other, keen to embrace legal protection of press freedom.

The aim of the 'Op-Eds' is to provoke: they are critical, they are sceptical and they challenge, not only the media's representation of human rights, but also the very foundation of these rights. Colm O'Cinnéide's chapter tackles the controversial nature of UK human rights law head on. Exploiting the Brexit-induced hiatus in the long running debates over repealing or retaining the Human Rights Act, the chapter assesses the current state of play. O'Cinnéide provides a critique of the arguments in favour of retaining the status quo and concludes that its proponents should focus on providing answers that persuade the public of the merits of our current arrangements. Emphasising the authority and the special status of human rights law is insufficient. Michael Gordon provides a democratic rights sceptical take on the current debates. He evaluates how media representation of legal human rights is framed in what, he argues, are binary terms; the 'good' press embracing the principles underpinning human rights law and the 'bad' press distorting and rejecting rights claims. According to Gordon, both the 'good' and 'bad' press instrumentalise human rights claims – unsurprisingly, as rights are an instrumental tool – for different ends and, as a consequence, little space is left for public debate to be influenced by democratic scepticism about human rights law. Gordon argues, ultimately, in favour of embracing democratic rights scepticism as a means of thinking through the limits, problems and shortfalls of human rights law. In the final chapter, Michelle Farrell and Edel Hughes argue that hostility towards the Human Rights Act is underpinned by its perceived foreignness, due to it giving further effect to the European Convention. They examine how the political establishment has invoked Magna Carta and Britain's tradition of rights, paradoxically, to argue for repeal. But British rights are an 'invented tradition', one that has been embraced by the media. This is particularly evidenced in the run up to the 2015 celebrations of the 800th anniversary of Magna Carta. The disdain for the Human Rights Act but, equally, the fetishisation of that Act, filtered through an invented tradition, crowds out the space for critical engagement with history and with rights.

Not all readers will agree with the questions asked of the human rights framework – its foundations, its philosophy, its evangelism, even – but that is the purpose of an Op-Ed: to make us think, reflect and question our own positions. So, perhaps it is appropriate to end by returning to the final line of Billy Bragg's *It Says Here*, the inspiration behind the title of David Mead's opening chapter: 'Just remember there are two sides to every story'. The chapters brought together in this collection demonstrate that when we scrutinise, critique and nuance, there are *many more* than two sides to this story.

Part I

Headlines

1 'They offer you a feature on stockings and suspenders next to a call for stiffer penalties for sex offenders'

Do we learn more about the media than about human rights from tabloid coverage of human rights stories?

David Mead

Introduction

The Billy Bragg song 'It Says Here' is a coruscating attack on the power of the tabloids to shape popular opinion:

> If this does not reflect your view you should understand
> That those who own the papers also own this land
> And they'd rather you believe
> In Coronation Street capers
> In the war of circulation, it sells newspapers
> Could it be an infringement
> Of the freedom of the press
> To print pictures of women in states of undress?[1]

The song also contains the lyrics that feature in the title to this chapter, lyrics that highlight the Janus-like approach of many media outlets: titillation vying with indignation. We can see the same moral flexibility when it comes to questions of human rights. We see outrage at who the claimants are, or at what they are claiming – or at both – at the same time as, without a hint of irony, claims to the rights of free speech when editorial judgement or practice is called into question. It is quite a feat of ambidexterity for a newspaper just a few days after lauding the Prime Minister for pledging to repeal the Human Rights Act to rely on it as the basis for protecting its own journalists from intrusive surveillance, as *The Sun* did

1 Taken from 'Brewing Up With Billy Bragg' (Go! Discs, 1984).

after the so-called Plebgate saga.[2] Similarly, *The Daily Mail* opposed recovery of after-the-event insurance premiums as part of a libel award by setting up Article 10 as its defence.[3] That ambivalence is, however, not the subject of this piece. Instead, it explores the skewed and partial approach taken by (elements of) the mainstream print media to the reporting of human rights cases and issues.

Much has been written about the Human Rights Act (HRA) since it came into force in October 2000. Largely this has focussed either on the wording of certain key sections or on the scope of human rights protection in the UK, both creating what I have typified as a juriscentric approach to the topic.[4] There has been only very limited engagement with issues outside this paradigm. Certainly, there has been little account of the ability newspapers have – often under the guise of simple reportage – to steer and to direct, and to offer us slanted interpretations and an unbalanced diet.[5] This piece adds to that literature by discussing the relationship between the media – specifically the stories and cases it reports, or omits – and human rights protection, locating that analysis within a media and communications framework.

I ought to make a couple of points clear at the outset. While this chapter draws in parts on some empirical research that I have conducted, it is for the most part illustrative, designed to offer something a little more than anecdotal. By no means is it conclusive, generalised or (save in one instance, the content analysis on p.25) systematic. Secondly, the research into how human rights stories are actually reported has largely been done using on-line searches. I have looked at printed editions only rarely, on those few occasions where I had the foresight to purchase a copy. That said, the market for consuming news in hard copy is

2 LM Eleftheriou-Smith, 'Last week The Sun wanted to abolish the Human Rights Act, this week they want to use it to protect their journalists' *The Independent* (6 October 2014), available online at: www.independent.co.uk/news/uk/crime/last-week-the-sun-wanted-to-abolish-the-human-rights-act-this-week-they-want-to-use-it-to-protect-9778190.html

3 'Daily Mail loses Human Rights Act challenge to CFA success fees and insurance premiums' (Inforrm's blog, 5 February 2016) available online at: www.inforrm.wordpress.com/2016/02/05/news-daily-mail-loses-human-rights-act-challenge-to-cfa-success-fees-and-insurance-premiums/more generally, see www.inforrm.wordpress.com/2015/06/07/daily-mail-has-attacked-the-human-rights-act-whilst-also-seeking-to-shelter-behind-it-brian-cathcart/

4 D Mead, 'Outcomes Aren't All: Defending Process-Based Review of Public Authority Decisions under the Human Rights Act' [2012] PL 61, 63.

5 Outside the contributions in this book, examples would include D Mead, ''You Couldn't Make it Up': Some Narratives of the Media's Coverage of Human Rights' in K Ziegler, E Wicks and L Hodson, *The UK and European Human Rights: A Strained Relationship?* (Hart Publishing, 2015); L Gies, 'Human Rights, the British Press and the Deserving Claimant' in K Ziegler *et al.*, *The UK and European Human Rights*; L Gies, *Mediating Human Rights: Media, Culture and Human Rights Law* (Routledge, 2014); L Gies, 'A Villains' Charter?: The Press and The Human Rights' (2011) 7 *Crime, Media, Culture* 1; and L Gies, 'The Hard Sell: Promoting Human Rights' (2011) 24 *Int J for the Semiotics of Law* 405. More widely, and as just one example, Simon Cottle has written extensively on international humanitarian law and the duty to protect.

declining. Circulation has broadly halved in the past decade.[6] By contrast, the figures for digital viewing now dwarf those for print – in some cases many times over. The most recent daily unique browser numbers for the *Mail* on-line and *Guardian* are 14m and 8m respectively.[7] Be that as it may, this chapter does not consider any story in its original 'as printed' format, ignoring where in the paper the story features, and with what prominence.[8] It is that hypocritical journalistic juxtaposition of stories – offering 'a feature on stockings and suspenders next to a call for stiffer penalties for sex offenders' – that Billy Bragg alludes to in the lyrics that form the title to this chapter. Finally, my on-line searches have covered only traditional written news media – national newspapers – and not Buzzfeed, for example, nor the BBC news on-line.

The chapter is in three parts. The first two draw on some earlier work of mine, updating and expanding it. In short, these explain the ways in which human rights stories and cases are misportrayed and analyse the various techniques of distortion. The third part locates that discussion within a communications theory framework. It offers a content analysis of one small part of what is regular newspaper coverage – the (non) deportation of foreign criminals – and then considers the semiotics of one single media text, a photo from *The Sun*.

The false impression created by the media coverage would matter much less were the HRA itself on a more secure footing, but it seems it is not. We should surely be dismayed if the arguments for repeal or withdrawal from the Strasbourg scheme are grounded on falsity? This piece argues that they are. After many, many false starts, we are facing yet again a clamour for change. The Queen's Speech in May 2016 pledged to bring forward proposals for a British Bill of Rights. The main benefits would be to 'continue protect[ing] fundamental human rights while also better protect[ing] against abuse of the system and misuse of human rights laws, and restor[ing] common sense to their application'.[9] What is interesting, for this chapter, is, however, not the proposal – a repeat from 2015 – but its location. The pledge can be found in the section of the Speech entitled

6 *The Guardian* has dropped from 337,000 in the first six months of 2006 to 164,000 at the end of 2015; *The Daily Mail* from 2.228m to 1.498m over the same period, *The Telegraph* 858,000 to 464,000, *The Sun* from 3m to 1.727m and *The Times* from 634,00 to 378,00. All data can be accessed at www.nrs.co.uk/nrs-print/readership-and-circulation-trends/trend-charts/

7 MailOnline 13,954,521 (-0.61%) theguardian.com 8,923,129 (-4.01%), Mirror Group Nationals 4,643,612 (1.72%), *Telegraph* 4,342,570 (5.21%), *The Independent* 3,048,377 (-7.19%), *The Sun* 2,367,137 (0.97%), ABC data reported in *The Guardian* on-line J Jackson, 'Independent's digital audience drops to below level it was before paper closed' *The Guardian* (16 June 2016) available online at: www.theguardian.com/media/2016/jun/16/independents-digital-audience-drops-to-below-level-it-was-before-paper-closed

8 A fuller study of digital reporting could include analysis of algorithmic links, from story A to stories B C and D, and of 'below the line' comments – to assess readers' understandings: see further n 62 below.

9 Cabinet Office, 'Background Briefing Notes' (18 May 2016) available online at: www.gov.uk/government/publications/queens-speech-2016-background-briefing-notes

'Strengthening our National Security'. In the Conservative Party's 2015 election manifesto, the pledge appeared twice: the first in a section on 'Fighting Crime and Standing up for Victims'; the second can be found in 'Real Change in our Relationship with the European Union'.[10] This is highly instructive. Its location is reflexive – a function of the wider context – yet also creating, and reinforcing, a particular narrative of the scope of the HRA, and the beneficiaries of its protection, depicting it as a 'charter for chancers'.[11] That symbiotic relationship is the focus of this chapter.

Misrepresenting the truth

The essence of this general complaint is that the portrayal of human rights cases (and judgments) and more broadly of human rights issues suffers from bias, or lack of objectivity. It is no longer the simple relaying of event A to reader C through the words of journalist B. As Dennis McQuail puts it, 'the ruling norms of most western media call for a certain practice or neutral informative reporting of events, and it is against this positive expectation that much news has been found deficient'.[12] McQuail offers three criteria by which we might assess claims that (in our case) newspapers either are or are not biased or objective. The first is factuality – how far does an article provide correct answers to who, what, where, when and why questions? This is not the focus of what follows. The second is accuracy – does it conform to independent records? In short, is the reporting false? On that point, we are still no nearer to a situation whereby newspapers are able properly to distinguish between the EU and the ECHR. In an article about the possible 'quitting' of the human rights court, *The Daily Mail* asserted that the Attorney-General did not know if the UK would still be 'signed up to the EU Human Rights Law' in 2020.[13] *The Express* made the same mistake on 4 August 2015 in its piece 'EXCLUSIVE Immigrants will 'clog UK courts with

---

10 Labour's commitment in 2015 to retain the HRA was in the section of the manifesto headed 'Reforming government to give more power to people' ('Britain can be better' Labour Party Manifesto 2015, 67). The same pledge can be found in the Liberal Democrat manifesto in the section on 'Freedom and Opportunity' ('Stronger Economy, Fairer Society, Opportunity for Everyone' Liberal Democrat Manifesto 2015 114). The Greens placed their same commitment in 'Government and People' ('For the Common Good' The Green Party Manifesto 2015). The Conservative approach in 2017 is dealt with on p.39.

11 *Daily Mail* Comment, 'Don't let Tripoli turn into an other Baghdad' *MailOnline* (25 August 2011) available online at: www.dailymail.co.uk/debate/article-2029421/Libya-Dont-let-Gaddafi-Tripoli-turn-Baghdad.html

12 D McQuail, *Media Performance: Mass communications and the public interest* (Sage, 1992) 197.

13 J Slack, 'UK 'could quit human rights court': Britain's top legal officer admits he doesn't know if UK will still be signed up to laws by 2020' *Daily Mail* (16 September 2015). The on-line version was corrected sometime thereafter such that it now reads 'signed up to human rights law'. I have the uncorrected version on file. I have been unable to find a copy of the print version to see if the story was included; this of course would remain uncorrected. This highlights some of the difficulties of research in this area.

human rights cases to avoid eviction',[14] only to have to print the following one month later:

> This article was amended on 04 September 2015. It previously referred to EU Human Rights legislation which is incorrect. The European Convention on Human Rights is not EU law, and nor is the Human Rights Act, which is the law that will be used by migrants mentioned in the article.[15]

Clearly, we cannot know how many readers will have been misinformed (yet) again, but if a week is a long time in politics, a month is a long time in human rights misinformation. It would matter marginally less if this were a one-off or if journalistic lessons had been learned. They have not. On the day this chapter was being finalised, the same paper printed the following, purporting to be a transcript of an interview Michael Howard gave on BBC's *Newsnight* programme: 'people do not understand that the European Court of Human Justice now has the power to overrule acts of parliament'.[16] I thought it would be an unlikely confusion for a former Conservative Party leader, and QC, so I checked. In the interview, Howard very clearly refers, correctly, to the European Court of Justice.[17] Either transcribing is no longer a key journalistic skill, or there is something more mendacious at work.

However, an article may be accurate but still suffer from bias. This is where the third of McQuail's criteria comes into play, what he refers to as 'completeness': are the facts sufficient to constitute an adequate account? The remainder of this part contends that human rights reporting still suffers from incompleteness, and suggests three ways in which it does so.

An article might either marginalise or overemphasise the human rights elements of a case. This is something I have touched on in earlier work, describing it as 'where the narrative subtext being created is one that is suggestive of human rights marginalising more "traditional values" or defeating what would be a common sense outcome'.[18] Perhaps the most egregious example of trivialisation – stressing the peripheral factual elements of a case but entwining them closely with the human rights claim so the two are linked in the reader's mind – is what has come to be known as Catgate.[19] Such narratives leave readers thinking, 'surely human rights must be about more than this?' The case originally led the Home Secretary to discuss the case at the 2011 Tory Party conference. The

---

14 S Campbell, 'Immigrants will clog UK courts with human rights cases to avoid eviction' *Express* (4 September 2015) available online at: www.express.co.uk/news/uk/596086/migrant-crisis-illegal-immigrants-eviction-landlord-law-asylum-seeker-Britain-courts-legal

15 The correction can be found at the foot of the on-line copy above (n 14).

16 C Peat, 'Former Tory leader Michael Howard tells UK to "take back its democracy" and back a Brexit' *Daily Express* (21 June 2016).

17 BBC *Newsnight* aired on 20 June 2016.

18 Mead, 'You couldn't make it up' (n 5) 457.

19 *Ibid.* (n 5) 463–4.

case concerned a gay Bolivian man who had succeeded in resisting deportation based on his same-sex relationship, and thus on Article 8 grounds.[20] The Home Secretary proclaimed that he avoided deportation because he and his partner (in her words) 'and I am not making this up – had a pet cat.'[21] It is abundantly clear from the first instance judgment of Judge DeVittie that the cat was simply one further piece of evidence of their shared commitment to each other. He talks of the joint acquisition of the cat reinforcing his conclusion about the strength of their shared life together.

Another piece illustrating the point is *The Daily Telegraph*'s coverage of Beth Warren's case against the Human Fertilisation and Embryology Authority.[22] While it was not legally inaccurate to declare that 'Widow wins High Court battle over dead husband's sperm',[23] the piece failed anywhere to explain that the reason for her success was the HRA. The judgment makes very clear that Article 8 was behind the re-interpretation, and thus relaxing, of the strict time limits on using the sperm of a dead partner contained in the Human Fertilisation and Embryology Act 1990.[24] By contrast, when the *Daily Mail* came to inform its readers about the *Gilbert* case in April 2015,[25] foremost in its introduction and discussion were the human rights of violent offenders. The piece began by telling its readers that the ban on sending high-risk violent prisoners to open jails had been dramatically overturned 'following a human rights challenge'. Later, it reported that the successful challenge came after claiming that the absconder policy 'breached his right to a fair hearing under European human rights laws'.[26] Both aspects are true; these were his claims and challenge but not in their entirety and the latter was certainly not the reason Gilbert won his case. The change in absconder policy, which would have rendered him ineligible for transfer to open conditions, was inconsistent with a previous Home Office order. In other words, the case was won on ordinary common law judicial review principles. While it is true that the *Daily Mail* did make clear some way through the piece that the High Court did not rule on the legality of the banning policy on human rights grounds, the thrust and emphasis belies that reading. We see the same with the following *Daily Mail* headline, this time covering the Home Secretary's failure to deport a Somali criminal: 'Foreign criminal who attacked his friend with knife is

20 The original decision was by Judge Devittie on 24 September 2008 and upheld on appeal by Senior Immigration Judge Gleeson on 1 December 2008, case IA/14578/2008. Original judgments with the author.

21 'Theresa May under fire over deportation cat claim' BBC News on-line (4 October 2011) available online at: www.bbc.co.uk/news/uk-politics-15160326

22 *Warren v Care Fertility (Northampton) Ltd* [2014] EWHA 602 (Fam).

23 H Dixon, 'Woman wins High Court battle over Dead Husband's Sperm' *The Telegraph* on-line (6 March 2014) available online at: www.telegraph.co.uk/news/uknews/law-and-order/10680897/Widow-wins-High-Court-battle-over-dead-husbands-sperm.html

24 *Warren* above n 22 at [124] and [142].

25 *R (oao Gilbert) v Secretary of State for Justice* [2015] EWHC 927 (Admin).

26 'Violent Criminals who go on run CAN be sent to open jails' *Daily Mail* 2 April 2015.

freed as holding him longer would breach HIS human rights'.[27] While the *Mail* headline lays the blame squarely on the Human Rights Act, this was but a minor factor in the reasoning. Indeed, further on – if readers get that far, a serious question surely? – the paper reported why Mrs Justice Lang ordered his release: Home Office 'incompetence', a poor standard of investigation by the UK Border Agency and a lack of 'due diligence' had prolonged his detention unreasonably. Why does the headline focus readers' attention – and their ire – on something that was not a causal factor, we might ponder.

A paper might acontextualise the legal issues such that it misleads. This is the second way in which a report might paint an incomplete picture for readers. *The Daily Mail* reported the case of *R (Johnson) v Secretary of State for the Home Department*[28] with this headline: 'Drug-dealing killer jailed for nine years for manslaughter cannot be deported because he's illegitimate.'[29] Readers could easily be forgiven for assuming that it was his status per se that led to the decision but the picture is more nuanced. Johnson's mother was Jamaican and his father English but since his parents were not married at the time of this birth, he did not automatically obtain British citizenship, something that would have conferred immunity from deportation. Rectifying that would have been a formality for anyone aged under 18 but Johnson had failed to do so. The decision then was not 'because he's illegitimate' but because that illegitimacy created an unwarranted discrimination. Similarly, while in the *Mail*'s coverage of *Reilly No.2*, the Poundland case,[30] it was true, as the headline put it, that a retrospective change in benefits legislation was held to breach human rights, that very much sidelined the factual matrix. An alternative conception would be this: Government held to have acted unlawfully again in denying an earlier successful litigant the fruits of victory by using its parliamentary majority to overturn a previous Court of Appeal ruling it had also lost by retrospectively changing welfare benefits law. Not as snappy a headline but a more informed portrait of the case. In that light, it seems strange for the paper to be rallying quite so much against governmental abuse of power, and against fair procedure.

The third way in which a newspaper might fail to provide an adequate account is to misrepresent the likely impact of whatever case is being discussed. A standard approach is to convey an example at the extreme as in fact situated in the

---

27 A Willis, 'Foreign criminal who attacked friend with knife freed as holding him longer would breach HIS human rights' *MailOnline* (18 December 2013) available online at: www.dailymail.co.uk/news/article-2525738/Foreign-criminal-attacked-friend-knife-freed-holding-longer-breach-HIS-human-rights.html c.f. 'Home Office officials' "incompetence" led to failed deportation of Somali criminal' *The Daily Telegraph* (18 December 2013).

28 [2014] EWHC 2386 (Admin), now decided by the Supreme Court [2016] UKSC 56.

29 E Glanfield, 'Drug-dealing killer jailed for nine years for manslaughter can't be deported because he's illegitimate' *MailOnline* (19 July 2014) available online at: www.dailymail.co.uk/news/article-2698154/Drug-dealing-killer-jailed-nine-years-manslaughter-deported-hes-illegitimate.html

30 [2014] EHWC 2182 Admin.

mainstream, thus distorting the 'reach' of any decision. Consider the *Daily Mail* headline – 'Rapist wins prisoners the right to vote by 2011' – and the assertion: 'The Government was ordered … to give all convicts the vote by May 2011. Legal experts say even the country's most reviled and dangerous inmates will now get the vote – including child-killers Ian Huntley, Rose West and Roy Whiting.'[31] Let us disregard the fact that this is plainly and simply wrong – the European Court has never ordered that 'all convicts' be given the vote – the story misleads massively on the likely scope of the judgment. Which legal experts were consulted will always be a mystery but it is simply inconceivable that the UK would have been forced to respond to the cases at issue – *Greens* and *Hirst* – by giving the vote to 'the country's most reviled and dangerous inmates'.[32] The Strasbourg judgments have been clear and limited: the absolute ban is unlawful. They have never mandated which categories of prisoner should be excluded but the Voting Eligibility (Prisoners) Draft Bill of 2012 – still, at the time of writing, luxuriating in the Westminster long grass – has a choice of four years or six months as the longest minimum sentence before the ban is applied. Child killers do not get as little as four years.

Another example of over-reach are the headlines, and articles, that greeted the Strasbourg case of *Bărbulescu v Romania*, in which the legality – in Article 8 terms – of an employer monitoring an employee's internet use while at work was the issue.[33] 'Bosses Free to Spy on Emails' was splashed across the front page of the *Daily Mail*, while the *Daily Express* warned readers 'Your boss can now read EVERY Facebook and WhatsApp message you send at WORK' and *The Sun* asserted that your 'Boss can snoop on your private emails'.[34] The problem is that this is far from what was decided. The facts lead to a much narrower ratio – Mr Bărbulescu's contract had a specific term forbidding personal use of computers

31 Daily Mail Reporter, 'Rapist wins prisoners the right to vote by 2011: European human rights court sets six month deadline for Britain' *MailOnline* (25 November 2010) available online at: www.dailymail.co.uk/news/article-1332539/Rapist-Robert-Greens-wins-prisoners-vote-Cameron-given-6-months-comply.html

32 *Greens v UK* (2011) 53 EHRR 21; *Hirst v UK* (2006) 42 EHRR 41.

33 *Bărbulescu v Romania* App 61496/08 ECtHR judgment 12 January 2016, though reversed by the Grand Chamber (5 September 2017).

34 K Rushton, 'Bosses Free to Spy on Emails' *Daily Mail* (14 January 2016), A Brown, 'Your boss can now read EVERY Facebook and WhatsApp message you send at WORK' *Daily Express* (14 January 2016) available online at: www.express.co.uk/life-style/science-technology/634269/WhatsApp-Facebook-Employer-Romania-European-Court-of-Human-Rights C Pollard, 'Boss can snoop on your private emails in shock Big Brother-style clampdown' *The Sun* (14 January 2016) available online at: www.thesun.co.uk/archives/news/126275/bosses-can-snoop-through-private-emails-in-shock-big-brother-style-clampdown/ It is worth noting that *The Daily Mirror* provided considerable context to the decision including a lengthy summary from a practitioner, explaining the limitations and scope of the judgment: S Curtis, 'Your boss can now legally read your private emails and social media messages – should you be worried?' (14 January 2016) *Mirror* on-line, available online at: www.mirror.co.uk/news/technology-science/technology/your-boss-can-now-legally-7179928

and the Yahoo messenger account that his employer had monitored was set up specifically for Mr Bărbulescu to deal with sales enquiries. Only after he denied using the account for personal emails did his employer then undertake the monitoring, something limited to that account only. The identity of the personal recipients was never disclosed to the Romanian employment tribunal where the case ended up, after Mr Bărbulescu was sacked. We can argue the toss over quite how limited the ruling is but it is abundantly clear that it is simply not a licence to snoop as is portrayed here. The headlines so worried the Court and Council of Europe that they put out a press release accusing the British press, or significant sections of it, of 'setting something of a new benchmark ... [for] inaccurate scare stories'.[35]

Techniques of distortion

In my earlier work I have offered some reflections on the journalist's armoury, the tools by which they are able to persuade their readers. I have asked, in other words, how are we misled? I categorised these as the sins of omission and the sins of commission. The former covered those stories omitted from the daily news diet, in particular – the dog that didn't bark – the non-reporting of European Court of Human Rights judgments, especially those where the UK succeeded. I divided the sins of commission into four: pre-emption (reporting of cases too early in their life cycle but portraying them as establishing a binding ruling), prominence, partiality (in sources) and phrasing of stories. I shall come back to that last aspect later in this chapter.

This part has two sections. The first updates an empirical study of the reporting of Strasbourg judgments.[36] The second offers analyses of three further reporting techniques: the use of statistical data, repetition for reinforcement and an adaption of Bertolt Brecht's *verfremdungseffekt* or alienation effect.

From January 2014 to May 2015, 18 cases against the UK reached the European Court for judgment. In four, the Court found a violation; 14 were findings in favour of the UK. Of those 18, eight (44%) were not reported anywhere – in only one of those eight cases was there a finding of a violation.[37] Five (28%) were reported in only one or two media outlets (including local/regional newspapers), two (11%) were reported in three or four outlets, and only three (17%) were

35 K Rawlinson, 'UK press accused of "misinformed media storm" over email spying story' *The Guardian* on-line (16 January 2016) available online at: www.theguardian.com/technology/2016/jan/16/uk-press-accused-of-misinformed-media-storm-over-email-spying-story

36 Mead 'You couldn't make it up' (n 5) 462.

37 Methodology: the names of all cases that reached the Court were discovered from the Council of Europe's HUDOC database. Then a Nexis search was carried out taking the date of judgment as the start point against 'All UK Newspapers' using the name of the applicant thus Gough 'human rights' and as a cross-search the subject matter of the claim thus 'safety interview' 'human rights'. All research was carried out on or around 19 May 2015. It is not 100% accurate: the *Hutchinson* case was, to my knowledge, discussed in *The Daily Telegraph* yet coverage by that newspaper did not show up on the search.

reported in five or more outlets.[38] The three cases with the greatest coverage were: *Firth*, where it was decided that those prisoners unlawfully denied the vote would not be entitled to compensation (reported in six outlets),[39] *Hutchinson*, when the question of whole life tariffs returned to Strasbourg,[40] a success for the UK Government (that was featured in 14 outlets) and *Gough* – the naked rambler – the subject of interest in 31 papers![41]Among those cases given no coverage at all were *RMT v UK*[42], *Ibrahim,* [43] and *Dillon.*[44] In *RMT,* the Court upheld as lawful the UK's ban on secondary picketing. In *Ibrahim,* 'safety interviews' were held not to involve a violation of any right.[45] In *Dillon,* the Strasbourg Court decided that there had not been an unreasonable delay in providing an IPP lifer (a prisoner serving an indeterminate sentence for public protection) with access to rehabilitation courses. The UK won in each case and, in the latter two, the UK succeeded in defending critical areas of national criminal justice/counter-terrorism policy. In short, these are cases which, had details been reported, might have led concerned citizens to re-evaluate their assessment of the Convention and the Court – as not necessarily being a criminal's charter.[46]

There is a disproportionate focus in the media on cases where the UK loses. Of the four cases in the period where the UK was found in violation, all bar one was reported – a reporting 'rate' of findings of a violation of 75%. Of the 14 cases in the period where the UK was found not to have violated the Convention, only seven, or 50%, were reported. Of the ten cases that were reported, three were reports of violations, and seven were findings of no-violation. From that, we might sensibly conclude that regular readers of UK national newspapers might themselves draw certain conclusions:

i) The UK loses about 30% of the human rights cases lodged at Strasbourg (following from the fact that three of the ten reports were of violations).
ii) The UK loses more cases than it wins: 50% of the non-violation cases were reported whereas 75% of the violation cases were reported.

---

38 These are all set out in Appendix 1 of this chapter.
39 *Firth v UK* [2014] ECHR 540.
40 *Hutchinson v UK* (2015) 61 EHRR 13.
41 *Gough v UK* (2015) 61 EHRR 8. The case was brought by G, who has walked the length and breadth of the UK unclothed, reflecting his view that nudity is not offensive, and followed his arrest for breach of the peace.
42 *RMT v UK* (2015) 60 EHRR 10.
43 *Ibrahim v UK* (2015) 61 EHRR 9.
44 *Dillon v UK* [2014] ECHR 1190.
45 A safety interview is one that can be conducted urgently for the purposes of protecting life or preventing serious property damage, and which under the Terrorism Act 2000 can occur without a solicitor and without the opportunity to seek legal advice.
46 See as one example of the use of the term Comment 'Human rights is a charter for criminals and parasites our anger is no longer enough' *MailOnline* (15 July 2012) available online at: www.dailymail.co.uk/debate/article-2173666/Human-rights-charter-criminals-parasites-anger-longer-enough.html

Neither is backed up by the evidence, as we shall see below. Where the regular diet of reporting on an issue is out of line with its likelihood, it is little wonder many might feel disillusioned with the system of human rights protection? The journalistic selection of cases – and near total (absolute?) exclusion of inadmissibility decisions – means the gap between 'reality' and reception of that reality is massive, and shapes public debate. I think that diet of case-law reporting helps explain perceived public antipathy to the Convention and the UK's continued membership in two ways. Not only does it generate the view that the UK is generally on the receiving end of Strasbourg judgments, it means that the public is generally poorly informed about the range of human rights law, and thus what a protective framework might mean for them as individuals. I develop some of that latter in the parts to come.

Let us now turn to the various techniques of misreporting. The first is the old adage about lies, damned lies and statistics. For example, a headline from *The Sun* states: 'Euro judges go against UK in 3 out of 5 cases'.[47] From that, surely any numerate reader would probably conclude a 'success' rate for applicants of about 60%? The *Daily Mail*, in 2012 (some two years before) asserted the figure to be 75%: 'Europe's war on British justice: UK loses three out of four human rights cases, damning report reveals'.[48] This is very far from the truth, or (putting it slightly more favourably to *The Sun* and *The Mail*) is very much the lesser of two possible truths, and one that tells us far less about what is really going on. It is true that of all the 540 cases *that reached the Court for final outcome* between 1959 and 2016, there was a finding of at least one violation in 312 cases, a 'loss' rate of almost exactly 60% or three in five. This tells, at best, only part of the story of the UK before the European Court. In that 57-year period, 23,781 applications against the UK were decided, that is were allocated to a judicial formation. Of those, 21,599 were either struck out or declared inadmissible – about 91%, or a 'loss' rate of about 7%.[49] If we consider those 312 cases where the government was held to be in breach as a percentage of all cases lodged against the UK and which end up being heard by the Court (i.e. those case which reached some form of judicial disposal), the success rate for applicants is about 1.3%.

A more egregious example comes from *The Daily Express*. Under the headline 'Millions paid out to criminals thanks to the European Court of Human Rights', it reported that Britain had lost 202 cases to criminals, according to figures obtained by Conservative MP Philip Davies and placed in the Commons

47 C Woodhouse, 'Euro judges go against UK in 3 out of 5 cases' *The Sun* (24 August 2014).

48 J Slack, 'Europe's War on British Justice: UK loses three out of four human rights cases, damning report reveals' *MailOnline* (11 January 2012) available online at: www.dailymail.co.uk/news/article-2085420/Europes-war-British-justice-UK-loses-human-rights-cases-damning-report-reveals.html

49 The statistics and data can be found through searching here on the Council of Europe website 'Violations by Article and State 1959–2016' and 'Overview ECHR 1959–2016' here: www.echr.coe.int/Pages/home.aspx?p=reports&c=#n1347956867932_pointer

library.[50] The original furore, including a rebuke from the court itself[51], over this piece and many others like it were that readers were not being told that of the total £4.4m paid out (an average of £22,00 per claimant) most was not compensation but legal fees and expenses. However, *Express* readers could also quite reasonably assume that of the cases against the UK where a violation had been found, 202 had been brought by, and thus had been lost, to criminals.[52] That is not confirmed by the facts. The influential human rights campaigning project, RightsInfo, undertook painstaking analysis of all cases brought against the UK and its conclusion was that of the (then, in 2015) 297 losses, only 94 – a third – were to those we could properly categorise as being either a criminal, terrorist or prisoner, leaving 203 benefitting what they called 'others'.[53] As significant – in terms of human rights reporting – is the fact that regular readers will rarely – if ever, and certainly not in blaring headlines – be exposed to other data that might cast the Court and the Convention in a different, and more positive, hue. For example, and again drawing on RightsInfo's hard work, data shows that the UK had the third equal lowest violation rate, with five cases lost per million population over the period 1959–2013. It also shows that from the years 2013–2015, it had a lower rate of applications allocated to a judicial function (that is, passed on to the court for a determination of some sort), per head of population, than Germany or France. In two of those three years, its rate was better than Denmark, while in the third year, it was only marginally worse.[54] More accurate reporting

50 O Bennett, 'Millions paid out to criminals thanks to the European Court of Human Rights' *Express* on-line (8 October 2013) available online at: www.express.co.uk/news/uk/435258/Millions-paid-out-to-criminals-thanks-to-the-European-Court-of-Human-Rights The paper was deposited on 10 September 2013 and can be found here DEP2013–1541: www.parliament.uk/business/publications/business-papers/commons/deposited-papers/?fd=2013-09-09&td=2013-09-11&house=1#toggle-1541 Given that the data includes cases up until 9 July 2013, it is hard to see why the figure of 202 differs so much from the figure of 297 in the *ECHR Overview 1959–2013* (above n 46).

51 Council of Europe, 'Court concern at "seriously misleading" UK news articles' (11 October 2013) available online at: www.humanrightseurope.org/2013/10/court-concern-at-seriously-misleading-uk-news-articles

52 *The Daily Telegraph* originally reported along the same lines but its on-line version now asserts merely that 'Britain has lost 202 cases in the European Court of Human Rights including to murderers, terrorists, paedophiles and rapists': H Dixon, 'Human rights cases in Europe have cost Britain more than £4m' and continues' *Telegraph* on-line (7 October 2013) available online at: www.telegraph.co.uk/news/uknews/law-and-order/10362563/Human-rights-cases-in-Europe-have-cost-Britain-more-than-4m.html What is interesting in the context of digital vs. printed versions of reports (see above n 8) is that the original deceptive wording still appears in the search result list: 'Britain has paid out millions to criminals in human rights cases' even though the text of the copy, if you link through to it, has been altered.

53 See the data behind card 10 'All the People?' (Rightsinfo.org) available online at: www.rightsinfo.org/infographics/human-rights-uncovered/

54 For the years 2013, 2014 and 2015 the figures were for the UK 0.14, 0.11, 0.09, and for Germany 0.19, 0.13, 0.10, for France 0.23, 0.17, 0.16 and for Denmark 0.15, 0.12, 0.08 respectively: see European Court of Human Rights Analysis of Statistics 2015

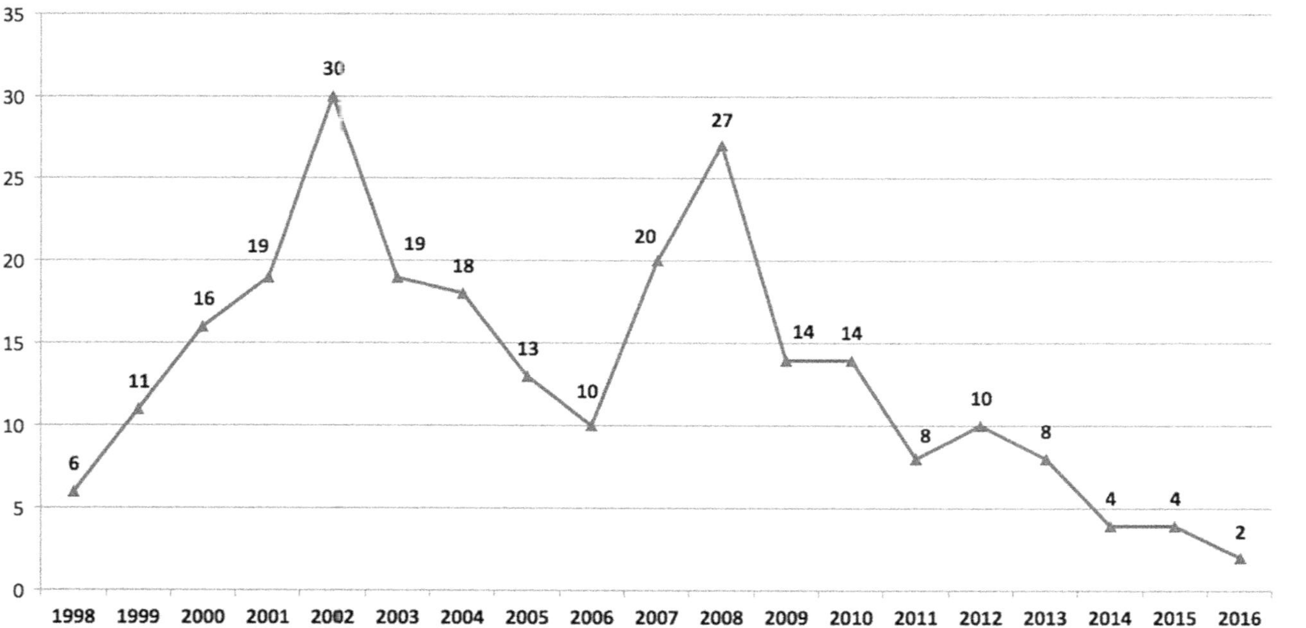

Note: one judgment may concern more than one application.
A violation judgment is one in which at least one violation has been found in respect of at least one application.

Table 1.1 Judgments delivered in 1998–2016 with at least one violation in the United Kingdom (12 April 2016)

Taken from Harvey & McCormick 'Only 1 in 200 European Court of Human Rights Cases Are from The UK. Here's Why That Matters' RightsInfo blog 24 May 2016 available online at: www.rightsinfo.org/0-4-european-court-cases-uk-heres-matters/

might too have allowed us to read about the decreasing number of cases against the UK where the court has found a violation, a figure that is, and has been, in single figures for several years.

Simply put, the daily diet of data is skewed to portray a particular vision of the ECHR and a particular version of human rights protection generally.

The second technique relates to the phrasing: repetition and reinforcement. I'm reminded here of the old Monty Python Word Association football sketch[55] – the near automated connection of words and phrases. Again, drawing on some other, basic empirical research I conducted in 2015 – interrogating the *Daily Mail* on-line database for 12 months – we see a familiar pattern emerging: 'terrorists murderers and rapists' is a phrase, when linked to 'human rights' in a search, featured in 11 *Daily Mail* stories with a UK focus. 'Paedophiles, rapists and murderers' (again linked to 'human rights') brought up ten stories, and 'murderers and rapists' led to 27, almost all in the context of prisoners' rights/deportation. Lastly 'rapists and killers' and 'human rights' returned 12 reports of domestic cases or stories. Initially, this 'continual production of familiarity',[56] as Keith Negus termed it, might seem to create a tension with news values, the search for something out of the ordinary to retain and attract readers. Why are there so many deportation and terrorist stories when newspapers depend on novelty? We find the solution in the work of Stan Cohen and Stuart Hall. In *Policing the Crisis*[57] Hall draws on Cohen's idea from 1973 of moral panic,[58] in which Cohen writes about the amplification of stories concerned with mugging leading to an orchestrated climate of fear. This, in turn, leads us to consent to (greater) repression by the ruling class, allowing it to maintain its hegemonic control.

The third and last technique requires a little understanding of the playwright Bertolt Brecht's dramatic technique. His *verfremdungseffekt*, or alienation effect, involves telling the audience what is going to happen, so they focus on superstructural whys and wherefores, not the whats or hows.[59] The removal of suspense encourages the audience to think more widely and deeply. Newspapers seem to do this in reverse – an *unverfremdungseffekt* perhaps? They leave the reader waiting – and many may never get to the end. Of course, some may only

---

Table 2, 11 available online at: www.echr.coe.int/Pages/home.aspx?p=reports&c=#n13479 56867932_pointer

55 Available online at: www.youtube.com/watch?v=WwdYCX60GRk accessed 27 June 2016 which starts with John Cleese introducing his talk as follows: 'Tonight's the night I shall be talking about of flu the subject of word association football. This is a technique out a living much used in the practice makes perfect of psychoanalysister and brother and one that has occupied piper the majority rule of my attention squad by the right number one two three four the last five years to the memory.'

56 K Negus, *Music Genres and Corporate Cultures* (Routledge 1999).

57 S Hall *et al.*, *Policing the Crisis Mugging, the State, and Law and Order* (MacMillan, 1978).

58 S Cohen, *Folk Devils and Moral Panics* (McGibbon and Kee, 1972).

59 See generally P Thomson and G Sacks (eds), *The Cambridge Companion to Brecht* (CUP, 1994).

catch a headline in the newsagents. If this 'reveal' then turns the story on its head, the opportunity to disabuse its readers of their misinformed notions is lost. The *Daily Telegraph* covering the Strasbourg whole-life challenge in *Hutchinson v UK* provides a good example of this.[60] The headline is 'Triple killer behind the latest Strasbourg ruling'. Within the first few lines, we have been told three times about how the applicant/claimant had been able to bring a human rights challenge: 'Arthur Hutchinson dubbed himself "The Fox" after committing his heinous crimes, and went on to bring the latest in a series of controversial appeals in the European Court of Human Rights'. Yet, it is only with the last six words of the 375-word piece that we learn that it was 'an appeal he has now lost'.[61] The journalist in question offered (in correspondence with me) that this was only 'an explainer', providing background material for readers of the main story, found elsewhere – and averred that the actual report of the judgment made the fact that he had lost more clearly much sooner.[62] That is so. However, during the course of that single day (3 February 2015), I made several searches of the *Telegraph*'s webpage using ' "whole life" Hutchinson'. Each search still produced the explainer, not the actual report of the judgment, at the top of the list. This must raise a further concern in the context of digital consumption? Another example of delayed information was one we saw above, the discussion of the Somali knife criminal,[63] where the real reason for the Home Secretary's failure to deport was nothing to do with his human rights at all. It has links to what I have earlier called 'pre-emptive' reporting, where newspapers report 'claims' or that something was 'argued in court' – as we saw in the coverage of the *Gilbert* case (above p. 14), creating a real risk that this passes into the public domain as what the law is.

Media theory

This part offers an alternative perspective of the foregoing discussion by viewing human rights reporting within a media and communications framework, specifically looking at media content. We will undertake a more detailed content analysis of one important category of human rights cases, the deportation of foreign national offenders (FNOs) before subjecting a single media text – a photo in *The Sun* – to semiotic analysis.[64]

---

60 *Hutchinson v UK* (n 40).

61 D Barrett, 'Triple killer behind the latest Strasbourg ruling' *The Telegraph* on-line (3 February 2015) available online at: www.telegraph.co.uk/news/uknews/law-and-order/11386311/Triple-killer-behind-the-latest-Strasbourg-ruling.html

62 D Barrett, 'Strasbourg judges back-track on "whole life" tariff human rights ruling' *The Telegraph* on-line (3 February 2015) available online at: www.telegraph.co.uk/news/uknews/law-and-order/11386190/Strasbourg-judges-back-track-on-whole-life-tariff-human-rights-ruling.html

63 Above n 27.

64 The term 'foreign criminal' is defined by s.32(1) of the UK Borders Act 2007.

According to one of its early pioneers, the study of mass communication is the study of 'who says what to whom through what channel and with what effect'.[65] This was put more expansively later as the attempt 'to understand the production, processing and effects of symbols and signaling systems [and to] explain the phenomenon associated with that production, processing and effects'.[66] The concern of communications theory is not with the text itself, or rather not solely and not in isolation, but with the meaning(s) generated by that text, meaning(s) produced by its audience – separately from each other and from the author – as a result of the process of reading. Meaning is, thus, not something embedded in the text but is the product of a multi-stage process: the act of witness, the act of reporting and the act of interpreting.

A precursor though to all this, in the case of news reporting, is an event. Something needs to happen (or not happen), something needs to be said first – in order to be reported, in order for that report later to be given some meaning by a reader. Most 'events' are witnessed by very, very few. The terrorist attack in Paris, New Order on the main stage at Glastonbury, a Donald Trump speech in Ohio were spectacles missed by billions more than those who saw and heard them first-hand. There are untold billions of 'events' occurring every day, the world over – an infinitesimally small number are both witnessed *and* reported more widely; they have a degree of 'newsworthiness'. Broadly speaking, almost all events have no newsworthiness – the fact that I am making a cheese and pickle sandwich for lunch today is of no interest, I would guess, to anyone else. Thus, a main concern – of media and communication scholars – is the process of selection – both the journalist choosing which event to witness and which events then to report, and the factors that dictate which events make it to the news.[67] In reporting an event, the journalist, through choice of words and text – by a process of exclusion/inclusion – confers meaning on it, but not a meaning that is single, fixed, immutable and intrinsic. The meaning of news text (as with all) is dependent both on its wording and on its reception, in turn a function of a whole host of variables. This part plots two different approaches to the study of media content: quantitative – content analysis – and structuralist – semiotics. The former is wrapped up with the issue of selection – which events make it into the news pages – while the latter informs our understanding of what a text 'means'.

According to its founder, content analysis is a research technique for the systematic, objective and quantitative description of the manifest content of communication.[68] It is a technique for discovering meaning by 'simply' counting the frequency of references in a text. Such is, of course, problematic – numeric repetition is not (necessarily) any measure of significance or of meaning. This piece

65 H Lasswell, 'The Structure and Function of Communication in Society' in L Bryson (ed.), *The Communication of Ideas* (Harper and Row, 1948).

66 C Berger and S Chaffee, 'The Study of Communication as a Science' in C Berger and S Chaffee (eds) *Handbook of Communication Science* (Sage, 1987) 17.

67 In this process of selection, organisational issues, structural factors and ideological concerns would also come into play.

68 B Berelson, *Content Analysis in Communication Research* (Free Press, 1952) 18.

though will not be utilising content analysis to assert the meaning of any newspaper text; it is used for a different purpose – to assess the incidence of reporting of phenomenon X as against verifiable data relating to that same phenomenon as a means to test the accuracy of its representation. Semiotics, on the other hand, is concerned with latent – or connotative – textual meanings. De Saussure posited that meaning is conveyed through signs: the signifier – what we actually read – and the signified – the socio-culturally imposed meanings we attach to them. Roland Barthes, one of the leading exponents of semiotics, for example, in *Mythologies*, considered the cover of *Paris-Match* depicting a young black Frenchman in uniform, saluting, with his eyes uplifted.

> All this is the *meaning* of the picture. But, whether naively or not, I see very well what it signifies to me: that France is a great Empire, that all her sons without any colour discrimination faithfully serve under her flag and that there is no better answer to the detractors of an alleged colonialism than the zeal shown by this Negro in serving his so-called oppressors.[69]

For the semioticist, newspaper (and other) text is decoded by inscribed readers[70] – an interpretative community with a shared *Weltanschauung* that is both historically and culturally located and derived – using a range of interpretative repertoires. To that extent, reading a text is a reflexive process. The meaning the reader gives to the text both shapes and is shaped by them. We shall develop much of this below when we consider a single front cover from *The Sun* from 2015.

So why does all this matter for law, and lawyers, and for human rights law, and human rights lawyers? Most of us, the vast majority indeed, can have no direct experience of human rights adjudication – of legal 'events'. Our understanding of the scope of protection, of its beneficiaries, and of its sticking points comes from what we read in various news media. There has historically been at best only passing engagement between lawyers and communications theorists,[71] yet, how a story is reported – how the reality of a case or judgment is (re-)produced – is pivotal to our understanding of it and, thus, of its meaning. What a media report means to me or to you informs our understanding of the subject matter, thence to our support, and is, thus, critical to the overall success of the human rights framework.

Content analysis

I carried out a small-scale study to test the following hypothesis: media reporting of FNOs successfully avoiding deportation on human rights grounds portrays a

69 R Barthes, *Mythologies* (A Lavers tr. Paladin, 1973) 125.

70 C Sparks and M Campbell, 'The "Inscribed Reader" of the British Quality Press' (1987) 2 *European Journal of Communication* 445.

71 See generally (n 5) and E Balabanova, *The Media and Human Rights: The Cosmopolitan Promise* (Routledge, 2014).

far higher success rate for individuals than is borne out by the official data. In other words, does the evidence support Richard Littlejohn's assertion, in the *Daily Mail* that judges 'go out of their way to side with criminals – especially foreign criminals – against the interests of the law-abiding majority'.[72]

Partly given those assertions, and partly for reasons of logistical practicality – sample size and ease of access – I took as my sample population only one media source, the *Daily Mail* on-line (*MailOn-line*). It is thus not a study of media reporting but of reporting by one media outlet only. These data could then be married against a second dataset, official figures on FNO appeals, specifically, numbers lodged, numbers that succeeded and numbers that succeeded on human rights grounds. This gives us, if not the 'real' figure on the likelihood of success, then at least one that is acceptable and on which it would be reasonable to rely, for these comparative purposes. On 10 November 2014, Dominic Raab MP tabled a written parliamentary question, asking how many and what proportion of appeals lodged over the last five years by FNOs against removal from the UK were based wholly or in part on either Article 8 or on human rights grounds.[73] On 17 November, while acknowledging the imperfections in the data, junior Home Office minister James Brokenshire, provided a written answer (set out below) outlining for the five and a half year period January 2009–July 2014, the number of FNO appeals lodged, the number of those appeals allowed and the number of those appeals allowed on human rights grounds.

If we consider the three years 2010–2012, the three-year average 'success' rate – appeals allowed as a percentage of appeals lodged – for avoiding deportation on human rights grounds is 19.1%. In 2010, it was 19% (i.e. 363 out of 1908), in 2011, it rose slightly to 20.7% and, in 2012, it dropped to 17.6%,

72 R Littlejohn, 'Robber spared deportation: When did 'family' mean some bird I met in the pub?' *MailOnline* (18 May 2011) available online at: www.dailymail.co.uk/debate/article-1387770/Super-injunctions-privacy-law-When-did-family-mean-bird-I-met-pub.html

73 Written question 213969, Hansard 17 November 2014 Written Questions and Answers and Written Statements available online at: www.parliament.uk/business/publications/written-questions-answers-statements/written-question/Commons/2014-11-10/213969/ Even this data is not accurate. In a written answer some eleven months before, in January 2014, the Home Office supplied figures that were broadly the same but not wholly so, and differed by a handful in most cases ...though it did not alter the success rate significantly, see HC Deb, 17 January 2014, Col 720W available online at: www.publications.parliament.uk/pa/cm201314/cmhansrd/cm140117/text/140117w0002.html *The Daily Mail*, on the other hand, consistently misportrays this official figure. In a piece on 27 October 2011, headed '4,000 foreign criminals set free to fight deportation including murderers, rapists and child sex offenders', it asserted, first, that in 2010 576 FNOs 'used the Human Rights Act to prevent being kicked out' and secondly that the government lost one in three cases. Neither is made out by the official statistics in that House of Commons answer. See J Doyle, '4,000 foreign criminals set free to fight deportation including murderers, rapists and child sex offenders' *MailOnline* (27 October 2011) available online at: www.dailymail.co.uk/news/article-2053981/4-000-foreign-criminals-set-free-fight-deportation-including-murderers-rapists-child-sex-offenders.html

Q Asked by **Mr Dominic Raab** (Esher and Walton) [N] Asked on: 10 November 2014

Home Office ⓒ 213969

Offenders: Deportation

To ask the Secretary of State for the Home Department, how many and what proportion of appeals lodged by foreign national offenders against their removal from the UK were based wholly or in part on (a) Article 8 of the European Convention on Human Rights and (b) human rights grounds in each of the last five years.

▶ **A** Answered by: **James Brokenshire** Answered on: 17 November 2014

Data on unsuccessful appeals against deportation is only held at the level of coordinated paper case files or within the notes section of the Case Information Database (CID). Such data is not aggregated in national reporting systems, which would mean these questions could only be answered through a disproportionately expensive manual case search to collate the data.

We can provide the following data

Table 1: Foreign National Offender (FNO) appeals lodged, with outcomes, 1 January 2009 to 16 July 2014

Year appeal lodged	2009	2010	2011	2012	2013	2014
Number of FNO appeals lodged	1,781	1,908	1,740	2,147	2,441	1,135
Number of appeals allowed	433	623	555	670	416	10
Appeals allowed on HR grounds	234	363	360	378	133	2

(1) The figures quoted have been derived from management information from the Home Office databases and are therefore provisional and subject to change. This information has not been quality assured under National Statistics protocols.

(2) A Foreign National Offender (FNO) is defined as an individual with a criminal case, on the Home Office's Case Information Database.

(3) Data relates to appeals lodged in the specified years. Appeal outcomes may have occurred in the same or subsequent years.

(4) Appeals allowed on Human Rights grounds may have been granted under one or more articles.

(5) Allowed appeals is based on the latest appeal outcome which includes those allowed at both the lower and upper tiers.

(6) Data extracted on 16 July 2014.

Figure 1.1 Home Office Written Answer 17 November 2014: FNO appeals January 2009–July 2014

leading to that average of 19% overall. There was a considerable drop between 2012 and 2014, and, in that final year, a massive drop. It is hard to tell whether this might be due to

(i) the fact that figures are for cases lodged per year, with appeals possibly taking some time to work their way through the system – meaning they might not have been resolved by the time the data were compiled – or

(ii) changes in substantive immigration rules that took effect on 9 July 2012, the avowed aim of which was to reduce reliance on Article 8, or to a combination of both.[74]

If we could be sure that the reductions were solely due to (ii), then we could use the full dataset as our baseline. Since we cannot, this content analysis was done using the more secure data of a two-year period, 2010–2011.

The methodology was straightforward. The *Mail* on-line website was interrogated using the search terms '"human rights" deportation' over the two-year period. This produced 221 news or comment items, each of which was read fully for further filtering using the following inclusionary criteria:

(i) an individual was either named or sufficiently identified in the piece even if the piece was not written solely about that individual, such as in a wide-ranging comment piece on human rights or on criminals;
(ii) the individual was not a UK citizen;
(iii) the piece clearly indicated that an individual had committed a specific non-immigration crime in the UK and been convicted or made subject to some criminal justice sanction;
(iv) the piece clearly identified that the individual was relying in whole or in part on one or more Convention right to avoid deportation in the legal proceedings, usually Article 8 (the right to family and private life) but occasionally Article 3 (the prohibition on torture and degrading treatment);
(v) there had been a conclusive determination of the individual's immigration status.[75]

The content analysis was designed to test whether about one in every five (i.e. the 19% figure above) of all deportation cases reported showed an applicant FNO succeeding on human rights grounds, with four in five or so showing success for the Home Secretary. This was a deliberately cautious approach, so as to produce

74 HC 395 (as amended from 9 July 2012). The effect of the change was to some extent nullified by *MF (Article 8 – new rules) Nigeria* [2012] UKUT 00393 (IAC) which (re-)asserted the *statutory* Article 8 framework given effect by s.6 of the HRA. This led to a change in the law, s.19 of the Immigration Act 2014 amending the Nationality, Immigration and Asylum Act 2002.

75 There are two caveats here, both due to possible temporal mismarriages in the data. The annual 'success' rate is a function of the first and third rows of data yet an appeal lodged in December 2010 would appear as an appeal heard in (say) 2011. Secondly, in many of the newspaper reports, it was not clear when the deportation determination was i.e. was it within the 2010–2012 period? Both risk conflating dissimilar data. As to the first, a three-yearly average of the success rate on human rights grounds – 19%, as we saw above – reduces quite considerably any time lags. Both in fact are marginal concerns. The aim of the research was simpler and different – to assess whether or not the preponderance of the *Daily Mail*'s coverage indicated a likelihood that an FNO would be deported at the end of sentence and, if it did, whether that likelihood matched, in broad terms, the scale of the official data.

the best 'fit' with the official data. It was designed, in lay terms, to capture all those stories where readers could properly conclude, having read the piece fully, that X, a foreign national offender, had been allowed to remain in the UK or, alternatively, had been ordered to leave and, in either case, had tried to argue that their human rights would be violated if they were deported. Thus, the content analysis excluded reports on those who were being deported following a failed asylum claim[76] or reports about Abu Qatada or Abu Hamza who had not been convicted of any crime in the UK[77] or reports that concerned someone being extradited. Since the focus was on determinations of immigration status, it excluded reports of prisoners suing (and in some cases being awarded compensation) for the manner or length of their detention pending deportation[78] or where someone had been sentenced but not yet subjected to deportation proceedings.[79]

It also meant excluding cases where it was not clear from the report that human rights were behind the deportation/failure to deport, such as in the case of Tarique Manahod, who 'remains in Britain because the Algerian consulate did not accept he was an Algerian citizen',[80] or of Alphonse Semo, who avoided deportation because of a Home Office mistake relating to his impending marriage.[81] Lastly, *Daily Mail* reports of two ECHR cases against the UK, decided

76 S Bruce, 'Failed asylum seeker who has dodged deportation for a decade told he can stay ... because he goes to the GYM' *MailOnline* (14 October 2011) available online at: >www.dailymail.co.uk/news/article-2052714/Failed-asylum-seeker-Amir-Beheshti-stay-goes-GYM.html>.

77 T Shipman and D Martin, '35 radicals trained for terrorism at British mosques, Guantanamo files reveal' *MailOn-line* (26 April 2011) available online at: www.dailymail.co.uk/news/article-1380564/35-radicals-trained-terrorism-British-mosques-Guantanamo-files-reveal.html

78 Daily Mail Reporter, 'Lying illegal immigrant who committed a string of crimes set to receive thousands in compensation for being "falsely imprisoned"' *MailOnline* (14 May 2011) available online at: www.dailymail.co.uk/news/article-1387027/Lying-illegal-immigrant-committed-string-crimes-set-receive-thousands-compensation-falsely-imprisoned.html

79 J Doyle, 'So what DOES it take to deport a criminal? Judge cuts drug-dealing migrant's sentence so he won't get kicked out' *MailOn-line* (16 August 2011) available online at: www.dailymail.co.uk/news/article-2026222/UK-immigration-Drug-dealing-Vincent-Millers-sentence-cut-wont-kicked-out.html

80 C Fernandez, 'Sex attacker we can't deport gets £1,000 a month in handouts (... and, guess what, the father of two says it's his human right to live in Britain)' *MailOnline* (2 August 2011) available online at: www.dailymail.co.uk/news/article-2021305/Sex-attacker-deport-gets-1-000-month-handouts.html

81 M Seamark and C Fernandez, 'Rapist who dumped victim on rubbish tip escapes deportation after judge says he "has right to stay and marry in UK"' *MailOn-line* (31 March 2010) available online at: www.dailymail.co.uk/news/article-1262243/Rapist-facing-deportation-allowed-stay-UK-married.html Others include Jaswinder Singh jailed for murder in June 2011. He arrived from Germany in 2002 where he had been jailed for glassing his then girlfriend, and had three further convictions in the UK for assault. Each time the deportation process was commenced, but it never ran its course though there is no indication in the report as to why that might be, see J Slack, 'Jailed for murder, Jaswinder Singh, immigrant who should have been deported in 2002' *MailOnline* (9 June 2011) available online at: www.dailymail.co.uk/news/article-2001193/Jailed-murder-immigrant-deported-2002.

in the two-year period – in both of which violations of Article 8 or Article 3 were found in the context of deportation of FNOs[82] – were excluded as these could not shed light on individual deportation decisions taken domestically by the Home Secretary or by the UK Border Agency (UKBA) or by the Immigration Appeals Tribunal (IAT).

The results were surprising. Over the two-year period, of the 221 stories overall, there were 42 stories in the *MailOn-line* which portrayed a named or identifiable individual subject to a deportation order who was claiming or relying on a Convention right. The vast majority were news items, with a few cases mentioned within comment pieces by *Mail* staffers such as Richard Littlejohn. Only four of those 42 pieces were about a human rights claim that had failed. That, in percentage terms, is the staggeringly low figure of 9.5 %. That is to say, in only 9.5% of its news coverage of FNO deportations would readers of the *Mail* on-line have read that a foreign criminal, having served their sentence, would be or indeed had been deported. The preponderance of *Daily Mail* reporting is skewed towards showing that, broadly speaking, FNOs avoid deportation on human rights grounds. Indeed, it is overwhelmingly skewed, painting a picture for readers that almost all FNOs avoid deportation by playing the human rights card.

A modicum of caution is needed here. In a handful of pieces, it might not have been sufficiently clear to the reader what the outcome may have been or, indeed, if there had been a definitive outcome. Take this piece from 10 July 2011, under the headline: 'Fugitive foreign killers use your money to avoid being deported'.[83] It considers one named Albanian murderer, Vullnett Mucelli, and two unnamed others, all three of whom were seeking to avoid being returned home by laying claim to Article 6, arguing they would not there have a fair trial. Technically this was an extradition case – and so outwith the parameters of the analysis. That said, even those readers aware of the subtle legal distinction between deportation and extradition were led to believe this case constituted one of the former: the opening lines informed them that 'fugitive foreign killers sheltering in Britain are costing taxpayers millions by exploiting human rights legislation to escape deportation'. Another case concerned William Danga, a Congolese asylum seeker and mainstay of *Daily Mail* coverage over the years. The paper very clearly steers to one conclusion with its headline 'Child rapist used "human rights" to fight deportation – then struck again', leaving readers in no doubt that this is one of the 90.5%

html Similarly, a story about French paedophile Phillipe Gandus at large in the UK was excluded as there was no indication on what grounds the original successful deportation order had been made, see Daily Mail Reporter, 'French drifter who tried to snatch child, 3, in Hamleys toyshop sneaks back into UK two years after he was deported' *MailOnline* (22 June 2011) available online at: www.dailymail.co.uk/news/article-2006902/Philippe-Gandus-tried-snatch-child-3-Hamleys-sneaks-UK.html

82 *Sufi and Elmi v UK* (2012) 54EHRR 9 and *AA v UK* [2011] ECHR 1345.

83 I Gallagher, 'Fugitive foreign killer use your money to avoid being deported' *MailOn-line* (10 July 2011) available online at: www.dailymail.co.uk/news/article-2013071/Fugitive-foreign-killers-use-money-avoid-deported.html

where a human rights argument succeeds.[84] The picture is less clear cut for those who read the whole piece which is actually about his most recent sentencing where the judge ordered he again be deported. A close reading of the newspaper report does not indicate clearly that, at any time, he has succeed avoiding deportation on human rights grounds – only that he used these grounds to seek to avoid it.

There are seven of these 'unknown' or 'pending' cases in our dataset of 42 applicants. If we exclude these, so as to present the *Daily Mail*'s coverage in the most favourable light, we reach the following conclusion. In four of 35 cases, the paper's coverage indicated that the Home Secretary was able to deport someone despite their raising human rights arguments. This equates to a government success 'rate' of 11.4% (that is, appeals allowed as a percentage of appeals lodged), and, thus, a success rate for FNOs of 88.6%. *Daily Mail* coverage presents us with an almost mirror image of reality – slightly worse in fact. If we compare this with the official statistics, we see that the gross disparity remains. As we saw, these indicate an annual average success rate (over that three-year period 2010–2012) *for the Home Secretary* of 81%. In only 19% of cases did an FNO successfully avoid deportation by arguing that their human rights would be infringed – not 88.6%!

That is a huge difference. It would be fair to assume that our views about the truth of X are informed by the volume of stories we read that purport to show proposition X is true. If so, the view that readers of the *Daily Mail* would have from that paper's on-line coverage would be that of every nine FNOs the Home Office tries to deport, eight are able to avoid deportation by arguing it would breach their human rights, usually Article 8. Only one in nine (11.4%) is ever deported. The official data shows that the Home Office succeeds in about four of every five cases (81%) – with FNOs succeeding only about 19% of the time. Though clearly other factors are at play, such inaccurate representations of the legal reality must contribute to explaining the view that certain sections of the public (or certain readerships) have of the role human rights should play.

The problem for *Daily Mail* readers is not that they are unaware of the official data. During the two-year period of the analysis, there was regular mention of the fact that '200 foreign criminals, including killers, won appeals against deportation [in 2010] using Article 8 of Labour's insidious Human Rights Act'.[85] Most reliable commentators agree that Article 8 comprises the bulk of human rights arguments, successful or otherwise, so, given that the official data for 2010, in the parliamentary answer, set out a figure of 234 FNOs successfully avoiding deportation on human rights grounds, that 200 figure in the Daily Mail is probably broadly correct. The problem is viewing that in isolation. Having the data in

84 C Greenwood and J Doyle, 'Child rapist used 'human rights' to fight deportation – then struck again' *MailOn-line* (18 November 2011) available online at: www.dailymail.co.uk/news/article-2063439/Child-rapist-used-human-rights-fight-deportation—struck-again.html

85 J Slack, 'The number one excuse: Right to a family life lets foreign convicts stay in UK' *MailOn-line* (12 March 2011) available online at: www.dailymail.co.uk/news/article-1365489/Human-Rights-Act-let-foreign-convicts-stay-UK.html

context – as it is for legal reporting – is as important for what we earlier considered as 'completeness'. In the way it was put by McQuail, are the facts sufficient to constitute an adequate account? The answer here must be a resounding 'no'.

A more recent content study of mine provides evidence that readers of different newspapers are provided with differential coverage of human rights issues – which may come as little surprise – but which, I would argue, indicates readers will have a skewed, and narrow, view of the scope of human rights guarantees. Using the NEXIS newspaper database, I searched 'Human Rights Act', (for a three-month period 1 October 2017 to 9 January 2018), and limited the results further by restricting analysis to identifiable cases or clear issues.[86] My analysis shows that for readers of two right-leaning tabloids/mid-range papers (*The Express* and *The Sun*) in that period the diet of HRA stories was solely about criminals, criminal justice, or terrorists and for readers of a third (*The Daily Mail*), almost entirely so: two of its seven stories were on the deportation of a Guatemalan wife and mother of two, and mention of the human rights issues surrounding the taking of photos at office Christmas parties (in a light-hearted piece by Rachel Johnson). Readers of *The Guardian* and *The Independent* had a more varied diet: the former had stories about the Grenfell Inquiry, (non-) disclosure of financial affairs on the Isle of Man, and the decision by TfL to ban taxis having 'Free Balochistan' adverts. In fact, the preponderance of stories in *The Independent* was on other issues. As well as the TfL decision, the paper covered the High Court PIPs decision,[87] surrogacy and the HFEA, NHS data-sharing, and the challenge to the abortion laws in Northern Ireland. *The Times* featured only two – the JR challenge to remove a 14-year-old boy's name from the police database following his 'sexting' photos, and in a piece on the release of John Worboys, there was mention of the successful HRA challenge by his victims.[88] Such vastly disparate coverage must be a cause for concern, given the way that it must inform (partially at least) readers' views on the cogency and value of human rights protection.

Semiotics

We will have as our focus this single front page from *The Sun*, urging the UK to jettison its European human rights commitments.[89]

Most striking perhaps – and most obvious – is the ethnic divide down the middle. There are, it seems, no white terrorists or murderers whom the HRA and the ECHR has helped, though we need think no further than John Hirst, the usual red-top bête noire, who successfully claimed that the absolute ban on

86 The full results can be found in my submission to the Joint Committee on Human Rights Inquiry 'Human Rights: Attitudes for Enforcement' available online at: www.parliament.uk/business/committees/committees-a-z/joint-select/human-rights-committee/inquiries/parliament-2017/defending-rights-17-19/publications/

87 *RF v SoS for Work and Pensions* [2017] EWHC 3375 Admin.

88 *DSD v Commissioner of Police for the Metropolis* [2014] EHC 436 QB, now decided [2018] UKSC 11.

89 The Sun Says 'Their Rights …Or Yours? *The Sun*, 27 May 2015.

THE Sun JUST 40p

Wednesday, May 27, 2015 BRITAIN'S BEST-SELLING PAPER thesun.co.uk

HOLS FROM £15

TOKEN 5: PAGE 18

EUROPEAN COURT PUTS TERRORISTS & MURDERERS FIRST. WHY IS CAMERON DITHERING OVER ENDING THIS FARCE?

KILLER

RAPIST

DAVE, 53

ZAFREEN, 17

THEIR RIGHTS ...OR YOURS?

PAEDO RAPIST

TERRORIST

CARINA, 25

WILKES, 76

THE Sun SAYS

DAVID Cameron will let foreign criminals aided by Europe's human rights judges dodge deportation for at least another year, The Sun can reveal.

Sun readers want to stop them taking Britain for a ride. So do millions more ordinary people, including those we spoke to above. The Prime Minister vowed that a British Bill of Rights would do it.

So it is a bitter disappointment that, despite firm pledges in the Tory manifesto,

Continued on Page Eight

RIGHTS OLD MESS...SUN READERS HAVE THEIR SAY: PAGES 8 & 9

Figure 1.2 The Sun 27 May 2015

prisoner voting was unlawful,[90] or Douglas Vinter, behind the challenge to whole life sentences at Strasbourg.[91] There is a host of narratives at play here. Blacks

90 *Hirst* (n 32).

91 *Vinter v UK* (2016) 63 EHRR 1.

and members of other ethnic minorities fit the bill of 'terrorists and murderers'; white Anglo-Saxons do not. This conflation of blackness with badness is a trope oft played out in the pages of that paper and many other right-leaning outlets.

It suggests a further bifurcation of human rights as 'goods'. Not only are they not for ordinary (generally white) Britons, the image portrays a singularly narrow conception of them in terms of the scope of the Convention – that is, both 'for' terrorists and murderers and thus 'about' criminal justice, torture and deportation – and the protection offered.

There is simply no sense – if we decode that front page – that swathes of people have taken full advantage of the human rights framework, either in the UK before our domestic courts or at Strasbourg under the ECHR itself, of whom very few indeed are terrorists and murderers (or even, more widely, criminals).[92] We need think no further than Mark Neary, who used Article 5 to effect the release of his 21-year-old autistic son from a positive behaviour unit where he had spent not three days as planned but almost a year,[93] or the parents of Joanna Michael, whose common law claim in negligence against South Wales police failed but whose Article 2 claim left open the possibility of accountability for failing to prevent her death.[94] It is easy to portray the HRA as a criminals' charter – as that image implies – but it is simply untrue to view it in such stark polarised terms. Not only were the Michaels helped, so were the victims of police incompetence after officers failed to prevent the so-called black cab rapist, John Warboys, from attacking again.[95] Losing the idea of the centrality of human rights to everyday life and for everyday people – its very normality and quotidianity – and letting it be shifted, onto more hostile terrain for debate is probably the greatest failing of pro-rights campaigners in the UK.

The Sun portrays human rights as something not currently of value for ***individuals*** like you and me – all those on the right of the picture, the silent majority, are identified by first names (and ages) to facilitate that assimilation – but as something that protects people who are distinguished only by some ***collective*** shared criminal identity, necessarily demarcating them as outsiders, as having rejected society and its norms. *The Sun* wants us to know these are clearly wrong 'uns. That front page presents us again with the idea of human rights as not for 'us' – but for the undeserving underclass. Constructing a divide between individual and the collective – and through its headline, exhorting us to see ourselves

92 *The Daily Express* illustrated its 19 August 2015 piece 'Look at the people who benefit from human rights law' with a single mid-page photo of Abu Qatada alongside photos of John Hirst, the prison vote applicant, and an Algerian illegal immigrant. As an aside, it was factually wrong on so many levels; the paper was forced to publish a lengthy correction piece on 28 September. The correction is available at <>www.express.co.uk/news/clarifications-corrections/608426/Human-Rights-Correction>. The original piece is no longer available in the paper's website.

93 *London Borough of Hillingdon v Neary* [2011] EWCOP 137.

94 *Michael v Chief Constable of South Wales* [2015] UKSC 2.

95 *DSD* (n 88).

on only one side, the correct side, of the line – is something, of course, that has resonance more widely for a newspaper like *The Sun*, as part of its greater political reconstitutive enterprise. Is there not something shady, suspicious, institutionalised about the four on the left? One is captured face half hidden by a cigarette, another looking downwards. A third is caught with a bare wall as a backdrop – a prison most likely. The four on the right are photographed outside. Trees seem to be the uniform backdrop for each, and most of them are smiling or engaging with the camera. How like us they are – and the four criminals 'the other'.

We can also detect in that image a very clear sense of the Chomskian notion of worthy and unworthy victims.[96] We see this as a running thread through much human rights coverage in the media. Media stories in papers such as *The Sun* and the *Daily Mail* are almost always visually represented by unworthy victims – such as in the photo above – even when there is no natural connection between the focus of the story and the image selected. Why, for example, would *The Sun* choose to illustrate its discussion of the UK's success rate before the European Court ('Euro judges go against UK in 3 out of 5 cases') with a photo of Thompson and Venables, the notorious killers of two-year old James Bulger?[97]

That narrative of the worthy claimant pervades much media coverage. This example from the *Daily Telegraph*, on the successful action brought by Beth Warren against the Human Fertilisation and Embryology Authority illustrates that narrative: 'Widow wins High Court battle over dead husband's sperm'.[98] What no reader would glean from that report is that the court held for Mrs Warren, by virtue of her right, under Article 8, to decide to become a parent by her deceased husband and – utilising s.3 of the HRA – read an extension into the time limit for storage (i.e. the point at which the sperm would have been destroyed).[99] There is not a single mention of the term 'human right' in the report.[100] Mrs Warren is a young, white, professional – a physiotherapist – and her late husband was a ski instructor, facts put into the public domain in the reports and accompanying photos. The impression we have is of human rights – again, as with the photo – reserved for 'the other'. The word 'battle' evokes a taking of sides, of good and evil or right and wrong, of David and Goliath perhaps, and we readers should know where we stand. Similarly, Victoria Wasteney – a young, white, Christian occupational therapist – bucked the trend in the *Daily Mail*'s usual coverage and narratives: 'Devout Christian NHS worker launches appeal after being suspended

96 E Herman and N Chomsky, *Manufacturing Consent: The Political Economy of the Mass Media* (Pantheon Books, 1988).

97 C Woodhouse, 'Euro judges go against UK in 3 out of 5 cases' *The Sun* (24 August 2014).

98 Dixon, 'Widow wins High Court battle' (n 23).

99 *Warren* (n 22).

100 The *Daily Mail*, on the other hand, did mention human rights: E Harding, 'Widow, 28, elated to win High Court battle to keep her late husband's sperm preserved so she can have his children' *MailOnline* (6 March 2014) available online at: www.dailymail.co.uk/news/article-2574777/Widow-28-wins-High-Court-battle-late-husbands-sperm-preserved-children.html

for inviting a Muslim colleague to church'.[101] The tribunal found that she had 'bullied' a Muslim colleague by praying for her and inviting her to church, leading Ms Wasteney to launch her human rights appeal, laying claim to her own right of freedom of religion and conscience under Article 9. There is nowhere the rejectionist, dismissive use of quotation marks that typifies much reporting. Ms Wasteney is seeking to assert her human rights, not her 'human rights', where the parenthetic phrase 'so-called' is noises off,[102] let alone her 'yuman rites', a dismissive turn of phrase beloved of *Daily Mail* columnist Richard Littlejohn over the years.[103]

The Sun front page presents human rights not as something universal but as belonging to – and claimable by – only certain groups, asserted by the word THEIR leaping out from the page. This is a standard divisive technique – the *Daily Mail* has previously presented '102 foreign criminals we can't deport ... because of THEIR "right to a family life"' and 'Foreign criminal who attacked friend with knife freed as holding him longer would breach HIS human rights'.[104] Not only that, the photo presents us with a false dichotomy – that of 'your' rights or 'theirs'. While, on one hand, this must be true – if *you* are able to exercise your right of privacy, someone else (a journalist) will not be able to exercise their rights of free speech – this is not the sense being conveyed here, which is something far more both abstract and absolute. The photo conveys an all or nothing. Either your side enjoys rights (all of them) or the other side has them (all). *The Sun* front page encourages us to see ourselves as permanently in the losing camp while 'they' always win. There is no sense of rights in constant contestation, or of a rights framework as a negotiated balance between a whole host of competing interests and rights, where some will win sometimes and others will win other times.

101 E O'Flynn, 'Devout Christian NHS worker launches appeal after being suspended for inviting a Muslim colleague to church' *MailOnline* (5 April 2015) available online at: www.dailymail.co.uk/news/article-3026259/Devout-Christian-NHS-worker-launches-appeal-suspended-inviting-Muslim-colleague-church.html

102 Examples of this are rife: see, for example, D Barrett, 'Immigration Judges Block Foreign Killer's Deportation on "Human Rights" Grounds' *The Daily Telegraph* (12 May 2014) available online at: www.telegraph.co.uk/news/uknews/immigration/10824715/Immigration-judges-block-foreign-killers-deportation-on-human-rights-grounds.html J Slack, 'Terrorists and Murderers "Should Get the Vote" ... But Only Six Months Before Release: Plans to Protect "Human Rights" of Prisoners' *MailOnline* (18 December 2013) available online at: www.dailymail.co.uk/news/article-2525566/Terrorists-murderers-vote-months-release-Plans-protect-human-rightsprisoners.html

103 R Littlejohn, 'Robber spared deportation' (n 63). Given the discussion above on the *Daily Mail*'s coverage of deportation cases, the following is a useful example of a worthy victim in this context: Daily Mail Reporter, '"You're an illegal alien": Grandmother who's lived in Britain since she was six months old is threatened with deportation' *MailOnline* (20 November 2010) available online at: www.dailymail.co.uk/news/article-1331274/Grandmother-whos-lived-UK-6-months-old-gets-deportation-threat.html

104 Willis, 'Foreign criminal attacked' (n 27).

The last matter signified by the image is the conflation of human rights with wickedness and malevolence. As Peter Hitchens put it 'wherever there's trouble, you'll find Human Rights'.[105] It is worth quoting his piece in a little more detail:

> For too long we have failed to notice the nasty revolutionary origins and the nasty purpose of this noble-sounding idea. Human Rights, closely related to the ideas behind the bloodthirsty, ruthless revolutions in France and Russia, are now being used to give our own Left-wing elite the power to override a thousand years of tradition, national independence and freedom, in the name of something that sounds noble but is in fact sordid and ugly. In the past 30 years I can think of only one instance – a group of railwaymen who refused to be forced into a union closed shop – where Human Rights have been used in the interests of real freedom.

There is simply no sense of the Human Rights Act and the ECHR, and human rights more widely, ever being a force for good, and for welcome social change.

Conclusion

In the last few days of the 2016 EU referendum debate, and using the infamous Zinoviev letter of 1924 as his base, *Guardian* journalist, Martin Kettle, wrote – in a piece on the *Daily Mail*'s coverage:

> No newspaper in this country's history has more consistently, and at times more rabidly, pursued political objectives than the Mail – from war with Germany in the early 20th century, to the promotion of Hitler, Mussolini and British fascism in the interwar period, to the drive to get Britain out of the EU in our own lifetimes – along with the defeat of Labour at all times, by fair means or foul.[106]

This chapter has argued and shown that the *Daily Mail* has an ideological line on human rights. It is by no means alone. Large segments of the British press contribute to the spread of misinformation – often on a daily basis. We considered both the types of misrepresentation and some of these techniques above.

The way the *Daily Mail* has handled the case of Mohammed Ibrahim, an Iraqi asylum seeker who avoided deportation (and whose applications had long been rejected), sheds much light on many of the themes and points made throughout this chapter. His is an horrific story. While driving his car, he hit – and killed – a 12-year-old girl, and then fled the scene. He was convicted for driving

105 Peter Hitchens, 'Whereever there's trouble, you'll find Human Rights' *MailOnline* (28 May 2011) available online at: www.dailymail.co.uk/debate/article-1391861/PETER-HITCHENS-Wherever-s-trouble-ll-Human-Rights.html

106 M Kettle, 'The EU referendum is a battle of the press versus democracy' *The Guardian* on-line (17 June 2016) available online at: www.theguardian.com/commentisfree/2016/jun/17/eu-referendum-battle-press-versus-democracy

while disqualified and failing to stop after an accident but – and even bearing in mind that he had committed other crimes interim – attempts to deport him failed. Having a family in the UK meant he was able to lay claim to Article 8.

Ibrahim is an iconographic figure in the context of human rights reporting, a regular mainstay in the pages of the *Daily Mail* and elsewhere (such as top left in *The Sun* front page above) – often simply referred to by the shorthand epithet 'hit and run killer'.[107] His name alongside details of his non-deportation and his crime, feature in 27 Daily Mail pieces from 2009 onwards, often appearing within another piece on some wider aspect of human rights and/or deporting criminals.[108] Not solely so; he was dragged into a piece that looked primarily at sham marriages: 'Crackdown on sham marriages: Migrants who wed to settle here must wait five years for benefits'.[109]

His case provides a very particular frame through which the public perceive human rights. We can see by the way his case is reported how well it illustrates Entmann's conceptualisation of framing: it promotes a particular problem definition, causal interpretation, moral evaluation and/or treatment recommendation.[110] Let us consider just one report in which he features.

> A major review of the human right to a 'family life' will be launched this week amid mounting evidence that it is undermining Britain's immigration system.... In one case, Iraqi immigrant Aso Mohammed Ibrahim was allowed to stay after killing Amy Houston, 12, by running her over while disqualified and leaving her to 'die like a dog' under his car. The failed asylum seeker could not be deported because, the judge said, he had started a relationship with a woman in Britain and had two children. Amy's father, Paul, shouted to the judges: 'What about my right to a family life?'

The wrong people are benefitting – there is a very clear association of human rights with the undeserving 'other' – and this is all due to what is usually called 'Labour's hated Human Rights Act'[111] or its 'insidious Human Rights Act'.[112]

107 It is important in this context to note that he was not convicted of causing death by dangerous driving or similar.

108 See, by way of one example, Willis, 'Foreign criminal attacked' (n 27). Cf 'Home Office officials' "incompetence" ' (n 27).

109 Daily Mail Reporter, 'Crackdown on Sham Marriages: Migrants who wed to settle here must wait five years for benefits' *MailOnline* (13 July 2013) available online at: www.dailymail.co.uk/news/article-2014156/Immigration-crackdown-sham-marriages-force-foreigners-wait-years-benefits.html

110 R Entmann, 'Framing: Toward Clarification of a Fractured Paradigm' (1993) 43(4) Journal of Communication 51–58.

111 J Slack, 'Why Michael Gove must not fail to axe Labour's hated Human Rights Act' *MailOnline* (11 May 2015) available online at: www.dailymail.co.uk/news/article-3076095/Why-Michael-Gove-not-fail-axe-Labour-s-hated-Human-Rights-Act-JAMES-SLACK-offers-15-reasons.html Interestingly, the Conservatives and right-leaning press never seem to refer to Labour's National Health Service Act.

112 Daily Mail Comment, 'No room for dogma in these hard times, *MailOnline* (17 August 2011) available online at: www.dailymail.co.uk/debate/article-2026857/UK-inflation-No-room-dogma-hard-times.html

Of those 27 items about him, there was just one single mention of an alternative explanation of why his case succeeded, an explanation that was arguably the *sine qua non* why Ibrahim was able to remain in the UK. For six years, the Home Office failed to deport him, giving him the time and opportunity to create the 'family life' that he then used to found his Article 8 case.[113] In other words, the UK is unable to deport him partly or largely because of official incompetence, dilatoriness and mis-management. To repeat, this made the news in just one story – blink and you would miss it. In terms of moral evaluation, readers are left in no doubt where their sympathies should properly lie – who would leave a young girl to 'die like a dog'? The solution is clear – end this human rights 'farce' and 'crazy' human rights,[114] and return to common sense and British values, all, in Entmann's words, 'highly salient' terms.[115] Praise is always reserved for judges who 'see sense' and rule against someone's rights[116], and disdain dispensed when sense and rights clash: 'the remote, unaccountable European Court of Human Rights ... is synonymous with judgments that fly in the face of common sense and the interests of the British people'.[117]

This piece has painted a sorry picture. Between them *The Sun* and the Daily *Mail*, where much of the focus of this piece has been directed, have a daily circulation of about 3.3m, while the *MailOn-line* has on average 14.3m browsers.[118] That is, on anyone's estimation, a large number of people being misled (or potentially misled) about the state of human rights protection in the UK. It is clear, following the EU referendum decision in late June 2016, that human rights reform will remain on the agenda. The current Prime Minister, Theresa May, is on record as urging withdrawal from the Convention.[119] The Conservative Manifesto going

113 That was in the report on 8 April 2011. R Evans, ' "What about my family rights?" Father's despair as appeal court refuses to deport failed asylum seeker who killed his daughter' available online at: www.dailymail.co.uk/news/article-1374970/Court-Appeal-refuses-Government-bid-deport-failed-asylum-seeker-killed-daughter.html

114 J Slack, 'End of human rights farce: In a triumphant week for British values, Tories unveil plans to give Parliament and judges power to IGNORE the European Court and its crazy decisions' *MailOnline* (3 October 2014) available online at: www.dailymail.co.uk/news/article-2778720/End-human-rights-farce-In-triumphant-week-British-values-Tories-unveil-plans-Parliament-judges-power-ignore-European-Court-crazy-decision-making.html

115 R Entmann, 'Cascading Activation: Contesting the White House's Frame after 9/11' (2003) 20 Political Communication 415–432.

116 J Slack, 'At last, judges see sense over human rights: Chinese robber who claimed right to family life is kicked out' *MailOnline* (13 October 2014) available online at: www.dailymail.co.uk/news/article-2791109/chinese-thief-deported-despite-claims-impact-human-rights-british-children-judge-rules.html

117 Daily Mail Comment, 'Put UK back in charge of human rights laws' *MailOnline* (2 October 2014) available online at: www.dailymail.co.uk/debate/article-2778788/DAILY-MAIL-COMMENT-Put-UK-charge-human-rights-laws.html

118 J Jackson, 'Independent, Mirror, Express and Star suffer sharp fall in traffic' *The Guardian* on-line (17 March 2016) available online at: www.theguardian.com/media/2016/mar/17/independent-mirror-express-and-star-suffer-sharp-fall-in-traffic

119 A Asthana and R Mason, 'UK must leave European convention on human rights, says Theresa May' *The Guardian* on-line (25 April 2016) available online at: www.theguardian.com/

into the 2017 General Election pledged not to leave the ECHR for the duration of the 2017–2022 Parliament, and put plans for repeal or replacing the HRA on hold while Brexit negotiations were underway, but asserted there would be a consideration of the human rights framework when that process was concluded.[120] The least the HRA deserves is a clean fair fight – not one encumbered by misreporting, misconception, and the misconstruction of reality.[121]

Bibliography

E. Balabanova, *The Media and Human Rights: The Cosmopolitan Promise* (Routledge, 2014).

R. Barthes, *Mythologies* (A Lavers tr. Paladin, 1973).

B. Berelson, *Content Analysis in Communication Research* (Free Press, 1952).

C. Berger and S Chaffee, 'The Study of Communication as a Science' in C Berger and S Chaffee, (eds) *Handbook of Communication Science* (Sage,1987).

S. Cohen, *Folk Devils and Moral Panics* (McGibbon and Kee, 1972).

R. Entmann, 'Framing: Toward Clarification of a Fractured Paradigm' (1993) 43(4) *Journal of Communication* 51.

R. Entmann, 'Cascading Activation: Contesting the White House's Frame after 9/11' (2003) 20 *Political Communication* 415.

L. Gies, 'Human Rights, the British Press and the Deserving Claimant' in K Ziegler, E Wicks and L Hodson, *The UK and European Human Rights: A Strained Relationship?* (Hart Publishing, 2015).

L. Gies, *Mediating Human Rights: Media, Culture and Human Rights Law* (Routledge, 2014).

L. Gies, 'A Villains' Charter?: The Press and The Human Rights' (2011) 7 *Crime, Media, Culture* 1.

S. Hall, C Critcher, T Jefferson, J Clarke and B Roberts, *Policing the Crisis Mugging, the State, and Law and Order* (MacMillan, 1978).

E. Herman and N Chomsky, *Manufacturing Consent: The Political Economy of the Mass Media* (Pantheon Books, 1988).

H. Lasswell, 'The Structure and Function of Communication in Society' in L Bryson (ed), *The Communication of Ideas* (Harper and Row, 1948).

D. McQuail, *Media Performance: Mass Communications and the Public Interest* (Sage, 1992).

D. Mead, ''You Couldn't Make It Up': Some Narratives of the Media's Coverage of Human Rights' in K Ziegler, E Wicks and L Hodson, *The UK and European Human Rights: A Strained Relationship?* (Hart Publishing, 2015).

K. Negus, *Music Genres and Corporate Cultures* (Routledge 1999).

C. Sparks and M Campbell, 'The "Inscribed Reader" of the British Quality Press' (1987) 2 *European Journal of Communication* 445.

P. Thomson and G Sacks (eds), *The Cambridge Companion to Brecht* (CUP, 1994).

politics/2016/apr/25/uk-must-leave-european-convention-on-human-rights-theresa-may-eu-referendum

120 Available online at: www.conservatives.com/manifesto, 37

121 I am contorting slightly Berger and Luckmann's title, see P Berger and T Luckmann, *The Social Construction of Reality: A Treatise in the Sociology of Knowledge* (Anchor Books, 1966).

Appendix 1

Nexis searches of 'uk national newspapers'

Case	*Result*	*Search terms*	*Reported in*	*Total outlets*
Magee & Duffy	No violation Art 5	Duffy 'human rights' Magee 'human rights'	*Daily Mail* *Scottish Daily Mail* *Belfast Telegraph* *Glasgow Herald*	4
Piper	Violation Art 6	Piper 'human rights' confiscation 'human rights'	Nothing	0
O'Donnell	No violation Art 6	O'Donnell 'human rights'	Nothing	0
Hutchinson	No violation Art 3	Hutchinson 'human rights' 'whole life' 'human rights' 'whole life' 'human rights'	*Guardian* *Independent* *Mirror online* *Daily Mail online* *Belfast Telegraph* *Glasgow Herald* *Daily Post North Wales* *The Star Sheffield* *Western Mail* *Evening Standard* *Hartlepool Mail* *Mail on-line* *Mirror online* *Yorkshire Post*	14
Ibrahim	No violation Art 6	Ibrahim 'human rights' 'safety interview' 'human rights'	Nothing	0
Horncastle	No violation Art 6	Horncastle 'human rights' hearsay 'human rights'	Nothing	0
McDonnell	Violation Art 2	Mcdonnell 'human rights' Mcdonnell and 'human rights' investigative delay	*Times Law Report* *Guardian* *Ulster Star*	3

(*Continued*)

Appendix 1 (Continued)

Case	*Result*	*Search terms*	*Reported in*	*Total outlets*
Armstrong	No violation Art 6	Armstrong 'human rights' jury bias 'human rights'	*Liverpool Echo*	1
Thomas Dillon	No violation Art 5	Thomas 'human rights' IPP 'human rights' 'Parole Board' 'human rights'	Nothing	0
	No violation Art 5	Dillon 'human rights' IPP 'human rights' 'Parole Board' 'human rights'	Nothing	0
Gough	No violation Art 10	Gough 'human rights' 'naked rambler'	*Oxford Mail* *Glasgow Herald* *The People* *Mirror* *Birmingham Evening Mail* *Mail on-line* *Independent on Sunday* *Independent* *Sunday Times* *The Express* *Independent i* *Scottish Daily Mail* *The Times* *Coventry Eve Telegraph* *Daily Telegraph* *Daily Mirror* *Metro* *Glasgow Herald* *Liverpool Echo* *Evening Times Glasgow* *Plymouth Herald* *The Sun* *Belfast Telegraph* *Western Morning News* *Daily Echo* *Hampshire Chronicle* *Evening Standard* *Scotsman* *Edinburgh Evening News* *Daily Star* *Huddersfield Daily Examiner*	31

Case	*Result*	*Search terms*	*Reported in*	*Total outlets*
Hassan	No violation Arts 2, 3 and 5	Hassan 'human rights' ba'ath 'human rights' Hussein 'human rights'	*Express* *Times Law Report*	2
Firth	No violation A3P1	Firth 'human rights' votes 'human rights'	*Scotsman* *Daily Mail* *The Guardian* *Glasgow Herald* *Times Law report* *Daily Record & Sunday Mail*	6
Mcdonald	Violation Art 8	Mcdonald 'human rights'	*Daily Telegraph* *Times Law Report*	2
Paulet	Violation A1P1		*Daily Telegraph*	1
RMT	No violation A11		Nothing	0
Church of Latterday Saints	No violation A9		Nothing	0
Jones	No violation A6		*Evening Standard* *Guardian*	2

2 It's not me, it's you

Examining the print media's approach to 'Europe' in Brexit Britain

Stephanie Reynolds[1]

Introduction

Regardless of the United Kingdom's history of grudging participation in European integration, the British electorate still 'stunned the world'[2] when, in June 2016, it voted to withdraw from the European Union (EU/Union). This because, irrespective of the UK's longstanding Euroscepticism, the odds appeared stacked against the Leave campaign. As the *Mirror* neatly reflected in its decision to back Remain, the newspaper 'simply [could not] ignore the combined weight of every living Labour leader, every living Prime Minister ... the country's biggest unions, most major employers, nine out of 10 economic experts ... and almost three quarters of businesses'.[3] When the UK went to the polls, however, 52% of the voting public disagreed.

Those who had charted the evolution of press attitudes to Europe and the connected mainstreaming of Euroscepticism in UK public debate over the four decades since the EU question was last put to the vote were perhaps less surprised.[4] Writing before the campaign, Daddow argued that then-Prime Minister David Cameron's referendum strategy would 'be on the back-foot from the outset since he is unlikely to alter press positions'.[5] And indeed, on the day of the referendum result certain quarters of the press were content to claim a decisive role in the Leave victory. Less than an hour after the outcome was declared, the editor-in-chief of

1 I am grateful to the editors of this collection for their useful feedback on earlier drafts. Particular thanks are owed to Sarah Price, who provided invaluable research assistance during the formulations of the findings that inform this chapter. Any errors remain my own.

2 Anon, 'Brexit vote stuns world' *Philippine Inquirer* (25 June 2016) 1.

3 Editorial, 'Why the Mirror is Backing Remain for the Sake of our Great Nation' *Mirror* (22 June 2016).

4 O. Daddow, 'Strategising European Policy: David Cameron's Referendum Gamble' (2015) 160(5) *The RUSI Journal* 4–10

5 *Ibid.*

the pro-Leave *Sun* newspaper reportedly told the Remain-supporting *Guardian*, 'so much for the waning power of the print media'.[6]

Drawing on a primary investigation of two pro-Remain (*The Mirror* and *The Guardian*) and two Leave-supporting (*The Daily Mail* and *The Telegraph*) newspapers, across three pre-[7] and three post-referendum[8] periods, this chapter interrogates that claim and asks what it signifies for meaningful democratic debate on emotive yet highly complex issues.[9] The investigation establishes three pertinent findings. First, though the Brexit press was extremely vocal during the referendum campaign, its influence stems from a much longer-term shaping of the UK's EU-related debates. When the referendum campaigns were launched, Euroscepticism had long been the working language of British public discourse.

Second, the Brexit debate is, nevertheless, a clear example of the *continuing* and significant role and reach of print media in setting the parameters of public dialogue, despite declining sales. This raises important questions about the undeniable centrality of a free press to democratic debate on the one hand, and the potential risks to the quality of those same deliberations, on the other, when a heavily partisan press shapes them.

Third, irrespective of previous approaches, one might expect that a Leave victory would create the elbow room for all quarters of the British press to scrutinise internal and external Brexit processes with rigour. Arguably the explicit commitment of the Conservative government and the Labour opposition to realising the referendum result relieves any perceived pressure for a more rhetoric-driven strategy on those publications dedicated to UK withdrawal. Not so. Now more than ever the needs of an apparently homogenous UK public are pitted against the demands of an equally homogenised European bloc, reducing the opportunity for vital, nuanced debate about what policy choices must be made, and how, in the course of British departure. This has repercussions beyond Brexit, including the issue of whether stepping back from Europe also means distancing

---

6 J. Martinson, 'Did The Mail and The Sun Help to Swing the UK towards Brexit?' *The Guardian* (online) (24 June 2016), available online at: www.theguardian.com/media/2016/jun/24/mail-sun-uk-brexit-newspapers (last accessed 5 May 2017).

7 The first three timeframes – 15–25 April; 14–24 May; 13–23 June 2016 – span the beginning, middle and end of the referendum campaign.

8 The second three periods focus on key post-referendum events: 3–4 November (High Court judgment in *R (Miller) v Secretary of State for Exiting the European Union* [2016] EWHC 2768); 17–18 January (Theresa May's Lancaster House Speech); 24–25 January (Supreme Court judgment in *R (Miller) v Secretary of State for Exiting the European Union* [2017] UKSC 5)

9 Substantive focus was on 1) EU citizens and 2) the Court of Justice. However, these subjects commonly co-habited with a plethora of other recurring topics. The data therefore provided a rich resource for broader comment. The writer nevertheless exercises caution, given this methodology. Quantitative claims are cross-referenced against wider research and the emphasis is on qualitative analysis supported by illustrative examples.

the UK from the separate European Convention on Human Rights (ECHR/the Convention).

Are you Leave or Reform? A polarising campaign without polar opposites

> You know the most depressing thing about the campaign to Bremain? It is that there is not a shred of idealism.... The EU, they say, is crap but we have no alternative.[10]

Admittedly, when one considers that the Remain campaign was prefaced by Cameron's pre-referendum negotiations for a 'reformed EU',[11] this statement from Conservative Leave campaigner, Boris Johnson rings true. Yet an historical understanding of attitudes to the EU since UK accession, within interconnected media, political and public discourse, demonstrates why a Europhilic strategy appeared fraught with risk. The pre-existence of a dominant Eurosceptic narrative had two consequences. First, since much of the media has long cast British citizens as the victims, rather than the beneficiaries, of 'Brussels diktats', space for discussions about the potential positives of EU law and policy, for different societal groups, was constrained. Second, conversely, the ability of critical pro-Europeans to voice their own concerns about, for instance, the Union's democratic legitimacy or neo-liberal foundations was circumscribed.

A traditionally Eurosceptic nation reading an increasingly Europhobic press

The UK could never really have been described as an enthusiastic participant in the European project. Having declined invitations to co-found the European Economic Community, the UK came late to the party and for reasons widely accepted to be rooted in its relative economic decline as a non-Member State.[12] Indeed, it was arguably the message of 'jobs + influence' conveyed not only by political voices but, crucially, by the vast majority of the British press, which convinced a public perceived to be wary of the EEC to vote for continued membership in 1975.[13]

10 N. Watt, 'Boris Johnson Labels David Cameron "the Gerald Ratner of politics"' *The Guardian* (15 April 2016).

11 D. Cameron, 'A New Settlement for the United Kingdom in a Reformed European Union' *Letter to Donald Tusk* (10 November 2015).

12 Daddow, *Referendum Gamble* (above n. 4) 7

13 O. Daddow, 'The UK Media and 'Europe': From Permissive Consensus to Destructive Dissent' (2012) 88(6) *Institutional Affairs*, 1219–1236, 1222. Of course, Euroscepticism is not a uniquely British phenomenon, I. Garcia-Blanco, 'A Victory of the Nation State: the EU Referendum in the Southern European Press', *EU Referendum Analysis*, available online at:

Such a weak, instrumentalist form of pro-Europeanism in the UK was clearly vulnerable to being overwhelmed including by changes in press attitudes to the Union. Such a shift occurred. Daddow pinpoints the rise of the Murdoch empire, with its strong ideological opposition to the EU coupled with a dogged commitment to securing sales, as 'an essential – perhaps the essential – explanation for the broader media drift from permissive consensus to destructive dissent' as regards UK/EU relations.[14] By assuming the position of the straight-talking 'common man' (and it was 'man') against 'establishment elites', and by asking its competitors why 'Britain is wrong and foreigners right', the *Sun*, in particular, pushed Eurosceptic newspapers towards more sensationalist reporting and the Euro-friendly press towards 'a qualitatively different tone', with increased focus on threats to British sovereignty and identity.[15] From a legal perspective, Treaty reforms that birthed a European Union with political and social aims,[16] preceded by Margaret Thatcher's reference to a 'European superstate exercising new dominance from Brussels',[17] provided fertile ground for this new narrative to take root.

By the time of the 2016 referendum campaign, then, Euroscepticism was already the common tongue of UK newspapers. Leave publications could continue to utilise longstanding rhetorical techniques to make their case, many of which were, potentially inadvertently, also long-used in newspapers backing Remain. Specifically, the debate was largely structured around an 'us' versus 'them' narrative, which adopted two main persuasive tools.

First, the European Union, its institutions, and its Member States were routinely presented as a uniform bloc under the label 'Brussels' or 'Europe',[18] contributing to the depiction of the EU as a foreign bureaucracy engaged in 'power grabs'.[19] Admittedly, 'Brussels' might furnish journalists with useful shorthand in much the same way as 'Westminster' does for UK parliamentary activity. Nonetheless, 'for the British at least and for Eurosceptics in general – the primary location [of the EU institutions] in Brussels inevitably evokes the notion of "foreignness"'.[20] The site of the EU's Court of Justice (CJEU) in Luxembourg is

www.referendumanalysis.eu/eu-referendum-analysis-2016/section-3-news/a-victory-of-the-nation-state-the-eu-referendum-in-the-southern-european-press/

14 Ibid., 1235

15 Daddow, *Destructive Dissent* (above n. 13) 1231–1233

16 Treaty on European Union (1992) OJ C191/1

17 M. Thatcher, Speech to the College of Europe (20 September 1988) available online at: www.margaretthatcher.org/document/107332

18 C. Hope and C. Turner, 'Gove: European Courts Control Who We Can Deport' *Telegraph* (20 April 2016).

19 J. Groves, 'And Claims Boris Doesn't Really Want to Leave EU' *Daily Mail* (20 May 2016); P. Johnston, 'In Brussels No Never Means No' *Telegraph* (22 June 2016).

20 N. Dugalès and G. Tucker, 'Representations of representation: European institutions in the French and British press' in P. Bayley and G. Williams (eds.), *European Identity: What the Media Say* (2012) (Oxford Scholarship Online), ch. 2, 47.

similarly utilised to emphasise its operation as a 'foreign court'.[21] Routine use of 'Brussels' also abrogates, in the eyes of some UK newspapers at least, the need to explain the actualities of the EU's institutional framework. Instead, as this legally inaccurate extract from the *Telegraph* demonstrates, since the institutions are impenetrably complex, focus is restricted to their ability to undermine British sovereignty:

> E is for European Council, the Council of Europe, the Court of Justice of the European Union, the European Commission, and all those other baffling bodies which have the power to overrule the wishes of the British people and their Parliament.[22]

This serves both to homogenise the EU and separate it from the UK.[23] *Daily Mail* readers were told, for example, that, upon exit, the UK could secure trade deals with the EU 'without having to accept free movement of *its citizens* or pay into Brussels' coffers' [emphasis added].[24] This despite the extensive involvement of UK representatives in the formation of the Union budget, which funds a collective project,[25] and the availability of free movement rights to British citizens.[26] The preserve of 'foreigners',[27] seeking access to benefits[28] or free healthcare in the UK,[29] free movement existed only to be 'abused'[30] and 'exploited'.[31] 'Brussels' also separated the UK from a wider, singular EU within the Remain press. *The Guardian* explained that, during pre-referendum negotiations 'Cameron wanted

21 S. Glover, 'Why is Obama Telling Us to Give Up on our Sovereignty When He'd Never Surrender a Drop of his Own? *Daily Mail* (21 April 2016).

22 A. Pearson, 'The Referendum Campaign? Ah Yes, I Remember It Well' *Telegraph* (22 June 2016). One example of the legal inaccuracy in this quotation is the inclusion of the Council of Europe, a separate organisation, within the EU's institutional framework. Where newspapers do seek to distinguish the EU's institutions from one another, focus is on the Commission as the 'undemocratic' 'heart of EU governance', Dugalès and Tucker (above n. 20) 31–32. E.g. J. Slack, 'Migrants Spark Housing Crisis' *Daily Mail* (20 May 2016).

23 In the context of TV news, see J. Thornborrow *et al.*, 'Discourses of European Identity in British, Italian and French TV News' in P. Bayley and G. Williams (eds), *European Identity: What the Media Say* (2012) (Oxford Scholarship Online) ch. 4.

24 J. Slack, 'Gove: Brexit Will Make Us Freer, Fairer and Richer' *Daily Mail* (20 April 2016); see also N. Komami, 'Brexit is Only Way to Control Immigration, Campaigners Claim' *Guardian* (25 April 2016).

25 Art. 314 TFEU.

26 Arts 20, 21 and 45 TFEU.

27 B. Glaze, 'Record 2.2m EU Migrants in Work in UK' *Mirror* (19 May 2016). See also J. Shaw et al, *Getting to Grips with EU Citizenship* (Edinburgh: Charlesworth 2013) 27–28.

28 M. Holehouse, 'UK Wins Migrant Benefits Case' *Telegraph* (15 June 2016); Anon, 'Cam's Vital Court Victory on Foreigner's Benefits' *Mirror* (15 June 2016).

29 J. Doyle, 'Health Tourists' NHS Loophole' *Daily Mail* (16 April 2016).

30 *Ibid.*

31 I. Drury, 'Migrant Workers Blow to Cameron' *Daily Mail* (19 May 2016).

politicians in Brussels to agree to change several key things [emphasis added]'.[32] Though some Remain-oriented articles sought to argue that free movement led to a net contribution by EU citizens to the public purse,[33] and even the taking up of jobs seemingly beneath the British,[34] EU immigration was generally accepted as inherently problematic. European Economic Area membership, for example, was described by the *Mirror* as 'being lumbered with the worst of all worlds, having to accept EU migrants but with no say at the top table'.[35]

That is not to say that the UK was routinely presented as an active contributor to EU law and policy. Instead, 'Brussels' imposed Union legislation[36] on a 'common sense' UK.[37] Frustration of the British will in Europe is commonly communicated via the second rhetorical tool: the framing of UK/EU relations through the language of war and imprisonment. Consequently, France and Germany are afforded independence from an otherwise uniform European bloc in order to cast aspersions on their motives, usually by reference to past continental conflict. The most striking illustration comes from the *Telegraph*:

> While Mr Johnson is not arguing that the bureaucrats of Brussels are Nazis attempting to bring back Hitler's Reich, his comparison is startling. Clearly he sees parallels between the choices that confronted his beloved Churchill, and Britain, during the Second World War and the decision facing voters next month.[38]

A long-term phenomenon, Daddow explains that, increasingly, Germanophobic rhetoric accompanied the Maastricht Treaty negotiations. *The Sun*, for example, described then-Labour leader Neil Kinnock as 'shaking the clenched fist of Europower … warbling "Deutschland über Alles"'.[39] Noting a similar approach to

32 J. Elgot, 'EU Referendum: Guide to the UK's Biggest Political Decision of the Century' *Guardian* (23 May 2016).

33 A. Travis, 'Are EU Migrants Really Taking British Jobs and Pushing Down Wages?' *Guardian* (20 May 2016).

34 J. Sawers, 'There Is No Simply Way to Make Britain Safer' *Telegraph* (17 June 2016).

35 Editorial, *Mirror* (above n. 3).

36 M. Howard and R. Aikens, 'The EU's Court is Picking Away Our Laws', *Telegraph* (23 June 2016).

37 Johnston, *Telegraph* (above n. 19)

38 T. Ross, 'Britain Can Be the Hero By Stopping the EU from Getting Out of Control' *Telegraph* (15 May 16); see also J. Slack, 'Project Fear? It's a Patronising Fantasy', *Daily Mail* (20 April 2016). WWII references also featured in pro-Remain articles e.g. Sawers, *Telegraph* (above n. 34): '[Britain] would inevitably be drawn back into try to sort out [renewed conflict caused by] Europe sliding back to extreme of Left and Right' following a Brexit'.

39 Daddow, *Destructive Dissent*, (above n. 13) 1234; see also P. Baranowska, 'The Coverage of the Eurozone Economic Crisis in the British Press' (2014) 15(4) *Perspectives on European Politics and Society* 500–517, 508.

the French government, Hawkins postulates that a lack of detail from the press strengthens rather than undermines its message:

> Little is said about the precise reasons why the European Commission or the French or German governments want to undermine the UK's independence beyond a general assertion that it is in their interests [or why] … the UK … is singled out for this apparently unique treatment. Yet it is precisely because the motives of the European 'other' remain vague and impenetrable to us that they appear so menacing.[40]

The language of imprisonment is employed in much the same way. The *Daily Mail*, for instance, exclaimed that [i]f we vote to stay we are hostages to their agenda'.[41] This imprisonment also prevents the UK from reaching its potential:

> are we seriously being told that a great nation like ours has no alternative other than to be manacled in perpetuity to a failing, undemocratic, self-obsessed, dysfunctional political edifice that even the Remain side can hardly bring itself to support?[42]

However, when dominant media voices presented the EU, before the idea of a referendum was even conceived, as a homogenous, foreign leviathan against whom the UK must go into battle, it is easy to see why 'Reform' was chosen over a more Europhilic form of Remain. Thus, pro-EU newspapers sought to convince through a strategy of 'coming clean' about the fact that the 'European Union is a difficult organisation to support with great enthusiasm',[43] arguing that 'we have to swallow short-term irritations and focus on long-term interests'.[44] Remain-campaigning politicians adopted the same approach, the clearest example being Cameron's pre-referendum pledge only to campaign for membership of a *reformed* EU[45] and his continued self-identification as a 'proud Eurosceptic' during the campaign.[46]

Yet, while being seen to address the Eurosceptic concerns that had long preoccupied British public discourse seemed the only available strategy, such an approach also underestimated the entrenched accounts of Europe in much of

40 B. Hawkins, 'Fantasies of Subjugation: a discourse theoretical account of British policy on the European Union', (2015) 9(2) *Critical Policy Studies* 139–157, 150.

41 Slack, 'Project Fear', *Daily Mail* (above n. 38); see also D. Raab, 'Madness of Brussels Rule that Weakens Our Borders', *Daily Mail* (19 May 2016); R. Mason and A. Asthana, 'Michael Gove Likens Remaining in the EU to Hostage Situation', *Guardian* (19 April 2016).

42 Johnston, *Telegraph* (above n. 19); see also R. Littlejohn, 'Our Last Chance to Escape from the Disaster Movie Unfolding Across Europe' *Daily Mail* (21 June 2016).

43 Editorial, *Mirror* (above n. 3); A. Asthana, 'UK Must Leave European Convention on Human Rights, says Theresa May' *Guardian* (25 April 2016).

44 Sawers, *Telegraph* (pro-Remain article) (above n. 34).

45 Cameron, *Letter to Donald Tusk* (above n. 11).

46 Groves, *Daily Mail* (above n. 19).

the British press. Specifically Cameron's tactic that his renegotiation 'positively [would], and normatively should, return powers to Britain' risked being undermined in the subsequent media edit.[47] Indeed, Cameron's pre-referendum renegotiation was ultimately portrayed by the Brexit press as confirming European contempt for the UK,[48] while even pro-EU newspapers implied that Cameron had gone back on his word in campaigning to Remain, given the outcome.[49] This despite the surprise of EU law experts as to what the renegotiations had achieved within the confines of the Union legal framework.[50] For instance, because Cameron's requested restriction on access to social assistance for newly arriving EU workers would have discriminated against them, as compared with UK nationals, it was widely believed, before the renegotiation, that this would require Treaty change. Amending the Treaties was unlikely to be achievable within the time constraints imposed as a result of the UK referendum. Unexpectedly, however, the 'emergency benefits brake', foreseen by the renegotiation, would have been introduced more swiftly via secondary Union legislation.[51]

Following this, the Remain campaign focused on the negative impact of a Brexit on the British economy and security, in which business had one of the loudest voices.[52] Yet this arguably contributed to, rather than undermined, what Hawkins identifies as a longstanding, 'impoverished [media] conception of the EU [w]hich precludes any meaningful discussion of the benefits which may derive from EU membership for different groups in society'.[53]

Imperial outrage: inching out positive policy developments

Just as the 'us versus them' structuring of UK/EU relations, by the British press, presents the Union as a singular entity, it serves equally to homogenise the UK public, which is frequently presented as having a uniform stance towards Europe.[54] This limits opportunity for discussion about the competing pros and cons of membership for a diverse British public. Two mechanisms enabled this. First, Leave-supporting newspapers juxtaposed 'elites' – encompassing the 'big

47 Daddow, *Referendum Gamble,* (above n. 4) 3.
48 Groves, *Daily Mail* (above n. 19).
49 Elgot, *Guardian* (above n. 32); Komami, *Guardian* (above n. 24).
50 M. Dougan, 'The Draft Deal on UK Membership of the EU' *The Liverpool View* 03 February 2016 available online at: https://news.liverpool.ac.uk/2016/02/03/the-liverpool-view-the-draft-deal-on-uk-membership-of-the-eu/
51 European Council Conclusions, 19/02/15, EUCO1/16, 23. For analysis of the legality of introducing the emergency benefits brake via secondary legislation, see. S. Reynolds, '(De) constructing the Road to Brexit: Paving the Way to Further Limitations on Free Movement and Equal Treatment?' in D. Thym (ed.), *Questioning EU Citizenship: Judges and the Limits of Free Movement and Solidarity in the EU* (London: Hart 2018) ch. 4.
52 Predicted by Daddow, *Referendum Gamble,* (above n. 4) 4–5.
53 Hawkins (above n. 40) 147.
54 E.g. P. Dominiczak, 'Bill to Give Parliament Supremacy over EU Courts Killed' *Telegraph* (19 May 2016).

corporates', the British 'political and educated classes' and the 'Brussels oligarchy'[55] – against 'ordinary working people excluded from the … the corridors of power and condemned to suffer the worst excesses of the EU juggernaut'.[56] In this way, the uniform 'will of the people' could be depicted as routinely frustrated by the 'unelected … people who run the show'.[57]

The Remain camp rarely addressed this. Rather than seek to broaden discussions to cover the pros and cons of EU membership for different (inter)sections of society, it focused on the projected negative impact of withdrawal on the UK economy, perhaps because of the knock-on effects this could be presented as having on everyone. *The Guardian*, for example, reported on then-Chancellor George Osborne's speech, backed by the IMF, OECD, Bank of England and London School of Economics, which combined arguments about the deleterious effects of a Brexit on the economy with the accusation that Leave considered 'allowing people to be poorer [to be] a price worth paying'.[58]

In the age of austerity and precarious work, however, this arguably simply played into the hands of the Leave press.[59] Readers were told that Remain's funders did not care about the loss of school, housing and hospital places, purportedly as a result of EU immigration, by 'ordinary people' because the 'big banks, the big corporates and oil companies don't use those services'.[60] Though the Remain press also employed an anti-elites narrative,[61] Levy et al. postulate that the Remain camp's focus on economic risks and expert endorsement might have 'compounded the sense that they represented an elite'.[62] This could be contrasted with the more 'emotive pull of the Leave campaign's approach, their hostility to experts … and their very effective slogan of retaking control of the country, which neatly brought together concerns about sovereignty and migration'.[63]

The second tool used to homogenise the UK public was to assess the Union's democratic legitimacy through a distinctly national lens. At worst, readers were

55 Pearson, *Telegraph* (above n. 22).

56 Littlejohn, *Daily Mail* (above n. 42); see also C. Moore, 'Trade Deals Are Red Herrings in EU Debate', *Telegraph* (25 April 2016).

57 Ibid.

58 A. Asthana et al, 'Remain Campaigners Treat Public Like "Mere Children"' *Guardian* (19 April 2016); Anon, 'All EU Need to Know' *Mirror* (13 June 2016).

59 See also J. Firmstone, 'Newspapers' Editorial Opinion', *EU Referendum Analysis 2016*, available online at: www.referendumanalysis.eu/eu-referendum-analysis-2016/section-3-news/newspapers-editorial-opinions-during-the-referendum-campaign/

60 Slack, 'Housing Crisis' *Daily Mail* (above n. 22); see also J. Aitken, 'It Saw Off the Normans and Nazis, Now the Defiant Patriotism of my Kent Stomping Ground Might See Off the EU Too! *Daily Mail* (21 June 2016); Pearson, *Telegraph* (above n. 22).

61 Asthana et al, *Guardian* (above n. 58); Editorial, *Mirror* (above n. 3)

62 D. Levy *et al.*, 'The Press and the Referendum Campaign', *EU Referendum Campaign Analysis 2016,* available online at: www.referendumanalysis.eu/eu-referendum-analysis-2016/section-3-news/the-press-and-the-referendum-campaign/ E.g. J. Groves, 'Fury Over Plot to Let 1.5m Turks into Britain', *Daily Mail* (13 June 2016).

63 Levy *et al.*, *ibid.*

told that Union legislation is generated at the 'whim of unelected bureaucrats'.[64] At best, they were informed that UK representation within the EU institutions was minimal: 'the UK can be outvoted in the Council of Ministers [where] we have 8% of the votes'.[65] *The Telegraph* went furthest, descending into blatant untruth: 'Z is for zero. The number of times EU law has been changed because Britain has raised objections. This has not been for want of trying'.[66] Of course, the UK can lose out during the EU's law-making processes. Indeed, Hix and Hagemann found that the UK was the most frequently outvoted Member State in the Council between 2009 and 2015.[67] Nevertheless, they also emphasised that, in practice, the Council makes the majority of its decisions by consensus and the UK remained on the 'winning side' 86.7% of the time.[68] This is without mentioning the various opt-outs/opt-ins the UK enjoys, including from the Euro[69] and in the Area of Freedom, Security and Justice.[70]

Crucially, the consequence of reducing EU law-making to a series of UK 'wins and losses'[71] is that 'sectoral, class-based analyses of specific policy issues are marginalised at the expense of the dominant narrative of the national interest'.[72] At the supranational level, this approach also fails to reflect the need to balance Union objectives against the wishes of sovereign Member States against the views of EU citizens, as the EU's Commission–Council–Parliament decision-making triangle seeks to do, even if the success of that framework is rightly the subject of rigorous debate.[73] Instead, EU legislation can be unvaryingly presented as bad for Britain and favourable to foreigners.

Despite newspapers' anti-elites narrative, press portrayal of Union law-making as disadvantageous to a uniform UK invariably focused on the effects of EU legislation on business rather than people. For example, one *Telegraph* article cited business costs as the sole reason why EU regulations were undemocratic:

---

64 Watt, *Guardian* (above n. 10); see also Howard and Aikens, *Telegraph* (above n. 36).

65 Anon, *Mirror* (above n. 58).

66 Pearson, *Telegraph* (above n. 22).

67 S. Hix and S. Hageman, 'Does the UK Win or Lose in the Council of Ministers?' *The UK in a Changing Europe Blog* (2015) available online at: http://ukandeu.ac.uk/explainers/does-the-uk-win-or-lose-in-the-council-of-ministers/.

68 *Ibid.* For European Parliament votes, see S. Hix, 'UK MEPs Lose Most in the European Parliament' *The UK in a Changing Parliament Blog*, available online at: http://ukandeu.ac.uk/explainers/uk-meps-lose-most-in-the-european-parliament/ Moreover, UK influence is clearly about more than just final votes. For broader analysis, see S. Hix, 'Is the UK at the Top Table in EU Negotiations?' *The UK in a Changing Europe Blog*, available online at: http://ukandeu.ac.uk/is-the-uk-at-the-top-table-in-eu-negotiations/

69 Protocol (No 15) to the TFEU on Certain provisions Relating to the United Kingdom of Great Britain and Northern Ireland.

70 Protocol (No 21) to the TFEU on the Position of the United Kingdom and Ireland in respect of the Area of Freedom, Security and Justice.

71 Arguably also the inevitable result of intergovernmental cooperation.

72 Hawkins, (above n. 40) 144; 148.

73 A. Follesdal and S. Hix, 'Why There is a Democratic Deficit in the EU: A Response to Majone and Moravcsik' (2006) 44(3) *JCMS* 533–562

'Democracy – Each year, 2,500 new Brussels Regulations cost business £600m'.[74] EU 'red tape' was depicted as necessary only for those companies who wished to export 'over there' and as pointlessly burdensome for the many that do not.[75] Rhetorical force was delivered to this argument by communicating a form of outrage at the impact of EU legislation that would otherwise seem paradoxical. Specifically, newspapers highlighted EU involvement in farcically low-level minutiae on the one hand, whilst emphasising the attack on British sovereignty that this represented on the other. Of course, the 'Metric Martyr ... who defied Brussels edicts by insisting on his right to sell his wares by the pint and inch',[76] was mentioned as well as restrictions on 'high performance vacuums'.[77]

Absent from much of these discussions[78] is adequate examination – regardless of any final conclusions – of the potential benefits of, for instance, health and safety, consumer or environmental rules, business costs aside. Remarkably, the Leave campaign was able to argue in the *Mirror* that 'some rules, such as forcing small firms to carry out health and safety checks could be axed to help business',[79] with no independent journalistic assessment of whether the rules referred to were actually less necessary within smaller companies. In short, the homogenisation of the British public, pitted against the singular 'Union' can result in the representation of wide-ranging EU law and policy as unwanted red-tape that operates to the detriment of the UK as a whole.

This press approach is reflective of the wider referendum campaign, which largely boiled down to a three issue poll on the economy, immigration and the campaign itself.[80] Deacon et al. report that the 'marginalisation of ... major issues, including the environment, taxation, employment, agricultural policy and social welfare was striking' and that there was a 'remarkable absence' of devolution from the discussion.[81] Clearly, this is frustrating given the consid-

74 Ross, *Telegraph* (above n. 38); c.f. P. Forster, 'Euro Rivals Will Use Brexit to Harm City' *Telegraph* (16 June 2016).

75 Slack, 'Gove', *Daily Mail* (above n. 24).

76 Aitken, *Daily Mail* (above n. 60).

77 Anon, *Mirror* (above n. 58).

78 *The Guardian* did offer a number of sector-specific assessments of Brexit, though these sometimes arguably still over-emphasised business: Guardian Small Business Network, 'Would Brexit Affect my Business's IP Rights?' *Guardian* (20 May 2016); D. Campbell *et al.*, 'What Would Brexit Mean for the NHS, Social Care and Disabled People?' *Guardian* (14 June 2016); P. Landau, 'What Would Leaving the EU mean for your Employment Rights' *Guardian* (24 May 2016).

79 Anon, *Mirror* (above n. 58).

80 D. Deacon et al, 'The Narrow Agenda: How the News Media Covered the Referendum' *EU Referendum Analysis 2016*, available online at: www.referendumanalysis.eu/eu-referendum-analysis-2016/section-3-news/the-narrow-agenda-how-the-news-media-covered-the-referendum/ ; S. Cushion and J. Lewis, 'Scrutinising Statistical Claims and Constructing Balance: Television News Coverage of the 2016 EU Referendum', *EU Referendum Analysis 2016*, available online at: www.referendumanalysis.eu/eu-referendum-analysis-2016/section-3-news/scrutinising-statistical-claims-and-constructing-balance-television-news-coverage-of-the-2016-eu-referendum/

81 Deacon *et al.*, *ibid.*

erable constitutional challenges now facing the devolved nations. Moreover, Northern Ireland offered an excellent case study of the broader practical challenges of realising Brexit. Prior to the referendum, the Northern Ireland Affairs Select Committee had highlighted the clash between the desire both to leave the Single Market and Customs Union and increase cross-border trade; and between the call to end financial contributions to the EU and maintain subsidies for farmers.[82]

If EU law was wholly detrimental for a uniform UK, any advantages were the strict reserve of non-British EU citizens. Further, if stories in UK newspapers were proportionate to reality, their readers would be forgiven for thinking that the EU citizenry was almost entirely comprised of 'benefit tourists'[83] and criminals. In a number of pieces, the *Daily Mail* reported that 'Brussels rules dictate that the UK can't bar EU nationals unless they present a serious, credible and present danger to national security';[84] and consequently 'a string of murders and rapists have been allowed in'.[85] Since Directive 2004/38 was passed by Council and the European Parliament, both institutions in which the UK sits, and allows EU citizens to be refused entry on grounds of public policy, public health, and public security, the newspaper's claims are at best inaccurate.[86] Public policy comfortably covers murder and sexual offences,[87] while the Court of Justice defines 'public security' considerably more broadly than 'national security'.[88]

This homogenisation of the British public not only narrowed the debate as regards the potential positives of EU membership for different sections of society. It also left little room for the critical Remainer, which arguably also impacted on the perceived legitimacy of the Remain campaign.

What place for the critical Remainer?

It might, at first, seem contradictory to argue, on the one hand, that the Remain campaign was built on reform and posit, on the other, that the debate limited

82 House of Commons Northern Ireland Select Committee, *Northern Ireland and the EU Referendum* 2016–17 HC48, paras.57, 73 and 69.

83 Above n. 28.

84 Raab, *Daily Mail* (above n. 41); Komami, *Guardian* (above n. 24). For stories on EU law operating to protect terrorists, see J. Slack, 'EU Makes Us Give Secret Evidence to Terrorists' *Daily Mail* (19 May 2016); Hope, *Telegraph* (above n. 18).

85 J. Slack, 'EU Makes It Harder for Us to Control Migration, admits Home Secretary' *Daily Mail* (25 April 2016).

86 Art.27, Directive 2004/38 of the European Parliament and of the Council of 29 April 2004 on the rights of citizens of the Union and their family members to move and reside freely within the territory of the Member States OJ L158/77. After five years continuous legal residence removals are restricted to serious grounds of public policy or public security; after 10 years to imperative grounds of public security (Art. 28).

87 *NYK* [2013] CSOH 84

88 *PI* (C-348/09) EU:C:2012:300. C.f. A. Travis, 'Does the EU Really Allow Dangerous Criminals Free Entry to the UK', *Guardian* 24/05/16, which accepted judges were unlikely to overturn decisions relating to murder and rape and focused instead on ongoing issues with EU information-sharing.

space for the critical Remainer. Nonetheless, the terms of that reform were arguably set by the longstanding live issues within British Eurosceptic discourse. In calling, amongst other things, for a reduction in the burden of over-regulation on business; a 'formal, binding and irreversible' exception from ever-closer union; restrictions on EU citizens' access to in-work benefits; a 'crackdown on the abuse of free movement by fraudsters'; and stronger powers to deport criminals,[89] Cameron's renegotiation, for instance, spoke directly to entrenched press positions on 'red tape', the threat to British sovereignty posed by a 'superstate', and the exploitation of free movement rules by EU 'benefit scroungers' and criminals.

Yet many of these concerns do not bear out in practice, since the Union is either already aware of the problem or evidence puts its very existence into doubt. On 'red tape', the Commission had already launched its Better Regulation Agenda in May 2015,[90] focused on effectiveness and efficiency. As for 'ever closer union', Gordon points out:

> Anxiety about the future sovereignty of the UK as a nation state has been projected onto these three words notwithstanding the fact that … they clearly do not commit the UK to inevitable absorption into a federal EU, with the possibility of differentiated membership increasingly well established in practice.[91]

Finally, beyond some instances of localised pressure, academic assessment of EU immigration consistently points to a positive impact on the British economy.[92]

Consequently, much of the 'renegotiation' reaffirmed existing mechanisms. It pledged to 'repeal unnecessary legislation'[93] and exclude the UK from 'ever closer union', whilst stating that the phrase did not compel Member States to aim for a common destination.[94] Member States' ability to remove EU citizens for reasons of public policy and public security and to tackle abuse of free movement rights was reiterated. Nevertheless, the introduction of an emergency brake as part of the renegotiation, which would have allowed the UK, under certain conditions, to limit newly-arrived EU citizens' access to in-work benefits was genuinely new. Traditionally, EU workers have long enjoyed equal treatment rights in their host

89 Cameron, *Letter to Donald Tusk* (above n. 11).

90 European Commission, 'Better Regulation Agenda: Enhancing Transparency and Scrutiny for Better Law-Making' IP/15/4988 (19 May 2015).

91 M. Gordon, 'The UK's Sovereignty Uncertainty' *UK Const. L. Blog* (11 February 2016) available online at: https://ukconstitutionallaw.org/2016/02/11/mike-gordon-the-uks-sovereignty-uncertainty/

92 C. Dustmann and T. Frattini, 'The Fiscal Effects of Immigration to the UK' (2014) 124 *Journal of the Royal Economic Society* 593–643

93 European Council Conclusions (19 February 2015) EUCO1/16, 15.

94 *Ibid.*, 17.

Member State as regards access to social assistance.[95] Crucially, despite a lack of empirical evidence,[96] the renegotiation explicitly accepted 'the pull factor arising from a Member State's in-work benefits scheme' as the underlying rationale for the emergency benefits brake.[97] Moreover, the renegotiation documents explicitly accepted that the UK was experiencing the 'exceptional situation' the emergency brake was intended to cover.[98] In this way, the renegotiation legitimised popular claims about 'benefit tourism', despite the fact that academic studies have found little evidence of this.[99]

Though Cameron and the EU had little choice but to be seen to address the perceived issues with the Union that had long featured on the front-pages of British newspapers,[100] the combination of the mere affirmation of existing mechanisms with the use of language that endorsed popular claims about immigration left the renegotiation ripe for attack by the Leave press. If mentioned at all, the renegotiation was simply presented as 'two thirds of diddly squat', and evidence of EU contempt for Britain.[101]

Furthermore, shaped by popular reservations about the Union, the renegotiation failed to engage in more meaningful EU reform, even accepting that this would have been ambitious within the time and situational constraints created by the UK referendum. Two examples demonstrate this point.

First, despite vociferous vilification of the CJEU by the Leave press,[102] its broad-brush criticism of the Court's 'sovereignty-stealing' nature precluded a deeper conversation about its power. Remain newspapers countered Leave's assertions by focusing on the technicalities of CJEU procedure. The Court, readers were told 'deals with requests from national courts for clarification of legal principles.... [It doesn't] decide the case ... over the years other competences have come within the field of EU law ... by common agreement of EU states'.[103] Yet, the Leave press is far from alone in questioning the Court's approach. As Nic Shuibhne rightly highlights: '[T]he Court frequently pronounces so prescriptively in preliminary rulings that it is effectively deciding on the facts ... [and]

95 Above n. 93, 19; *Even* (C-207/87) EU:C:1988:409.

96 See S. Currie, *Migration, Work and Citizenship in the Enlarged European Union* (Cornwall: Ashgate 2008) 45; Eurofound Report, 'Social Dimension of Intra-EU Mobility: Impact on Public Services' December 2015.

97 Above n. 93, 23.

98 Above n. 93, 34.

99 Above n. 96.

100 E.g. G. Sheldrick, 'Benefits Britain Here We Come!' *Daily Express* (1 January 2014); J. Slack, 'Migrants Handed £1m a Week for Children Back Home' *Daily Mail* (4 February 2013).

101 B. Johnson, 'Do Bremainers Really Think Voters will be Cowed by the Likes of Obama?' *Telegraph* (24 April 2016).

102 T. Ross, 'Obama 'ignorant' of Harm EU Does to Our Joint Security, says Minister', *Telegraph* (24 April 2016); Glover, *Daily Mail* (above n. 21).

103 O. Bowcott, '"We Don't Decide National Cases": ECJ Veteran Swipes Away Eurosceptic Barbs', *Guardian* (19 April 2016).

does not always consider the downstream systemic effects or implications of its decisions for broader national regulatory priorities.'[104]

Indeed, the CJEU's expansive approach to what constitutes 'the scope of EU law' has seen the free movement provisions affect national rules on, amongst other things, industrial relations,[105] social security,[106] non-EU immigration,[107] and housing.[108] More broadly, the Court's introduction of direct effect and supremacy,[109] and the primary law status of its judgments, have rendered the EU's political institutions less central to internal market developments and less able to respond to domestic reactions to EU case-law.[110] This has inhibited some of the political means of securing the Union's democratic legitimacy, even accepting the centrality of seminal CJEU judgments to the contemporary functioning of the internal market.[111]

Second, since press analysis of the Union's democratic legitimacy was principally conducted through a national lens, little attention was paid by UK newspapers to the growing dominance of national executives within the Union's institutional framework, particularly following the sovereign debt crisis.[112]

In sum, against a longstanding 'us' versus 'them' narrative, within British media and public discourse, which pits a singular 'Europe' against a homogenised UK, it was always going to be difficult to present the positives of membership to the electorate. Conversely, nuanced critique of the Union's democratic profile is also inhibited by this reductive approach to UK/EU relations. Of course, correlation and causation are very different things and it is difficult to measure, particularly as a lawyer, the impact of the print media on wider public discourse, the reform agenda, and the vote itself. Nevertheless, it is clear that the press, working in partnership with certain politicians, enjoys substantial societal voice, which in turn gives newspapers the power to influence the tone of EU-related debate.

Tomorrow's chip paper? Assessing the reach and role of the Brexit press

In the social media age, in which newspaper sales are in decline, analysis of print media might seem outdated. However, research suggests the press still enjoys

104 N. Nic Shuibhne, *The Coherence of EU Free Movement Law: Constitutional Responsibility and the Court of Justice* (Oxford: OUP, 2013) 60.

105 *Laval* (C-341/05) EU:C:2007:809.

106 *Grzelczyk* (C-184/99) EU:C:2001:458.

107 *Carpenter* (C-60/00) EU:C:2002:434.

108 *Libert* (Case C-197/11) EU:C:2013:288.

109 *Van Gend en Loos* (C-26/62) EU:C:1963:1; *Costa v ENEL* (C-6/64) EU:C:1964:66.

110 G. Davies, 'Legislative Control of the European Court of Justice' (2014) 51 *CMLRev* 1579.

111 D. Grimm, 'The Democratic Costs of Constitutionalisation: The European Case' (2015) 21 *ELJ* 460.

112 C.f. J. Slack, 'Corbyn Says We Can't Limit EU Migrants' *Daily Mail* (20 June 2016); see M. Ruffert, 'The European Debt Crisis and European Union Law' (2011) 48 *CMLRev* 1777–1806.

significant reach. Given the rhetorical approaches newspapers employ, outlined above, this raises questions about their role. On the one hand, a free press is pivotal to a functioning democracy; on the other, a heavily partisan press might pose risks to high-quality debate. This difficult balancing act is arguably best approached by viewing newspapers as political actors and by assessing whether there are sufficient checks and balances across the democratic landscape to ensure the wider discourse reflects the complexity of the issue at hand. However, the wider media, and in particular broadcasters, allow their own communications to be strongly influenced by newspapers' agendas, markedly limiting their ability to act as a check on a persistently powerful press. That said, the UK press does not act alone in shaping debate. It is often ably assisted by political actors, creating a press/politics partnership that severely inhibits the capacity of newspapers to meet their democratic function and hold politicians to account.

'It is smaller, weaker and less profitable than before but [Fleet Street] still bites'[113]

For some media commentators, the referendum result demonstrates the current conundrum that 'as the print media decline in circulation ... their power has never seemed greater'.[114] However, a long-term analysis arguably once again indicates why this is the case. Over the three main loci of EU-related debate – the individual, the broader media, and political spaces – the influence of the press far pre-dates the referendum campaign.

At the individual level, British newspapers have historically benefited from healthy readership figures. Indeed even as numbers wane, they still enjoy, relatively speaking, considerable direct reach. In 2014, over 12 million people in the UK still bought a newspaper every day.[115] Moreover, those figures do not include readers who read their paper 'second-hand', nor do they include online editions. Crucially, while individual titles were divided fairly evenly across Leave and Remain, the readerships of the latter are significantly smaller than the former.[116] Even before the referendum, the proportion of UK readers consuming Eurosceptic coverage vastly outweighed those taking in 'neutral' or pro-European messages.[117] Demographics are also a factor: older voters were more likely to buy a newspaper, and one which was pro-Leave, turn out to vote, and to opt for exit.[118]

Of course, this raises the question of whether the press simply preaches to the choir. Certainly, the drivers behind newspapers' increased Euroscepticism appear at least part-commercial,[119] leading *The Guardian* to question the power of the

113 J. Gapper, 'Fleet Street's European Bite Remains Sharp' *Financial Times* (22 June 2016).
114 J. Seaton, 'Brexit and the Media', (2016) 87(3) *The Political Quarterly*, 333–337, 334.
115 Baranowska, (above n. 39) 501
116 Daddow, *Referendum Gamble* (above n. 4) 6; Deacon *et al.* (above n. 80).
117 *Ibid.*
118 Levy *et al.* (above n. 62).
119 Daddow, *Destructive Dissent* (above n. 13) 1225.

Brexit press, since it 'reflected what their readers thought to begin with'.[120] Nevertheless, research suggests that newspapers hold considerable sway over their consumers. Prolonged exposure to the media's evaluative messages can either gradually influence predispositions or entrench negative views, particularly as regards the EU, about which the media is often citizens' primary source of information.[121] Ultimately, while commercial drivers might have contributed to more sensationalist reporting, this in turn allows proprietors and editors with their own ideological positions to capitalise on readers' general wariness towards 'Europe' by suggesting that the Union is responsible for readers' wider concerns about anything from the NHS to national security.[122]

Newspapers also enjoy an agenda-setting function as regards the wider media. Section one demonstrated that a Eurosceptic discourse structured discussions even in Remain newspapers. More broadly, broadcasters have been slow to respond to diminishing newspaper sales, offering the press a disproportionate role in shaping their own communications and allowing the print media to influence the information imparted even on those who no longer reach for their morning paper.[123] As Seaton notes, 'it took two days from the actress Emma Thompson coming out in favour of "Remain" through the Sun's headline "Shut Yer Cakehole", to Evan Davies on Newsnight saying that Remain had a "Luvvie" problem'.[124]

Finally, the historical power of the UK press has also influenced political discourse over the longer term. Hawkins reports that Government ministers have long-employed the same 'us versus them' narrative as British newspapers, depicting the EU 'not as a mechanism through which the UK manages its relations with other member-states but as a threat from which the UK must be protected'.[125] At the very least, this suggests a 'subtle, subconscious process of socialisation'[126] of political discourse by the press. However, politicians have often also made a conscious choice. According to Daddow, as the media became more hostile to the EU, 'politicians came to believe that serious and sustained political discussion of European affairs was dangerous to their personal careers and party political fortunes'.[127] This was not, however, just about abandoning pro-European positions. Increasingly politicians have sought to cultivate an image of being tough on Europe, whether that be Blair's stance on the EU Charter of Fundamental

120 P. Preston, 'The People Have Spoken on Brexit: But Did the Media Tell Them the Truth?' *The Guardian* 13 October 2016.

121 P. Desmet *et al.*, 'Discussing the Democratic Deficit: Effects of Media and Interpersonal Communication on Satisfaction with Democracy in the European Union' (2015) 9 *International Journal of Communication* 3177–3198; 3192. Other significant factors include interpersonal communications and political 'sophistication'.

122 J. Slack, 'Exposed: Cameron's EU Sham' *Daily Mail* (17 May 2016); Ross, *Telegraph* (above n. 102).

123 Seaton (above n. 114) 335.

124 *Ibid.*

125 Hawkins (above n. 40) 152.

126 *Ibid.*

127 Daddow, *Destructive Dissent* (above n. 13) 1236.

Rights and labour law,[128] or the competition between politicians on both sides of the referendum campaign to display their Eurosceptic credentials.[129]

There is also evidence of more explicit attempts by newspapers to influence political figures. John Major told the Leveson Inquiry that:

> In the run-up to the 1997 election ... [Murdoch] made it clear that he disliked my European policies which he wished me to change. If not, his papers could not and would not support the Conservative Government ... it's not often that point is directly put to a prime minister in that fashion.[130]

Evidence to the Inquiry also suggested indirect forms of influence by the Murdoch press on Labour during the Blair years and, later, on the Conservative party by means of steer from Murdoch as regards what policies would win his newspapers' general election support,[131] or via friendships between editors and political figures.[132]

While attempts by newspaper proprietors to influence individual politicians see varying degrees of success,[133] newspapers and their owners clearly enjoy continuing capacity to shape public discourse. As regards the referendum, the press clearly 'intervened in the debate with the strategic aim of influencing politicians, campaigners and readers'.[134] This raises difficult questions. On the one hand, a free press is central to functioning democracy. On the other, since 'the media plays a crucial role as the electorate's main source of information about politics, and particularly about the EU',[135] a heavily partisan press risks the inhibition of varied debate. The examination of newspapers as political actors[136] offers a useful means of assessing whether press partiality poses a democratic problem and, if so, the extent of it.

Newspapers as political actors

Scrutiny of the press as a political actor is two-fold. First, newspaper conduct should be assessed. Second, the efficacy of current checks and balances must be considered. On conduct, partiality is not, of itself, problematic. Indeed, the

128 Hawkins (above n. 40) 152–153.
129 Groves, *Daily Mail* (above n. 19).
130 Lord Leveson, *An Inquiry into the Culture, Practices and Ethics of the Press: Report* (2012) Vol. III, 1131.
131 *Ibid.*, 1139–1143.
132 Leveson, (above n. 130) 118.
133 John Major refused to change his EU policies and lost the support of *The Sun* in the 1997 General Election; Daddow argues that pressure from Murdoch influenced Blair's U-Turn on a referendum on the now defunct EU Constitutional Treaty, *Destructive Dissent* (above n. 13) 1229.
134 Firmstone (above n. 59).
135 Hawkins (above n. 40) 154.
136 See also Firmstone (above n. 59).

Leveson Inquiry recognised the right of the press to be partisan and the legitimate influence this can have on the choice of story and the angle from which it is reported.[137] The survey sample for this study indicates, in this regard, that the Leave press was simply better at writing persuasively,[138] and invested more of its resources into the campaign.[139] More importantly, there are numerous examples of newspapers providing useful scrutiny of Brexit debates and developments despite, or as part of, their ideological position. The *Daily Mail*, for example, reported on a leaked letter suggesting Cameron was 'plotting with a multinational firm on how to hammer home the Remain case while still claiming he was prepared to campaign for Leave'.[140] The *Telegraph* questioned whether law and politics could ever be as separate as the High Court claimed in *Miller*,[141] in which it was held that parliamentary authorisation was needed for Theresa May to trigger UK withdrawal from the Union.

Press conduct becomes a cause for concern, however, when newspapers misreport EU legal issues as a result of poor practice or conscious choice.[142] An infamous example of a blatant lie during the referendum campaign was the *Daily Mail's* 'We're From Europe – Let Us In' story which falsely implied that a 'lorry-load of migrants sneaking into Britain' claimed to be from Europe.[143] Though the *Telegraph* stated that the individuals were from Iraq, it chose nonetheless to place the story within a wider piece on EU immigration.[144] Over the course of the campaign, *Telegraph* and *Daily Mail* readers were also told, *inter alia*, that Britain has never been able to influence EU law;[145] that Union legislation emanates solely from the European Commission;[146] and that continued EU membership meant the prospect of '77m Turks' coming to Britain.[147] Establishing that this is a longer-term phenomenon, the Leveson Inquiry found evidence of 'wilful

137 Leveson (above n. 130) Vol. II 688; see also Independent Press Standards Organisation, *Editors' Code of Practice*, (2016) preamble.
138 Eurosceptic newspapers were more likely to sandwich counter-arguments between arguments supportive of their stance e.g. compare Hope and Turner, *Telegraph* (above n. 18); Slack, *Daily Mail* (above n. 24) with Mason and Asthana, *Guardian* (above n. 41); Komami, *Guardian* (above n. 24).
139 Firmstone (above n. 59).
140 Slack, 'Exposed' *Daily Mail* (above n. 122).
141 P. Johnston, 'The Judges Should Have Stayed Out of This and Left it to the Politicians' *Telegraph* (4 November 2016); *Miller* (above n. 8) para.5; see also on the UK opt-out from the EU Charter of Fundamental Rights, Howard and Aikens, *Telegraph* (above n. 36).
142 See Slack, 'Secret Evidence' *Daily Mail* (above n. 84), in which the author did not discuss the various allowances made for national security in CJEU case-law or provide readers with the name of the judgment discussed (presumably *ZZ v SSHD* (C-300/11) EU:C:2013:363).
143 J. Slack and J. Groves, 'We're From Europe – Let Us In' *Daily Mail* (16 June 2016).
144 S. Swinford and K. McCann, 'May Calls for Extra Curbs on Migrants' *Telegraph* (16 June 2016).
145 Pearson, *Telegraph* (above n. 22).
146 Howard and Aikens, *Telegraph* (above n. 36).
147 J. Doyle, 'Boris: Beware 77m Turks Coming Here' *Daily Mail* (18 April 2016).

blindness to the (lack of) truth of stories which fit a newspaper's adopted viewpoint' as regards the EU.[148] It also emphasised that factual inaccuracies, such as the *Sun*'s 'Swan Bake' headline, which alleged Eastern Europeans were eating swans, can seem trivial but the 'cumulative impact' can have serious consequences for policy options and democratic discussions about policy choices.[149]

More troubling still is the decision of newspapers to descend into xenophobic, sexist or homophobic language,[150] which is often used as a rhetorical device to reinforce the 'us versus them' narrative of the Brexit press and to dramatise the legal situation at hand. Thus, the *Daily Mail* described the EU as 'an unruly and disputatious club of strange foreigners',[151] and implied that it was in some way problematic that one of the High Court judges in *Miller* was 'openly gay'.[152] Both the *Daily Mail* and the *Telegraph* rarely mentioned the *Miller* litigation without reference to the births of the applicants in the case, Gina Miller and Deir Dos Santos, in Guyana and Brazil respectively.[153] Christine Lagarde was presented to readers not simply as the head of the International Monetary Fund, but also as 'George Osborne's cougar friend'.[154] Once again, these approaches are longstanding; the referendum was merely an opportunity for concentrated examples. Wring considers the 1986 Single European Act to be the watershed moment in this regard. Importantly, he highlights that, while the *Sun* led the way by encouraging its readers to tell the 'feelthy French to FROG OFF … jingoism was not confined to the "redtop" papers. One Telegraph report suggested a breakthrough in the Channel Tunnel's construction would allow the British to smell the "first whiffs of garlic" '.[155]

The duration of this press conduct, and the ongoing ability of newspapers to set the parameters of wider media debate, appears to have impacted on the effectiveness of checks and balances by the broader media. As regards inaccurate reporting, a number of fact-checking bodies, such as FullFact.org, seek to scrutinise newspapers' factual claims but enjoy considerable less reach than Britain's most popular dailies. Journalistic enterprises such as InFact directly challenge EU-related articles before the Independent Press Standards Organisation (IPSO), but their impact can be limited. For example, since the *Daily Mail* entered into a dialogue over its infamous 'We're From Europe – Let Us In' headline, no action was

148 Leveson (above n. 130), Vol. II, 672.

149 Leveson (above n. 130), Vol. II, 688.

150 Notwithstanding that the right to offend might fall within the freedom of expression, this should be balanced against the rights of others (Art 8(2) ECHR).

151 Glover, *Daily Mail* (above n. 21).

152 J. Slack, 'Enemies of the People' *Daily Mail* (4 November 2016).

153 E.g. K. McCann, 'Brexit Could Be Delayed for a Year By Remainers' *Telegraph* (4 November 2016); R. Littlejohn, 'We Can't Let Brexit Be Derailed by a City Slicker and a Brazilian Crimper' *Daily Mail* (4 November 2016).

154 Pearson, *Telegraph* (above n. 22); see also Q. Letts, 'His Creamy Dimples Beamed with Self-Pleasure' *Daily Mail* (25 January 2017).

155 D. Wring, 'Going Bananas Over Brussels: Fleet Street's European Journey' *The Conversation* (21 June 2016).

taken against the paper for its breach of the Editors' Code. Instead, a correction was published on page two and was therefore likely to reach far fewer readers.[156] Likewise, *The Guardian's* scrutiny of inaccurate reporting in other newspapers is unlikely to be read by many of those who saw the original piece.[157]

Very blatant racism was still expressly condemned in the newspapers surveyed, suggesting that an intangible combination of constraints – such as readers' reactions, laws around incitement of racial hatred, and the individual boundaries of journalists and editors – offers something of a (potentially fragile) safeguard against openly racist abuse. The *Telegraph* condemned the UK Independence Party's 'Breaking Point' poster, describing it as 'triggering echoes of Nazi propaganda ... and [going] well beyond the bounds of decency'.[158] More broadly, the wider reaction to the *Daily Mail's* 'Enemies of the People' front page,[159] following the High Court judgment in *Miller* had a visible effect on that paper's subsequent approach to the Supreme Court ruling.[160]

Yet, these constraints themselves risk distracting from more subtle and pervasive press attacks. Indeed, the same *Telegraph* article that denounced the Breaking Point poster, argued that a Leave vote would free us from 'having a lot of shouty Eastern European blokes standing outside B&Q'.[161] The more tempered *Daily Mail* article on *Miller* still referred to Gina Miller as the 'gloating 'Guyana[n]'.[162] While the pro-Remain press offered some scrutiny here, asking Miller 'whether she believed a white man would have received similar levels of hate'[163] – the long-term Eurosceptic angle of the British press led those newspapers to adopt some questionable techniques of their own. *The Guardian* sought to reassure its readers about EU free movement rules, for instance, by claiming that 'the more typical EU migrant today is a French or Italian graduate working in the City ... than a Polish plumber'.[164] The contrast between *The Guardian's* approach here and its treatment of Miller raises larger questions about the considerable societal voice one seemingly needs to enjoy before the opportunity to challenge entrenched narratives even arises.

Of course, checks and balances need not be internal to the press. One would expect a range of views to contribute to democratic debate – and informed

---

156 D. Ponsford, 'Daily Mail breached Editors' Code with inaccurate WE'RE FROM EUROPE – LET US IN! front page' *Press Gazette* (7 October 2016).

157 R. Greenslade, 'Daily Mail Publishes Correction to Misleading EU Migrants Story' *Guardian* (24 May 2016).

158 Pearson, *Telegraph* (above n. 22); see also J. Blanchard, 'Deluded and Dangerous: Brexit Vote Fury as Farage Claims He's a Victim' *Mirror* (20 June 2016).

159 Slack, 'Enemies', *Daily Mail* (above n. 152).

160 J. Doyle, 'Champions of the People' *Daily Mail* (25 January 2017) (focused on the dissenting judgments)

161 Pearson (above n. 22).

162 Comment, 'This Was Not a Good Day for Democracy' *Daily Mail* (25 January 2017).

163 A. Ross, 'Gina Miller: the Woman behind the Article 50 Challenge', *Guardian* (3 November 2016); Anon, 'Gina's Victory over the Odds ... and Trolls' *Mirror* (25 January 2017).

164 A. Travis, 'Is Michael Gove's Points-Based System for Immigration Realistic?', *Guardian* (19 April 2016).

decision-making – across, rather than simply within, media outlets. In that regard, broadcasters achieved greater parity than newspapers ahead of the referendum.[165] However, concern about meeting their impartiality obligations, in a campaign that did not cut neatly across party political lines, also seems to have led broadcasters to rely more than ever on newspapers to set the parameters of debate,[166] calling into question the capacity of news media to offer an effective counter-balance to the Eurosceptic press. More broadly, this rigid approach to impartiality led, first, to an over-emphasis on 'balance' between Remain and Leave, with little independent journalistic scrutiny of the due weight to be given to individual claims depending on their veracity;[167] second, to the categorisation of evidenced-based expertise as simply falling on one side or the other of a political argument;[168] and, third, to the over-representation of Conservative voices, since that party was more openly split, to the detriment of left-of-centre cases for Remain.[169] Similarly alienating was the lack of diversity in media representations of the campaign. According to Harmer, women accounted for just 25.3% of all individual expert sources in television coverage and 15.4% in press reports, as compared to 48.1% and 39.1% respectively in features drawing on vox-popping.[170] Moreover, Priti Patel MP and London Mayor, Sadiq Kahn, were the only black, Asian and minority ethnic campaigners to appear in the top 30 most featured campaigners.[171] In keeping with the wider findings here that the referendum merely reflects longstanding phenomena, there is evidence that this is a longer-term issue within the UK media coverage of EU issues.[172]

Overall, then, while a free, and even partisan, press is essential to healthy democratic debate, its power, and the societal influence newspapers offer to individual proprietors and editors,[173] also requires that they be scrutinised as political actors. While a number of mechanisms exist, the limited reach of, for instance, fact-checking services and corrections, following IPSO complaints, calls into question their effectiveness. Similarly, though the formal impartiality of broadcasters appears to offer a counter-balance to a partisan press, the reliance of TV news on newspapers to set the parameters of debate and an overly-rigid utilisation of 'balance' to achieve impartiality can undermine journalistic scrutiny and narrow debate. If broadcaster focus on balance led to an under-scrutiny of political

165 Deacon *et al.* (above n. 80).
166 Levy *et al.* (above n. 62).
167 Cushion and Lewis (above n. 80).
168 Seaton (above n.114), 335–336.
169 J. Lewis and S. Cushion, 'BBC Brexit Bias' Claims Need to Be Based on Hard Evidence' *The Conversation* (23 March 2017).
170 E. Harmer, 'Brexit Mansplained: News Coverage of the EU Referendum' *EU Referendum Analysis 2016*, available online at: www.referendumanalysis.eu/eu-referendum-analysis-2016/section-3-news/brexit-mansplained-news-coverage-of-the-eu-referendum/
171 *Ibid.*
172 BBC Trust Review of the Breadth of Opinion Reflected in the BBC's Outputs (July 2013) 41.
173 On Murdoch's editorial influence at *The Sun*, see Leveson (above n. 130) Vol. I, 108.

claims, however, newspapers went further, working together with the political actors to co-write Brexit.

Co-writing Brexit: the press/politics partnership

It has already been established that Euroscepticism had become the 'stock national style of debating European affairs' far ahead of the referendum, including within political discourse.[174] At best, this was because pro-European politicians demonstrated 'a lack of leadership on European issues since accession' or, at worst, it was the result of 'a cunning political game' designed to appease the Murdoch press for party political gain on what was once considered a low-salience issue.[175] Eventually though, as section one outlined, this political mainstreaming of Euroscepticism left Remain with few strategic options beyond Reform when the issue of membership came to a head at the referendum.

However, the long-term nature of the UK's Eurosceptic narrative notwithstanding, the referendum was nevertheless a flashpoint for closer synergies between like-minded political and media actors. Writing in the pre-referendum era, Hawkins argued that politicians expressed their Euroscepticism 'in very different terms to the "obscene" components of Euroscepticism articulated by commentators in the tabloid press',[176] whose tactics were unavailable to the political mainstream. By calling upon politicians to choose a side, and inviting them to campaign, the referendum appears to have broken down this barrier. Indeed, politicians were often in the driving seat, providing Leave newspapers with more than enough material to communicate their message, or even writing on their behalf, whether to disseminate inaccurate information or, more troublingly, to join newspapers in the use of xenophobic language.

Thus, as well as emblazoning it on the side of a bus, in an interview with the *Telegraph,* Boris Johnson claimed that upon exit 'we would have £350m more a week to spend on our priorities, such as the NHS'.[177] Politicians were at the forefront of claims that EU law is imposed by the European Commission,[178] and that EU citizens can only be refused entry to the UK for reasons of national security.[179] Of course, newspapers provide an important mechanism for political expression. However, where politicians are providing copy that speaks to a publication's editorial stance, the opportunity for journalistic scrutiny of (inaccurate) political claims becomes narrower. Admittedly, as far as MPs were concerned, Leave politicians were in the minority, certainly in terms of Cabinet ministers. They nevertheless enjoyed considerable voice, arguably out of proportion with the number of parliamentary figures actually supportive of withdrawal. This is

174 Daddow, *Destructive Dissent* (above n. 13) 1236.
175 *Ibid.*
176 Hawkins (above n. 40) 149.
177 Ross, *Telegraph* (above n. 38).
178 Howard and Aikens (above n. 36).
179 Raab, *Daily Mail* (above n. 41).

arguably because, while Remain relied on expert endorsement, Leave was more likely to forefront political figures,[180] which suited the media's presidential-style campaign coverage[181] and gave media-savvy politicians such as Boris Johnson a considerable platform.[182]

Some politicians also engaged more openly in xenophobic language than was historically the case. For instance, though Second World War references have long been a rhetorical staple of the Eurosceptic press, politicians have traditionally been expected to be more discreet. When, in the early 1990s, Nicholas Ridley, then Secretary of State for Industry, described progress towards economic and monetary union as 'like giving it up to Hitler' in a 'German racket designed to take over the whole of Europe', he was forced to resign.[183] A leaked document nevertheless suggested wider Cabinet and prime ministerial distrust of the 'German character'.[184] While Daddow rightly argues that we should not underestimate the impact of off-the-record Germanophobic sentiment shared between certain political and media actors, come the referendum there was seemingly no need for such caution. In an interview with the *Telegraph*, for example, Boris Johnson described the Union as the latest attempt to unify Europe: 'Napoleon, Hitler, various people tried this out, and it ends tragically'.[185] He pointed to the Italian motor-manufacturing industry, which 'ha[s] been absolutely destroyed by the euro – as was intended by the Germans'.[186]

Arguably, then, the synergies between a powerful Brexit press and high-profile Leave politicians, employing increasingly similar approaches to presenting UK/EU relations, allowed them to play their considerable part in co-writing Brexit. Nevertheless, Leave's unexpected referendum victory might have brought an end to this partnership, giving the Eurosceptic press the elbow room to scrutinise the withdrawal process in exercise of its democratic function.

If it ain't broke they are unlikely to fix it: lessons for the Convention from the Brexit referendum

Rather than provide opportunity for a fresh approach by newspapers to UK/EU relations, the referendum result has instead further entrenched pre-existing press practices. In particular, the print media has utilised the exit negotiations

180 Lewis and Cushion, *Hard Evidence* (above n. 169).
181 Deacon et al, (above n. 80).
182 Ross, *Telegraph* (above n. 38), which argued that only Johnson could match Cameron 'for sheer star quality [and] influence'.
183 D. Lawson, 'Saying the Unsayable about the Germans – Dominic Lawson Meets Nicholas Ridley, *The Spectator* (14 July 1990).
184 Anon, 'Portrait of the Week' *The Spectator* (21 July 1990).
185 Ross, *Telegraph* (above n. 38).
186 *Ibid.* Though it printed the interview, the *Telegraph* was critical of Johnson's interview elsewhere, Forster, *Telegraph* (above n. 74). The *Daily Mail* instead chose to criticise those who had condemned Johnson's remarks, Groves, *Daily Mail* (above n. 19).

to entrench further its 'us versus them' narrative and is often joined by Leave-supporting politicians who find endorsement in the wider political discourse. This presentation of the UK/EU relationship operates to the detriment of nuanced democratic debate about the various, and often conflicting, policy choices that the UK must make as it progresses towards exit. The longevity and tenacity of newspapers' approach to the EU is arguably indicative of how future discussions about the UK's relationship with the separate ECHR might play out. The rhetorical devices employed by the print media in its EU and Convention-related discussions have long been interchangeable and politicians have adopted comparable strategies in response. Consequently, any future debates about the UK's engagement with the ECHR, with or without a referendum, seem pre-destined to be structured and conducted in much the same way as those on Brexit, leaving those who wish the UK to maintain its current approach to Convention rights in a difficult position.

Getting the best deal for Britain: a homogenous Europe versus a uniform UK

In maintaining an 'us versus them' structure to its presentation of UK/EU relations, the British press continues to utilise well-established rhetorical devices such as the use of 'Brussels' to homogenise the Union. Following Theresa May's Lancaster House speech – in which she outlined her Government's overall ambitions for the UK's exit from and future relationship with the EU – the *Mirror*, a Remain newspaper, speculated on what would happen if 'Brussels refuses to cooperate'.[187] France and Germany, however, continue to be singled out as being particularly eager to jeopardise negotiations.[188] The language of war and imprisonment is still employed to reinforce this dynamic. For instance, a *Guardian* article critical of Boris Johnson's decision to compare then French president François Hollande to a German guard in a Second World War film, was nonetheless entitled 'Battle Lines Harden after Article 50 Ruling'.[189] For the *Daily Mail*, Theresa May's Lancaster House speech demonstrated her capacity to 'extract us from the claws of Brussels'.[190]

Similarly, the UK public is presented as having a uniform stance on Brexit, via the same 'anti-elites' narrative that juxtaposed 'Remainers' and 'ordinary British

187 J. Beattie, 'What May Happen? Brexit Plan: Deal or No Deal with Europe?' *Mirror* (18 January 2017); see also A. Brummer, 'Speech Sent Pound Soaring No Wonder the City Cheered' *Daily Mail* (18 January 2017).

188 D. Sandbrook, 'Daring. Decisive. A Hint of Steel. Truly, May's Momentous Speech was like Watching the Iron Lady in Full Flight' *Daily Mail* (18 January 2017); Anon, 'Blueprint to Free Britain from Brussels' *Daily Mail* (18 January 2017).

189 J. Henley and J. Elgot, 'Brexit Weekly Briefing: Battle Lines Harden after Brexit Ruling' *Guardian* (24 January 2017) referring to M. Safi and P. Wintour, 'No 10 Defends Boris Johnson Over "Brexit Punishment Beatings" Quip' *Guardian* (18 January 2017).

190 Q. Letts, 'A Curse on Branson and his Plot to Hijack Brexit with his Cash and his Bemoaning Chums' *Daily Mail* 24 January 2017; see also Anon, *Daily Mail* (above n. 188).

people'[191] before the referendum, and regardless of the fact that Remain secured 48% of the vote. The *Miller* proceedings only strengthened these accusations. '£30m Gina'[192] formed part of a 'smug, self-selecting, so-called "elite"',[193] that 'sticks two fingers up at 33 million Britons whichever way they voted'.[194] This, too, is underpinned by the language of war and imprisonment. According to the *Daily Mail* 'fanatical Remainers [want] to keep Britain locked in the EU'. Its readers should 'be under no illusion', though 'there may not be tanks on the streets … we're seeing … an attempted coup designed to overthrow the will of the British people'.[195]

Of course, the legal framework for Member State departure now provides some justification for press presentation of UK/EU relations as oppositional and the EU as singular. Under Article 50(2) TEU, the UK negotiates its exit with the EU as though already a third party. Moreover, the EU27 have accepted that this provision gives the Union horizontal competence over all substantive policy areas falling within negotiations, regardless of whether the EU would ordinarily have exclusive competence in the particular field.[196] Consequently, the Union does negotiate as a single 'bloc'. However, this legal backdrop is unlikely to be the root cause of newspapers' continuing depiction of the UK and the EU as diametrically opposed. Press focus is not on the EU's now far-reaching negotiating powers but on two more emotive issues. Newspapers frequently assert, first, that the EU is united in its desire to punish the UK for leaving,[197] and second, that 'to many EU leaders, stopping the project unravelling matters more than anything else, including a beneficial Brexit deal'.[198]

The print media's 'us versus them' presentation of UK/EU dynamics is endorsed even more heavily in the political discourse post-referendum than it was in the decades prior to it. Theresa May's Lancaster House speech homogenised the UK public by promising 'the right deal for Britain', achieved through 'the strength and support of 65 million people willing us to make it happen'. The speech implicitly endorsed accusations of 'Brussels diktats' and the language of imprisonment by declaring that post-exit, the UK could once again be an

---

191 Letts, *ibid.*

192 Anon, 'Lawyer Lives a Grand Prix Life' *Mirror* (4 November 2016).

193 Littlejohn, *Daily Mail* (above n. 153).

194 D. Raab, 'Wrecking Tactics Will Only Backfire' *Daily Mail* (4 November 2016).

195 Littlejohn, *Daily Mail* (above n. 153); see also Slack, 'Enemies' *Daily Mail* (above n. 152).

196 European Council, ANNEX to Council Decision (EU, Euratom) 2017 authorising the opening of negotiations with the United Kingdom of Great Britain and Northern Ireland for an agreement setting out the arrangements for its withdrawal from the European Union, 22/05/17 XT 21016/17 ADD 1 REV 2, 3

197 J. Blanchard, 'No Deal is Better than a Bad Deal' *Mirror* (18 January 2017); A. Asthana et al, 'May's Brexit Threat to Europe' *Guardian* (18 January 2017); Anon, *Daily Mail* (above n. 188).

198 P. Johnston, 'May's Plan is Good for Everyone but Will the EU Have the Sense to See it?' *Telegraph* (18 January 2017); see also D. Roberts, 'Theresa May's Brexit Speech: Key Clues to Look Out For' *Guardian* (17 January 2017).

'independent' and 'self-governing' country where 'laws would be made in Westminster, Edinburgh, Cardiff and Belfast'.[199] Furthermore, May made explicit reference to the apparent EU motivators of punishment and deterrence: 'I know there are some voices out there calling for a punitive deal that punishes Britain and discourages other countries from taking the same path'.[200] Elsewhere, pro-Brexit Conservative politicians have enthusiastically adopted the language of the newspapers for which they write, limiting the cohort of 'Remoaners'[201] to 'die-hard elites'[202] within the Houses of Parliament whose primary goal is to thwart the will of the British people.[203]

As was the case before the referendum, an 'us versus them' narrative in public discourse is problematic for three reasons. First, the discursive space is reduced for nuanced debate about the diverse policy areas affected, in different ways, by various forms of Brexit. Soon after the Leave vote, Eurosceptic newspapers began distinguishing a 'hard Brexit', which would include departure from the Single Market and the Customs Union, from a 'soft Brexit', which could be implemented through continued membership of the European Economic Area. In arguing that anything other than the former would frustrate the will of the British public,[204] the UK is presented as internally homogenous at the expense of honest debate about the various policy choices that might benefit some sectors or groups over others.

Second, the legal complexities of withdrawal are overlooked and presented, instead, as barriers fabricated by a Union with an ulterior motive. Having correctly predicted exit from the Single Market, *The Guardian* advanced that 'losing preferential access ... is another thing entirely. Ideally, the government would negotiate replacement trade arrangements but European leaders wish to limit these to deter others from leaving'.[205] Though protecting the continuity of the Union is a clear EU priority,[206] obstacles to the UK's post-exit access to the Single Market are more practical in nature. By exiting the Single Market and 'taking back control of its own laws', the UK leaves a system of regulatory convergence and mutual recognition that makes the depth and breadth of intra-EU free trade possible in practice. In leaving the customs union, 'Global Britain' places itself outside a goods border relevant not just to tariffs but to ensuring that goods about to circulate freely within a market of 500 million consumers meet regulatory standards. By reducing the complex legal and regulatory frameworks,

199 T. May, 'The Government's Negotiating Objectives for Exiting the EU: PM Speech' (17 January 2017).

200 *Ibid.*

201 I. Duncan-Smith, 'Judicial Activism is Taken to a New Level' *Telegraph* (4 November 2016).

202 Raab, *Daily Mail* (above n. 194).

203 J. Rees-Mogg, 'Only a Foolhardy MP Would Challenge Voters' *Telegraph* (4 November 2016).

204 J. Slack, 'A Great Nation is Reborn' *Daily Mail* (18 January 2017).

205 Roberts, *Guardian* (above n. 198).

206 White Paper on the Future of Europe, COM (2017) 2025 (1 March 2017).

which are integral to the functioning of the Union, down to mere political game-playing by a vindictive EU, newspapers on both sides of the Remain/Leave divide deprive their readers of information that is crucial to their understanding of the negotiations.

Third, driven by an ideological goal, large sections of the UK press continue to underachieve as democratic checks on political activity. There was some evidence of journalistic scrutiny of Theresa May's Lancaster House speech. The *Mirror* called it 'rich on policy but short on detail', especially as regards May's approach to the customs union.[207] The *Daily Mail* questioned whether May could keep her promise to protect workers if she were forced to carry out her threat to slash regulation to attract business.[208] For the most part, however, the Brexit press in particular failed to scrutinise the Lancaster House speech with any real rigour. May's unexplained claims – that UK citizens residing in other Member States would retain their current rights; that the UK could retain preferential access to the Single Market; and that new customs arrangements could be forged – were simplistically depicted as a 'direct rebuke to European leaders who have repeatedly claimed that Britain will have to compromise on freedom of movement'.[209] Moreover, parliamentary attempts to scrutinise the Brexit process are frequently depicted in Eurosceptic newspapers as 'wrecking amendments by saboteurs'.[210] In this way, the press aligned Theresa May's vision for Brexit, as outlined in the Lancaster House speech, with the 'will of the people', while parliamentary involvement is characterised as an attempt to 'dictate our negotiating stance'[211] and to 'thwart the will of the people', language also employed by then-Secretary of State for Exiting the EU, David Davies.[212]

Thus, though a Leave vote might have been viewed as giving the Eurosceptic press space to scrutinise the intricacies of UK withdrawal from the Union with rigour, instead it has continued with existing approaches, working alongside pro-Leave politicians and the post-referendum Conservative governments in seeking to co-write a 'hard Brexit'. The continuity of the press's rhetorical devices arguably has wider ramifications for media representations of UK relations with 'Europe' more broadly.

---

207 Blanchard, *Mirror* (above n. 197); Beattie, *Mirror* (above n. 187).

208 Anon, *Daily Mail* (above n. 188); see also C. Hope, 'The Brexit Deal Will Be a Legacy of our Time, says May' *Telegraph* (18 January 2017).

209 P. Dominiczak, 'May: My 12-Point Plan for Brexit' *Telegraph* (17 January 2017); see also, J. Slack, 'Theresa's New Free Britain' *Daily Mail* (17 January 2017).

210 D. Raab, 'Our Path to the Exit Door Remains Clear' *Telegraph* (25 January 2017); see similarly, P. Dominiczak and C. Hope, 'May in a Hurry to Carry Out Will of the People' *Telegraph* (25 January 2017); c.f. J. Beattie, 'May Court Out' *Mirror* (4 November 2016), which quoted a Labour MP's argument that by 'asking what Brexit might mean for the economy, jobs or standards of living … MPs … will be doing their job'.

211 Littlejohn, *Daily Mail* (above n. 153).

212 A. Asthana et al, '"Straightforward" Brexit Bill Likely to be Published on Thursday' *Guardian* (24 January 2017)

Ready for round two: the legacy of the Brexit debate for the ECHR

One of the most frustrating errors in media coverage of 'Europe', for anyone with a basic understanding of EU law and the Convention, is conflation of the two systems. Mead and Gies both found numerous examples of this in their contributions to this volume.[213] Analysis of the EU referendum campaign also demonstrates more subtle media amalgamation of the Union and the ECHR, which suggests that, without a change in approach, the UK's relationship with the Convention is on a similar trajectory to its EU membership.[214]

First, the ratcheting up of anti-European sentiment by the Eurosceptic press, as Brexit negotiations progress, is likely to cross-contaminate into ECHR discussions since these are built upon the same rhetorical structures used in EU-related debates. This is facilitated by the media's frequent use of 'Europe' as 'rather nebulous terminology'[215] to refer to both systems. United by their 'Europeanness', these separate regional polities are presented, whether inadvertently or deliberately, as sharing institutional frameworks, problems, supporters and detractors.[216] Consequently, the Euroscepticism that has become the working language of British public discourse is not limited to the EU but extends also to the ECHR. Accordingly, the well-entrenched nature of press antipathy towards the EU is mirrored in similarly longstanding hostility towards the ECHR.[217] Opposition to the Convention is structured around the same 'us versus them' presentation of UK/EU relations, and expressed through identical persuasive tools. A homogenous Britain of 'ordinary hardworking citizens' is forced, by the 'elite',[218] into membership of a human rights system that offers no benefits for UK citizens, whilst working, much like EU free movement rules, exclusively in favour of 'foreigners' and 'terrorists'.[219] If the Convention does have something to offer British citizens, this remains limited to 'unworthy' individuals such as paedophiles and murderers.[220] UK/ECHR interactions are frequently portrayed through the language of war and imprisonment.[221]

Second, the shaping of British public discourse about the ECHR around the same 'us versus them' structure as UK/EU relations indicates that those wishing to stay within the Convention framework are likely to opt for the same 'reform

213 D. Mead, ch. 1 in this volume, 12–13; L. Gies, ch. 3 in this volume, 85–86.

214 In line with the Conservative's 2017 Manifesto (www.conservatives.com/manifesto), Brexit has pushed debate about the Human Rights Act and the UK's participation into the long-grass, but only for the duration of exit negotiations and the 2017–2022 parliament.

215 Gies (above n. 213) 87.

216 Doyle, *Daily Mail* (above n. 160); Dominiczak, *Telegraph* (above n. 209).

217 Gies (above n. 213), 82–86.

218 Mead (above n. 213) 37.

219 Mead (above n. 213) 22; In this way, Drywood and Gray's cogent arguments about the 'doubly foreign' depiction of the ECHR is equally applicable to the EU, see ch. 5 in this volume.

220 Mead, (above n. 213), 16.

221 Gies, (above n. 213), 91.

and remain' strategy used for the EU referendum, when the issue of ECHR participation is inevitably back on the table. Indeed, such an approach is already in play. After Theresa May called for exit from the ECHR over the EU during the referendum campaign, a spokesperson for David Cameron said 'the PM has made clear that he wants to see reform of the ECHR and has ruled out absolutely nothing if we don't achieve that'.[222] Moreover, the emphasis of proposed ECHR reform on the need to 'restore common sense' and 'prevent abuse of the system'[223] is starkly reminiscent of Cameron's pre-EU referendum focus on 'the need to crack down on abuse of free movement'.[224] Crucially, just as the discussion here establishes that the UK/EU pre-referendum renegotiation focused on issues fore-fronted by the British press, Gies' analysis of the ECHR reforms sought by the British Government at the 2012 Brighton Conference identifies a similar relationship between the Government's demands and those issues that were regularly featured in newspapers.[225] In particular, the emphasis was on the politically sensitive issues – such as the deportation of terror suspects and prisoner voting – that have long received disproportionate press attention as compared with their occurrence before the ECtHR.[226] Though Cameron is no longer Prime Minister, the longevity of opposition to the ECHR in media and wider discourse makes it difficult to envisage any case being made for continuing ECHR membership that is not rooted in reform. As Mead posits, 'letting [the idea of human rights] shift onto more hostile terrain is probably the greatest failing of pro-rights campaigners in the UK'.[227] Now that that ship has sailed, like the EU Remain campaigners before them, those in favour of continued UK participation in the Convention are likely to find themselves cornered by an opposition comfortable with its internal contradictions. Specifically, the latter would accuse the former either of being part of an elite too privileged to see the failings of the system or of being unable to make a positive case for the ECHR.

Third, as was the case with the EU referendum, any 'Leave or Reform' structure to future debate about the UK's ECHR membership is likely simultaneously to narrow opportunities, first, to present the potential positives of participation for a diverse UK, on the one hand, and, second, to critique the evidence-based failings of the Convention system on the other. As Mead argues, the non-reportage of ECHR judgments in which the UK won the case, or where the action did not concern 'foreign criminals' means that readers rarely have the opportunity to 're-evaluate their assessment of the Convention ... as a criminal's charter'.[228] Conversely, Murray advances that 'Strasbourg's supposed transgressions [in the

222 Asthana, *Guardian* (above n. 43).
223 Background Briefing Notes to the Queen's Speech 2016, 48, available online at: www.gov.uk/government/publications/queens-speech-2016-background-briefing-notes
224 Cameron, *Letter to Donald Tusk,* (above n. 11) 5.
225 Gies (above n. 213).
226 Gies (above n. 213) 88.
227 Mead (above n. 213) 34.
228 Mead (above n. 213) 18.

Hirst prisoner-voting case-law] are 'small beer' compared to the substance of some of its other decisions'.[229]

Consequently, if balance is to be at least partially restored to UK human rights debates prior to the reappearance of the question of the UK's ECHR membership, regardless of whether that involves a referendum, the ability of British newspapers, as political actors, to set the tone of discussion must be assessed. When it comes to human rights, the print media is not 'merely reporting the parliamentary debate [but] ... forming, leading and directing the content',[230] arguably motivated, at times, by its own agenda.[231] A free press remains vital to functioning democracy, and has the right to be partisan as part of its freedom of expression. However, since it is also a political actor it is necessary to ensure that it is subject to sufficient checks and balances. An adequate diversity of voices must be fully heard across the democratic landscape.

Yet at present, the same weakness of checks and balances is visible in the Convention context as it is in respect of the EU. Murray points out that though the Convention's institutions seek to offer an alternative source of information about Strasbourg judgments, these have limited reach as compared with the British press.[232] He also argues that the print media continues to set the tone for broadcasters, who struggle with impartiality as regards the ECHR since, just like EU membership, views on it do not neatly align with party politics. There is an over-emphasis on a mathematical 'balance' of views rather than giving due weight to evidence-based positions.[233] Finally, politicians have been increasingly reluctant to challenge press accounts, either because they are sympathetic to newspapers' positions or wise to the potential impact on personal or party political fortunes of making a positive case for the ECHR. A clear example of this is Cameron's oft-quoted claim that giving prisoners the vote would make him 'physically ill'.[234] And, of course, political actors have not simply avoided addressing inaccurate press narratives. In their own communications, they have often consciously used similar rhetorical devices as the press. Theresa May, for example, employed the press tactic of over-emphasising certain aspects of a human rights case, for sensationalist effect, when she told the Conservative conference that a non-British citizen had been permitted to remain in the UK because he had a pet cat.[235]

In sum, unless something changes across the broader democratic landscape, newspapers' parallel approaches to the EU and the ECHR – which foster a

229 C. Murray, Ch. 4 in this volume, 108.

230 D. McNulty et al, 'Human Rights and Prisoners' Rights: The British Press and the Shaping of Public Debate' (2014) 53 *Howard Journal of Criminal Justice* 360, 374.

231 Murray points to press concerns about the impact of Art. 8 ECHR on press freedoms (above n. 229) 103.

232 Murray (above n. 229) 112–119.

233 *Ibid.*

234 Cameron MP, HC Deb, vol. 517, col. 921 (3 Nov 2010).

235 Mead (above n. 213) 13–14; Drywood and Gray (above n. 218).

Eurosceptic narrative in the broader discourse – mean that the process of withdrawing from the EU is unlikely to push debates about the Convention into the long grass. Instead, the Brexit process might well strengthen anti-ECHR sentiment whilst (further) weakening the quality of human rights debate.

Conclusion

One needed only to glance across newspapers' front pages during the referendum campaign to see the virulence of much of the British press towards the EU. Yet given declining newspaper sales, and the fact that Remain had the backing of the then-British Prime Minister, the vast majority of his Cabinet, much of business and many trade unions, one might have questioned the contemporary reach of the UK's print media prior to the referendum. Following the Leave vote, however, the influence of UK newspapers seems as strong as ever.

A long-term analysis of press approaches to the Union demonstrates why its power pervades. Though of course extremely vocal during the campaign itself, the British press had already significantly contributed to the establishment of Euroscepticism as the working language of UK public discourse well before the referendum. EU-related discussions, even in newspapers that would come out for Remain, commonly adopt an 'us versus them' structure, underpinned by rhetorical devices, such as the language of elites, war and imprisonment. This left the Remain campaign with few strategic choices beyond 'Reform', even while that focus left it open to criticism for failing to make a positive case for EU membership. More importantly, the pitting of an homogenised UK against a singular 'Europe', as a consequence of the 'us versus them' narrative inhibited both nuanced discussion about the potential advantages of EU law and policy for different societal groups and, conversely, deeper assessment of whether the evolution of Union law has been sufficiently democratic.

The considerable societal voice that newspapers clearly enjoy when asserting their ideological positions raises important democratic questions. While on the one hand a free, and even partisan, print media can be central to functioning democracy, press pursuit of a particular political position at the expense of accurate reporting can pose a risk to the quality of debate, or worse, incite racist, sexist and xenophobic sentiment. This difficult balancing act can be approached by assessing newspapers as political actors and examining whether there are sufficient checks and balances across the media and broader democratic landscape to reflect the complexity of the issue at hand. In the context of the referendum, however, where broadcasters seem to have struggled with how to meet their impartiality requirement, they appear to have relied more than ever on newspapers to set the parameters of debate. Ultimately, though, the press has not acted alone. Over the longer-term, politicians, wary of what the question of 'Europe' means for their parties' fortunes have often utilised the same rhetorical devices as the press in their EU-related discussions. During the campaign, Leave-supporting politicians were often behind many of the inaccurate claims about UK/EU relations that appeared in the press and, at times, provided newspapers with material that reinforced growing, and more open, xenophobia. This press-politics partnership itself undermines newspapers' roles as democratic checks on political actors.

Post-referendum, a Leave victory has not created the elbow room for rigorous scrutiny of internal and external Brexit processes. Indeed, the position of the UK as a third country in withdrawal negotiations seems, instead, to have reinforced the 'us versus them' narrative of UK/EU relations. Newspapers and a number of high-profile politicians continue to pit a uniform 'Europe' against a homogenous British public, reducing the opportunity for vital debate about what type of Brexit the UK should seek, and how, given the potential (and often conflicting) pros and cons for diverse stakeholders.

That this approach continues provides a strong indication of how future debate about the UK's membership of the separate ECHR might proceed. Convention-debates in the UK have the same historical and rhetorical underpinnings as those surrounding EU membership. This – in a similar way as it does in EU-related discussions – works to the detriment both of nuanced debate about the advantages of membership and detailed consideration about problems with the ECHR framework. Since the EU and the ECHR fall under the same label of 'Europe' in British newspapers, rather than pushing the debate about the Convention into the long grass, the process of withdrawing from the EU might well strengthen anti-ECHR sentiment whilst further weakening the quality of human rights debates. To seek to avoid this it is vital to continue to scrutinise the press as a powerful political actor in its own right.

Bibliography

BBC Trust Review of the Breadth of Opinion Reflected in the BBC's Outputs (July 2013).

P Baranowska, 'The Coverage of the Eurozone Economic Crisis in the British Press' (2014) 15(4) *Perspectives on European Politics and Society* 500–517.

S Currie, *Migration, Work and Citizenship in the Enlarged European Union* (Cornwall: Ashgate, 2008).

O Daddow, 'Strategising European Policy: David Cameron's Referendum Gamble' (2015) 160(5) *The RUSI Journal* 4–10.

O Daddow, 'The UK Media and 'Europe': From Permissive Consensus to Destructive Dissent' (2012) 88(6) *Institutional Affairs*, 1219–1236.

G Davies, 'Legislative Control of the European Court of Justice' (2014) 51 *CMLRev* 1579.

P Desmet, J van Spanje and C de Vreese, 'Discussing the Democratic Deficit: Effects of Media and Interpersonal Communication on Satisfaction with Democracy in the European Union', (2015) 9 *International Journal of Communication* 3177–3198.

N Dugalès and G Tucker, 'Representations of representation: European institutions in the French and British press', in P. Bayley and G. Williams (eds) *European Identity: What the Media Say* (Oxford Scholarship Online, 2012).

C Dustmann and T Frattini, 'The Fiscal Effects of Immigration to the UK', (2014) *Journal of the Royal Economic Society*, 593–643.

Eurofound Report, 'Social Dimension of Intra-EU Mobility: Impact on Public Services' (December 2015).

A Follesdal and S Hix, 'Why There is a Democratic Deficit in the EU: A Response to Majone and Moravcsik', (2006) 44(3) *JCMS* 533–562.

D Grimm, 'The Democratic Costs of Constitutionalisation: The European Case' (2015) 21 *ELJ* 460.

B Hawkins, 'Fantasies of Subjugation: a discourse theoretical account of British policy on the European Union', (2015) 9(2) *Critical Policy Studies* 139–157.

Lord Leveson, An Inquiry into the Culture, Practices and Ethics of the Press: Report (2012).

D McNulty, N Watson and G Philo, 'Human Rights and Prisoners' Rights: The British Press and the Shaping of Public Debate', (2014) 53 *Howard Journal of Criminal Justice* 360.

N Nic Shuibhne, *The Coherence of EU Free Movement Law: Constitutional Responsibility and the Court of Justice* (Oxford: OUP, 2013).

S Reynolds, '(De)constructing the Road to Brexit: Paving the Way to Further Limitations on Free Movement and Equal Treatment?' in D. Thym (ed.) *Questioning EU Citizenship: Judges and the Limits of Free Movement and Solidarity in the EU* (London: Hart, 2018).

M Ruffert, 'The European Debt Crisis and European Union Law' (2011) 48 *CMLRev* 1777–1806.

J Seaton, 'Brexit and the Media', (2016) 87(3) *The Political Quarterly* 333–337.

J Shaw, N Miller and N Fletcher, *Getting to Grips with EU Citizenship: Understanding the Friction between UK Immigration Law and EU Free Movement Law* (Edinburgh: Charlesworth, 2013).

J Thornborrow, L Haarman, and A Duguid, 'Discourses of European Identity in British, Italian and French TV News', in P Bayley and G Williams (eds), *European Identity: What the Media Say* (Oxford Scholarship Online, 2012).

3 British human rights scepticism through the lens of European newspapers

Lieve Gies

Introduction

The British press, with a few exceptions, has shown itself to be very hostile to the Human Rights Act 1998 (HRA) and, by extension, the European Convention on Human Rights (ECHR). *The Sun* newspaper has in the past openly campaigned for the HRA to be repealed[1] and the European Court of Human Rights' ('the European Court' hereafter) judgments have come under sustained criticism in both tabloids and broadsheets, with specific flashpoints including prisoners' voting rights and the deportation of terrorism suspects.[2] This chapter asks whether Britain is an outlier in this regard by examining newspaper coverage in other signatory states. Do the anti-ECHR sentiments underpinning much of the criticism targeted at the HRA in the British press strike a chord with other European media?

Following the 2016 referendum in which almost 52% of the UK electorate voted in favour of leaving the European Union, the possibility of a chain reaction across Europe threatening the stability of the European Union has become a real concern. Similarly, in relation to the ECHR and the rights scepticism pervading sections of the British press and also, it should be said, government, a possible side effect of a future withdrawal from the Convention by the UK could be to prompt other states to follow its example. Furthermore, there are concerns that a UK withdrawal could provide states with a poor human rights record (e.g. Russia) with a further incentive to disobey human rights laws, impacting human rights standards far beyond the UK.[3] This fear of a domino effect suggests that the UK's stance on European human rights law has important ramifications for the way in which human rights are perceived across Europe and possibly throughout the world. However, such a hypothetical chain reaction rests on a number of suppositions; for example, about the UK's moral authority, but also about the

1 L Gies, *Mediating Human Rights: Media, Culture and Human Rights Law* (Routledge 2014).

2 *Hirst v United Kingdom* (no 2) (2006) 42 EHRR 41. *Othman v United Kingdom* (2012) 55 EHRR 1.

3 D Grieve, 'Is the European Convention working?' (2015) 6 EHRLR 584.

degree to which other countries are receptive to the UK's Euroscepticism in its many different guises. In the wake of the Brexit vote there is mounting evidence that public hostility towards the EU is not an exclusively British phenomenon, but much less is known about the way in which the ECHR is perceived in other European countries.

More specifically, this chapter examines how the UK's human rights scepticism is portrayed in the European press. To what extent does the anti-ECHR agenda, which is firmly embedded in British public discourse, register with European newspapers and what does the coverage reveal about the possibility of an anti-human rights climate taking hold elsewhere in Europe? How does the kind of rights scepticism that is very much in evidence in the British national media compare with coverage in Europe? Is there any support for the British agenda to scale back the ECHR? The empirical part of this chapter involves an analysis of newspaper coverage of the Brighton Conference in the British, Dutch, French, German, Italian and Irish national press in 2012. Under the UK's presidency, this conference of ECHR signatory states culminated in the Brighton Declaration outlining some limited reforms of the European Court. The conference took place against the backdrop of the political fallout in the UK over prisoners' voting rights and the extradition of the Muslim cleric Abu Qatada to Jordan. Considering that the Brighton conference directly involved all 47 signatory states and was a very direct expression of the UK Government's frustration at the power held by the European Court, it could be reasonably assumed that this event would be particularly newsworthy across Europe, resulting in a significant amount of coverage.

However, this study found that the Brighton conference attracted comparatively little attention in the European press. Its lack of newsworthiness can be explained with reference to a broad literature documenting the non-existence of a genuinely European public sphere and the limited extent to which news media in Europe have undergone a process of 'Europeanization'. The limited coverage that is available suggests that dissatisfaction with the ECHR was very much seen as a domestic British problem, but the fact that it only involved a handful of articles also reveals a failure to appreciate how deep anti-ECHR sentiments run in parts of British society. While Britain's attempt to reform the European Court was portrayed as a failure, the coverage revealed some support for its reform agenda, for example, in the Dutch and French press. An important lacuna is the notable absence, with a few exceptions, of a strong defence of the ECHR against British rights scepticism. The focus of this chapter is therefore twofold: it explores the relative absence of European newspaper discourse about the ECHR and it will highlight the paucity of articles in defence of human rights.

The Brighton conference in a UK policy context

To say that the HRA is a divisive issue in British public life would be something of an understatement. The Act incorporating the ECHR into UK law already encountered press hostility before it was even placed on the statute book.[4] Since it came into force public criticism of the legislation has only intensified. It comes from a broad cross-section of society, including politicians, citizens and the press but also some senior judges and lawyers, and the target of the criticism is equally diverse. Klug has argued that anti-HRA arguments revolve to a large extent around the idea that the Act is only interested in protecting 'foreigners, terrorists, and paedophiles'.[5] In an age in which social media have joined forces with the mass media to provide seemingly unlimited space for public commentary and analysis, there are a host of platforms for making such arguments. However, it is the traditional press that has been the most vocal in this regard: not bound by the impartiality rules that apply to broadcasters, newspapers are at much greater liberty to be partisan in their coverage.[6] Media-based criticism of human rights also extends to the ECHR and the European Court itself, prompting one judge to qualify the debate as 'progressively frantic and ill-informed'.[7] A familiar trope is that European judges unduly interfere with internal British matters and pose a threat to sovereignty, echoing Eurosceptic arguments grounded in the notion of an existential threat to the nation-state.

The HRA has also been a thorn in the side of successive governments, including, it should be said, the Labour Government whose brainchild it was. In opposition, the Conservatives were very sceptical about the legislation.[8] In government, their drive for reform was tempered initially by being in a coalition with the pro-HRA Liberal Democrats from 2010 to 2015. The Brighton Declaration coincided with this period of relatively moderate reform but it did not settle the issue: when the 2015 general election returned an all-Conservative Government, it created scope for a more radical scenario, including withdrawal from the ECHR, something which the then Justice Secretary Michael Gove refused to rule out.[9] Brexit produced a change of Prime Minister and a drastic government reshuffle: at the time of writing, it is not clear whether reforming human rights law will be a priority in a political landscape dominated by the fallout from the referendum decision to leave the EU. Prime Minister Theresa May was not exactly a supporter of the HRA during her tenure as Home Secretary. Not only did she do battle with the European Court to extradite the terrorism suspect Abu Qatada to Jordan, she also very publicly ridiculed the HRA when she (wrongly)

4 Gies (above n 1).

5 F Klug, 'A Bill of Rights: do we need one or do we already have one?' [2007] PL 701, 714.

6 A parallel can be drawn here with the Brexit campaign in which the newspapers were able to openly declare whether they wished Britain to remain in or leave the EU. See D Levy, B Aslan and D Bironzo, 'The press and the Referendum Campaign' in D Jackson, E Thorsen and D Wring (eds), *EU Referendum Analysis 2016: Media, Voters and the Campaign* (The Centre for the Study of Journalism, Culture and Community Bournemouth University 2016).

7 B McCluskey, 'Human Rights, governments and judicial independence' (2012) 5 EHRLR 479.

8 See e.g. D Raab, *The Assault on Liberty: What Went Wrong With Rights* (Fourth Estate 2009).

9 Grieve (above n 3).

claimed at the 2011 Conservative Party conference that an illegal immigrant had been allowed to stay because he had a pet cat and to deport him would violate his right to a family life,[10] a story that was grist to the mill of an already rights-sceptical press. During the Brexit referendum campaign, May's view was that the UK should withdraw from the ECHR but remain in the EU. However, whilst campaigning to become Prime Minister she offered reassurances that the UK under her premiership would not seek to withdraw from the ECHR.

Conservative government policy has so far consisted of a two-pronged approach: reform of the HRA by replacing it with a 'homegrown' Bill of Rights and reform of the European Court. The reason for this dual strategy is that simply passing a new Bill of Rights with the aim of lowering or scaling back existing human rights safeguards would leave the door open for claimants to pursue their case before the Strasbourg Court. A Bill of Rights has yet to be introduced in Parliament, but an opportunity to reform the European Court presented itself in the form of the Brighton Conference. The reform pursued by the British Government was based around the notion of greater subsidiarity, 'meaning that sensitive political issues should be determined by national Parliaments, not the Court'.[11] This was meant to give a clear signal to the Court that it should refrain from interfering with issues that had already been duly considered by national institutions.

With only limited support from other signatory states, the gains made in the final drafts of the Brighton Declaration were only modest, with the text stating that the Conference: 'Reiterates the invitation made by the Interlaken and Izmir Conferences to the Committee of Ministers to apply fully the principle of subsidiarity by which the States Parties may choose how to fulfil their obligations under the Convention'.[12] The Declaration also pledged to include the principle of subsidiarity in the Preamble of the Convention[13] (12. B), with the Committee of Ministers charged with adopting the amendment by the end of 2013. Other reforms included measures to reduce the backlog of cases facing the Court, something that also furthered the UK's reform agenda by ensuring that cases without merit could be struck out more quickly. The former Attorney-General Dominic Grieve, who played an active part in the Brighton negotiations, recognised that these were only modest reforms, noting that:

> We would have achieved more and changed the text of the Convention itself if our fellow signatory governments, who shared our analysis and our goals,

10 A Wagner, 'Catgate: another myth to trash human rights' *The Guardian* (London, 4 October 2011) www.theguardian.com/law/2011/oct/04/theresa-may-wrong-cat-deportation (accessed 3 October 2016).

11 H Fenwick, 'The Human Rights Act or a British Bill of Rights: creating a down-grading recalibration of rights against the counter-terror backdrop? [2012] PL 468, 485.

12 Council of Europe, *High Level Conference on the Future of the European Court of Human Rights Brighton Declaration* (2012) para 29 b, available online at: www.echr.coe.int/documents/2012_brighton_finaldeclaration_eng.pdf (accessed 16 November 2016).

13 *Ibid.* para 12 b.

> had not been deterred by their domestic NGOs from full cooperation with our agenda because of a fear that we wished to diminish and not improve the Court's effectiveness.[14]

He argued that the reforms had nevertheless been effective and criticised the Conservative Government's continuing desire for further reform: 'in pressing for a wholesale reform of our relationship with the Convention and the Court, the government is in danger of fighting yesterday's battle'.[15] There is an obvious parallel to be made with Brexit in that some factions within the Conservative party would presumably only regard a complete withdrawal from the ECHR to be an effective way of preventing government policy being continually frustrated by 'Europe'.

Media coverage of the ECHR in the European public sphere

Writing about the ECHR in French law, Grewe notes: 'how modest French public debates on Convention rights have been. On the whole, these debates gained only the attention of specialists as they are related to quite technical subjects.... Some serious problems have failed to attract wider public interest'.[16] Similarly, Rackow observes how cases similar to the ones that have sparked heated public debate in the UK have failed to generate the same level of public discussion in Germany.[17] Specialist discussion aside, it appears that the ECHR is not routinely or frequently a topic of public debate in signatory states, with Britain being the one notable exception. That said, little is known about the extent to which the Council of Europe and the European Court are the subject of media debate across Europe as empirical data is simply lacking. However, there is a sizeable amount of research involving the not dissimilar question of how the institutions of the European Union fare in European media.

This issue has to be seen against the backdrop of a longstanding debate regarding the existence, or rather non-existence, of a European public sphere. A European public sphere, just like the original model developed by Habermas,[18] would require pan-European *Öffentlichkeit* aimed at monitoring and developing a common discourse regarding European issues, a discourse that is predominantly but not exclusively geared towards the European Union.

14 Grieve (above n 3) 593.

15 *Ibid.*, 594.

16 Constance Grewe, 'The ECHR in French Law: Status, Implementation and Debates' in K S Ziegler, E Wicks and L Hodson (eds), *The UK and European Human Rights: A Strained Relationship?* (Hart 2015) 359.

17 J Rackow, 'From Conflict to Cooperation: The Relationship Between Karlsruhe and Strasbourg' in K S Ziegler, E Wicks and L Hodson (eds), *The UK and European Human Rights: A Strained Relationship?* (Hart 2015) 398.

18 J Habermas, *The Structural Transformation of the Public Sphere: An Inquiry into a Category of Bourgeois Society* (MIT Press 1989).

The function of the public sphere in a democratic society is to allow civil society to engage in a sustained exercise to monitor political institutions closely and hold them to account without usurping their role. A prominent, if imperfect, manner in which the ideal-typical public sphere manifests itself in practice is through the mass media, as these provide the channels facilitating the kind of informed and rational debate that is necessary to promote political accountability. Empirically, the public sphere is very much in evidence in democratic countries through the fact that there is a degree of open discussion about matters of public concern, albeit that the system has several shortcomings, such as the lack of media access for disenfranchised groups, hampering their participation in public debate.

Equivalent arguments apply to the European Union: ideally, its institutions should be subjected to a process of close monitoring in order to ensure a degree of transparency and accountability to the peoples of Europe, if only to prevent the so-called democratic deficit that features prominently in criticism targeted at the EU. Just as in national politics, one would reasonably assume that media infrastructures across Europe have an important role to play in achieving a well-functioning European public sphere. According to Statham:

> Media performance is central to any debate about a European public sphere, since media actors are entrusted with making the European level visible and accessible to citizens. Without an effective media providing a supply line of political information, which allows people the opportunity to see, think, and make decisions about the European level, it would matter relatively little if institutional-fix solutions were applied to strengthen the link between the supranational level of governance and citizens.[19]

However, there are number of obstacles that stand in the way of a European public sphere. There is a lack of truly European media, that is, media platforms that have a pan-European reach and target audiences in all, or at least several, member states.[20] Language barriers and significantly differing media systems are two of the most obvious obstacles preventing the emergence of a European public sphere. At first glance, the internet should be capable of facilitating some level of pan-European public debate, at least for those who possess the necessary skills, such as the ability to converse in a non-native language.[21] Nevertheless, there seems to be a dearth of media channels through which citizens from across

---

19 P Statham, 'Introduction: Europe's Search for a Public', in R Koopmans and P Statham (eds) *The Making of a European Public Sphere: Media Discourse and Political Contention* (Cambridge University Press 2010) 4.

20 M Machill, M Beiler and C Fischer, 'Europe-Topics in Europe's Media: The Debate about the European Public Sphere: A Meta-Analyses of Media Content Analysis' (2006) 21 *European Journal of Communication* 57. L Novy, *Britain and Germany Imagining the Future of Europe: National Identity, Mass Media and the Public Sphere* (Palgrave 2013).

21 R Koopmans and P Statham (eds.) *The Making of a European Public Sphere: Media Discourse and Political Contention* (Cambridge University Press 2010).

Europe can communicate with each other to debate matters of common concern. According to Novy: 'This, then, is the rub: the European peoples do not "talk" to each other'.[22]

In the absence of an overarching, Europe-wide communication system, a proxy measure involves the extent to which the content of national news media has been 'Europeanized' by incorporating European issues. Europeanization principally takes on two different forms.[23] In its vertical dimension Europeanization in an EU context means the extent to which national media cover the politics and policies of 'Brussels', whereas in its horizontal dimension it involves national media covering domestic political debates that take place in other European countries. Vertical Europeanization is about the extent to which media across Europe report on the central, overarching institutions that impact on the lives of all European citizens; horizontally, it is about the extent to which national public spheres pay attention to one another, for example, how much interest British media take in the domestic affairs of France, Germany, Italy, Poland, and so on. Other features of Europeanization include the synchronisation of news agendas[24] or 'congruence'[25] in what passes for news in different countries.

On the ground, European media display a mixed record in relation to both vertical and horizontal Europeanization. There is relatively little attention on the EU,[26] with 'bread and butter issues' often treated as too technical and too complex, resulting in an over-emphasising of crisis moments at the expense of day-to-day aspects.[27] This, in turn, cements the image of the EU as perpetually in crisis. There is also limited coverage of domestic politics in other EU countries. To some extent, this picture depends on the type of media – for example, quality newspapers versus tabloids – although this difference may not be as great as is often assumed.[28] There are also important differences between countries, meaning that some national media systems are more cosmopolitan in their outlook compared to others. A British quality newspaper like *The Times*, for example, has been noted for its 'parochial' perspective,[29] neglecting much of what is going on in continental Europe, whereas its French counterpart *Le Monde* ranks among the most cosmopolitan newspapers in Europe. Ironically, this does not prevent *The*

22 Novy (above n 20) 2.

23 M Brüggemann and K Kleinen-von Königslöw, 'Let's talk about Europe: Explaining vertical and horizontal Europeanization in the quality press' (2009) 24 *European Journal of Communication* 27.

24 Novy (above n 20) 63.

25 B Pfetsch, S Adam and B Eschner, 'The Media's Voice over Europe: Issue Salience, Openness, and Conflict Lines in Editorials' in R Koopmans and P Statham (eds) *The Making of a European Public Sphere: Media Discourse and Political Contention* (Cambridge University Press 2010) 153.

26 Machill, Beiler and Fischer (above n 20).

27 L van Noije, 'The European paradox: a communication deficit as long as European integration steals the headlines' (2010) 25 *European Journal of Communication* 259.

28 Pfetsch *et al.* (above n 25) 157.

29 Brüggemann and Kleinen-von Königslöw (above n 23).

Times from being the newspaper that is most frequently cited by other European newspapers,[30] which suggests that it occupies a very influential position as an international opinion maker. Another important difference between the British and European press is that the former tends to be more political about European issues whereas the latter is more likely to approach them from a more 'technical and expert viewpoint'.[31] Empirical research among EU correspondents found that 'Many of the British journalists pointed to the media specifically in France and Germany … as examples of profoundly different styles. Both were seen as less vigorous, more reserved or 'boring', and much less likely to deal with controversial issues than are British media'.[32]

It is clear that UK media representations of the EU are in a league of their own: the jury is still out when it comes to the role of the media in the outcome of the Brexit referendum but prima facie it appears to have been considerable.[33] As far as the issue of EU integration is concerned, UK media frames are very distinct: for example, the sovereignty theme figures much more prominently in the British press than it does in the European press.[34] Moreover, media coverage has become progressively more hostile over time. One author argues that there has been a remarkable transition from 'permissive consensus' when the UK first joined the EEC in the early 1970s to present-day 'destructive dissent' in its media.[35] Another one points to a 'plethora of oversimplified and hostile stories about the EU in the British press, even in the quality papers'.[36] While Britain does certainly not have a monopoly over Euroscepticism, it is much more pronounced in British media described as holding 'the very hardest of "hard" variants of Eurosceptical opinion'.[37] 'Europe has nearly always been reported as a "problem", not as a good thing', noted Seaton[38] in the aftermath of the Brexit referendum. It is little surprise, therefore, that strong scepticism about the EU has also had a tendency to spill over in unrelated areas loosely grouped together under the same umbrella of 'Europe'.

Media accusations that judges at the European Court unduly interfere with British domestic affairs have distinct echoes of related anxieties about a loss of sovereignty in an EU context. At the same time, in line with the lack of horizontal

---

30 G A Veltri, 'Information flows and centrality among elite European newspapers' (2012) 27 *European Journal of Communication* 354.

31 P Preston, *Making the News: Journalism and News Cultures in Europe* (Routledge 2009) 157.

32 *ibid* 153.

33 J Seaton, 'Brexit and the Media' (2016) 87 *The Political Quarterly* 333.

34 J D Medrano and E Gray, 'Framing the European Union in National Public Spheres' in R Koopmans and P Statham (eds) *The Making of a European Public Sphere: Media Discourse and Political Contention* (Cambridge University Press 2010) 206.

35 O Daddow, 'The UK media and 'Europe': from permissive consensus to destructive dissent' (2012) 88 *International Affairs* 1219.

36 van Noije (above n 27) 261.

37 Daddow (above n 35) 1220.

38 Seaton (above n 33) 336.

Europeanization, it should come as no surprise that, as the ECHR is hardly at issue in a wider European context, British domestic concerns about the ECHR attract comparatively little coverage in the European press. The absence of an equivalent political agenda means that the topic is not one that readily lends itself to being domesticated for audiences outside Britain. An international event such as the Brighton conference potentially holds broader European relevance, but its technical remit and its complexity may explain why it failed to dominate the European news agenda.

The Brighton Declaration in the British national press

Before examining coverage of the Brighton conference and the British reform agenda in the European press, it is useful to establish first to what extent this constituted a newsworthy event in the UK national press. After all, newspapers in Britain were the most invested in the reforms precisely because of their intertwinement with domestic issues and, therefore, provide a good yardstick with which to assess coverage in other European papers where the topic would have had less salience. The sample examined here was obtained through the newspaper database Nexis focusing on coverage between 1 April and 31 May 2012. The keywords 'Brighton conference' and 'Brighton declaration' were used to obtain as precisely a match as possible with the actual event and provide a basis for comparison for the European press analysis.

Electronic newspaper databases are not without their pitfalls: it is clear that they lend themselves best to keyword searches involving objects that can be specifically pinpointed (e.g. places and events), rather than abstract themes that are difficult to capture by inputting key words.[39] In this study, the key words acted as a proxy for obtaining a relevant sample of coverage involving the more abstract theme of reform of European human rights law. Another potential issue is that, apart from returning duplicate items, the Nexis database does not always consistently identify all relevant coverage, meaning that items may be missed.[40] Nevertheless, Nexis is a widely used tool in newspaper content analysis; however, the fact that it is not guaranteed to be exhaustive means that the number of results returned cannot be seen as an exact measure of the coverage.

Even allowing for the possibility of 'low-level' omissions, it is clear that the Brighton event was a newsworthy event in the British press. More precisely, there was a spike in the coverage on 19 and 20 April, dates that coincided with the actual conference. The event was covered by all the national broadsheets (*The Daily Telegraph*, *The Independent*, *The Guardian*, *The Times*) and some of the tabloids (*Daily Mail*, *Express* and *The Sun*) in both their print and online editions. The importance of the Brighton conference can be seen not just from the fact that it exercised the minds of reporters across the broadsheet/tabloid spectrum

39 D Deacon, 'Yesterday's Papers and Today's Technology: Digital Newspaper Archives and 'Push Button' Content Analysis' (2007) 22 *European Journal of Communication* 5.
40 *Ibid.*

but also from the fact that the coverage featured several complementary articles on the same day within the same publication, notably in *The Independent* and *The Guardian*, evidence of more in-depth coverage. *The Sun* even devoted an editorial to the Brighton declaration, which, even allowing for the tabloid tradition of irreverent commentary, was strong-worded and very outspoken, as can be seen from the headline:

> YOU DIRTY BRATZ;
> OUTRAGE AT BOSS OF JUDGES WHO FREED QATADA
> Rights court chief slams shake-up bid
> Cleric may sue for 'wrong arrest'
> MP's demand: Kick him out now [41]

'Bratz' refers to the then President of the European Court, Sir Nicolas Bratza, who was critical of the proposed Brighton reforms; Abu Qatada is the Jordan Muslim cleric who was the subject of protracted extradition proceedings at the time. Another detail to note is the erroneous reference to 'EU court' in at least two of the headlines,[42] a small but significant slip-up that is revealing of an inability to distinguish between the EU and the ECHR and is indicative of the confusion that is inherent to the rather nebulous terminology involving 'Europe'.

Another qualitative feature of the coverage is that it was embedded in a larger narrative framework with frequent allusions and references being made to other news stories. This suggests that the Brighton conference was by no means a one-off news event but part of a serial narrative about human rights. One story running directly in parallel with the Brighton reporting concerned the protracted legal proceedings to extradite Abu Qatada to his native Jordan.[43] The European Court was seen as instrumental in frustrating attempts to have him extradited:

> There has also been fury over the ECHR blocking the removal of dangerous terrorists such as Abu Qatada and foreign criminals.[44]

> Europe's court jesters; Britain threatens exit from European Court of Human Rights as Home Office mix-up over deadline lets Abu Qatada win again.[45]

---

41 Editorial, 'YOU DIRTY BRATZ; OUTRAGE AT BOSS OF JUDGES WHO FREED QATADA' *The Sun* (London, 20 April 2012) 10. Compare this with the rather sedate headline in the *Daily Mail* 'Judges defy UK bid to overhaul European Court' in an article featured on the same day. Jack Doyle, 'Judges defy the UK bid to overhaul European Court' *Daily Mail* (London, 20 April 2012).

42 M Beckford, 'Clarke hails EU court reform … but its leader says nothing has changed', *The Daily Telegraph* (London, 20 April 2012) 5. T Judd, 'Clarke clashes with EU court chief over reforms' *Independent.co.uk* (London, 19 April 2012) online.

43 *Othman* (above n 2).

44 Doyle (above n 41).

45 S Coates, R Ford and F Gibb, 'Europe's court jesters; Britain threatens exit from European Court of Human Rights as Home Office mix-up over deadline lets Abu Qatada win again' *The Times* (London, 19 April 2012) 1.

Another story that was mentioned in tandem with the Abu Qatada saga was that of the European Court's ruling against the blanket ban on prisoners' right to vote.[46] Once again, the story, which informed the background to the Brighton reporting, offered an opportunity to cast the European Court as the nemesis of the UK Government:

> Today's agreement comes in the wake of the continuing furore over Government attempts to deport terror suspect Abu Qatada and after European Court of Human Rights (ECHR) judges ruled that the UK must give some prisoners the right to vote.[47]

> Ministers had seen the summit, held as Britain chairs the Council of Europe, as a once-in-a-generation attempt to reform the European Court of Human Rights following rulings that have gone against Government policy and supported the rights of criminals and terror suspects. One case brought by a convicted axe killer ended with ministers being told to give prisoners the right to vote, while another saw the Al-Qaeda suspect Abu Qatada released from jail rather than being deported.[48]

Both the Qatada and the prisoners' voting stories served a very important purpose in the coverage, which was to turn a topic, involving the powers and procedures of a European court, that is very abstract and of limited interest to a lay audience, into a talking point drawing on the highly emotive issue of how much rights 'criminals' should have.

As we will see, in other European newspapers such a powerful backstory was not widely available, which could explain why the Brighton conference did not make for particularly gripping reading. The reforms were presented as a British initiative driven by British domestic problems that would require a considerable effort to explain to audiences who were not privy to the prolonged coverage that readers in Britain had been exposed to for years. Foreign audiences lack the contextual and intertextual knowledge in order for them to 'get' the story in a few words. Indeed, as van Dijk points out in relation to news texts:

> In order to summarize and globally understand the text (…), we must have a vast amount of political knowledge, knowledge that is not spelled out in the text, but presupposed by it.… Thus, we may need complex social and political knowledge schemata, or *scripts* to understand what this text is about.[49]

---

46 *Hirst* (above n 2).

47 W Johnson, 'Talks will lead to 'substantial' ECHR reforms, says Justice Secretary Kenneth Clarke' *Independent.co.uk* (London, 19 April 2012) online.

48 M Beckford, 'Human rights reform 'doomed to fail'' *The Daily Telegraph* (London, 18 April 2012) 4.

49 T A Van Dijk, *Discourse and Communication: New Approaches to the Analysis of Mass Communication Discourse and Communication* (De Gruyter 1985) 76–77.

Furthermore, news discourse routinely relies on readers already having 'a model of the situation' from exposure to previous news stories.[50] Evidence of such a model of the situation is replete in the UK media coverage of Brighton, for example, through the very fact that very few words were expended to explain the two cases that loomed large in the story, relying on shorthand such as 'hate cleric',[51] 'radical cleric and terror suspect'[52] and 'prisoner-voting gate'[53] and 'UK ban on prisoners voting'.[54]

Another noteworthy aspect of the coverage in the UK press is the use of specific frames to interpret and evaluate the event. This is important as it took the reporting beyond the level of stating key facts and enabled the Brighton conference to be assessed in a particular way, even in places that were not explicitly signposted as opinion pieces. A frame in a news context amounts to the 'central organizing idea'[55] conveyed by a news item. It refers to 'the ability of a text – or a media representation – to define a situation, to define the issues, and to set the terms of a debate'.[56] It is more than just a theme in that it has an evaluative dimension, for example, designating a particular cause or solution to a particular issue. The frame works to give salience to particular aspects of the story:[57] this means that different media may throw a very different light on a particular event, depending on the frame that is being promoted, or, on the contrary, news reports may demonstrate striking similarities, for example, because of a successful effort on the part of a news source to promote a particular narrative. The components that make up a frame are potentially manifold: lexical choices or the use of specific phrases and metaphors, along with quotes, all serve to give a frame its particular flavour and orientation.[58] Equally, a frame can be merely implied, for example, by ordering the components of a story in a specific way.

As de Vreese[59] notes, the frame of conflict is one of the most dominant in news making, not just because a story in which different actors clash is infinitely more interesting than one in which everyone agrees, but also because it

---

50 *Ibid.*, 81.

51 Editorial (above n 41).

52 F Gibb, 'Clarke attacks European court's 'scandalous' delays' *The Times* (London, 20 April 2012) 6.

53 T Lyle, 'Is the European Court of Human Rights the villain it is being presented as?' Independent.co.uk (London, 19 April 2012) online.

54 T Parfitt, 'European Court of Human Rights reforms could have 'devastating' effect in Russia' telegraph.co.uk (London, 17 April 2012) online.

55 W A Gamson and A Modigliani, 'Media discourse and public opinion on nuclear power: A constructionist approach' (1989) 95 *American Journal of Sociology* 1, 3.

56 J W Tankard, 'The Empirical Approach to the Study of Media Framing' in S D Reese, O H Gandy Jr and A E Grant (eds) *Framing Public Life: Perspectives on Media and Our Understanding of Social Life* (Taylor and Francis 2001) 96.

57 C H de Vreese, 'New Avenues for Framing Research' (2012) 56 American Behavioral Scientist 365.

58 Tankard (above n 56).

59 de Vreese (above n 57) 369.

is a classic mechanism for balancing a story by showing that there are two sides to the argument. In a similar vein, a dominant theme of the Brighton coverage was the extent of disagreement between various parties over the success/failure of the proposed reforms, along with an assessment of whether these parties would either impede or aid the implementation of the reforms. The headlines, visually the most prominent part of any newspaper story, almost speak for themselves in this regard, as a few examples demonstrate:

> 'Human rights summit "doomed" to failure'.[60]
> 'Council of Europe set to endorse UK-led reforms of human rights court'.[61]
> 'Human rights humiliation 1: Judges to defy UK bid to overhaul European Court'.[62]
> 'Clarke hails European court reforms despite its leader saying nothing has changed'.[63]
> 'Clarke's bid in tatters'.[64]

The identity of the various parties who were considered instrumental to the success/failure of the reforms in the coverage perhaps holds little surprise: the axis mainly revolved around politicians versus judges and the UK versus Europe, and, as noted above, this is backed up by the illustrative power of two other familiar stories that were explicitly associated with the reform debate through repeated cross-referencing.

Finally, what about the Europeanization aspect of the coverage? As previously discussed, Europeanization has both a vertical and a horizontal dimension. While the vertical dimension was very much in evidence in the Brighton coverage in that the story manifestly paid attention to proposed reforms of a key European institution, the horizontal aspects of the story were less pronounced. The focus was overwhelmingly on the UK's stake in seeing the European Court reformed, with only very limited reference to the position of other signatory states. Very few articles engaged with the question of how the reforms would be viewed by citizens and governments elsewhere in Europe: Russia was quoted in the coverage by an Amnesty International source as a country that would be incentivised to disregard human rights further by the proposed changes, resulting in a deteriorating human rights record. Similar concerns were raised by the Secretary-General of the Council of Europe, Thorbjørn Jagland, in an article by

60 Beckford (above n 48).
61 O Bowcott, 'Council of Europe set to endorse UK-led reforms of human rights court' *guardian.co.uk* (London, 18 April 2012) online.
62 J Doyle, 'Human rights humiliation 1: Judges to defy UK bid to overhaul European Court' *MailOnline* (London, 19 April 2012) online.
63 M Beckford, 'Clarke hails European court reforms despite its leader saying nothing has changed' *telegraph.co.uk* (London, 20 April 2012) online.
64 Anonymous, 'Clarke's bid in tatters', *The Express* (London, 20 April 2012) 5.

the Guardian's legal correspondent.[65] However, in general, the coverage was relatively parochial, failing to promote 'identification beyond the local or national realm'.[66] The failure to see the issue of reform of the European Court from the perspectives of other countries and the transnational level more broadly fuelled the us/them narrative encapsulated by the frame of a battle between the UK and the rest of Europe. A prime example is the way in which European judges were portrayed as going out of their way to block the extradition of Abu Qatada just to frustrate the UK national interest. Human rights as a cosmopolitan good only featured in the margins of this all too familiar story of the UK against Europe.

The Brighton Declaration in the European press

A definite feature of the coverage of the Brighton conference in the European press is that it was by no means extensive, a finding that is supported by the Europeanization literature pointing to a lack of a European public sphere. For this part of the study, coverage of Brighton in the Dutch, French, German, Italian and Irish national press was observed. In the first instance, the search term 'Brighton' was submitted to Nexis, with additional search terms in the relevant languages used to widen the net as appropriate. The initial focus of the search was on the period 1 April to 31 May 2012, but this was broadened to the entire year if no results were found for this particular period. As previously noted, Nexis sometimes fails to capture relevant news items. To counter the problem of false negatives, the websites of a sample of individual publications were searched for triangulation purposes. For example, no relevant coverage could be retrieved from Italian newspapers through Nexis and a further search of the websites of *La Corriere de la Sera* and *La Repubblica*, two of the main Italian national newspapers, also failed to uncover any relevant articles, confirming the lack of coverage.[67] On the other hand, the French national newspaper *Libération* did not show up in Nexis but a further search of the newspaper's website did yield four articles.

The overall volume of retrieved coverage remains very small, even allowing for the fact that some coverage may have slipped through the net. Take the Republic of Ireland, a country that has very close historical, economic, political and geographical ties with the UK. A reasonable assumption is that its national press would take an interest in the reform package closely pursued by its direct neighbour. Nevertheless, only one relevant article could be retrieved: this involved an opinion piece in *The Irish Times* by the Executive Director of Amnesty

---

65 J Rozenberg, 'Draft Brighton declaration is a breath of fresh air' *guardian.com* (London, 19 April) online.

66 M Brüggemann and K Kleinen-von Königslöw, 'Explaining cosmopolitan coverage' (2013) *European Journal of Communication* 361, 362.

67 One of the reasons for including Italy in the study is that its government was a party to the prisoners' right to vote case of *Scoppola v Italy* (no 3) (2013) 56 EHRR 19. Consequently, it seems reasonable to presume that its press would show an interest in an issue that caused so much anger in the British press.

International Ireland making the case that Ireland should support the European Court in the face of the challenges posed by the British reform agenda.[68] Coverage of the Brighton reforms was the most extensive in the French press. After the Irish press, it was the German press that featured the least amount of coverage (as measured by the number of articles). The event was also reported in three main national Dutch dailies (*NRC Handelsblad*, *de Volkskrant* and *het Parool*).

Starting with the frames that were used to make sense of Brighton, the notion of conflict and disagreement along with the purported success/failure of the reforms were once again central in organising the story. The centre-right paper *Le Figaro* in one of its headlines referred to an attack by David Cameron on the European Court and designated the conflict 'a new apple of European discord',[69] a powerful metaphor drawn from Greek mythology. The same paper also used the frame of undue interference by the European Court in two of its headlines to identify the cause of the conflict. Interestingly, the paper suggested that despite its official pro-ECHR stance, France 'discreetly' supported the UK in its struggle with the 'interfering' European Court, a thought reflected in its headline: 'English (sic) and French stand shoulder to shoulder on reforms'.[70] It also hinted that there were several other countries that shared the UK's dissatisfaction with the Court: 'In reality, if the English (sic) have set the tone, they are not alone in criticising the increasing interference of the ECtHR in national jurisdictions'.[71] On the other hand, the paper also argued that the British reform agenda was driven by 'domestic political tactics once again making Europe the scapegoat'.[72] *Le Figaro* also featured an opinion piece by the then Justice Secretary, Ken Clarke, setting out the case for reform.[73] Furthermore, quite remarkably, it included an article portraying the European Court as having had a negative impact on French law.[74] Although *Le Figaro* did not appear to carry any reports of the Brighton conference itself, of all the European newspapers surveyed, it signalled the strongest support for the UK's reform agenda and showed itself the most sceptical about the European Court. In a similar vein, the Dutch *NRC Handelsblad* asserted that the Netherlands was considered a 'very useful ally' by British diplomats and

68 C O'Gorman, 'Ireland should champion Strasbourg court' *The Irish Times* (Dublin, 2 April 2012) 6.

69 F Collomp, 'Cameron s'attaque a la Cour des droits de l'homme' *Le Figaro* (Paris, 26 January 2012) 8.

70 L de Charette, 'Anglais et Français main dans la main pour reformer' *Le Figaro* (Paris, 30 January 2012) 10.

71 *Ibid.*

72 *Ibid.*

73 K Clarke, 'Pour une véritable Europe des droits de l'homme' *Le Figaro* (Paris, 8 April 2012) 17.

74 L De Charette, 'Quand la CEDH défait le droit français' *Le Figaro* (Paris, 26 January 2012) Opinions 15. In contrast, the left-leaning paper *Libération* featured an article documenting the beneficial impact of the Court on rights in France. S Faure, 'Garde à vue, "double peine" des immigrés.... Les décisions de la Cour des droits de l'homme ont permis de faire avancer notre législation' *Libération* (Paris, 17 April 2012) online.

that the country shared Britain's displeasure at the 'activist' tendencies of the Court.[75] Such a portrayal stands in marked contrast with the 'UK against the rest of Europe' frame pursued by elements of the British press and effectively reframes the conflict to 'the European Court against several nation-states'.

As for the actual reforms achieved in Brighton, the principal suggestion was that they were at best a modest success and at worst a failure. *Le Monde*'s headline was unequivocal: 'Britain fails to reduce the powers of the ECtHR'.[76] The *NRC Handelsblad* concurred: 'Brits fail to put Strasbourg in its place'.[77] The reforms were framed as 'watered down'[78] (*Libération* and *NRC Handelsblad*), enabling the UK to 'save face but not much else' (*Le Monde*[79]). The reaction of the British press was itself a yardstick for measuring the success: 'The British tabloids are unhappy with the outcome of the negotiations' (*NRC Handelsblad*[80]). The British media and public opinion more generally were identified as a key factor in driving the UK's dissatisfaction with the European Court. *Libération*, the most supportive of the ECHR of all the publications surveyed here, accused the British press of wrongly claiming that Britain was always held to have been in the wrong by the European Court.[81] Reporting on the prisoners' voting rights issue, *Le Monde* stated that 'the court expects to be at the receiving end of a cartload of insults from the English (sic) press'.[82] The German paper *Die Welt* explained that 'in the British public sphere, the charter of the ECHR has long been considered 'a charter for law-breakers'.[83] The outsider's perspective of the European press allowed for the British press and public opinion to become an explicit part of the news frame as newspapers tried to enlighten their readers of the reasons why the ECHR and the European Court were such bones of contention in the UK. This need for explanation further illustrates that the ECHR and the European Court are not much of a talking point in their own national public spheres.

The Abu Qatada case that provided an important focus for the reporting on Brighton in the UK press also featured in the European press coverage. The sample of reporting surveyed also made mention of the prisoners' franchise, that other cause célèbre, but overall this featured less prominently. In an article in

75 T Ketelaar and M Beunderman, 'Britten krijgen Hof in Straatsburg niet klein' *NRC Handelsblad* (Amsterdam, 20 April 2012) 14.

76 F Johannès, 'L'Angleterre échoue a réduire les pouvoirs de la Cours européenne des droits de l'homme' *Le Monde* (Paris, 21 April 2012) 10.

77 S Delesalle-Stolper, Cour européenne des droits de l'homme: projet de réforme et polémiques. Ketelaar and Beunderman (above n 75).

78 Ketelaar and Beunderman (above n 75).

79 Johannès (above n 76).

80 Ketelaar and Beunderman (above n 75).

81 M Semo and S Delesalle-Stolper, 'La Cour des droits de l'homme en accusation' *Libération* (Paris, 17 April 2012) online.

82 F Johannès, 'La Cour de Strasbourg somme Londres de moduler la suppression du droit de vote pour les condamnés' *Le Monde* (Paris, 24 May 2012) 5.

83 T Kielinger, 'Hass auf Staatskosten; England darf nach dem Urteil seiner Gerichte einen Islamisten abschieben' *Die Welt* (Berlin, 23 April 2012) 95.

the Dutch newspaper *Het Parool* the main focus was on the struggle to extradite Qatada.[84] The Brighton conference came secondary in the story as it was confined to just one paragraph, amounting to just 81 out of 617 words. Similarly, *Die Welt* devoted almost an entire article to explaining the British frustration with the Qatada case, a piece that essentially acted as a lengthy introduction to the why of the Brighton conference.[85] The article evoked British anger at the European Court by opening and closing with a 'frustrated' David Cameron who, according to the report, woke up every morning asking himself how it could possibly be that Qatada was still in the country. The coverage provided in such articles clearly suggests that the 'script' or 'schemata' accompanying the reporting in the British press was not as established as a narrative in the European press, hence the need for a lengthy explanation. The criteria of newsworthiness typically encompass many different values and preferences.[86] One of the reasons why the Brighton conference did not attract much coverage in the European press is arguably that the topic required too much explanation for an audience unfamiliar with the decade-long news coverage of European human rights law found in the UK press. The story lacked potential to be domesticated because it overlapped only sparingly with national issues in the countries surveyed.

By the same token, the modest volume of coverage could also be seen as illustrative of the limited extent to which news media in Europe take an interest in shared European matters. Similar to the institutions of the EU, the day-to-day operations of the European Court that were at the heart of the Brighton negotiations are possibly both too complex and too technical to dominate the news on a wide scale. As for the horizontal aspect of Europeanization, the dearth of coverage illustrates how little news value a key issue dominating the political agenda of one country holds to the press in other countries. At the same time, within the limited reporting that was generated, a visible effort was made to see the issue from a British perspective. This transpired in the few articles that tried to explain in some detail what the UK's concerns were in regard to the European Court. It was also reflected in the fact that two key newspaper titles offered a platform to British voices to explain the reforms: in the case of *Le Figaro*, this took the form of an opinion piece authored by Ken Clarke,[87] while, in the *NRC Handelsblad*, it involved an interview with the Attorney General Dominic Grieve.[88] Oppositional voices were also heard in *Libération* featuring an interview with the former president of the European Court, Jean-Paul Costa,[89] and in *The Irish Times*, where it was Amnesty International which was given a platform to outline its concerns about the reform package.[90] In summary, there were pockets of cosmopolitanism,

84 Anonymous, 'Britse regering is Europees hof beu' *Het Parool* (Amsterdam, 20 April 2012) 9.
85 Kielinger (above n 83).
86 J Hartley, *Understanding News* (Routledge 2013).
87 Clarke (above n 73).
88 M Beunderman, 'Mensenrechtenhof in Straatsburg moet minder zaken aannemen' *NRC Handelsblad* (Amsterdam, 5 April 2012) Buitenland section.
89 Semo and Delesalle-Stolper (above n 81).
90 O'Gorman (above n 68).

involving explicit support for the ECHR, to be detected in what otherwise testifies to a parochial neglect of an issue of Europe-wide significance.

Conclusion

This chapter has focused on European and British press coverage of a significant event, the Brighton conference, with the aim of generating insight into the way in which British (media) discourse about human rights is perceived elsewhere in Europe. There appears to be neither great interest in nor alarm about British human rights scepticism, at least not as far as these particular reforms were concerned. There were some murmurings of support for the United Kingdom in its desire to reform the European Court but this hardly amounts to strong evidence that anti-ECHR sentiments are catching on elsewhere. Neither can it be said that the European press came out in strong defence of the ECHR, with a few notable exceptions. Most importantly, the analysis reveals a failure on the part of the European press to appreciate how strong anti-human rights sentiments are in the British public sphere and how much of a threat these potentially constitute to the cosmopolitan human rights ideal.

These findings are consistent with research documenting the lack of a European dimension in Europe's media content and the absence of public discussion about the Convention in other signatory states. It could be surmised that this is merely a sign that there is little to be debated and points to a tacit yet unbroken public consensus about the legitimacy of the Convention and its institutions. It also suggests that the kind of media narrative portraying human rights as the root cause of many contemporary problems, from immigration to crime, does not have particular purchase elsewhere in Europe. However, it would be rash to conclude that this therefore means that people in Europe are not equally concerned about these various issues and that these do not have the potential to collide with human rights at some point in the future. The invisibility of rights in European media means that public opinion is not particularly well informed about the system of human rights protection currently on offer through the ECHR. This ignorance creates a knowledge vacuum that can be exploited for different ideological purposes: the UK is a case in point of how human rights went from being low profile to becoming one of the most controversial topics in its national media coalescing around a particular type of narrative.

Inevitably, there is a parallel to be drawn with Brexit and the limited coverage of European matters in Europe's media. Early analysis suggests that Brexit did attract a huge amount of coverage in various European countries,[91] but one could say that this came as too little too late: British Euroscepticism has been an issue for several decades but it only managed to take centre stage when a full-blown

91 I Garcia-Blanco, 'A victory of the nation state: the EU Referendum in the Southern European Press' in D Jackson, E Thorsen and D Wring (eds), *EU Referendum Analysis 2016: Media, Voters and the Campaign* (The Centre for the Study of Journalism, Culture and Community Bournemouth University 2016).

crisis was looming that could no longer be averted. Such a crisis point has not yet been reached as far as Britain's membership of the ECHR is concerned, but with Government ministers openly toying with the idea of withdrawal, there is yet again the possibility that this issue will only become part of the European news agenda at the point of no return. As with Brexit, the danger is that rampant rights scepticism in the UK press will continue to go both unnoticed and unchecked in the European press. This is not to argue that the only legitimate narrative is one that is unequivocally supportive of the ECHR; rather, the argument concerns the lack of public debate and the absence of media frames offering a variety of perspectives.

Bibliography

M Brüggemann and K Kleinen-von Königslöw, 'Let's talk about Europe: Explaining vertical and horizontal Europeanization in the quality press' (2009) 24 *European Journal of Communication* 27.

M Brüggemann and K Kleinen-von Königslöw, 'Explaining cosmopolitan coverage' (2013) *European Journal of Communication* 361, 362.

Council of Europe, *High Level Conference on the Future of the European Court of Human Rights Brighton Declaration* (2012) para 29 b, available online at: www.echr.coe.int/documents/2012_brighton_finaldeclaration_eng.pdf (accessed 16 November 2016).

O Daddow, 'The UK media and 'Europe': from permissive consensus to destructive dissent' (2012) 88 *International Affairs* 1219.

CH de Vreese, 'New Avenues for Framing Research' (2012) 56 *American Behavioral Scientist* 365.

D Deacon, 'Yesterday's Papers and Today's Technology: Digital Newspaper Archives and 'Push Button' Content Analysis' (2007) 22 *European Journal of Communication* 5.

S Delesalle-Stolper, Cour européenne des droits de l'homme: projet de réforme et polémiques.

H Fenwick, 'The Human Rights Act or a British Bill of Rights: creating a down-grading recalibration of rights against the counter-terror backdrop? [2012] PL 468.

I Garcia-Blanco, 'A victory of the nation state: the EU Referendum in the Southern European Press' in D Jackson, E Thorsen and D Wring (eds) *EU Referendum Analysis 2016: Media, Voters and the Campaign* (The Centre for the Study of Journalism, Culture and Community Bournemouth University 2016).

W A Gamson and A Modigliani, 'Media discourse and public opinion on nuclear power: A constructionist approach' (1989) 95 *American Journal of Sociology* 1.

L Gies, *Mediating Human Rights: Media, Culture and Human Rights Law* (Routledge 2014).

C Grewe, 'The ECHR in French Law: Status, Implementation and Debates' in K S Ziegler, E Wicks and L Hodson (eds), *The UK and European Human Rights: A Strained Relationship?* (Hart 2015) 359.

D Grieve, 'Is the European Convention working?' (2015) 6 *EHRLR* 584.

J Habermas, *The Structural Transformation of the Public Sphere: An Inquiry into a Category of Bourgeois Society* (MIT Press 1989).

J Hartley, *Understanding News* (Routledge 2013).

F Klug, 'A Bill of Rights: do we need one or do we already have one?' [2007] PL 701, 714.

R Koopmans and P Statham (eds), *The Making of a European Public Sphere: Media Discourse and Political Contention* (Cambridge University Press 2010).

D Levy, B Aslan and D Bironzo, 'The press and the Referendum Campaign' in D Jackson, E Thorsen and D Wring (eds) *EU Referendum Analysis 2016: Media, Voters and the Campaign* (The Centre for the Study of Journalism, Culture and Community Bournemouth University 2016).

M Machill, M Beiler and C Fischer, 'Europe-Topics in Europe's Media: The Debate about the European Public Sphere: A Meta-Analyses of Media Content Analysis' (2006) 21 *European Journal of Communication* 57.

B McCluskey, 'Human Rights, governments and judicial independence' (2012) 5 *EHRLR* 479.

J D Medrano and E Gray, 'Framing the European Union in National Public Spheres' in R Koopmans and P Statham (eds) *The Making of a European Public Sphere: Media Discourse and Political Contention* (Cambridge University Press 2010) 206.

L Novy, *Britain and Germany Imagining the Future of Europe: National Identity, Mass Media and the Public Sphere* (Palgrave 2013).

B Pfetsch, S Adam and B Eschner, 'The Media's Voice over Europe: Issue Salience, Openness, and Conflict Lines in Editorials' in R Koopmans and P Statham (eds) *The Making of a European Public Sphere: Media Discourse and Political Contention* (Cambridge University Press 2010) 153.

P Preston, *Making the News: Journalism and News Cultures in Europe* (Routledge 2009).

D Raab, *The Assault on Liberty: What Went Wrong With Rights* (Fourth Estate 2009).

J Rackow, 'From Conflict to Cooperation: The Relationship Between Karlsruhe and Strasbourg' in K S Ziegler, E Wicks and L Hodson (eds), *The UK and European Human Rights: A Strained Relationship?* (Hart 2015) 398.

J Seaton, 'Brexit and the Media' (2016) 87 *The Political Quarterly* 333.

P Statham, 'Introduction: Europe's Search for a Public', in R Koopmans and P Statham (eds) *The Making of a European Public Sphere: Media Discourse and Political Contention* (Cambridge University Press 2010) 4.

JW Tankard, 'The Empirical Approach to the Study of Media Framing' in S D Reese, O H Gandy Jr and A E Grant (eds) *Framing Public Life: Perspectives on Media and Our Understanding of Social Life* (Taylor and Francis 2001).

TA Van Dijk, *Discourse and Communication: New Approaches to the Analysis of Mass Communication Discourse and Communication* (De Gruyter 1985).

L van Noije, 'The European paradox: a communication deficit as long as European integration steals the headlines' (2010) 25 *European Journal of Communication* 259.

GA Veltri, 'Information flows and centrality among elite European newspapers' (2012) 27 *European Journal of Communication* 354.

Part II

Features

4 Monstering Strasbourg over prisoner voting rights

C. R. G. Murray[1]

Introduction

On 12 February 1950 a Ronald Niebour cartoon accompanying a *Daily Mail* article pictured a smiling inmate sitting in his prison cell being vigorously canvassed by two politicians above the caption 'Blimey – Roll on February 23' (polling day for the forthcoming general election). This story followed strenuous efforts by the Prison Commission to ensure that prisons across the country informed their inmates that if they had been sentenced to imprisonment for under 12 months they were eligible to use the new system of postal votes to vote in their constituency of ordinary residence.[2] The accompanying reporting, even if it expressed surprise at this development, did not intimate that the collapse of the UK's parliamentary democracy was imminent.[3] A limited prison franchise would remain in place for the next two decades until it was abolished, without any substantive parliamentary debate, under the Representation of the People Act 1969.[4] Over half-a-century later, however, the mere thought of giving any prisoners the vote in response to the European Court of Human Rights' judgment in *Hirst v United Kingdom*[5] was sufficient to leave Prime Minister David Cameron feeling 'physically ill'.[6]

A complex combination of factors has transformed prisoner voting from an issue that excited virtually no attention in the post-war era to an intractable stand-off between successive UK governments and the Strasbourg Court. Considerable attention has been devoted to the influence of the press when the

1 My thanks to, Daithí Mac Síthigh (Queen's University Belfast), Aoife O'Donoghue (Durham) and Hélène Tyrrell (Newcastle) for their encouragement and comments upon earlier drafts of this article. Any errors remain my own.

2 See UK National Archives, PCOM 9/1362 K. Paice (Secretary, Prison Commission), 'Circular to all Establishments: Parliamentary General Election of 1950, Prisoners and Borstal Inmates Voting by Post' (14 Feb 1950).

3 Daily Mail Reporter, 'They can Post their Votes from Jail' *Daily Mail* (12 Feb 1950).

4 Representation of the People Act 1969, s.4. See G. Zellick, 'Prisoners' Rights in England' (1974) 24 UTLJ 331, 334.

5 *Hirst v United Kingdom (no.2)* (2006) 42 EHRR 41 [GC].

6 D. Cameron, MP, HC Deb., vol. 517, col. 921 (3 Nov 2010).

Figure 4.1 Blimey – Roll on February 23

Human Rights Act (HRA) is at issue. Prisoner voting has undoubtedly formed a prominent part of the 'outspoken anti-HRA agenda'[7] pursued by a swathe of the UK's national print media, and in particular the *Sun*, *Star*, *Express*, *Daily Mail*, *Times* and *Telegraph*. The *Daily Mail*, in particular, has insisted that '[w]ith our sovereignty at stake ... the blanket ban must remain'.[8] Although the *Hirst* saga

7 L. Gies, *Mediating Human Rights: Media, Culture and the Human Rights Act* (Routledge, 2014) 4. See also 44–46.

8 Daily Mail Comment, 'Cameron's Chance to Deliver for Britain' *Daily Mail* (23 May 2012). See also J. Slack, 'Euro Judges trample UK sovereignty and insist: You WILL give Prisoners the Vote' *Daily Mail* (13 Apr 2011).

has been a dominant feature of these newspapers' criticisms of the UK's human rights commitments,[9] their assault on the HRA is in large part motivated by the impact of privacy rights upon press freedoms.[10] In advancing this agenda these outlets 'are not merely reporting the parliamentary debate, they are actually forming, leading and directing the content'.[11] Ministerial reluctance to reform the UK's blanket ban is often attributed to the sway of these newspapers.[12] Such claims, however, maintain attention upon tabloid influence over policy debates, glossing over just how, in an era of new media, declining newspaper sales and impartiality requirements upon broadcast news, this supposed influence has been sustained.[13]

This contribution places the agenda of right-of-centre newspapers within a multi-media context in an effort to understand how prisoner voting was transformed into a 'totemic' issue in contemporary UK politics.[14] I begin by reconsidering the *Hirst* judgment and the requirements it placed upon the UK, analysing the decision in light of some of the early reporting on the issue. This sets up my examination of the developing treatment of prisoner voting through news websites, print media and broadcast media. This account is based upon the systematic analysis of coverage of prisoner voting in the *Telegraph*, the *Daily Mail* and on the *ConservativeHome* website. These outlets have covered the issue of prisoner voting extensively, but this coverage has often adopted skewed representations of Strasbourg's jurisprudence. I thereafter analyse politicians and think tanks' efforts to generate support for their policy positions through these outlets. The resulting account lays bare the networks of power (mis)shaping public discourse. It challenges some of the shibboleths underpinning deliberative accounts of democracy; the "monstering" of the *Hirst* judgment indicates that truth will not necessarily win out 'in the competition of the market [of ideas]'.[15] Moreover, the conception

---

9 See Joint Committee on the draft Voting Eligibility (Prisoners) Bill, *Oral and Written Evidence* (2013) 629 (Adam Wagner). Available online at: www.parliament.uk/documents/joint-committees/Draft-Voting-Eligibility-Prisoners-Bill/prisonervoting-evidvol%20(4).pdf See also M. O'Boyle, 'The Future of the European Court of Human Rights' (2011) 12 *German LJ* 1862, 1862.

10 See B. Hale, 'What's the point of Human Rights?' (Warwick University, 28 Nov 2013) 20. Available online at: www.supremecourt.uk/docs/speech-131128.pdf

11 D. McNulty, N. Watson and G. Philo, 'Human Rights and Prisoners' Rights: The British Press and the Shaping of Public Debate' (2014) 53 *Howard Journal of Criminal Justice* 360, 374.

12 See, for example, P. Mason, 'Misinformation, Myth and Distortion: How the Press construct Imprisonment in Britain' (2007) 8 *Journalism Studies* 481 and Gies (above n.6) 18–21.

13 See C. Sunstein, *Republic.com 2.0* (PUP, 2007) 200–201 and M. Dean, *Democracy under Attack: How the Media Distort Policy and Politics* (Policy Press, 2013) 421.

14 Joint Committee Evidence (above n.8) 224 (Chris Grayling).

15 *Abrams v United States* (1919) 250 US 616, 630 (Holmes J). See also J. Habermas, 'Political Communication in Media Society: Does Democracy still enjoy an Epistemic Dimension? The Impact of Normative Theory on Empirical Research' (2006) 16 *Communication Theory* 411, 413.

of broadcasting as a particularly 'immediate and powerful'[16] vehicle for shaping public discourse may now be more truism than truth.

The trouble with *Hirst*

In 2016 the right-wing think tank Policy Exchange established the "Judicial Power Project" to highlight the propensity of the UK's domestic courts and of those international courts which impact upon the UK's Constitution to overreach the boundaries of the "proper" judicial role.[17] The project team enlivened their task by canvasing opinions on the worst examples of judicial overreach. Their resultant Top 50 list enthroned the *Hirst* judgment as the most egregious example of judicial overreach in UK constitutional history. This listing caps a decade-long academic debate over whether *Hirst* should be characterised as a subtle and 'sensitive' judgment[18] or one which took 'unnecessary risks'.[19] Given that the Strasbourg Court has subsequently tied itself into knots over the circumstances in which punitive franchise restrictions contravene Article 3 of Protocol 1 (A3P1), the critics would seem to have had the better of the argument. Far from amounting to a power grab, however, the shortcomings of this jurisprudence stem primarily from Strasbourg's cautious approach to its role in protecting human rights.

Some of the most trenchant criticism of *Hirst* has focused upon the decision as an example of Strasbourg's 'living instrument' doctrine, by which the Court interprets the European Convention on Human Rights (ECHR) with particular regard to contemporary values in contracting states and not in light of the drafters' intentions.[20] The right to vote has been described as being 'fabricated by judicial innovation,'[21] through the Court 'making a judgment in an area that is basically nothing to do with it'.[22] For the Judicial Power Project *Hirst* 'stretches the "living instrument" approach to interpretation to breaking point'.[23] This account of the Grand Chamber's decision has become so pervasive that it is

16 See *Jersild v Denmark* (1995) 19 EHRR 1, [31] and *Murphy v Ireland* (2004) 38 EHRR 13, [69].

17 This venture can be seen as a transfer of the activity of the United States' 'conservative legal movement' into the UK, with the fixation of groups such as the Federalist Society on 'judicial restraint'; S. Teles, *The Rise of the Conservative Legal Movement: The Battle for Control of the Law* (PUP, 2008) 154.

18 C. Murray, 'Playing for Time: Prisoner Disenfranchisement under the ECHR after *Hirst v United Kingdom*' (2011) 22 *KLJ* 309, 315.

19 E. Bates, 'Analysing the Prisoner Voting Saga and the British Challenge to Strasbourg' (2014) 14 *HRLRev* 503, 537.

20 *Tyrer v United Kingdom* (1978) 2 EHRR 1, [31].

21 D. Raab, *Strasbourg in the Dock: Prisoner Voting, Human Rights & the Case for Democracy* (Civitas, 2011) xiii. See also D. Raab, HC Deb, vol. 523, col. 582–583 (10 Feb 2011).

22 Joint Committee Evidence (above n.8) 140 (Jack Straw).

23 Judicial Power Project, '50 Problematic Cases: 1. Hirst v United Kingdom No.2 (2006)' (Policy Exchange, 2016). Available online at: http://judicialpowerproject.org.uk/50-problematic-cases/

difficult to resist explaining the decision in light of the idea of the ECHR as a living instrument.[24] The *Hirst* judgment, however, did not explicitly invoke this doctrine.[25] Indeed, the Court acknowledged that no common European approach to prisoner enfranchisement had developed since the drafting of the ECHR.[26] The Court's explanation for its conclusion that 'the right to vote is not a privilege' instead drew upon extensions to the UK's parliamentary franchise which mostly took place before the UK ratified the ECHR.[27] It did not insist that a twenty-first century account of A3P1 required universal suffrage, but that 'the presumption in a democratic state must be in favour of inclusion'.[28] This observation would have been as salient when the ECHR was drafted. The Court was not creating a right to vote where none had previously existed. It had recognised that the notion of a free and fair election contained within it a justiciable right to vote nearly two decades earlier in *Mathieu-Mohin and Clerfayt* (again, without reference to the living instrument doctrine).[29] This decision navigated the ECHR's *Travaux Préparatoires* and because these contain no specific guidance on prisoner disenfranchisement, there was no need to repeat the exercise in *Hirst*.[30]

The Grand Chamber drew further criticism from senior Labour politician Jack Straw for refusing to apply interpretative tools which it had historically used to inflate the margin of appreciation available to ECHR states.[31] The majority considered that claims that prisoner voting would offend public opinion could not influence its interpretation of the A3P1 Right.[32] By 'severing' its interpretation of human rights from such 'majoritarian preferences', the majority was responding to concerns that such preferences inevitably undermine the rights of small and unpopular groups within society, such as prisoners.[33] This narrowing of the

24 See, for example, Joint Committee on Human Rights, *Enhancing Parliament's Role in relation to Human Rights Judgments* (9 Mar 2010) HL 85/HC 455, para. 117 and Joint Committee on the Draft Voting Eligibility (Prisoners) Bill, *Draft Voting Eligibility (Prisoners) Bill* (18 Dec 2013) HL 103/HC 924, para. 37.

25 The dissent of Judges Wildhaber, Costa, Lorenzen, Kovler and Jebens noted that the majority had not referenced the case law on 'a dynamic and evolutive approach' to the ECHR rights; *Hirst* (above n.4) O III, [6].

26 *Ibid.*, [81].

27 *Ibid.*, [59].

28 *Ibid.*, [59]. As Claudio López-Guerra observes, prisoners 'continue to be subject to the laws, and their basic interests continue to depend on the decisions of elected officials'; C. López-Guerra, *Democracy and Disenfranchisement: The Morality of Electoral Exclusions* (OUP, 2014) 112.

29 *Mathieu-Mohin and Clerfayt v Belgium* (1988) 10 EHRR 1, [49]-[50]. The Court did note an evolution in the manner in which the Human Rights Commission had interpreted the right in its earlier decisions, at [51].

30 *Ibid.*, [52].

31 J. Straw, *Aspects of Law Reform: An Insider's Perspective* (CUP, 2012) 28.

32 *Hirst* (above n.4) [70].

33 See G. Letsas, 'The ECHR as a Living Instrument' in A. Føllesdal, B. Peters and G. Ulfstein (eds.), *Constituting Europe: The European Court of Human Rights in a National, European and Global Context* (CUP: 2013) 106, 123.

margin of appreciation in *Hirst*, relative to the approach employed in the Human Rights Commission's earlier decisions on prisoner disenfranchisement,[34] is therefore justifiable. Issues which were live in *Hirst*, including the blanket nature of the UK's ban and the claimant's particular status as a post-tariff life prisoner, had not previously been subject to adjudication. Even the dissenting judges accepted the possibility that the UK's 'restrictions may be disproportionate in respect of minor offences and/or very short sentences'.[35] The *Hirst* case is therefore an example of Strasbourg engaging with a novel issue, rather than the Court partaking in novel modes of interpretation.[36] These issues reached Strasbourg when they did because the HRA had opened up avenues for human rights challenge in the UK courts, for the first time allowing John Hirst a meaningful domestic route to remedy.[37]

Other courts which had challenged restrictions upon the prison franchise, in particular the Canadian Supreme Court, dismissed out-of-hand official justifications for such measures, including claims that removing the vote promotes civic responsibility and helps to deter crime.[38] The Chamber judgment in *Hirst* had specifically cast doubt on the validity of the UK Government's account of the policy objectives behind the ban, noting that the removal of the ability of some prisoners to vote had not been subject to debate in Parliament in 1969.[39] The Grand Chamber's majority, however, accepted that these were legitimate aims for the UK to pursue through legislation.[40] It instead ruled that instituting a blanket ban was disproportionate to these aims, as it 'applies automatically' to prisoners 'irrespective of the length of their sentence and irrespective of the nature or gravity of their offence and their individual circumstances'.[41] In adopting this approach the Court granted the UK considerable leeway for responding to the judgment in light of these aims. To comply with the ruling the UK Government needed to explicitly inform Parliament of the purposes behind new restrictions on sections of the prison franchise. Such restrictions could well conform to A3P1's requirements, subject to future consideration by the Court. The majority hinted that they would prefer the sentencing judge to deprive a convicted criminal of their vote as an additional punishment to incarceration in certain cases, but judicial authorisation was not a prerequisite for a system of restrictions to be A3P1

34 See, for example, *X v Netherlands*, App. No.6573/74 (1974) 1 DR 87.

35 *Hirst* (above n.4) O-III, [8].

36 As the then Lord Chancellor, Lord Falconer, explained *Hirst* at the time, '[t]he European Convention allows everyone to vote. It does not say "everyone, bar prisoners"'; BBC News, 'Convicts "will not all get the Vote"' (6 Oct 2005). Available online at: http://news.bbc.co.uk/1/hi/uk/4315348.stm

37 *R (Pearson and Martinez) v Secretary of State for the Home Department and Others; Hirst v Attorney General* [2001] EWHC Admin 239. On the counter-majoritarian role of the UK courts in the HRA context, see P. Sales, 'Partnership and Challenge: The Courts' role in Managing the Integration of Rights and Democracy' [2016] PL 456, 467.

38 *Sauvé v Canada* [2002] 3 SCR 519, [49] (McLachlin CJ).

39 *Hirst v United Kingdom* (2004) 38 EHRR 40, [47].

40 *Hirst* (above n.4) [75].

41 *Ibid.*, [82].

compliant.[42] The Court did not give specific guidance on how the UK should reform its restrictions on the prison franchise, or set out what minimal compliance with A3P1 would involve, precisely because the UK could respond to the judgment in 'number of different ways'.[43] In a final concession to the UK Government the Grand Chamber awarded Hirst no damages to compensate him for the breach of his rights.[44]

Strasbourg's finding that the UK's blanket ban was disproportionate did not, however, necessarily provide the UK, and other similarly affected states, with as much leeway as the majority intended. A blanket ban well might be 'general, automatic and indiscriminate',[45] as the Court asserted, but then so too is 'a rule disqualifying all persons sentenced to 10 years ... for homicide'.[46] Both rules involve exercises in line drawing which can impact upon some prisoners more seriously than others as a result of the timing of elections relative to their incarceration. One dissenting judgment identifies this problem with the majority's proportionality rationale, a weakness compounded by the Court's lack of guidance 'as to what would be solutions compatible with the Convention'.[47] The resultant uncertainty even led later chambers to assume that the Grand Chamber had required judicial imposition of a restriction on voting.[48] John Finnis has therefore accused the majority in *Hirst* of ignoring the 'statutory ends it had pretended to accept'.[49] Instead, the Grand Chamber gives rather too much weight to ends which the UK Government claimed the statutory ban pursued, but which were not articulated when the ban was imposed in 1969 or when it was transposed into its current form in 1983.[50] Strasbourg recognised Parliament's lack of substantive consideration of the blanket ban on prisoners voting and ruled that the right to vote could not be displaced in an offhand manner. There were no 'statutory ends' that it ignored, just *ex post facto* rationalisations which it accepted the UK could use in redrawing its restrictions on the prison franchise. Far from 'depriving the State of all margin and all means of appreciation',[51] the majority's concern for the need to respect a margin of appreciation in this context led to it compromising the integrity of its judgment.

The shortcomings in Strasbourg's approach to prisoner disenfranchisement therefore stem from the Court's 'timidity',[52] as opposed to any overweening

42 *Ibid.*, [77].
43 *Ibid.*, [84].
44 *Ibid.*, [94].
45 *Ibid.*, [82].
46 J. Finnis, 'Judicial Power: Past, Present and Future' (Gray's Inn Hall, 20 Oct 2015) 21. Available online at: http://judicialpowerproject.org.uk/wp-content/uploads/2015/10/John-Finnis-lecture-20102015.pdf See also Bates (above n.18) 509.
47 *Hirst* (above n.4) O-III, [8].
48 See *Frodl v Austria*, App. No. 20201/04 (8 Apr 2010), [18].
49 Finnis (above n.45) 21.
50 Representation of the People Act 1983, s.3.
51 *Hirst* (above n.4) O-IV, [9] (Judge Costa).
52 R. Ziegler, 'Voting Eligibility: Strasbourg's Timidity' in K. Ziegler, E. Wicks and L. Hodson (eds), *The UK and European Human Rights: A Strained Relationship* (Hart, 2015) 165.

aggrandisement of its jurisdiction. But few of the Court's critics have reflected upon the substance of its A3P1 jurisprudence and instead invoke *Hirst* because they are uncomfortable with the outcome. When, as Lord Chancellor, Chris Grayling was asked why *Hirst* had so undermined his faith in Strasbourg, his response 'set aside this particular case' and instead discussed how *Animal Defenders v United Kingdom* showed that the Court was straying 'too far away from the original intentions of its creators'.[53] In essence, Strasbourg's supposed transgressions in *Hirst* were 'small beer' when compared with some other decisions on less emotive subject matter.[54] For all that *Hirst* has become emblematic of an international court exceeding its remit, little about the decision sustains such criticism. We must therefore explore other factors which account for this judgment's prominence in the UK's human rights debate.

Making a monster of *Hirst*

As every pressure group embarking upon a campaign to change the law through the courts is aware, a claimant who elicits a sympathetic response from a court can influence a test case's outcome. Such a claimant can humanise the issues at stake for judges and can help to translate the publicity generated by a case into a media campaign capable of influencing Parliament.[55] The campaign for prisoner voting rights was not, however, fronted by such a claimant. This is, of course, because at the outset there was no campaign to extend the right to vote to prisoners, organised by the likes of the Howard League for Penal Reform or the Prison Reform Trust. There was John Hirst, a man who kept himself busy for over two decades in prison by studying law and using this knowledge to challenge aspects of his prison treatment.[56] Hirst, as has so often been repeated in media accounts of prisoner voting rights, was serving a sentence of life imprisonment for the manslaughter of his landlady when he commenced his A3P1 challenge. Having been released from prison he maintained that he was not remorseful for his crimes and revelled in the problems which his challenge had caused the UK Government.[57] Hirst was not only an unsympathetic claimant, his challenge involved the complex claim that because he had served the tariff element of his sentence and was no longer being held for retributive purposes, but for public protection,

53 *Animal Defenders International v United Kingdom* (2013) 57 EHRR 21; Joint Committee Evidence (above n.8) 215.

54 N. Phillips, 'European Human Rights – A Force for Good or a Threat to Democracy?' (17 Jun 2014) 12. Available online at: www.kcl.ac.uk/law/newsevents/newsrecords/2013-14/assets/Lord-Phillips-European-Human-Rights—A-Force-for-Good-or-a-Theat-to-Democracy-17-June-2014.pdf

55 See C. Harlow and R. Rawlings. *Pressure Through Law* (Routledge, 1992) 9.

56 See A. O'Hagan, 'It's not like I'm Killing Someone Now because there's no Lid for my Jam Jars' *The Guardian* (18 Nov 2006).

57 R. Edwards and M. Beckford, 'John Hirst faces Police Investigation over YouTube Video' *The Telegraph* (4 Nov 2010).

there was no punitive rationale for depriving him of his vote.[58] These were not telegenic arguments. Indeed, to the frustration of the Grand Chamber's minority, the majority were not explicit as to whether any reform of the UK's law would have to extend voting rights to prisoners in Hirst's position.[59] But Strasbourg's willingness to gloss over these shortcomings in Hirst's application to enable it to tackle a widespread infringement of the right to vote subsequently contributed to the hostile reception of its decision.

The misreporting of human rights stories by failing to accurately 'convey either the full or proper human rights dimension', has been commonplace since the HRA's enactment.[60] Even though Strasbourg's pronouncement that a blanket ban was 'general, automatic and indiscriminate'[61] could have been intelligibly communicated to the general public, reporting on the Chamber and Grand Chamber decisions in *Hirst* devoted little attention to the judges' reasoning and focused instead on spurious claims that Strasbourg had required that all prisoners be enfranchised.[62] If the collapse in the number of dedicated legal correspondents in UK newsrooms contributed to the shortcomings in this reporting,[63] some of the blame also lies with the Grand Chamber's refusal to explicitly state what reforms would satisfy A3P1.[64] Given this vagueness, reports that all prisoners would have to be enfranchised were always likely because John Hirst, convicted of a serious violent offence, had won his case.[65] By overstating the decision's requirements, and maintaining a sensationalist focus on Hirst's crimes rather than the wider issue of prisoner voting, this early reporting set the tone for subsequent public debate. It effectively 'reconstructed and reduced the narrative [on prisoner voting] around a discourse of violence and fear'.[66] When the *Financial Times* returned to the premise, which had so titillated *Daily Mail* readers 55 years earlier, of prisoners being canvased by would-be parliamentarians, its putative prisoner "Slasher" was serving time for attempted murder and GBH.[67]

---

58 *Hirst* (above n.4) [45].

59 *Ibid.*, O-III, [8].

60 D. Mead, '"You Couldn't Make It Up": Some Narratives of the Media's Coverage of Human Rights' in K. Ziegler, E. Wicks and L. Hodson (eds.), *The UK and European Human Rights: A Strained Relationship* (Hart, 2015) 453, 455.

61 *Hirst* (above n.4) [82], paraphrasing the Chamber judgment (above n.38) [49].

62 See S. Doughty, 'Convicted Criminals Given Right to Vote by Europe' *Daily Mail* (1 Apr 2004).

63 See Joint Committee Evidence (above n.8) 625 (Joshua Rozenberg and Adam Wagner).

64 For the Labour Government's efforts to rectify these misconceptions, see Department of Constitutional Affairs, *Review of the Implementation of the Human Rights Act* (HMSO, 2006) 34.

65 For confusion as to *Hirst's* requirements, even amongst well-advised bodies like Parliament's JCHR, see; C. Murray, 'We need to talk: "Democratic Dialogue" and the Ongoing Saga of Prisoner Disenfranchisement' (2011) 62 NILQ 57, 61–62.

66 P. Mason, 'Lies, distortion and what doesn't work: Monitoring Prison Stories in the British Media' (2006) 2 *Crime, Media, Culture* 251, 255.

67 R. Shrimsley, 'How to Vote? The Prisoner's Dilemma' *Financial Times* (7 Oct 2005).

From the Chamber judgment onwards, *Hirst* was also the subject of manoeuvrings between the UK's main political parties. The Conservative leadership stoked speculation surrounding the case, with the shadow Attorney General informing the BBC that '[i]f convicted rapists and murderers are given the vote … many people will see it as making a mockery of justice'.[68] Before the 2005 general election the Liberal Democrats expressed their support for the UK responding to the judgment.[69] Labour responded by defending disenfranchisement as an important additional penalty to a prisoner's loss of liberty.[70] The Blair and Brown administrations thereafter did everything they could to delay complying with the *Hirst* decision. As substantive legislative changes were required for the UK to fulfil its A3P1 obligations the *Hirst* saga began to accumulate its own process stories. Two public consultations were prolonged and intentionally 'inconclusive'.[71] Labour candidates once again ramped up the rhetoric on prisoner voting as they fought Liberal Democrat challengers in the 2010 general election.[72] Following that election the Coalition Government faced an issue at boiling point. Tensions between the governing parties on the issue saw a draft bill on prisoner voting published, but outside of select committee no parliamentary time was allocated to debate the proposals. Any pretence that the terms of the draft bill were being actively considered was abandoned with the Conservative victory in the 2015 general election.[73]

Hirst, in short, became a controversial judgment more because of its subject matter rather than its reasoning. It put Strasbourg at odds with the eagerness of many UK politicians to reflect 'what they believe to be the public's generally punitive stance' towards convicted criminals.[74] *Hirst* was not the first time that the ECHR has impacted upon UK penal policy,[75] but the misconception that Strasbourg had required the UK to extend the vote to all imprisoned "murderers, rapists and paedophiles" dovetailed with accounts of the Court as an overweening institution seeking to 'aggrandise its jurisdiction and to impose uniform rules on Member States'.[76] *Hirst* enabled some politicians and commentators to con-

68 BBC News, 'Convicts "will not all get the Vote"' (6 Oct 2005). Available online at: http://news.bbc.co.uk/1/hi/uk/4315348.stm

69 See 'Live chat with Liberal Democrat Simon Hughes' *Mail Online* (10 Apr 2005). Available online at: www.dailymail.co.uk/debate/article-343273/Live-chat-Liberal-Democrat-Simon-Hughes.html

70 See 'Controversy over Prisoner Voting Plans' *politics.co.uk* (4 Mar 2005). Available online at: www.politics.co.uk/news/controversy-over-prisoner-voting-plans-$30136.htm

71 J. Straw, *Last Man Standing: Memoirs of a Political Survivor* (Macmillan, 2012) 538.

72 See BBC News, 'Labour's "Votes for Paedophiles" Leaflet sparks Row' (19 Apr 2010). Available online at: http://news.bbc.co.uk/1/hi/uk_politics/election_2010/8630001.stm

73 See D. Barrett, 'David Cameron on verge of landmark victory over prisoner voting as ministers shelve reforms' *The Telegraph* (10 Dec 2015).

74 A. Bottoms, 'The Philosophy and Politics of Punishment and Sentencing' in C. Clarkson and R. Morgan (eds), *The Politics of Sentencing Reform* (OUP, 1995) 17, 40.

75 See V. Treacy, 'Prisoners' Rights Submerged in Semantics' (1989) 28 Howard Journal of Criminal Justice 27 and J. Schone, 'The Short Life and Painful Death of Prisoners' Rights' (2001) 40 *Howard Journal of Criminal Justice* 70.

76 L. Hoffmann, 'The Universality of Human Rights' (2009) 125 *LQR* 416, 424.

nect their populist approach to penal policy, their opposition to pan-European institutions and their belief that human rights law was undermining the UK's criminal justice system. A *Telegraph* opinion piece by former Conservative minister (and former prisoner) Jonathan Aitken exemplifies this nexus:

> To pretend that voting is something as 'basic' as the right of access to a lawyer is at best special pleading and at worst judicial meddling in the right of EU member states to decide how they will punish their criminal offenders.[77]

With little regard for the facts Aitken connected the issue of prisoner voting to the UK's fraught relationship with the European Union and disregarded the existence of the UK's commitments under A3P1, making it appear that the European Court had no basis for issuing its ruling. He proceeded to raise the improbable spectre of prisoners influencing penal policy by extracting promises from candidates.[78] And as such claims brought further notoriety to *Hirst* it became such a useful rallying cry for opposition to the UK's commitments to European legal orders that accounts of the judgment slipped any remaining mooring in fact. During the 2016 EU referendum campaign Vote Leave cynically exploited popular awareness of *Hirst* to make prominent claims that 'EU judges have already overruled UK laws on … whether prisoners should be allowed to vote'.[79] Ironically, in *Delvigne*, the Court of Justice (CJEU) had pointedly refused to be drawn into the territory of *Hirst* by ruling that EU law had not been breached by France denying the vote to a convicted murderer over a decade after the end of his incarceration.[80] We must therefore consider how such flagrant misrepresentations of *Hirst* have been so pervasive and resilient within public discourse.

The echo chamber

'Justice is not a cloistered virtue' proclaimed Lord Atkin,[81] and UK law has followed his lead in permitting vigorous political and media criticism of the courts.[82] The treatment of *Hirst*, however, has lurched into a realm of 'post-truth politics' in which an argument's factual basis is less important than whether its target

77 J. Aitken, 'Prisoners Don't Care about their Right to Vote' *The Telegraph* (14 Dec 2006).

78 See also S. Doughty, 'Convicted Criminals Given Right to Vote by Europe' *Daily Mail* (1 Apr 2004).

79 Vote Leave, 'Briefing: Taking back control from Brussels' (2016). Available online at: www.voteleavetakecontrol.org/briefing_control

80 Case C-650/13 *Delvigne v Commune de Lesparre-Médoc* (CJEU Grand Chamber, 6 Oct 2015). This case provoked considerable discussion before the European Union Select Committee over how the CJEU would react in the event that it heard a challenge to the UK's voting restrictions; see European Union Committee, *The UK, the EU and a British Bill of Rights* (2016) HL 139, para. 103–112.

81 *Ambard v Attorney-General for Trinidad and Tobago* [1936] AC 322, 335 (Lord Atkin).

82 For examples, see A. Bradley, 'Judicial Independence under Attack' [2003] PL 397 and O'Boyle (above n.8) 1862.

audience accepts it as credible.[83] The 'post-truth politics' label came out of the climate change debate, and has been dismissed as a faddish attempt to caricature right-of-centre politicians as exploiting 'the knee-jerk emotional responses and tribal loyalties of their followers'.[84] The prisoner voting saga, however, showcases how figures across the political spectrum can indulge in post-truth politics when it serves a "tough-on-crime" narrative, whereas judges 'do not have the last word in communicating the nature of their decisions to the public'.[85] Changes in the media environment have further distorted accounts of *Hirst*. As the then long-standing *Daily Mail* Editor Paul Dacre informed Parliament

> in a changing age, a 24-hour media age, an age of instant newse, an age in which there is generally a lack of reverence, judges must learn to expect more criticism and will need to think through how they are going to respond to that.[86]

Partisan news websites have added to this mix by sustaining focus on particularly emotive stories.[87] *Hirst* was one of the first controversial judgments to be subject to the full force of this new media context.

First, the media operations of judicial institutions have not kept pace with changes in the media environment. Far from being an issue that the courts have not 'thought through', as Dacre suggests, media management poses an irreducible problem for courts. Judges cannot both maintain the impartiality necessary to their function and contribute to politicised debates over the consequences of their decisions.[88] At the domestic level, the Minister of Justice is supposed to shield judges from ministerial criticisms which would undermine public confidence in the legal system.[89] Although this shield is not always robust, Strasbourg enjoys no equivalent protection. Chris Grayling's oath as Lord Chancellor did not prevent him from criticising *Hirst* in the strongest terms and encouraging the Committee on the Draft Voting Eligibility (Prisoners) Bill to adopt a position which he knew to be incompatible with the decision.[90] Ministers enjoy open season to criticise Strasbourg when they disagree with its judgments, and this ministerial criticism stands out for its ferocity against the backdrop of the respect generally shown to domestic judges. Neither domestic nor international judges are in a position to defend their decisions against misrepresentation in the press, meaning that they

83 See 'Art of the lie' *The Economist* (20 Sep 2016) 11.
84 T. Young, 'The Truth about 'Post-Truth Politics' *The Spectator* (7 Jul 2016).
85 F. Sauvageau, D. Schneiderman and D. Taras, *The Last Word: Media Coverage of the Supreme Court of Canada* (UBC Press, 2006) 227.
86 Constitution Committee, 'Relations between the Executive, the Judiciary and Parliament' (2007) HL 151, Q340.
87 See Sunstein (above n.12) 150.
88 For an insight into this problem in the context of the Canadian Supreme Court, see Sauvageau, Schneiderman, and Taras (above n.84) 204–207.
89 For detail of one Lord Chancellor's struggles to defend judicial independence, see J. Straw (above n.70) 498.
90 Joint Committee on the Draft Voting Eligibility (Prisoners) Bill (above n.23) para. 233.

are always at a disadvantage by comparison to other branches of government. Rather quaintly, press releases have been touted as a means by which Courts can reduce the likelihood of misrepresentation of their decisions. According to Parliament's Constitution Committee '[t]his kind of accessible and concise explanation increases the transparency of the decision and is to be commended'.[91] They do not, however, allow judges to address misrepresentations of their decisions. Indeed, Strasbourg's collegial judgments, in which multiple judges make contributions to a single text, can blur the reasoning behind a decision and exacerbate this problem.[92] The press release which accompanied *Hirst* could even have compounded confusion surrounding the complex decision by further truncating the Court's rationale.[93]

Following the post-*Hirst* backlash Strasbourg's Press Unit has devoted increasing attention to producing up-to-date summaries of jurisprudence in areas such as prisoner voting. Such factsheets, however, struggle to gain any attention in the face of post-truth accounts of its decisions. Confronted by a growing media storm the Court had to wait, impassive, until a new case arose which allowed it to clarify its position and reasoning. By the time that Strasbourg's Grand Chamber got this opportunity, in *Scoppola v Italy (No 3)*,[94] the *Daily Mail's* concern following *Hirst*, that serious violent criminals would be enfranchised, had given way to a strident injunction that 'there can be no compromise with the court – no clever-Dick move to satisfy the letter of its ruling by giving the vote to the barest minimum of prisoners'.[95] The Court was wrong-footed by the vociferousness of what had become a single-issue campaign against its jurisdiction:

> [T]he scale and tone of the current hostility directed towards the Court, and the Convention system as a whole, by the press, by members of the Westminster Parliament and by senior members of the Government has created understandable dismay and resentment among the judges in Strasbourg.[96]

In attempting to respond to criticisms of *Hirst*, however, the Grand Chamber introduced new inconsistencies into its prisoner voting jurisprudence in *Scoppola*, by accepting that disenfranchisement which continues after a prisoner's release

---

91 Constitution Committee (above n.85) para. 151.

92 See R. White and I. Boussiakou, 'Separate opinions in the European Court of Human Rights' (2009) 9 *HRLR* 37, 59.

93 The summary of the judgment neglected the Court's implicit recognition that the UK did not have to enfranchise all prisoners in response to *Hirst*; see Press Release 512 (2005), 'European Court of human Rights – Grand Chamber judgment *Hirst v. United-Kingdom* (No. 2)'. Available online at: https://wcd.coe.int/ViewDoc.jsp?p=&id=924847&Site=COE&direct=true

94 *Scoppola v Italy* (No 3) (2013) 56 EHRR 19 [GC].

95 Daily Mail Comment, 'Cameron's Chance to Deliver for Britain' *Daily Mail* (23 May 2012).

96 N. Bratza, 'The Relationship between the UK Courts and Strasbourg' [2011] EHRLR 505, 506.

can satisfy A3P1's requirements.[97] As Judge Thór Björgvinsson's dissenting judgment made clear, the Italian arrangements were no less blunt and indiscriminate than those in place in the UK.[98] Nonetheless, having reaffirmed that a broad range of approaches to prisoner voting would be acceptable under A3P1, in its subsequent *Firth v United Kingdom* and *McHugh v United Kingdom* decisions the Court refused to compensate UK prisoners for the ongoing breach of this right, maintaining that 'the finding of a violation constitutes sufficient just satisfaction for any non-pecuniary damage sustained by the applicants'.[99] It even refused payment of legal costs on the basis that lodging an application in a repeat case 'was straightforward and did not require legal assistance'.[100] The Court has allowed the UK to remain in perpetual breach of its obligations without applying any meaningful sanctions. *Hirst* was thereby rendered all but moot, especially as the Committee of Ministers has done no more than state its 'profound regret' at the UK Government's lack of action.[101]

Strasbourg's efforts to take the heat out of the story have scarcely registered with its critics. Time and again, the launch of repeat claims at Strasbourg has garnered considerable attention, only for the ultimate judgments to receive little coverage.[102] The *ConservativeHome* website, for example, followed up on the *Firth* decision with renewed warnings over the 'rise and rise of the judiciary'.[103] Such interventions speak to the second important feature of the media landscape in which the *Hirst* judgment has been debated; the emergence of a 'Fifth Estate' of blogs and digital news outlets which speak directly to particular ideological standpoints.[104] *Time* magazine might have named the public 'Person of the Year' 2006 for 'seizing the reins of the global media',[105] but concerns quickly mounted over the freedom of online platforms from established journalistic standards of objectivity[106] and, in the case of web based news channels, from any legal impartiality requirement. '[T]his freedom', the BBC Trust intoned, 'may become infectious'.[107]

97 *Scoppola v Italy* (above n.93) [109]. See E. Bates, 'Analysing the Prisoner Voting Saga and the British Challenge to Strasbourg' (2014) 14 *HRLRev* 503, 516–518.

98 *Ibid.*, O-I [8].

99 *Firth v United Kingdom* App.47784/09 (12 Aug 2014) [18].

100 *Ibid.*, [21]. See also *McHugh v United Kingdom* App.51987/08 (10 Feb 2015) [17].

101 Council of Ministers, '1243 DH meeting of the Ministers' Deputies' CM/Res DH (9 Dec 2015) 251.

102 See Mead (above n.59) 465–466.

103 H. Hill, 'The Rise of the Judges is a Failure of Democracy' *ConservativeHome* (14 Aug 2014). Available online at: www.conservativehome.com/thetorydiary/2014/08/the-rise-of-the-judges-is-a-failure-of-democracy.html

104 S. Cooper, *Watching the Watchdog: Bloggers as the Fifth Estate* (Marquette Books, 2006) 14.

105 *Time*, 'Person of the Year 2006' (13 Dec 2006).

106 See M. Schudson, 'The Objectivity Norm in American Journalism' (2001) 2 *Journalism* 149, 161–165 and M. Hampton, 'The "Objectivity" Ideal and its limitations in 20th-Century British Journalism' (2008) 9 *Journalism Studies* 477, 482–489.

107 BBC Trust, *From Seesaw to Wagon Wheel: Safeguarding Impartiality in the 21st Century* (BBC, 2007) 14.

The degree to which the marketplace of ideas requires regulatory stewardship has been hotly contested for a century,[108] but from its rarefied vantage point the BBC Trust regarded the emergence of unregulated new-media news with thinly concealed horror. This new media environment marginalised and discredited the voice of 'patrician experts' (including the courts) in matters of penal policy,[109] leaving politicians with 'far less room for manoeuvre in responding to public opinion'.[110] Savvy Conservative politicians have cultivated an activist following on *ConservativeHome* by emphasising particularly emotive aspects of the prisoner voting debate, such as the possibility of violent criminals voting and of compensation being payable to claimant prisoners.[111] Although such claims misrepresent Strasbourg's jurisprudence their continued prominence nonetheless demonstrates their effectiveness at engaging supporters.[112] A form of cognitive dissonance seems to be at work on these websites, which long prevented them from recognising Strasbourg's changed position on prisoner voting.[113] When *ConservativeHome* did, eventually, address the decrease in tensions between the UK and the Court it was to express dismay that this development undermined the case for the UK withdrawing from the ECHR, because 'it is precisely confrontations with it over controversial issues that raise that eventuality'.[114] Court decisions have always been contestable, but traditional media organisations are no longer in a position to act as gatekeepers over what factual disputes enter the public domain.[115]

The third factor in play is the degree to which newspapers have had to respond to the agenda shaped by social media and news websites. In this new environment traditional '[n]ews providers are no longer managers of a scarce resource, they are struggling to sustain a business and a role in an environment of information

108 See M. Whipple, 'The Dewey-Lippmann Debate Today: Communication Distortions, Reflective Agency, and Participatory Democracy' (2005) 23 *Sociological Theory* 156.

109 J. Pratt, *Penal Populism* (Routledge, 2007) 83.

110 See M. Ryan, 'Red Tops, Populists and the Irresistible rise of the Public' in P. Mason (ed.) *Captured by the Media* (Willan, 2013) 31, 32.

111 See N. Herbert, 'On prisoner voting, we shouldn't defy the ECHR, we should resile from it altogether' *ConservativeHome* (22 Nov 2012). Available online at: www.conservativehome.com/platform/2012/11/nick-herbert-on-prisoner-voting-we-shouldnt-sddefy-the-echr.html

112 These interventions amount to an effort to engage one of many 'issue publics'; Habermas (above n.14) 422.

113 Perceptions, once formed, can be particularly difficult to change in an era of 'selective exposure' in which many people get their news online, via service providers which use algorithms to filter content to suit the reader; see R. Garrett and N. Stroud, 'Partisan Paths to Exposure Diversity: Differences in Pro- and Counterattitudinal News Consumption' (2014) 64 *Journal of Communication* 680, 681–684.

114 P. Goodman, 'Raab Kicks Prisoner Votes towards the Long Grass' *ConservativeHome* (11 Dec 2015). Available online at: www.conservativehome.com/thetorydiary/2015/12/raab-kicks-prisoner-votes-towards-the-long-grass.html

115 S. Reilly, 'The Technology of Truth: Revisiting Areopagitica' (2013) 9 *International Journal of Technology, Knowledge & Society* 139, 140.

overload'.[116] In response newspapers have developed their own online platforms and used this capacity to devote an increased proportion of space to commentary as opposed to reportage.[117] Generating 'clickbait' content helps to staunch the flow of readers to ideologically driven websites.[118] Columnists and in-house bloggers allow newspapers to engage with their readerships' political preconceptions as they are not subject to the same professional expectations concerning fact handling as reporters.[119] Some editors have drawn a distinction between the expectations applicable to commentary and reporting on criminal justice,[120] but the imperative to respond to their readerships' preconceptions has also affected the nature of reporting. For example, when Jeremy Corbyn's spokesperson described his position on prisoner voting as being 'guided by the European Court', this statement was emotively reported as showing willingness to 'give way' to Strasbourg.[121] Under pressure from news websites which do not maintain expensive rosters of reporters, but instead rely on activists to generate content for free or 'aggregate' existing stories and package them with an ideological slant, many newspapers have pandered to public perceptions of 'an increasingly lenient judiciary, handing down lesser and lesser sentences for what many regard as serious crimes'.[122] Journalists have also sought shortcuts to generating stories by picking up ready-made copy. On the issue of prisoner voting, think tanks such as Policy Exchange[123] and Civitas[124] have been eager to oblige, producing partial accounts of Strasbourg's jurisprudence. These reports, adopting the model promoted by the conservative legal movement in the United States are designed to generate headlines and comment pieces when published and to provide fuel for Strasbourg's critics in subsequent debates.[125] When Civitas published a report by Dominic Raab on prisoner voting in 2011, the *Daily Mail* immediately exploited the opportunity to repeat its claims that 'the court – riding roughshod over our sovereign parliament – insists that votes must be given to prisoners'.[126]

---

116 R. Sambrook, *Delivering Trust: Impartiality and Objectivity in the Digital Age* (Reuters Institute, 2012) 10.

117 See BBC Trust (above n.106) 33.

118 See D. Rowe, 'Media and culture: Movement across the decades' (2014) 10 *International Journal of Media & Cultural Politics* 171.

119 See, for example, D. Hannan, 'There is no longer any possible reason to remain in the ECHR' *The Telegraph* (14 Mar 2012). Available online at: http://blogs.telegraph.co.uk/news/danielhannan/100075824/britain-should-withdraw-from-the-european-convention-on-human-rights/

120 Constitution Committee (above n.85) Q345 (Paul Dacre).

121 M. Wilkinson, 'Jeremy Corbyn: Let Prisoners have the Right to Vote' *The Telegraph* (26 Aug 2015).

122 Constitution Committee (above n.85) Q335 (Paul Dacre).

123 M. Pinto-Duschinsky, *Bringing Rights Back Home: Making Human Rights compatible with Parliamentary Democracy in the UK* (Policy Exchange, 2011).

124 Raab (above n.20).

125 See Teles (above n.16) 272.

126 Daily Mail Comment, 'European Court of Human Rights and Nick Clegg's Chilling Effect' *Daily Mail* (21 Apr 2011).

One obvious means of generating clickbait stories is to focus on content which will outrage readers (and which can also form the basis of comment pieces). Where prisoner voting is at issue, this has been achieved by presenting skewed accounts of the steps which are necessary to satisfy Strasbourg. Reporting has emphasised the possibility of violent criminals being enfranchised when *Hirst* imposed no such obligation on the UK. The *Telegraph* continued to report on the range of violent offenders involved in legal actions,[127] even when Strasbourg has repeatedly affirmed that the UK's breach of A3P1 lies in the blanket nature of its ban, and does not require such offenders' enfranchisement.[128] Newspapers have also prominently reported speculation over the possibility that Strasbourg could award compensation to prisoners. In 2010 the *Telegraph* reported that the bill for compensation could rise to more than £50 million if prisoners were not given the vote.[129] Such figures have continued to be bandied about despite the Court repeatedly refusing to award compensation (and latterly costs) in its prisoner voting decisions.[130] The day after the *Firth* judgment Richard Littlejohn thundered that '[w]e may kid ourselves that we live in a parliamentary democracy, but the reality is that we are ultimately governed by a judicial dictatorship, accountable to no one, with its power base in Strasbourg', a claim which could scarcely be squared with his acknowledgement that Strasbourg had 'ruled unexpectedly that British prisoners denied the vote are not entitled to compensation or legal costs'.[131] Pressure to be the first outlet to publish on a controversial case encourages journalism which predicts the outcomes of cases, even if it is not ultimately supported by 'a careful reading of the text of the decision'.[132]

We are often encouraged to believe that newspaper leader columns no longer have the capacity to shape national debate.[133] Radio and Television news can reach much more of the population than the fragmented readership of the print media or even news websites and are therefore required to conform to rules on

127 D. Barrett, 'Revealed: The Killers and Rapists among 1,000 criminals launching Compensation Claims over Prisoner Voting' *Telegraph* (9 Oct 2014).

128 For internal criticism of the manner in which the Court has addressed breaches of serious and violent offenders' A3P1 right, see *Firth* (above n.98) O-II [8] (Judge Wojtyczek).

129 A. Porter, 'Prisoners to get the vote for the first time' *Daily Telegraph* (1 Nov 2010).

130 See Mead (above n.59) 457. The prominence accorded to this story is such that even some academics have accepted as fact that Strasbourg has 'tried to force the hand of the British government by allocating monetary compensation to a new set of prisoners who were denied voting rights'; E. Voeten, 'Public Opinion and the Legitimacy of International Courts' (2013) 14 *Theoretical Inquiries in Law* 411, 418.

131 R. Littlejohn, 'Democracy? No, Britain's now a Judicial Dictatorship – and it's time for Revolution' *Daily Mail* (13 Aug 2014).

132 S. Reilly, 'The Technology of Truth: Revisiting Areopagitica' (2013) 9 *International Journal of Technology, Knowledge & Society* 139, 140.

133 See, on such claims, S. Barnett, 'Plurality and Public Service Broadcasting: Why and How PSBs Deserve Protection' in S. Barnett and J. Townend (eds.), *Media Power and Plurality: From Hyperlocal to High-Level Policy* (Palgrave, 2015) 45, 45–46.

impartiality and balance across their news and current affairs content.[134] Despite these requirements, the HRA's critics often claim that they struggle to get their voices heard in the face of favourable coverage of the legislation by the BBC. Paul Dacre has even pleaded that '[t]he BBC, which is the most powerful voice in Britain, which dwarfs the influence of Fleet Street, is very pro Europe and very pro the Human Rights Act'.[135] This view is reinforced by websites such as *BiasedBBC* and *Global Britain*, which according to the BBC Trust have 'focused a laser-like beam' on BBC programming with the intent of exposing a pro-European bias.[136] The former site maintains that in BBC programming 'debates are framed to ensure the BBC view always prevails – no one phones in to talk about the gross obscenities the ECHR seeks to provide – such as votes for convicts'.[137] Such claims are, of themselves, intended to pressurise broadcasters into altering their content. The fourth element of the media landscape in which prisoner voting rights have been analysed is therefore how susceptible broadcasters have become to such manipulation, for fear of the impact of accusations of bias upon trust in their output.

Concerns that the BBC's coverage of certain issues took too much of a lead from newspapers arose in the field of science reporting. A report by the geneticist Steve Jones for the BBC Trust concluded that on issues such as climate change, BBC reporting sometimes adopted an 'over-rigid' approach to impartiality guidelines in a 'fact-based' field, covering different perspectives on these issues as if they had equal weight of scientific opinion behind them.[138] New BBC Editorial Guidelines were therefore issued which built a consideration of 'due weight' of support for particular positions on controversial issues into the test for impartiality. A conception of broadcaster impartiality as requiring that 'minority views should not necessarily be given equal weight to the prevailing consensus',[139] however, does not always ensure broadcasting in the public interest. Within an intensely populist debate on penal policy it can marginalise voices which challenge the prevailing consensus and the factual claims upon which it is based. The impact of the print media's 'framing'[140] of the *Hirst* story can be seen in the BBC's wholesale acceptance by late-2010 that the Government was poised to 'give up' by removing 'the

134 For the rules covering commercial broadcasters, see the Communications Act 2003, s.320 and the Broadcasting Code, rule 5. Allegations that the BBC has breached its duties with regard to accuracy and impartiality are addressed by a separate BBC complaints system, and ultimately by the BBC Trust.

135 Constitution Committee (above n.85) Q348.

136 BBC Trust, *A BBC Trust Review of the Breadth of Opinion Reflected in the BBC's Output* (BBC, July 2013) 41.

137 D. Vance, 'Last Night a Human Rights Lawyer saved my Life' *BiasedBBC* (21 Aug 2011). Available online at: http://biasedbbc.org/blog/2011/08/21/last-night-human-rights-lawyer-saved-my/

138 BBC Trust, *BBC Trust Review of Impartiality and Accuracy of the BBC's Coverage of Science*' (BBC, July 2011) 67 and 87.

139 M. Lyons, *Editorial Guidelines* (BBC, 2016) 25.

140 Habermas (above n.14) 415.

blanket voting ban on British prisoners' in the face of the threat that litigation would 'cost the taxpayer hundreds of millions of pounds in compensation'.[141] Little wonder that BBC News has been accused, by its then Economics Editor, of being 'completely obsessed by the agenda set by newspapers'.[142] Such reporting suggests that broadcaster impartiality on social issues continues to be seen through the lens of party politics.[143] For as long as the Labour and Conservative leaderships accepted that the UK Parliament should not enfranchise any prisoners there was little impetus for the BBC, or other broadcasters, to challenge the misconceptions underpinning this consensus in their reporting of the UK Government's approach to Strasbourg's judgments.[144] Newspapers may increasingly be responding to an agenda set by new media, but in doing so their framing of a debate, and the policy-maker responses that this framing triggers, continues to shape broadcast news coverage.

Prolonging Strasbourg's monstering

If the theory of a marketplace of ideas posits that 'a process of robust debate, if uninhibited by governmental interference, will lead to the discovery of truth, or at least the best perspectives or solutions for societal problems',[145] then Strasbourg's monstering over prisoner voting calls into question whether this marketplace has become skewed. Not only have falsehoods concerning the Court's position been sustained, they characterise challenges to the UK's relationship with the ECHR and even the EU. While the marketplace of ideas should be a vehicle for tackling societal problems, a dysfunctional marketplace prevents such issues from being effectively addressed. In the wake of Strasbourg's pillory other institutions have been inhibited from addressing prisoner voting.

In the post-*Hirst* climate the UK's domestic courts have sought to remain aloof from the issue of prisoner voting. This might appear to be a strange claim in light of how vigorously the issue has been litigated before the courts of Scotland,[146] Northern Ireland,[147] and England and Wales[148] since the *Hirst* judgment. In

141 BBC News, 'Killer John Hirst on Prisoners getting the Vote' (3 Nov 2010). Available online at: www.bbc.co.uk/news/uk-politics-11686283

142 M. Brown and J. Deans, 'Robert Peston: BBC follows the Daily Mail's lead too much' *The Guardian* (6 Jun 2014).

143 See, for acknowledgment of concerns over this approach, BBC Trust (above n.135) 41.

144 For a warning about the dangers of 'consensus' issues for impartial reporting, see Lyons (above n.138) 29.

145 S. Ingber, 'The Marketplace of Ideas: A Legitimizing Myth' [1984] Duke LJ 1, 3.

146 *Smith v Scott* [2007] CSIH 9, 2007 SC 345; *Traynor and Fisher v Scottish Ministers and Secretary of State for Scotland* [2007] CSOH 78; *R (McGeogh) v The Lord President of the Council* [2013] UKSC 63, [2014] 1 AC 271; *Moohan v The Lord Advocate* [2014] UKSC 67, [2015] 1 AC 901.

147 *R v Secretary of State for Northern Ireland, ex parte Toner and Walsh* [2007] NIQB 18.

148 *Tovey v Ministry of Justice* [2011] EWHC 271, [2011] HRLR 17; *R (Chester) v Secretary of State for Justice* [2013] UKSC 63, [2014] 1 AC 271.

deciding these cases, however, the courts have spent as little time as possible addressing the principles underpinning prisoner disenfranchisement or the substance of A3P1 claims. None of the judges would contemplate reinterpreting section 3 of the Representation of the People Act 1983 to conform with *Hirst*; 'such a measure cannot be effected under the guise of interpretation, however supercharged by HRA s.3'.[149] Nor would the courts attempt to allay Strasbourg's concerns over UK electoral law. In spite of Strasbourg's Grand Chamber softening its stance in *Scoppola*, Lord Mance considered that any effort to persuade it to move further away from *Hirst* would be a wasted effort, because '[t]here is … no prospect of any further meaningful dialogue between United Kingdom Courts and Strasbourg'.[150] Given that *Hirst* resulted from a Divisional Court decision the lack of engagement with A3P1 claims by the UK's senior judiciary has denied Strasbourg valuable guidance in shaping its jurisprudence. Once the first court to address the issue following *Hirst* had issued a declaration of incompatibility, the UK's domestic courts have steered clear of repeating even this minimal step.[151] Of all of the domestic judges to have considered the issue post-*Hirst*, only Lord Sumption has engaged with the substance of Strasbourg's reasoning, and that was not to re-evaluate the Grand Chamber's treatment of the issue in the round, but to pull at threads in its jurisprudence.[152] The UK judiciary's overarching position, staked out by Laws LJ in *Chester*, remains that '[t]here are deep philosophical differences of view between reasonable people upon the question of prisoners' suffrage'.[153] This studied refusal to address the subject at the heart of these cases flies in the face of the idea, propagated with the earliest HRA jurisprudence, that judges should attempt 'to draw out the broad principles which animate the Convention'.[154] These decisions cannot be fashioned into a meaningful domestic jurisprudence on prisoner disenfranchisement. Indeed, the domestic courts have maintained that since Strasbourg has spoken, the issue is now one for Parliament to resolve.[155] Merris Amos has argued that when UK courts accept 'the clear and constant jurisprudence of the ECtHR' they can suffer a consequent 'loss in

149 *R (Chester) v Secretary of State for Justice* [2010] EWCA Civ 1439, [2011] 1 WLR 1436, [24] (Laws LJ).

150 *Chester and McGeoch* (above n.147) [34]. This stance paid rather too much attention to the fact that the Grand Chamber reaffirmed the *Hirst* judgment, in form if not in substance; *Scoppola* (above n.93) [95].

151 *Ibid.*, [42]. See M. Gordon, *Parliamentary Sovereignty in the UK Constitution: Process, Politics and Democracy* (Hart, 2015) 124–125.

152 *Ibid.*, [126]–[136].

153 *Chester* (above n.148) [32] (Laws LJ). See also I. Judge, 'Constitutional Change: Unfinished Business' (University College London, 4 Dec 2013) para. 48. Available online at: www.nottingham.ac.uk/hrlc/documents/specialevents/lordjudgelecture041213.pdf

154 *Aston Cantlow v Wallbank* [2001] EWCA Civ 713, [2001] 3 WLR 1323, [44] (Morritt VC).

155 *Chester and McGeoch* (above n.147) [42]. See Judge (above n.152) para. 44.

legitimacy'.[156] The prisoner voting cases could, however, indicate the UK courts adapting to such concerns over their own legitimacy. Although they followed Strasbourg's jurisprudence, their refusal to engage with Strasbourg's reasoning has prevented the furore surrounding the European Court from swallowing them.

Despite divesting themselves of any responsibility for finding a way out of the post-*Hirst* impasse senior domestic judges lined up after *Chester and McGeoch* to take pot shots at Strasbourg's approach in extrajudicial engagements. Even Baroness Hale, who acknowledged that prisoner voting provided a 'good example of why we need human rights legislation',[157] talked up the fact that she 'initiated another small rebellion against Strasbourg'[158] by refusing remedy to the claimants. This was not a particularly emphatic rebellion, as Strasbourg had already emphasised that *Hirst* should not be interpreted as requiring that all prisoners be enfranchised.[159] Moreover, her own leadership on this point is questionable, as she was essentially restating a point made by Langstaff J two years previously.[160] With the domestic courts' role under the HRA under sustained criticism, however, her speech could be characterised as burnishing the credentials of the UK's legal systems at Strasbourg's expense. Other judges used the issue of prisoner voting to explicitly critique the system of rights protection under the ECHR. For the avoidance of doubt, Laws LJ revisited the position which he in advanced in *Chester* in his 2013 Hamlyn Lectures: 'The historic role of the law of human rights is the protection of what are properly regarded as fundamental values. It is not to make marginal choices about issues upon which reasonable, humane and informed people may readily disagree'.[161] Not to be outdone, Lord Sumption proclaimed that for Strasbourg '[t]o give the force of law to values for which there is no popular mandate is democratic only in the sense that the old German Democratic Republic was democratic',[162] and Lord Judge warned that 'we should beware of the danger of even an indirect importation of the slightest obligation on Parliament to comply with the orders and directions of any court, let alone a foreign court'.[163] When it comes to extrajudicial pronouncements on politically controversial issues Lord Neuberger has suggested that '[c]omity and the separation of powers may well call

156 M. Amos, 'From Monologue to Dialogue – The relationship between UK courts and the European Court of Human Rights' in R. Masterman and I. Leigh (eds), *The UK's Statutory Bill of Rights: Constitutional and Comparative Perspectives* (OUP, 2013) 139, 155.

157 Hale (above n.9) 19.

158 *Ibid.*, 18.

159 *Scoppola* (above n.93) [83].

160 *Tovey v Ministry of Justice* (above n.147) [52].

161 J. Laws, 'The Common Law Constitution' (CUP, 2014) 83.

162 J. Sumption, 'The Limits of Law' (Kuala Lumpur, 20 Nov 2013) 11. Available online at: www.supremecourt.uk/docs/speech-131120.pdf

163 Judge (above n.152) para. 48.

for reticence'.[164] In the autumn of 2013, on the subject of prisoner voting, judicial reticence was in short supply.[165]

These interventions mark judges out as no longer being passive subjects of media attention, but as sophisticated media actors. These extra-judicial speeches functioned as ersatz press conferences, allowing judges to spin their position on prisoner voting in order to deflect criticism of their judgments and thereby avoid public loss of face. Sir John Laws, Lord Sumption and Lord Judge were all quoted with approval in the *Daily Mail*, whilst Baroness Hale was cast as out-of-step, being 'the most radical and feminist of the senior judiciary'.[166] This flurry of judicial comment came in the weeks before the Joint Committee reported on the Draft Voting Eligibility (Prisoners) Bill. Although the Supreme Court had remitted the issue to Parliament's consideration with a specific acknowledgment that the Committee's work was on-going,[167] these judges could not resist the temptation to have their cake and eat it too. The Committee was obliged to take their interventions into account,[168] and they clearly influenced the Chair's thinking on key issues.[169] Little wonder that throughout the Joint Committee's deliberations many commentators, including those who supported the UK's compliance with international human rights norms,[170] treated the parliamentary process as a delaying tactic which allowed ministers to put off addressing the issue.[171] The Committee's efforts to take on board evidence of media representations of human rights and to consider the portrayal of the prisoner voting issue counted for little. All of this noise surrounding the Committee's deliberations, however, can be contrasted with the comparative lack of commentary upon its majority recommendations that some prisoners should be enfranchised.[172]

---

164 D. Neuberger, 'Where Angels Fear to Tread' (Holdsworth Club, 2 Mar 2012) para. 50. Available online at: www.judiciary.gov.uk/wp-content/uploads/JCO/Documents/Speeches/mr-speech-holdsworth-lecture-2012.pdf

165 The approach of these judges can be contrasted with Lord Dyson's contemporaneous refusal to discuss the issue of prisoner voting rights; J. Dyson, 'Are the Judges too Powerful?' (Bentham Association, 12 Mar 2014) 13. Available online at: www.judiciary.gov.uk/wp-content/uploads/JCO/Documents/Speeches/mor-speech-have-judges-become-too-powerful.pdf

166 S. Doughty, 'UK Judge says Strasbourg must rule on Prisoner Votes: Deputy President of Supreme Court says they have the right to overrule Parliament' *Daily Mail* (6 Dec 2013).

167 *Chester and McGeoch* (above n.147) [19] (Lord Mance).

168 See Joint Committee on the Draft Voting Eligibility (Prisoners) Bill (above n.23) paras. 84, 95 and 151

169 N. Gibb, 'With respect, I disagree with my committee. Prisoners should not have the vote' *ConservativeHome* (18 Dec 2013). Available online at: www.conservativehome.com/platform/2013/12/nick-gibb-mp-with-respect-i-disagree-with-my-committee-prisoners-should-not-have-the-vote.html

170 See J. Rozenberg, 'Phrasing the Question on Prisoner Votes' *The Guardian* (6 Nov 2013).

171 Especially in light of the Prime Minister's insistence that 'prisoners are not getting the vote under this Government'; D. Cameron, MP, HC Deb., vol.551, col.923 (24 Oct 2012).

172 See Joint Committee on the Draft Voting Eligibility (Prisoners) Bill (above n.23) 67.

Having actively contributed to turning the issue of prisoner voting into a campaign against Strasbourg's jurisdiction, the Conservative Party has been eager to profit from the success of this approach in Government. This has meant delaying any response to the Joint Committee's recommendations which might suggest any compromise of the UK's blanket ban. From 'active consideration' of the Committee's recommendations in early 2014,[173] Coalition Government ministers proceeded to side-line the report. As a result the 2015 Conservative manifesto was able to trumpet that '[w]e have stopped prisoners from having the vote'.[174] In his subsequent stint as Lord Chancellor/Secretary of State for Justice, when asked directly for a response to the Joint Committee's report, Michael Gove failed to engage with its recommendations and fell back on the position that 'the last Parliament made its view very clear on the issue, and I cannot see, given the constitution of the new Parliament, that it would be likely to be dramatically different'.[175] In the saga of prisoner voting rights there is no room for multiple narratives. A Committee which may well have been instituted as a delaying tactic was all but airbrushed out of public debate after it produced an unexpected response.

At least, that is, until Brexit cooled the Conservative Party leadership's enthusiasm for picking simultaneous fights with both the Council of Europe and the European Union. The first sign that things could be changing came when the 2017 Conservative manifesto all-but abandoned tub thumping statements regarding the ECHR (with the exception of one re-heated pledge on its application to armed conflicts).[176] The absence of commitments on prisoner voting allowed the new Lord Chancellor/Secretary of State for Justice, David Lidington, to work up proposals for a "minimum-compliance" response to Strasbourg's judgments against the UK. The plans suggested enfranchising prisoners serving up to one-year sentences by day release, aligning neatly with the major Joint Committee proposal.[177] For an embattled and overburdened minority Government this approach could take advantage of the terms of the statutes barring prisoners from voting, negating the need for fresh legislation.[178] When the plans were, inevitably, leaked to *The Sunday Times*, the paper immediately attempted to push a recalcitrant

---

173 C. Grayling, 'Letter to the Chair of the Joint Committee on the Draft Voting Eligibility (Prisoners) Bill' (25 Feb 2014). Available online at: www.parliament.uk/documents/joint-committees/Draft-Voting-Eligibility-Prisoners-Bill/Grayling-letter-to-Chair.pdf.

174 Conservative Party, *The Conservative Party Manifesto* (2015) 60. Available online at: https://s3-eu-west-1.amazonaws.com/manifesto2015/ConservativeManifesto2015.pdf

175 Constitution Committee (above n.85) 17.

176 Conservative Party, *Forward, Together: The Conservative and Unionist Party Manifesto* (2017) 41. Available online at: https://s3.eu-west-2.amazonaws.com/manifesto2017/Manifesto2017.pdf

177 See Joint Committee on the Draft Voting Eligibility (Prisoners) Bill (above n.23) para. 239.

178 Under the terms of the Representation of the People Act 1983, s.3, a prisoner is only barred from voting 'during the time that he is detained in a penal institution in pursuance of his sentence', enabling the UK Government to pursue an administrative, as opposed to legislative, response.

government back into line by opening its reporting with the assertion that the plans 'will raise fresh questions about the government's approach to law and order'.[179] Against all of the evidence that Strasbourg wants to draw a line under the dispute the *Conservative Home* editor muttered darkly that the Court would soon push the UK for further concessions; 'we doubt that his (David Lidington's) manoeuvre will satisfy the court'. It was never given the chance; faced with a new furore over prisoner voting, the Government watered down the plans and enfranchised only those prisoners already on temporary release on polling day.[180]

Conclusion

Prisoner voting sits uncomfortably at the confluence of 'tough-on-crime' criminal justice narratives and opposition to pan-European institutions as a threat to the UK's sovereignty. A triumvirate of socially conservative think tanks, populist politicians and sections of the print media have exploited this context to use prisoner voting to upend the UK's relationship with the ECHR. Each element of this triumvirate mutually enhances the influence of the others upon political debate, marginalising divergent voices. Politicians and think tanks have exploited digital media to energise supporters by misrepresenting Strasbourg's jurisprudence, whilst newspapers have sustained the resulting narrative with clickbait articles. Having set the terms of public debate these actors have all but obliged broadcast news to follow their lead. Confronted with dominant post-truth accounts of Strasbourg's case law, successive UK Governments have either considered the issue too politically sensitive to address, or have actively participated in misrepresenting the position of the Court for electoral advantage. Even supposedly independent institutional actors have accepted the prevailing consensus that prisoner voting should not be accepted as a human rights issue. No UK judge has contemplated articulating what the right to free and fair elections means in the context of parliamentary elections, seemingly for fear of being accused of overreaching on this most fraught of issues.[181] Within academia the Judicial Power Project inflated the weaknesses in the *Hirst* judgment into a monstrous judicial power grab long after Strasbourg disavowed expansive interpretations of that decision. In the face of this 'resistance' Strasbourg has been cowed, resiling from the principles which underpinned *Hirst*.[182] In this debased public discourse all serving prisoners remain barred from voting, even in the absence of any meaningful official account of why this must be so.

---

179 T. Shipman and T. Harper, 'Prisoners Gain Vote in Human Rights U-Turn' *The Sunday Times* (29 Oct 2017).

180 P. Goodman, 'Remaining in the ECHR is a cost of leaving the EU' *ConservativeHome* (30 Oct 2017). Available online at: www.conservativehome.com/thetorydiary/2017/10/remaining-in-the-echr-is-the-price-for-leaving-the-eu.html

181 The ability to act 'independent' of the demands of the media and pressure groups is supposedly central to the judicial function; D. Heydon, 'Threats to Judicial Independence – The Enemy Within' (Inner Temple, 23 Jan 2012) 11. Available online at: www.innertemple.org.uk/downloads/members/lectures_2012/lecture_dyson.pdf

182 See O. Gerstenberg, '(The Failure of) Public Law and the Deliberative Turn' in N. Walker, C. Michelon and C. Mac Amhlaigh (eds), *After Public Law* (OUP, 2013) 218, 239.

Bibliography

M Amos, 'From Monologue to Dialogue – The relationship between UK courts and the European Court of Human Rights' in R Masterman and I Leigh (eds), *The UK's Statutory Bill of Rights: Constitutional and Comparative Perspectives* (OUP, 2013).

S Barnett, 'Plurality and Public Service Broadcasting: Why and How PSBs Deserve Protection' in S Barnett and J Townend (eds), *Media Power and Plurality: From Hyperlocal to High-Level Policy* (Palgrave, 2015).

E Bates, 'Analysing the Prisoner Voting Saga and the British Challenge to Strasbourg' (2014) 14 *HRLRev* 503.

A Bottoms, 'The Philosophy and Politics of Punishment and Sentencing' in C Clarkson and A Bradley, 'Judicial Independence under Attack' [2003] PL 397.

N Bratza, 'The Relationship between the UK Courts and Strasbourg' [2011] EHRLR 505.

S Cooper, *Watching the Watchdog: Bloggers as the Fifth Estate* (Marquette Books, 2006).

M Dean, *Democracy under Attack: How the Media Distort Policy and Politics* (Policy Press, 2013).

R Garrett and N Stroud, 'Partisan Paths to Exposure Diversity: Differences in Pro- and Counterattitudinal News Consumption' (2014) 64 *Journal of Communication* 680.

O Gerstenberg, '(The Failure of) Public Law and the Deliberative Turn' in N Walker, C Michelon and C Mac Amhlaigh (eds), *After Public Law* (OUP, 2013).

L Gies, *Mediating Human Rights: Media, Culture and the Human Rights Act* (Routledge, 2014).

M Gordon, *Parliamentary Sovereignty in the UK Constitution: Process, Politics and Democracy* (Hart, 2015).

J Habermas, 'Political Communication in Media Society: Does Democracy still enjoy an Epistemic Dimension? The Impact of Normative Theory on Empirical Research' (2006) 16 *Communication Theory* 411.

M Hampton, 'The "Objectivity" Ideal and its limitations in 20th-Century British Journalism' (2008) 9 *Journalism Studies* 477.

C Harlow and R Rawlings. *Pressure Through Law* (Routledge, 1992).

L Hoffmann, 'The Universality of Human Rights' (2009) 125 *LQR* 416.

S Ingber, 'The Marketplace of Ideas: A Legitimizing Myth' [1984] Duke LJ 1.

G Letsas, 'The ECHR as a Living Instrument' in A Føllesdal, B Peters and G Ulfstein (eds), *Constituting Europe: The European Court of Human Rights in a National, European and Global Context* (CUP: 2013).

C López-Guerra, *Democracy and Disenfranchisement: The Morality of Electoral Exclusions* (OUP, 2014).

P Mason, 'Lies, distortion and what doesn't work: Monitoring Prison Stories in the British Media' (2006) 2 *Crime, Media, Culture* 251.

P Mason, 'Misinformation, Myth and Distortion: How the Press construct Imprisonment in Britain' (2007) 8 *Journalism Studies* 481.

D McNulty, N Watson and G Philo, 'Human Rights and Prisoners' Rights: The British Press and the Shaping of Public Debate' (2014) 53 *Howard Journal of Criminal Justice* 360.

D Mead, '"You Couldn't Make It Up": Some Narratives of the Media's Coverage of Human Rights' in K Ziegler, E Wicks and L Hodson (eds), *The UK and European Human Rights: A Strained Relationship* (Hart, 2015).

R Morgan (eds), *The Politics of Sentencing Reform* (OUP, 1995).

C Murray, 'Playing for Time: Prisoner Disenfranchisement under the ECHR after *Hirst v United Kingdom*' (2011) 22 *KLJ* 309.

C Murray, 'We need to talk: "Democratic Dialogue" and the Ongoing Saga of Prisoner Disenfranchisement' (2011) 62 *NILQ* 57.

J Pratt, *Penal Populism* (Routledge, 2007).

M Pinto-Duschinsky, *Bringing Rights Back Home: Making Human Rights compatible with Parliamentary Democracy in the UK* (Policy Exchange, 2011).

D Raab, *Strasbourg in the Dock: Prisoner Voting, Human Rights & the Case for Democracy* (Civitas, 2011).

D Rowe, 'Media and culture: Movement across the decades' (2014) 10 *International Journal of Media & Cultural Politics* 171.

M Ryan, 'Red Tops, Populists and the Irresistible rise of the Public' in P Mason (ed) *Captured by the Media* (Willan, 2013).

F Sauvageau, D Schneiderman and D Taras, *The Last Word: Media Coverage of the Supreme Court of Canada* (UBC Press, 2006).

J Schone, 'The Short Life and Painful Death of Prisoners' Rights' (2001) 40 *Howard Journal of Criminal Justice* 70.

M Schudson, 'The Objectivity Norm in American Journalism' (2001) 2 *Journalism* 149.

S Reilly, 'The Technology of Truth: Revisiting Areopagitica' (2013) 9 *International Journal of Technology, Knowledge & Society* 139.

P Sales, 'Partnership and Challenge: The Courts' role in Managing the Integration of Rights and Democracy' [2016] PL 456.

R Sambrook, *Delivering Trust: Impartiality and Objectivity in the Digital Age* (Reuters Institute, 2012).

J Straw, *Aspects of Law Reform: An Insider's Perspective* (CUP, 2012).

J Straw, *Last Man Standing: Memoirs of a Political Survivor* (Macmillan, 2012).

C Sunstein, *Republic.com 2.0* (PUP, 2007).

S Teles, *The Rise of the Conservative Legal Movement: The Battle for Control of the Law* (PUP, 2008).

V Treacy, 'Prisoners' Rights Submerged in Semantics' (1989) 28 Howard Journal of Criminal Justice 27.E Voeten, 'Public Opinion and the Legitimacy of International Courts' (2013) 14 *Theoretical Inquiries in Law* 411.

R White and I Boussiakou, 'Separate opinions in the European Court of Human Rights' (2009) 9 *HRLR* 37.

M Whipple, 'The Dewey-Lippmann Debate Today: Communication Distortions, Reflective Agency, and Participatory Democracy' (2005) 23 *Sociological Theory* 156.

R Ziegler, 'Voting Eligibility: Strasbourg's Timidity' in K Ziegler, E Wicks and L Hodson (eds), *The UK and European Human Rights: A Strained Relationship* (Hart, 2015).

5 Demonising immigrants

How a human rights narrative has contributed to negative portrayals of immigrants in the UK media

Eleanor Drywood and Harriet Gray

Introduction

Immigrants of all types – asylum seekers, refugees, EU migrants, reunified family members – have suffered at the hands of a predominantly hostile press. Language is incendiary; the factual basis of stories is questionable; negative events dominate reporting. In this chapter, we explore the role of human rights in stories about migrants in the UK media. Through this exploration, we argue that a human rights narrative has exacerbated the negativity surrounding immigrants in the UK press. This may seem somewhat counter-intuitive given that human rights are often the very mechanism by which migrants have resisted aggressive control of borders and rampant destruction of non-nationals' legal status by European nation states.[1] In support of our core thesis, however, we advance a series of arguments which demonstrate that the legal architecture of human rights and their failings as a grassroots project have shaped a rhetoric which, in turn, has had a decidedly negative impact upon popular perceptions of immigration in the UK media.

In order to explore these dynamics, it is useful, first, to examine a now infamous example of media and political deception around immigration and human rights.[2] In October 2011, Theresa May (at that time, the Home Secretary of the

1 On this point, Costello cites Advocate-General Maduro of the Court of Justice of the European Union (in his Opinion on Case C-327/02 *Panayotova* [2004] ECR I-11055) who argues the importance of judicial protection of fundamental rights of third-country nationals under European Union law precisely because their minority status puts them outside the political community which determines their legal entitlements (C. Costello, *The Human Rights of Migrants and Refugees in European Law* (OUP 2006) 9.

2 For further exploration of 'misreporting, misconception and misconstruction' by the media in relation to human rights, see Mead in this volume: D. Mead, '"They offer you a feature on stockings and suspenders next to a call for stiffer penalties for sex offenders": do we learn more about the media than about human rights from tabloid coverage of human rights stories? in M. Farrell, E. Drywood and E. Hughes (eds), *Human Rights in the Media: Fear and Fetish* (Routledge 2019). See, also: D. Mead, '"You Couldn't Make It Up": Some Narratives of the Media's Coverage of Human Rights' in K. Ziegler, E. Wicks and L. Hodson (eds), *The UK and European Human Rights: A Strained Relationship* (Hart 2015).

United Kingdom) used her speech at the Conservative Party conference to slam the use of Article 8 of the European Convention on Human Rights (ECHR) by migrants to resist deportation. She told the now-infamous story of an 'illegal immigrant' who could not be deported 'because he had a pet cat': 'I am not making this up' she declared, to jeers and laughter from the floor.[3] The genesis of May's story was a series of factually dubious and incendiary press reports at the time of the original Asylum and Immigration Tribunal decision: 'Migrant facing deportation wins right to stay in Britain… … because he's got a cat' (*The Daily Mail*);[4] 'Immigrant allowed to stay because of pet cat' (*The Daily Telegraph*).[5] These headlines have come to represent the pinnacle of the absurdity of human rights reporting in the UK press, cited often by commentators as a particularly egregious example of inaccurate coverage of human rights in the UK media.[6] The case was an appeal to the Asylum and Immigration Tribunal at which the Home Office conceded that it had erroneously applied the law relating to the partners of British citizens.[7] The appellant in the case was a Bolivian man in a long-term relationship with his British partner. In the initial application, the couple had presented numerous pieces of evidence that they were in an enduring relationship, joint ownership of a pet cat being just one of these. The idea that this case created a legal precedent that immigrants can resist deportation on the basis of ownership of a cat, as suggested by many newspaper reports, is absurd. It is, however, reflective of an attitude prevalent in the UK press that immigrants' enjoyment of human rights is unfettered and a threat to British society, very often underpinned by a racist, xenophobic and divisive tone. Its repetition by May at the Conservative Party conference – and surrounding media furore – assured the case entry into the UK press's sorry history of immigration folklore, underpinning the

3 A. Wagner, 'Catgate: Another Myth Used to Trash Human Rights' *The Guardian* (London, 4 October 2011) available online at: www.theguardian.com/law/2011/oct/04/theresa-may-wrong-cat-deportation (accessed 12 June 2018).

4 'Migrant Facing Deportation Wins Right to Stay in Britain…Because He's Got a Cat' *The Daily Mail* (London, 19 October 2009) available online at: www.dailymail.co.uk/news/article-1221353/Youve-got-cat-OK-stay-Britain-officials-tell-Bolivian-immigrant.html (accessed 12 July 2018).

5 D. Barrett, 'Immigrant Allowed to Stay Because of Pet Cat' *The Daily Telegraph* (London, 17 October 2009) available online at: www.telegraph.co.uk/news/newstopics/howaboutthat/6360116/Immigrant-allowed-to-stay-because-of-pet-cat.html (accessed 12 July 2018).

6 See, for example: Wagner (n 3); E. Balabanova, 'Human Rights and Public Debate: The Media as a Scapegoat?' in M. Farrell, E. Drywood and E. Hughes (eds), *Human Rights in the Media: Fear and Fetish* (Routledge 2019).

7 For an excellent summary of both the appeal and the first-tier decisions, see D. Campbell '"Catgate" and the Challenge to Parliamentary Sovereignty in Immigration Law' [2015] Public Law 426. It has not been possible to provide a reference to the original judgment. Indeed, the reference provided by Campbell to the Asylum and Immigration Tribunal website is no longer active and has been replaced by a database that does not contain this decision, such that his secondary narrative (based upon primary documents) is the most comprehensive summary available at this time (July 2018).

symbiotic relationship between xenophobic rhetoric in UK politics, on the one hand, and the media's editorial choices around balance and tone, on the other.[8]

Beyond the hostile reporting of human rights in many parts of the press, any serious analysis will tell you that human rights play an important role in shaping the legal status of migrants.[9] Indeed, non-nationals in the UK have found legal solace in, amongst others, their right to family life, to be free of inhuman and degrading treatment and to claim asylum when fleeing persecution.[10] These are rights which are protected in international instruments, which have been interpreted and elaborated by domestic and international courts and which now allow migrants resident in the UK to engage more meaningfully with life in their host country than might otherwise be the case. That said, the failings of human rights law in relation to immigration are multifarious, with scholars having pointed to, amongst others: the limited ability of rights framework to protect non-members of a political society, stemming from Hannah Arendt's writings on the 'right to have rights';[11] the inherent tension between state securitisation and border control, on the one hand, and the full and enthusiastic recognition of the rights of individual migrants, on the other;[12] and, the failure of human rights to prevent ongoing migration-related humanitarian crises.[13] Our focus here, however, moves beyond these critiques, offering an analysis of how a human rights dimension impacts the reporting of immigration-related stories within the media. We argue that a human rights angle increases the level of negativity in reporting. We do not suggest that this makes human rights a bad thing for immigrants, instead we use the treatment of immigrants in the UK media to explore some of the weaknesses of the European human rights project of the past seventy years. This chapter, therefore, adds a new dimension to a rich literature scrutinising the relationship between immigration and human rights by considering, not just how these two legal frameworks map onto each other, but by assessing their relationship in popular rhetoric, as played out in the UK press. Crucially, we do this through a legal lens, seeking to understand what it is about law's structures which facilitates

8 R. Greenslade, 'Seeking Scapegoats: The coverage of asylum in the UK press', Asylum and Migration Working Paper 5 (Institute for Public Policy Research May 2005).

9 See, for example: Costello (n 1); N. Blake and R. Husain, *Immigration, Asylum and Human Rights* (OUP 2003)

10 Rights drawn from, respectively: Article 8 European Convention on Human Rights 1950, Article 3 European Convention on Human Rights 1950, 1951 Geneva Convention relating to the Status of Refugees and its 1967 Protocol.

11 For example: S. Benhabib, *The Rights of Others: Aliens, Residents and Citizens* (CUP 2004); H. Arendt, *The Origins of Totalitarianism* (Harcourt, Brace and Jovanovich, 1968 [1951]).

12 For example: V. Moreno-Lax, *Accessing Asylum in Europe: Extraterritorial Border Controls and Refugee Rights under EU Law* (OUP 2017); Costello (n 1).

13 For example: C. Harvey, 'Refugees and Human Rights: the Future of International Protection in the United Kingdom' (2015) 6 European Human Rights Law Review 603; B. McCloskey, 'Third-Country Refugees: the Dublin Regulation/Article 8 ECHR Interface and Judicial Remedies' (2017) 29(4) *International Journal of Refugee Law* 641.

such toxic reporting in relation to the human rights of immigrants, with an eye always on the wider social and cultural context of the UK media.

First, we identify a tone of what we are terming 'dual foreignness' to stories around immigration and human rights. We point to the tendency of human rights in the UK to be seen as not truly 'British'. When these rights, foisted on us by Europe, are used by non-citizens to enhance their legal status, the press cries 'foreign!': foreign rights from a foreign legislature for the benefit of foreign people. Second, we argue that what we term the 'legal anatomy' of human rights cases structures these claims such that they fuel a 'them and us' undertone to press coverage. In short: a human rights claim requires the applicant to pit their interests against those of the state, providing fertile ground for press reporting which emphasises the un-Britishness of migrants' human rights. Finally, we point to the failure of human rights as a grassroots cause, highlighting the absence of a belief in their value for 'everyday folk'. If rights are for 'other' people, a divisive undertone is particularly apt to take root when these individuals are not British. To support this argument, we consider the generally more positive tone of stories about migrants in local news media. These stories rarely mention human rights, something we argue reflects the perception that human rights are foreign, distant and for other people. Our conclusion, therefore, is that despite the many positive contributions that human rights instruments have made to the lives of immigrants resident in the UK, they have done nothing to soften the treatment of this group by the press.

Before we move onto our main analysis, a few notes on methodology and terminology in this chapter are necessary. First, we have made use of a rich literature from experts on media and communication to support our observations around the treatment of migrants in the UK press, but our analysis remains very much legal. Where we note 'trends' in reporting, we offer supporting literature, if appropriate, but some of our observations are more tentative – they are impressionistic and are used to support our analysis of the law, rather than to make any methodologically rigorous contribution to media and communication studies literature (though we hope we ask questions and raise issues of interest to this discipline). Second, whilst we use the word 'media' as an umbrella term to denote 'newspapers, radio and television, regarded collectively' (Oxford English Dictionary), our emphasis is on newspapers (or the equivalent term, the press). We have sought to include both tabloid and broadsheet newspapers in our analysis, however the focus has inevitably fallen on the former. This chapter addresses an incendiary attitude to immigration and disregard for accuracy in reporting which is more common amongst tabloid newspapers, particularly those on the right. Furthermore, tabloid newspapers have higher circulation: the three most popular tabloids (*The Daily Mail*, *The Daily Mirror* and *The Sun*, and their Sunday counterparts) all have more readers than the most popular broadsheet (*The Guardian*).[14] Indeed, amongst those who read a daily newspaper, no single

14 Ofcom, 'News Consumption in the UK: 2016' (29 June 2017) available online at: www.ofcom.org.uk/__data/assets/pdf_file/0016/103570/news-consumption-uk-2016.pdf (accessed 12 July 2018).

broadsheet is accessed by more than 10% of the population.[15] We use the terms 'immigrant' and 'migrant' largely interchangeably to denote anyone who does not enjoy an unconditional right of abode in the UK,[16] and where necessary we distinguish between various categories, primarily that of European Union (EU) citizen,[17] work/study-based migrant and family-based migrant etc. Furthermore, we make reference to particular issues around reporting of stories relating to asylum seekers – those who have fled persecution and have applied for refugee status, within the meaning of the Refugee Convention[18] – and 'refugees' – those who have been granted this status.[19]

The demonising of immigrants in the UK press

Immigration is a prominent issue in UK politics and news reporting, and has therefore generated significant academic scrutiny. In this section, we draw out key trends in this literature to build a picture of press treatment of immigrants, supplemented with examples from news stories. The tone of reporting on immigrants in the UK media is overwhelmingly hostile, which is perpetuated by repeated use of dehumanising metaphors. There is a particular focus on the most marginalised group, asylum seekers, but this is underpinned by a general dislike of all migrants and blurring of groups so that an issue with one seeps into the wider sense of distrust and negative perception of all. The potential impact of such negative trends is significant when evidence of the extent to which public opinion is shaped through news reporting is considered.

Discussion of immigration in the UK media is widely acknowledged to be characterised by negativity and even hostility. Balch and Balabanova refer to the 'broadly negative tone of public debate' of the UK's immigration policy.[20] Strabac *et al.* describe a press that presents ethnic minorities in negative and stereotypical terms and migrants as the embodiment of various threats to society.[21] Examples of such hostile reporting abound, including claims that migrants

15 *ibid.*

16 Immigration Act 1971, ss. 1 and 2.

17 For further discussion of the treatment of EU citizens post-Brexit by the UK press, see Reynolds in this volume: S. Reynolds, 'It's Not Me, It's You: Examining the Print Media's Approach to 'Europe' in Brexit Britain' in M. Farrell, E. Drywood and E. Hughes (eds), *Human Rights in the Media: Fear and Fetish* (Routledge 2019)

18 In UK law, an asylum seeker is a person who has submitted an application for permission to stay in a country other than her own as a refugee (Immigration Rules, 23 May 1994, HC 395 (as amended), para 327).

19 Convention relating to the Status of Refugees (Geneva, 28 July 1951) and its 1967 Protocol (New York, 31 Jan 1967). See Article 1A for the definition of a refugee.

20 A. Balch and E. Balabanova, 'Ethics, Politics and Migration: Public Debates on the Free Movement of Romanians and Bulgarians in the UK, 2006–2013' (2016) 36(1) *Politics* 19–35, 19.

21 Z. Strabac, K. Thorbjørnsrud and A. Todal Jenssesn, 'News Consumption and Public Opposition to Immigration Across Countries' in T. Aalberg and J. Curran (eds), *How Media Inform Democracy: A Comparative Approach* (Routledge 2012) 176–188, 176–177.

attempting to cross from Calais to Dover were not only a threat to the economy by delaying imports and exports, but also that the migrants were contaminating food: 'Millions of pounds worth of food are being destroyed because of contamination by migrants jumping into lorries'.[22]

This hostility is frequently conveyed through dehumanising metaphors. Cisneros explains that the most commonly used metaphors in reporting migration refer to images of 'flood', 'infestation' and 'burden',[23] and argues that 'pollutant' might also be added to this list.[24] None of these metaphors presents migrants and migration in a positive, or even neutral, light. The metaphor of 'flood' was particularly prevalent in reporting of the 'refugee/migrant crisis' in 2015–2016, transferring the disastrous threat to stability and security of a flood to migrants. For example, the Daily Express published an article titled: 'Migrant crisis getting worse: While politicians dither thousands more flood Europe', compounding the idea by accompanying it with pictures of overcrowded boats surrounded by water.[25] The *Sunday Express* used news of 'Illegal migrants flooding into EU' to support its campaign to have the UK leave the European Union.[26] The *Daily Mail* reported on a 'flood of young male migrants', which it linked to higher rates of 'aggression and, in particular, sexual violence'.[27] A particularly notorious example of the use of dehumanising metaphors is the British right-wing commentator Katie Hopkins' description of migrants crossing the Mediterranean as 'cockroaches'.[28] These metaphors represent migrants as non-human or less than

22 'Daily Mail Comment: It is time to end this migrant madness' *The Daily Mail* (London 30 July 2015) available online at: www.dailymail.co.uk/news/article-3179339/DAILY-MAIL-COMMENT-time-end-migrant-madness.html (accessed 12 July 2018).

23 J. D. Cisneros, 'Contaminated Communities: The Metaphor of "Immigrant as Pollutant" in Media Representations of Immigration' (2008) 11(4) Rhetoric and Public Affairs 569–602, 572.

24 *ibid*, 589–590.

25 M. Reynolds, 'Migrant crisis getting worse: While politicians dither thousands more flood Europe' *The Daily Express* (London 6 July 2016) available online at: www.dailymail.co.uk/news/article-3179339/DAILY-MAIL-COMMENT-time-end-migrant-madness.html (accessed 12 July 2018).

26 C. Dixon, 'Illegal migrants flooding into Europe: Record 1.8MILLION border breaches in one year' *The Sunday Express* (London 6 April 2016) available online at: www.express.co.uk/news/politics/658502/Record-illegal-migrants-entered-EU-ONE-year-Brexit (accessed 12 July 2018).

27 N. Afzal, 'Why Britain should be worried about this flood of young male migrants: Leading lawyer who's the son of migrants gives a stark warning' *The Daily Mail* (London 8 January 2016) available online at: www.dailymail.co.uk/news/article-3389734/Why-Britain-worried-flood-young-male-migrants-Leader-lawyer-s-son-immigrants-gives-stark-warning.html (accessed 12 July 2018).

28 K. Hopkins, *The Sun* (London 17 April 2015). A full reference to this piece is not available because it has been removed from the newspaper's website since publication, however, the original publication of the piece is reported in M. Duell, 'Cops get attack of common sense at last: Katie Hopkins will NOT face charges over allegations she incited racial hatred in migrant article' *The Daily Mail* (London 3 November 2015) available online at: www.dailymail.co.uk/news/article-3301963/Katie-Hopkins-not-face-charges-allegations-incited-racial-hatred-article-comparing-migrants-cockroaches.html (accessed 12 July 2018).

human. This adds to the dominant message that migrants are a threat and are to be looked down upon, and it creates a space for questioning whether migrants, if non-human, are deserving of human rights.

News media have been particularly hostile to asylum seekers. Philo *et al.* identify 'persistent and overwhelmingly hostile coverage of refugees and asylum' in national news media, including newspapers and television broadcasts, but note that these groups are largely confused with other groups of migrants.[29] There are many examples of this coverage, including a *Daily Express* article published a few days before Christmas in 2016 that proclaimed: '"The children were PETRIFIED" Asylum seeker STORMS nativity play to read from the Koran',[30] or 'Muslim asylum seeker jailed for life after killing "infidel" landlady in Germany'.[31] Through such reporting, the term 'asylum seeker' has become a pejorative way of describing a migrant, regardless of whether the person falls within the relevant legal definition.[32] The right to seek asylum is long enshrined in international law, intimately connected to the humanitarian aim of providing refuge for persecuted persons unable to access effective legal protection in their own state,[33] but under the gaze of such headlines, the term has become somewhat detached from its legal meaning and has become politicised, transformed into a label for a suspect and hated 'other'. Similar to the way in which 'Muslim' is used in the examples of newspaper reports we have cited in this section, what starts out as a neutral term to describe a conceptually clear group becomes a flag for racism, xenophobia and, in the case of these and similar examples, Islamophobia.

Balabanova argues that care should be taken with the terminology used to describe refugees and asylum seekers in particular, with some phrasing implying negative preconceptions.[34] Some commonly-used phrases are simply incorrect, such as 'illegal asylum seeker'. Under a correct reading of the law, everyone has the right to claim asylum so it cannot be illegal for person to lodge an application for asylum.[35] Beyond this, the Refugee Convention recognises that it may not always be possible for an asylum seeker to get advanced permission from her host country to seek asylum there, and so prohibits the imposition of penalties

29 G. Philo, E. Briant and P. Donald, *Bad News for Refugees* (Pluto Press 2013), 165.

30 J. Rogers, 'The children were PETRIFIED" Asylum seeker STORMS nativity play to read from the Koran' *The Daily Express* (London 21 December 2016), emphasis original, available online at: www.express.co.uk/news/world/745789/Asylum-seeker-Somali-Koran-Austria-Oberndorf (accessed 12 July 2018).

31 J. Rogers, 'Muslim asylum seeker jailed for life for killing 'infidel' landlady in Germany' *The Sunday Express* (London 1 March 2017) available online at: www.express.co.uk/news/world/773832/Muslim-asylum-seeker-life-sentence-murder-landlady (accessed 12 July 2018).

32 n 19.

33 J. Hathaway and M. Foster, *The Law of Refugee Status* (CUP 2014).

34 E. Balabanova, *The Media and Human Rights: The Cosmopolitan Promise* (Routledge 2015), 113.

35 Universal Declaration of Human Rights 1948, Article 14; Charter of Fundamental Rights of the European Union, Article 18; UK Immigration Rules, para 327A.

on refugees for illegal entry or residence.[36] In UK law, this is manifested in a legal defence to criminal charges relating to irregular entry where the entrance was to seek asylum.[37] In recognition of this, the National Union of Journalists advises against the use of legally inaccurate terminology,[38] though the steadfast endurance of such terms indicates that this guidance is not universally heeded.[39] Even putting these aside, Balabanova suggests that by referring to 'asylum seekers' rather than 'refugees', 'we raise a question regarding the authenticity of that individual's claim against the state, thus (re)asserting or privileging the state's role as the ultimate arbiter over the individual's status'.[40]

This is illustrated in a press article that refers in its headline to a 'young asylum seeker' whose family had been permitted to join him in the UK.[41] However, as the text of the article makes clear, the case, in fact, concerned a refugee in respect of whom the rules regarding family reunification had been (correctly) re interpreted to include parents. The tone of the article is negative, questioning the wisdom of this decision both on the basis that this would mean that other refugee children would also be permitted to bring their parents to the UK and, more perniciously, that we should question the veracity of the teenager's original asylum application. The article reports that he 'fled his native Eritrea where his father had been "imprisoned for political reasons"', using quotation marks to cast doubt on the basis for his refugee claim. The article creates the space to raise such questions by selecting the descriptor 'asylum seeker', a less definitive term – both linguistically and legally – than 'refugee'. By positing the illegitimacy of the boy's right to seek asylum, the article suggests that this is a situation in which human rights have exceeded their legitimate reach, as indicated by its inclusion of remarks from Lord Green of Deddington, chair of Migration Watch: 'Human rights considerations are important, but cannot be given free reign'.

In the wider context of migration across European media, Bennett *et al.* identify four themes in news stories about migrants: negative labelling and 'fuzzy' group designations; dominant portrayal of migrants negatively, including as victims; underrepresentation of migrants themselves and the overrepresentation of officials; and the relative absence of the European context in the discussion

36 Geneva Convention on the Status of Refugees 1951, Article 31.

37 Immigration and Asylum Act 1999, s. 31.

38 National Union on Journalists, *Fair Play: Refugees and Asylum Seekers in Scotland: A Guide for Journalists* (Oxfam, revised 2007), 13. Use of such terms is also in breach of s.1 of the Independent Press Standards Editors' Code of Practice available online at: www.ipso.co.uk/editors-code-of-practice/ (accessed 8 August 2016).

39 R. Wodak, "'Us' and 'them': inclusion and exclusion – discrimination via discourse" in G. Delanty, R. Wodak and P. Jones (eds), *Identity, Belonging and Migration* (Liverpool University Press 2008) 54–77, 73–74.

40 n 35, 133.

41 M. Beckford, 'Judge lets a young asylum seeker's family into the UK – opening the way for thousands more in legal precedent' *The Daily Mail* (London 12 June 2016) available online at: www.dailymail.co.uk/news/article-3637142/Judge-lets-young-asylum-seeker-s-family-UK-opening-way-thousands-legal-precedent.html (accessed 12 July 2018).

of migration.[42] Similarly, Wodak argues that the many factors that differentiate migrants are ignored in favour of constructing a single target for negative attention:

> Sometimes, however, all foreigners are assumed to belong to one single group and are classified as 'migrants or foreigners' although they arrive from different countries, with different motives and goals, with various educational backgrounds, religious and political affiliations, and (gendered) cultural traditions. Right-wing populist rhetoric attempts to merge all foreigners into one homogeneous group, which is subsequently stigmatized as a negative 'other'.[43]

This dehumanises migrants in the media further by removing personal and distinguishing characteristics. It is illustrated well by a report in *The Daily Telegraph* on the terminology used to discuss migrants. Its headline is: 'Don't call them "illegal immigrants", says Europe human rights commissioner', and the article proceeds to explain briefly the reasons behind this request – namely that 'illegal' implies criminality and denies humanity, and so 'irregular' is preferred – before detailing the Government's defiant rejection of this request.[44] In support of the Government's stance, the article offers long quotations from Conservative MP, Phillip Hollobone, through which the criminality implication is made explicit via direct allegations: 'This can be very much to the detriment of women, Jews and gay people in this country and others, as we saw in Cologne earlier this year when women were sexually assaulted by gangs of men'. The article then expands this threatening image to cover all migrants (as a homogeneous group) by reporting on projected numbers of overstaying international students, without explaining any link between this and the terminology issue at hand. By including reference to this group at the end, the message that all migrants are the same and all present a threat is reinforced. The European Commissioner for Human Rights' argument is in turn presented as over-sensitive and far removed from reality, or, as Hollobone is quoted as saying: 'The niceties and delicacies of the language this man suggests are lost on my constituents'.

This negativity is particularly significant when viewed in the context of a growing literature demonstrating the influence of the media's presentation and framing of migrants on public opinion. A 2011 Ipsos MORI poll demonstrated that

42 S. Bennett, J. ter Wal, A. Lipiński, M. Fabiszak and M. Krzyżanowski, 'The Representation of Third-Country Nationals in European News Discourse' (2013) 7(3) *Journalism Practice* 248–265, 249–250 and 253.

43 Wodak (n 39) 57, citing R. Wodak and A. Pelinka (eds) *The Haider Phenomenon in Austria* (Transaction Press 2002) and J. Rydgren (ed) *Moments of Exclusion* (Nova 2005).

44 D. Barrett, 'Don't call them "illegal immigrants", says Europe human rights commissioner' *The Daily Telegraph* (London 23 March 2016) available online at: www.telegraph.co.uk/news/2016/03/23/dont-call-them-illegal-immigrants-says-europe-human-rights-commi/ (accessed 12 July 2018).

people rely heavily on the media for information about immigration: news programmes on the television or radio, television documentaries, tabloid newspapers, and broadsheet newspapers were the top four most relied-upon sources, each ranked as more influential than personal experience or word of mouth.[45] Boomgaarden and Vliegenthart demonstrate that increased intensity of reporting on immigration issues in the news had a significant positive effect on support for anti-immigration parties in the Netherlands.[46] Although the study considers the salience of particular topics in the news rather than analysis of their tone, the impact of news about these topics leaves the authors confident in assuming that increased reporting often collides with negative reporting.[47] Together with the findings of a similar study conducted in Belgium,[48] they argue that these conclusions are transferable across European democracies.[49] Schemer's research supports the thesis that the tone of media reporting (negative or positive) impacts on the opinions of television viewers and newspaper readers,[50] but qualifies this with the finding that this influence is greater on less, or moderately, informed people and has less influence on the opinions of those well-informed about the issue at hand, namely immigration.[51]

On the other hand, Kaye argues that it is the repetition of negative stereotypes and phrases by the media *in itself* that is influential in creating or encouraging negative attitudes towards migrants, regardless of the tone of the article in which they appear.[52] Even if the piece is criticising the use of negative terminology such as 'bogus' in relation to asylum seekers, through repetition 'the reader becom[es] socialised to reading them, and com[es] to assume that the "genuineness" of refugees is a significant question'.[53] Greenslade explains that racist and xenophobic reporting on immigration is grounded in editors' belief that this reflects the attitudes of their readership:[54] 'A xenophobic press for a xenophobic people'.[55] He argues that such negative reporting is dangerous precisely because it arouses

45 B. Duffy and T. Frere-Smith, *Perceptions and Reality: Public Attitudes to Immigration* (Ipsos MORI Social Research Institute, January 2014), 92–93.

46 H. G. Boomgaarden and R. Vliegenthart, 'Explaining the rise of anti-immigrant parties: The role of new media content' (2007) 26 *Electoral Studies* 404–417, 413–414.

47 *Ibid.*

48 S. Walgrave and K. de Swert, 'The making of the (issues of the) Vlaams Blok: the media and the success of the Belgian extreme-right party' (2004) 21(4) *Political Communication* 479–500.

49 n 47, 415.

50 C. Schemer, 'The Influence of News Media on Stereotypic Attitudes towards Immigrants in a Political Campaign' (2012) 62(5) *Journal of Communication* 739–757, 751.

51 *Ibid.*, 751–752.

52 R. Kaye, 'Blaming the Victim: An analysis of press representation of refugees and asylum-seekers in the United Kingdom in the 1990s' in R. King and N. Wood (eds), *Media and Migration: Constructions of Mobility and Difference* (Routledge 2001), 53–70.

53 *Ibid*, 60.

54 n 8, 9–14.

55 *Ibid*, 9.

feelings that might otherwise lie dormant,[56] a conclusion that seems to be supported by psychological research on the same topic.[57]

Philo *et al.* are similarly convinced about the outcome of media's 'monstering' of asylum seekers:[58] division and hostility, particularly in those communities that are already facing the rough end of wealth inequalities.[59] Irrespective of which of these accounts of how media influences public perceptions of immigration, is more convincing, there is clear evidence to support the conclusion that the media is influential in cultivating, validating and encouraging attitudes that understand migrants as 'other'; as different to, and worse than, 'us'.

The media presents migrants as a homogenous group that should be regarded with suspicion and contempt. It does this by using dehumanising metaphors, by undermining migrants' legitimacy, particularly in respect of asylum seekers, and by implying criminality. This is especially damaging given the impact the media has on public perception of migrants and the public understanding of migration. The following sections explore how this negativity attached to 'otherness' or 'foreignness' offers fertile ground for growing a symbiotically 'anti-migrant' and 'anti-human rights' media.

The 'dual foreignness' of human rights and immigrants in the UK media

We argue in this section that press negativity in relation to immigration is exacerbated when a human rights element is introduced into the story. Human rights are presented as 'foreign' in both nature and origin, and, therefore, a threat to tabloid-fuelled notions of Britishness. The combination of 'foreign' human rights and 'foreign' beneficiaries (the immigrants who rely upon them in legal arguments) creates a 'dual foreignness' which leads to particularly toxic reporting. There are two especially potent ways in which the press invokes 'foreignness' in relation to human rights, which we identify to support our analysis: emphasis of the European, and, therefore, non-British origin of rights; and, the use of language which evokes a threat from abroad when describing rights.

Human rights are very often cast in the tabloid press as being inherently un-British and, by extension, as threatening national identity.[60] The Human Rights Act 1998 – as the UK expression of the European Convention on Human Rights 1950 – is presented as an unwelcome interference in the domestic legal system

56 *Ibid*, 29.

57 n 51, 741, citing E. T. Higgins, 'Knowledge activation: Accessibility, applicability and salience' in E. T. Higgins and A. W. Kruglanski (eds), *Social Psychology: Handbook of Basic Principles* (Guilford Press 1996) 133–168.

58 n 30, 166.

59 *Ibid*, 165–168.

60 See, further Farrell and Hughes in this volume: M. Farrell and E. Hughes, 'Magna Carta and the Invention of British Rights' Chapter 11. in M. Farrell, E. Drywood and E. Hughes (eds), *Human Rights in the Media: Fear and Fetish* (Routledge 2019).

by a European body, the Council of Europe (often confused or conflated with the equally unpopular EU).[61] Press coverage tends to invoke 'Europeanness' in its most pejorative form, pitting Britishness against Continental European ideas about human rights which are depicted as being as alien to the UK as bull fighting, siestas and salami. When, in the run-up to the 2015 UK general election, the Conservative Party announced its intention to repeal the Human Rights Act 1998 and renegotiate the terms of the UK's membership of the Convention, right-wing tabloids celebrated: 'Human rights madness to end: Europe's judges to be stopped from meddling in our affairs' (*The Daily Express*).[62] *The Daily Mail* declared it a 'triumphant week for British values'.[63]

Criticisms of human rights in the UK press often invoke what are presented as quintessentially British values, such as fairness, common sense and financial propriety, and present 'European' human rights as a threat to these. In a 2015 editorial criticising a High Court decision in which a suspected terrorist's monitoring conditions were relaxed on the basis of his rights under Articles 3 and 8 ECHR (the prohibition of torture and the right to respect for private and family life, respectively), *The Daily Telegraph* argued that 'Britain needs to return some *common sense* to these vexatious legal proceedings'.[64] Words such as 'quango' have been used in relation to human rights and related institutions by politicians to suggest excesses of administration,[65] invoking problematic traits such as 'shedding personal responsibility, rewarding friends, expanding the corporate state, diminishing the responsibility of Parliament … encourag[ing] patronage and invit[ing] corruption'.[66] This is linked to suggestions that the European Convention on Human Rights and its Strasbourg institutions are the cause of financial excesses which place a strain on the UK. Frequent reference is made to the cost to the public purse of a case which goes to the Strasbourg Court, and the burden of paying compensation when the UK loses, as though human rights are an

61 For further analysis of negative reporting around the EU see Reynolds in this volume (n 18).

62 M. Hall, 'Human Rights Madness to End: Europe's Judges to be Stopped from Meddling in our Affairs' *The Daily Express* (London, 3 October 2014) available online at: www.express.co.uk/news/uk/518143/Human-rights-judges-powers-removed-promise-Tories (accessed 12 July 2018).

63 J. Slack, 'End of Human Rights Farce: In A Triumphant Week for British Values, Tories Unveil Plans to Give Parliament and Judges Power to IGNORE the European Court and its Crazy Decisions' (London, 3 October 2014) available online at: www.dailymail.co.uk/news/article-2778720/End-human-rights-farce-In-triumphant-week-British-values-Tories-unveil-plans-Parliament-judges-power-ignore-European-Court-crazy-decision-making.html (accessed 12 July 2018).

64 'Telegraph View: This Human Rights Madness Must Come to An End' (London, 21 June 2015) available online at: www.telegraph.co.uk/news/uknews/law-and-order/11688595/This-human-rights-madness-must-come-to-an-end.html (accessed 12 July 2018).

65 'Conservative MPs' quoted in John Henley 'Why is the European Court of Human Rights hated by the Right?' *The Guardian* (London, 22 December 2013).

66 Phillip Holland MP writing in 1979 cited in L. Pliatzky, 'Quangos and Agencies' (1992) 70 *Public Administration* 555, 557.

indulgence which can scarcely be tolerated.[67] In a similar vein, the un-Britishness of the Convention and the Strasbourg Court is emphasised through painting these legal institutions as a threat to Parliament and parliamentary sovereignty. This was seen most acutely in the coverage of decisions around prisoners' voting rights, where the Strasbourg Court was presented as undermining Parliament's legislative autonomy and, thus, threatening a most-British institution: 'European judges rode roughshod over British sovereignty yesterday by ruling that prisoners must be allowed to vote'.[68]

The un-British trope attached to human rights is further fuelled by suggesting a foreign threat, through the use of language not dissimilar to that which, we have observed above, is used to describe immigrants. This is evidenced, for example, in straightforwardly racist presentation of Strasbourg judges. *The Daily Mail* columnist, Max Hastings, in an article calling upon his readers to 'remain angry' about 'Human Rights lunacy' (original capitalisation), writes: 'It seems intolerable that 16 Strasbourg judges should dictate to Britain how it addresses crime and punishment', emphatically adding, 'And what judges!'.[69] He then goes on to list the names of judges from Greece, Serbia, Georgia and Montenegro, all of whom have distinctly un-Anglo-Saxon names and hail from the Eastern and Mediterranean fringes of the European territory. The un-subtle suggestion is that these judges, with their foreign names and foreign training, lack the skills, qualifications and civilised values of their British counterpart(s). Emphasis is also placed on the unelected status of Strasbourg judges, as though this indicates their lack of accountability to the UK populous. This, of course, ignores the fact that judges are not elected in the UK either, but nonetheless succeeds in driving a wedge between 'them', judges with foreign values and interests, and 'us', the UK populous, the unwilling recipients of their decision-making.

Further negative language around the foreign threat of human rights is found in accusations about the 'creep' of the Convention. That is, the suggestion that through the zeal and creativity of its judges, the Convention's

---

67 See, for example: 'Just Send Him Away' *Daily Star* (London, 14 November 2012); H. Dixon, 'Human Rights Cases in Europe Have Cost Britain More Than £4m' *The Daily Telegraph* (London, 7 October 2013).

68 J. Slack, '"This Is For Britain to Decide": Cameron Pledges to Fight Diktat from Unelected European Judges Who Say Prisoners Must Get the Vote' *The Daily Mail* (London, 23 May 2012) available online at: www.dailymail.co.uk/news/article-2148208/Prisoner-vote-row-European-judges-insist-prisoners-MUST-vote.html (accessed 12 July 2018). For further discussion of the media's treatment of prisoner voting rights, see Murray in this volume: C. Murray, 'Monstering Strasbourg over Prisoner Voting Rights' in M. Farrell, E. Drywood and E. Hughes (eds), *Human Rights in the Media: Fear and Fetish* (Routledge 2019).

69 M. Hastings, 'The Danger is We've Become Immune to Human Rights Lunacy. It's Vital We Stay Angry, Says Max Hastings' *The Daily Mail* (London, 9 July 2013) available online at: www.dailymail.co.uk/debate/article-2359048/The-danger-weve-immune-Human-Rights-lunacy-Its-vital-stay-angry-says-MAX-HASTINGS.html (accessed 12 July 2018).

influence extends to ever increasing areas.[70] Thus, the Convention's status as a 'living instrument', one which can grow with the changing demands of the protection of human rights in Europe, provides fruitful ground for criticising its contemporary reach and influence.[71] The 'creep' of the European Convention mirrors the metaphor of a migrant population which also 'creeps' across Europe as it makes its way to British shores, one frequently invoked by tabloid newspapers when highlighting the threat of large scale migration.[72] Crucially, the word 'creep' (as defined by the Oxford English Dictionary) denotes both quiet and stealth movement, as well as the aim of eluding observation. It is a word, therefore, that very effectively suggests a threat which is especially menacing because it might slip under the radar if, these stories suggest, readers do not remain vigilant.

These allusions – and, indeed, explicit references – to the 'foreignness' of the Convention and its Court, underpinned by the use of language which evokes a threat from abroad, bear a striking resemblance to characterisations of the 'bad immigrant' played out in the UK press. Nikesh Shukla, as he introduces his seminal collection of essays exploring immigrant experience in the UK, cites Musa Okwanga on this polarising rhetoric: 'the biggest burden facing people of colour in this country is that society deems us bad immigrants – job-stealers, benefit-scroungers, girlfriend-thieves, refugees'.[73] The threatening language and constant othering – through emphasising difference and deviance – that underpins this depiction is very similar to what we have identified in relation to human rights in the UK press. The caricature is as follows: human rights creep steadily from continental Europe towards the UK, subsuming themselves in ever increasing areas of daily life; they might have embedded themselves in the UK's legal institutions, but they continue to betray their foreignness through a failure to uphold British values; the strain on the UK public purse is intolerable, wasting money and threating vital public services. This is remarkably similar to the 'bad immigrant' characterisation we have identified in this chapter. Indeed, we might substitute the word human rights for immigrants in the previous sentence and have an accurate summary of the dominant way of reporting of immigration in the UK press. The threat comes from Europe, either in the form of EU free movement rights, or in a failure of Mediterranean countries to stem the flow of refugees into Europe. The 'bad immigrant' is foreign, he (for he is a 'he') steals, scrounges, thieves (jobs, benefits and women, respectively),[74] fails to assimilate

70 'European Court of Killers' Rights', *The Sun* (17 August 2015).

71 See *Tyrer v United Kingdom* (1978) 2 EHRR 1, para 31: 'the Convention is a living instrument which … must be interpreted in the light of present-day conditions'. For a critique of the 'living instrument' approach of the European Court of Human rights, see: S. Theil, 'Is the 'Living Instrument' Approach of the European Court of Human Rights Compatible with the ECHR and International Law?' (2017) 23 (3) *European Public Law*, 587.

72 n 23, 26 and 27.

73 N. Shulka (ed.), *The Good Immigrant* (Unbound 2016).

74 *Ibid.*

to a British way of life and places a burden on public finances through a reliance on social welfare. The use of the same rhetorical devices by the press in relation to both immigrants, on the one hand, and human rights, on the other, creates a symbiosis when the two are used together in a story: all the negative connotations of one are invoked by the use of the other, and vice versa. Thus the potency of each (human rights, immigration) is enhanced when they are used in combination (the human rights of immigrants); they become greater than the sum of their parts: more othered, more threatening and more distant. This is the 'dual foreignness' which, we argue, is a crucial factor in explaining why the UK press's treatment of immigrants becomes especially toxic in stories which involve a human rights element.

The 'them and us' anatomy of a human rights claim as played out in the UK media

Two structural features of human rights within the UK immigration framework fuel the UK press's preoccupation with 'foreignness' and deviance when reporting cases in the area. Non-EU migrants' permission to enter and reside in the UK is governed by domestic law, principally the Immigration Rules.[75] The Immigration Rules, whilst submitted to very limited parliamentary supervision,[76] are subject to change by the Secretary of State for the Home Department.[77] In *Pankina*, their legal status is described as 'not merely unusual but unique':[78] despite being a non-legal source, they are considered to be binding on immigration decision makers.[79] Though these rules sometimes reflect human rights considerations – such as granting leave to remain for those facing human rights abuses should they be returned to their countries of origin,[80] or for family members who would not qualify on other grounds[81] – human rights neither motivate nor wholly explain the Immigration Rules. Indeed, they respond variously to security concerns, the exercise of state control through enforcement, and economic concerns. Applications for leave to enter and remain are determined by UK Visas and Immigration, a branch of the Home Office, under these rules. This framework has two important implications for the reporting of human rights and immigration in the media that are unpacked in this section. First, all immigration cases are challenges against a decision of the state, which pitches the state's interests against those of

75 Immigration Act 1971 ss. 1(2) and 1(4); Immigration Rules, 23 May 1994, HC 395 (as amended).
76 Technically in accordance with Immigration Act 1971 s. 3(2).
77 Immigration Act 1971 s. 3(2).
78 *Pankina v Secretary of State for the Home Department* [2010] EWCA Civ 719, [13].
79 *Ibid.*; confirmed in *R (on the application of Alvi) v Secretary of State for the Home Department* [2012] UKSC 33.
80 Immigration Rules Part 11: Asylum, paras 326A–352H.
81 Immigration Rules Part 8: Family Members, paras A277–319Y, Appendix FM and Appendix FM-SE.

the migrant, dichotomising 'Britishness' and 'foreignness'. Second, human rights are a last resort in immigration law, governing those cases which are by definition exceptional, those that do not fall within the standard parameters of the Immigration Rules. This allows the press to focus disproportionately on extreme cases and behaviour, which is in turn presented as inherently un-British. The legal anatomy of immigration cases based on human rights, therefore, contributes to their negative portrayal in the UK media.

Immigration decisions are an exercise of public law powers, carried out in the name of the Secretary of State. Immigration cases question these decisions, either on appeal or through judicial review, such that these cases are fundamentally set up as a challenge to the British state by a migrant. This immediately sets the migrant against the state and necessarily dichotomises their respective interests, framing the applicant's request as a contradiction to the will of the British people as represented by their political institutions.[82] This conceptual segregation is deepened by the legal limits that define the circumstances in which an appeal may be brought. Whilst previous provisions allowed for a wider variety of decisions against which appeal was permitted,[83] the Immigration Act 2014 limited the right to appeal to cases in which the Secretary of State has refused a protection claim, refused a human rights claim or revoked a protection status.[84] These remaining grounds for appeal only envisage appeals for human rights based applications, including asylum claims, excluding many everyday decisions on migration for work, study or family reasons from standard appeals procedures. This restriction responds both to 'anti-migrant' feeling as expressed in the press and the essential dichotomy imagined in immigration cases between the interests of migrants and 'Britishness'. According to the logic of this divide, restricting appeal rights and limiting the challenges that can be brought against the state strengthens its hand against its 'opponent', the migrant appellant. The reduction of grounds also forces migrants who have received a negative decision in cases outside those listed

82 This dichotomy might also be observed in other types of public law cases, such as social security appeals (recently, see, for example *Secretary of State for Work and Pensions v Carmichael* [2018] EWCA Civ 548; T. Royston and C. O'Brien, 'Court of Appeal Declares That Tribunals Must Apply Any Secondary Legislation That Breaches Human Rights' (2018) 25(2) *Journal of Social Security Law* D49). However, it is particularly acute in the example of immigration given the way that this framing is reproduced in media reports of these cases and the way in which questions as to the human rights of migrants have attracted media, political and popular attention.

83 Previously, appeals could also be made against many other decisions: refusal of leave to enter the UK; refusal of entry clearance, refusal of a certificate of entitlement (under s.10 Nationality, Immigration and Asylum Act 2002); refusal to vary leave to enter or remain if the result leaves the person with no leave to enter or remain; variation of leave to enter or remain if the result leaves the person with no leave to enter or remain; revocation of indefinite leave to enter or remain; removal decisions; decision to make a deportation order; refusal to revoke a deportation order.

84 Nationality, Immigration and Asylum Act 2002 s. 82(1), as amended by the Immigration Act 2014 s. 15.

to channel their complaints into the language of human rights in order to access a judicial assessment of their case.

Human rights play a residual role in immigration law, offering grounds to challenge decisions taken in line with the Immigration Rules, rather than acting as the primary basis for a decision. The Human Rights Act 1998 provides at section 6 that public authorities must act in accordance with the incorporated human rights, which includes officials making immigration decisions.[85] Section 84(1)(c) of the Nationality, Immigration and Asylum Act 2002 confirms that an immigration decision may be appealed on the basis that the decision is incompatible with the appellant's human rights. This means that all human rights claims by migrants are, by definition, exceptional (as standard applications are covered by the Immigration Rules) and a challenge to the British state by questioning its earlier decision.

An illuminating way to explore how these two factors – the dichotomising of state and individual interests, and the last resort nature of human rights claims – skew reporting is through deportation cases challenged under Article 8 ECHR, particularly where the applicant has a criminal record. This type of case is a press favourite: 'More than 1,300 foreign criminals, including killers, rapists and paedophiles have used human rights laws to stay in the UK';[86] 'Victory for Theresa May after drug dealer convicted of attempted murder loses human rights bid to avoid deportation';[87] and, less emotively, 'Tunisian criminal loses Supreme Court deportation challenge'.[88] These reports invariably emphasise the deviant behaviour of the applicant, highlighting their immigration status and their reliance on (foreign and un-British) human rights. The legal anatomy of such claims disproportionately focuses newspaper reporting on examples of behaviour which is both extreme and which the law requires us to classify as un-British through its emphasis upon state interests.

When a deportation decision is appealed under Article 8 ECHR, the court considers whether the right to respect for private and family life is engaged and interfered with and, if so, whether such interference is necessary to pursue a legitimate aim and whether the decision in question is proportionate to pursuing

---

85 Human Rights Act 1998 s. 6(3)(b).

86 I. Drury, 'More than 1,300 foreign criminals, including killers, rapists and paedophiles have used human rights laws to stay in the UK' *The Daily Mail* (London, 15 November 2016) available online at: www.dailymail.co.uk/news/article-3939970/More-1-300-foreign-criminals-including-killers-rapists-paedophiles-used-human-rights-laws-stay-UK.html (accessed 12 July 2018).

87 'Victory for Theresa May after drug dealer convicted of attempted murder loses human rights bid to avoid deportation' *The Daily Telegraph* (London, 25 May 2016) available online at: www.telegraph.co.uk/news/2016/05/25/drug-dealer-convicted-of-attempted-murder-loses-human-rights-bid/ (accessed 12 July 2018).

88 'Tunisian criminal loses Supreme Court deportation challenge' *The Belfast Telegraph* (Belfast, 16 November 2016) available online at: www.belfasttelegraph.co.uk/news/northern-ireland/tunisian-criminal-loses-supreme-court-deportation-challenge-35221073.html (accessed 12 July 2018).

this aim.[89] Recent changes to the Immigration Rules direct judicial reasoning in cases challenging the deportation of people who have been convicted of criminal offences, significantly restricting the circumstances in which such appeals will be accepted.[90] The importance accorded to the 'public interest in deportation' is paramount, with the Rules emphasising that this will only be outweighed by 'very compelling circumstances' which fall outside situations normally envisaged by the provisions.[91] Further stringent requirements relate to: a narrow reading of what constitutes a family member; significant duration of residence in the UK to be able to claim family life warrants protection; the exclusion of those with longer sentences from family life claims.[92]

The imposition of such stringent standards responds to the monstering of migrants and their human rights in the media, but it also perpetuates this approach. The test pits the interests of the British people against those of the applicant, by insisting that, by default, deportation will be in the public interest. It also sets the exceptions at such a high threshold that it ensures that cases testing them will be those with unusual circumstances. This has led to a skewed impression, within press reporting, that cases involving the sort of extreme circumstances that arise within the narrow confines of the current Article 8 framework are in some way indicative of the normal immigrant experience of the UK legal system.

This strictness has been tempered to a degree by the courts continuing to refer back to the case law preceding the changes. *JO (Uganda)*, decided in 2010, required the courts to consider all the relevant facts on a case by case basis in Article 8 cases.[93] In *Nagre* in 2013, the court rejected a challenge to the legality of the change to the Immigration Rules, but held that the framework for decision-making from case law pre-dating the change to the Rules should still be followed.[94] Similarly, in *MF (Nigeria)*, the court held that although the new rules did not expressly require the court to address all relevant factors in assessing proportionality, they did expressly envisage a balancing of the public interest in removal against 'other factors'.[95] These factors, the court held, implicitly included all relevant factors, even those not named in the provisions.[96] These judgments show the continued influence of Strasbourg jurisprudence on proportionality, which, in the media, is represented as the judges conspiring with immigrants in a plot to undermine the will of the British people and their Government.

---

89 *Razgar v SSHD* [2004] UKHL 27; *Huang and Kashmiri* [2007] UKHL 11.

90 Immigration Rules paras A398–399A.

91 Immigration Rules, para 398(c). The legal authority of this test was fortified by the Immigration Act 2014, which inserted equivalent provisions into the Nationality, Immigration and Asylum Act 2002. It states that the more serious the offence committed the greater the public interest in deportation is (Nationality, Immigration and Asylum Act 2002 s. 117C).

92 See: Nationality, Immigration and Asylum Act 2002 s. 177C(5); Immigration Rules, para 399A.

93 *JO (Uganda) and JT (Ivory Coast) v SSHD* [2010] EWCA Civ 10, [28].

94 *Nagre v SSHD* [2013] EWHC 720 Admin, followed in *Green (Article 8 – new rules)* [2013] UKUT 00254 (IAC).

95 *MF (Nigeria) v SSHD* [2013] EWCA Civ 1192, [38]-[39].

96 *Ibid.*

For example, in *The Daily Telegraph*, three immigration judges who had allowed appeals based on Article 8 ECHR were named and criticised: 'plans by Theresa May, the Home Secretary, to crack down on the way foreign criminals use human rights to avoid being deported risk being undermined in the courts'.[97] The ability of the court to refer back to the previous case law was further weakened by the repetition of the new standards in primary legislation.[98]

This example of the rules governing the deportation of foreign nationals convicted of criminal offences serves to demonstrate an important point for the role of human rights in UK immigration law and its reporting in the media. Despite the residual role they play in immigration law, human rights have become a significant target for popular discontent, spearheaded by right-wing media. This has resulted in tangible political efforts by the Government to restrict the scope for its decisions to be challenged on human rights grounds. The effect of this is that the legal anatomy of a human rights challenge to an immigration decision produces stories and arguments that are increasingly exceptional, making more atypical cases for the media to report. Thus we can observe a vicious circle: the legal framework encourages the press to focus on extreme cases, media outrage at these extreme cases follows, increasing public pressure to further restrict immigration regulation. Furthermore, this focus on cases at the margins of the legal framework, coupled with the toxic impact of 'dual foreignness' outlined in the previous section, results in an acutely 'othering' tone to stories on the human rights of immigrants. The focus of stories is on difference, deviance and distance – all three of which are found in popular rhetoric around both human rights and immigration, and which are facilitated by the legal anatomy of human rights claims within immigration law.

Human rights aren't for everyday folk: immigration and human rights in the local press

Our arguments so far have focused on national reporting of stories around immigration and human rights, exploring some of the reasons for their overwhelming negativity. In this section, our focus shifts to the local media. We identify a more positive tone to reporting of immigration-related stories at this level. Crucially, these stories almost never contain a reference to human rights. Whist there are structural and geographic reasons for this – not least that human rights claims tend to arise in appeal courts, whose work is most often the subject of analysis by the national media – it is also symptomatic of a failure of human rights to embed themselves at a grassroots level. The othering of immigrants is further achieved

97 D. Barrett and J. Ensor, 'Judges who allow foreign criminals to stay in Britain', *The Daily Telegraph* (London, 16 June 2012) available online at: www.telegraph.co.uk/news/uknews/immigration/9335689/Judges-who-allow-foreign-criminals-to-stay-in-Britain.html (accessed 12 July 2018).

98 Nationality, Immigration and Asylum Act 2002 s. 117C, as amended by the Immigration Act 2014 s. 19.

by an underlying perception that human rights are for people who 'aren't like us', are often deviant in some way, and are at the fringes of society. This is seen in two, interconnected ways. First, human rights have negative connotations in press reporting, therefore where the local press choose to run positive stories about immigration (often pointing to conduct on the part of non-nationals which makes them seem more 'like us') human rights language is avoided (either consciously or subconsciously) because of the damaging impact it may have on the tone and angle of the story. The journalist does not reach for human rights vocabulary because of its distancing effect. Second, human rights are less reported at a local level because they are not seen as being available in a grassroots sense: their mechanisms, their institutions and their vocabulary are not democratised. After exploring the treatment of immigrants by local press, we draw upon wider critiques of the failure of human rights at grassroots level to explore these arguments.

Immigration and the local press: a more sympathetic and humanitarian angle

Stories about migrants are generally more positive in the local press. This is not to suggest that none of the ills of incendiary reporting, questionable facts and dominance of negative events are found in regional newspapers – far from it – rather that, for a number of reasons, the local press is generally more willing to report good news stories about immigrants and asylum seekers and to pay closer attention to appropriate journalistic standards in this context. Studies which have reached this conclusion have focused on various regions – Scotland, South Wales, Bristol, for example – with this comment from a 2005 study carried out in London neatly encapsulating the different approach of local media to stories about refugees: '[London's local newspapers] do not tend to comment on policy and are mainly concerned with positive local interactions between individual asylum seekers/refugees and host community members'.[99]

Perhaps the most significant factor explaining the higher number of positive stories in the local press is a greater awareness of the impact on community cohesion of inflammatory pieces. The following observation was made in the context of a project which engaged migrants and representatives of the media to explore difficulties in reporting refugee and asylum issues at a local level:

> It was argued that local media have a heightened sense of their ethical obligations precisely because they are 'local'. They are part of the community, living amongst the people they serve, known by them and accountable to them. They can therefore be more responsive to people's feelings and are able to adapt their reporting when necessary.[100]

---

99 ICAR, *Reflecting asylum in London's communities: monitoring London's press coverage of refugees and asylum seekers: an analysis of press reporting January – February 2005* (ICAR 2005) 67.

100 N. Finney, 'The Challenge of Reporting Refugees and Asylum Seekers: ICAR Report on Regional Media Events Organised by the PressWise Refugees, Asylum Seekers and the Media (RAM) Project' (ICAR 2003) 16.

Similarly, a regional newspaper editor argued that there was simply no appetite for inflammatory reporting at a local level: 'If we produced a racist newspaper it won't sell in this city. Anything we do we have to live with it unlike the national newspapers.'[101] Indeed, this latter comment hints at a wider issue: that inaccurate reporting is straightforwardly harder to get away with at a local level because people are more immediately able to check the accuracy of a story against their own lived experiences. This can be particularly pronounced in relation to stories about immigration where a popular rhetorical device is that of 'floods' of immigrants placing an untenable burden on public services. Where this is reported nationally, it can easily stoke fears, even where the threat remains distant and hypothetical; if this is reported locally, readers can easily reference their own community-based experiences and question the story's veracity.

In some regions, we see examples of local newspapers going further and carrying-out an activist role through participation in projects which engage media in activities to promote integration of immigrants. In South Wales, the Merthyr Tydfil Council public affairs department worked with local press to foster greater support for and understanding of migrants following the recruitment of many Polish and Portuguese workers by a local meat production factory.[102] *Wales on Sunday*, for example, published stories which highlighted the migrants' contribution to the Welsh economy through a willingness to take on jobs that local residents did not want and their desire to learn English.[103] Similarly, the Asylum Positive Images Project in Scotland targets local media to influence content and portrayal of asylum, with activities including media awards, education of media students, training for asylum seekers and refugees on engaging with the media and community outreach activities.[104] Furthermore, Oxfam, the Refugee Council, Amnesty International and the National Union of Journalists have produced a guide for journalists working in Scotland on accurate and balanced reporting in relation to the asylum and refugee issues.[105] This was followed up by guidelines from the National Union of Journalists for the rest of the UK; however it is widely reported that the local media are keener observers of press regulatory standards than their national counterparts, particularly the tabloid newspapers.[106]

In addition to a greater awareness of community cohesion and a stronger inclination to observe good standards of journalism, local newspapers tend to focus

101 K. Smart *et al.*, 'Reporting Asylum: The UK Press and the Effectiveness of PCC Guidelines (January – March 2015)' (ICAR 2005) available online at: www.crimeandjustice.org.uk/sites/crimeandjustice.org.uk/files/ReportingAsylum.pdf (accessed 10 July 2018), 79.

102 As discussed in T. Threadgold, 'The Media and Migration in the United Kingdom, 1999 to 2009' (Migration Policy Institute 2009) 6.

103 'Foreign Workers Take Jobs Welsh Don't Want' *Wales on Sunday* (Cardiff, 20 February 2005) available online at: www.walesonline.co.uk/news/wales-news/foreign-workers-take-jobs-welsh-2406826 (accessed 12 July 2018).

104 Oxfam, 'Forward Together: Ideas for Working with Asylum Seekers, Refugees, the Media and Communities' (Oxfam GB 2008).

105 Oxfam, 'Fair Play. Refugee and Asylum Seekers in Scotland: A Guide for Journalists (Revised 2007)' (Oxfam GB 2007).

106 n 102, 80.

on human interest stories which emphasise immigrants as individuals. These stories cover areas such as cultural contributions, achievements in school ('Syrian refugee who arrived in the UK in a chip van wins place at Oxford University'),[107] work in the local community ('Foreign Workers Take Jobs Welsh Don't Want')[108] and cultural integration ('This Kurdish refugee took his wedding vows in Welsh after fleeing persecution and finding a home').[109] Equally, local newspapers are more likely to focus upon the hardship suffered by migrants, using a sympathetic and humanitarian lens, than national newspapers which cast immigrants as threatening. So, for example, we see stories on the negative lived-experiences of refugees or on support shown by local communities for immigrant populations ('Campaign to Save 10-Year-Old Glasgow Orphan from Deportation').[110] Similarly, pieces which depict threats of deportation are often found in the local press and tend to emphasise links that immigrants have forged with the local community ('Anger as Liverpool Asylum Family and Disabled Son Detained and Set to be Deported').[111] What stories in the local press very rarely feature, however, is any discussion of the human rights of migrants, a striking conclusion given the focus upon individuals.

Human rights, immigration and the local press: do human rights fail at a local level?

A simple review of local media coverage of migrants, refugees and asylum seekers reveals virtually no stories which contain any discussion of human rights. Migrants' everyday lives can be shaped in multifarious ways by rights derived from a number of international instruments: whether as the basis for the individual's residence in the UK, to resist deportation, to enjoy family life, or to access education, amongst others. In one respect, it is surprising that the local press – characterised by their tendency towards a human interest angle – does not provide a natural home for a

107 'Syrian refugee who arrived in the UK in a chip van wins place at Oxford University' *Oxford Mail* (Oxford, 16 January 2018) available online at: www.oxfordmail.co.uk/news/yourtown/oxfordshire/15841001.Syrian_refugee_who_arrived_in_the_UK_in_a_chip_van_wins_place_at_Oxford_University/ (accessed 12 July 2018).

108 n 104.

109 B. White, 'This Kurdish refugee took his wedding vows in Welsh after fleeing persecution and finding a home' *The Western Mail* (Cardiff, 21 September 2016) available online at: www.walesonline.co.uk/news/wales-news/kurdish-refugee-took-wedding-vows-11919698 (accessed 12 July 2018).

110 S. McNab, 'Campaign to Save 10-Year-Old Glasgow Orphan from Deportation' *The Scotsman* (Edinburgh, 1 June 2018) available online at: www.scotsman.com/regions/glasgow-strathclyde/campaign-to-save-10-year-old-glasgow-orphan-from-deportation-1-4748565 (accessed 12 July 2018).

111 L. Thorp, 'Anger as Liverpool Asylum Family and Disabled Son Detained and Set to be Deported' *Liverpool Echo* (Liverpool, 5 April 2018) available online at: www.liverpoolecho.co.uk/news/liverpool-news/anger-liverpool-asylum-family-disabled-14495412 (accessed 12 July 2018).

focus on rights. Indeed, it is the very foundation of liberal human rights that they are enjoyed on an individual basis.[112] However, the stories referred to above do not, for example, celebrate the right to access education of a child asylum seeker who goes on to gain a place to study at Oxford University. Nor is there acknowledgement of the right to be free from torture, human or degrading treatment or punishment, or the right to claim asylum from persecution, or the right to a private and family life, which can form the basis of a claim to resist deportation. In short, the local press, with their focus on stories about individual migrants, have not extended the goodwill shown in some aspects of their coverage of immigrants to a sympathetic discussion of the contribution that human rights play in shaping the lives of these individuals.

Of course, the legal anatomy of a human rights claim in the immigration context, as outlined above, goes some way to explaining their lack of coverage in the local press. Human rights claims occupy a residual role in UK immigration law. As such, they are most often used to challenge immigration decisions and are, therefore, the fodder of appeal courts. Legal reporting in local news outlets tends to focus upon first instance courts, with discussion of higher court rulings and supranational judgments falling to the national press. This is indicative of a broader tendency not to cover national or international immigration policy in the local press. And, in many ways, this is unsurprising: scrutiny of Westminster powers, and the influence of European and international law, is naturally going to fall to national newspapers. The result is that we see a contrast between grievances around hard legal rules derived from a 'foreign' source and applied by distant appeal courts, on the one hand, and far softer, more banal reporting of human interest stories drawn from the locality and containing relatable details, on the other. This distinction between the distant national news and the familiar local news is unsurprising – and is played out in relation to many areas, not just immigration stories – but its potential impact on perceptions of human rights is interesting.

First and foremost, it belies an underlying assumption that human rights are not something to be enjoyed on an everyday basis, nor something from which individuals who do not suffer routine human rights abuses benefit. If human rights condition state power, allowing individuals to live their lives through the enjoyment of liberties,[113] they are, by their very nature, extremely banal, local and everyday. Yet, this is not the public perception they enjoy. The infamous statement of Philip Davies, Conservative MP, that the ECHR is 'a charter for illegal

112 Articles 1 and 2 Universal Declaration of Human Rights (Universal Declaration of Human Rights (10 Dec. 1948), U.N.G.A. Res. 217 A (III) (1948). Critiques of the individual and universalist nature of human rights abound. See, notably: J. Bentham, *Anarchical Fallacies* (1789), as discussed in H. Bedau, '"Anarchical Fallacies": Bentham's Attack on Human Rights' (2000) 22(1) *Human Rights Quarterly* 261.

113 This view of rights as conditioning state power corresponds broadly to Dworkin's idea of rights as trumps (R. Dworkin, *Taking Rights Seriously* (Harvard University Press 1977), but the observation is factual, rather than ideological.

immigrants and criminals' is indicative of a belief that human rights are simply not relevant to most people.[114] As Davies also said: 'I'm not aware of my decent law-abiding constituents running off to the European Court of Human Rights.' Of course, the straightforward explanation for this is that those who enjoy a secure residence status in the UK, who do not come into contact with the criminal justice system, who are not members of minorities etc, are simply much less likely to suffer violations of their human rights. The reason they do not 'run off to Strasbourg' is not because human rights are not something they benefit from, it is because they are fortunate enough not to suffer human rights abuses. What is noteworthy here is that the human rights project of the twentieth and twenty-first century has largely failed to convey this message. Makau Matua, writing on the distinction between 'civil rights' and 'human rights' in a US context, makes the following observation: '"human rights problems" do not apply to "people like us" but rather to "backward" peoples or those who are "exotic"'.[115] The civil rights/human rights distinction is admittedly not one which readily translates to the UK context, but his observations here are nonetheless prescient. Where human rights are associated only with foreigners or those who engage in deviant behaviour, it becomes particularly easy to 'other' not just the individuals who benefit from them, but the content and the validity of the rights themselves.

Indeed, this observation resonates with some of the arguments of rights-sceptics around the failure of the post-Second World War human rights project to embed itself meaningfully at a grassroots level and its association with political and legal elites.[116] David Kennedy has written, in the context of the international humanitarian movement, about the Western-centric nature of the modern human rights movement and its tendency to favour those with existing political and economic means.[117] Human rights language, people and activities are often better established among social elites, which results in a lack of knowledge about human rights laws, concepts and mechanisms amongst the very people they ought to serve.[118] The result, therefore – presented as a fundamental failing of human

114 Dixon (n 67).

115 M. Mutua 'The Ideology of Human Rights' (1996) 36 *Virginia Journal of International Law* 589, 609.

116 For a useful summary of recent trends in human rights critiques, see O. Pedersen and C. Murray 'Examining Critical Perspectives on Human Rights: An Introduction' in R. Dickson *et al.* (eds), *Examining Critical Perspectives on Human Rights* (CUP 2016).

117 D. Kennedy, *The Dark Sides of Virtue: Reassessing International Humanitarianism* (Princeton University Press 2004) ch 8; see, also, in this volume, Gordon on the role of the media in challenging elitism, whether through human rights scrutiny, or wider democratic government accountability: M. Gordon, 'Instrumentalism in Human Rights and the Media: Locking Out Democratic Scepticism?' Chapter 10.

118 M. Banya, 'Human Rights for Whom? A Closer Look at Elitism and Women's Rights in Africa' (*Open Democracy*, 2 December 2013) available online at: www.opendemocracy.net/openglobalrights/moiyattu-banya/human-rights-for-whom-closer-look-at-elitism-and-women's-rights-in-a (accessed 10 July 2018).

rights by some commentators[119] – is a lack of consciousness within poor and marginalised communities of the rights that individuals enjoy.[120] Banya comments: '[j]ust because human rights *information* is concentrated among elites, human rights *protections* should not be similarly biased'(original emphasis), pointing to the need to involve disadvantaged groups in human rights planning and implementation.[121] Much of the work on the failures in human rights as a grassroots movement has been carried out in the context of developing countries, pointing to the limitations of an international movement which is the bread and butter of a Western, metropolitan elite, but has made limited inroads in the lives of 'the poor, the powerless and the oppressed' in Ghana, Mexico, Colombia, Morocco and India, for example.[122] This critique is fairly fatal to any view of the post-Second World War human rights movement as a success, pointing, as it does, to an enduring global and social inequality which was the very thing the movement sought to address.

For many, human rights have failed to embed themselves at a grassroots level and this is evidenced in part by the relative paucity of coverage of human rights within the local press. This failure of human rights at grassroots level has two consequences. First, that they are an insufficiently mobilising force for the individuals who suffer the most violations. Second, that there is limited cognisance amongst those who do not routinely suffer rights violations that human rights nonetheless benefit them. This benefit comes not via the capacity to challenge state activity in the face of a violation, but instead through enjoying a life free of violations by virtue of living in a country whose legal structures uphold those rights on an ongoing basis.[123] When we set this observation within the context of a local press that seems largely to overlook a human rights angle when covering

119 Open Global Rights, a website which facilitates learning and critical thought in relation to a range of human rights topics, hosts a discussion forum on the question of 'human rights: mass or elite movement?' with links to a range of articles debating this theme: www.openglobalrights.org/human-rights-mass-or-elite-movement/ (accessed 10 July 2018).

120 Bell offers a passionate rebuttal to some of Kennedy's ideas on an 'international human rights movement' made up of professionals, international NGOs, bureaucratic machinery and governments, identifying instead her own experiences as part of 'a movement of local activists ... ordinary people, often marginalised in terms of their politics and their identity, ethnicity or gender', and citing the importance of human rights paradigms in activism (C. Bell 'Human Rights and the Struggle for Change: A Study in Self-Critical Legal Thought' in Dickson *et al.* (eds), *Examining Critical Perspectives on Human Rights* (CUP 2016).

121 Banya (n 18).

122 J. Ron, D. Crow and S. Golden, 'The Struggle for a Truly Grassroots Human Rights Movement' (*Open Global Rights* 18 June 2013) available online at: www.openglobalrights.org/struggle-for-truly-grassroots-human-rights-move/ (accessed 12 July 2018).

123 We can, of course, observe that there is no country which benefits from the kind of utopian human rights framework which assures a violation-free existence for all individuals within its jurisdiction. Our point here is instead that the majority experience rights violations on a far less frequent basis than minority groups. Thus, rights become less relevant to their day-to-day existence not because they do not need the protections they offer, but because they already enjoy them.

immigration-related stories, we see that this is part of a wider tendency to downplay their value in everyday life. In short, we argue that human rights suffer from a PR crisis. Indeed, Moyn points to a lack of a rallying call, as compared to other globalising ideologies (citing, in particular, Christianity, nationalism and socialism): 'human rights have not succeeded in offering the world breviaries, flags or anthems'.[124] He argues, further, that this is a consequence of the relative infancy of the human rights movement, on the one hand, and the inevitable top-down nature of legal principles which require 'the propagation of norms of international law to domestic mobilisation', on the other. What is important here is that we see, once again, that the legal anatomy of human rights claims makes them seem removed from, and irrelevant to, the daily lives of most people. This offers some insight into the tendency of the local press not to give much coverage to the human rights angles of stories, particularly those of immigrants who are themselves often perceived as 'different' from the majority community.

Our observation that human rights dimensions rarely feature in positive news stories around immigration at local level has allowed us to identify a further factor which shapes press attitudes towards immigration, namely the limitations of a grassroots movement around human rights. That the language and philosophy of human rights has never really embedded itself in popular rhetoric in a local, community sense further distances this legal framework from those individuals who are the natural consumers of local media. This distancing effect is an additional potent influence on the othering of immigrants: where they rely upon rights, this can simply be cast as further evidence that they are not 'everyday folk'. If the ECHR is 'a charter for illegal immigrants and criminals' then reliance upon human rights must imply some sort of deviant behaviour. This third conclusion, therefore, is a natural corollary to the arguments made in previous sections, focusing as they did on recurring themes of deviance, difference and distance.

Conclusion

This chapter engages with the overwhelmingly hostile reporting of human rights in relation to immigrants in the UK media, and uses it is a base from which to explore reasons for it that are peculiar to the specific context – namely the 'dual foreignness' expressed by such cases and their particular legal anatomy – and how this fits into broader problems with the human rights project and its failure to gather grassroots support.

First, we identify that the tone of reporting on immigration in the UK press is overwhelmingly negative, noting key trends from media and communications literature, namely: the wide use of dehumanising metaphors; the particular focus on asylum seekers as an object of hostility, but in the context of inaccurate

124 S. Moyn 'Human Rights Are Superficial' (*Humanity Journal* 10 June 2014) available online at: http://humanityjournal.org/blog/human-rights-are-superficial/ (accessed 12 July 2018).

terminology and blurring of migrant groups together; and the strong role played by news reporting in shaping readers' opinion of immigration. This hostile landscape is the foundation of our analysis in the rest of this chapter: how does the idea of human rights fit in, and interact, with stories of immigrants in the UK media?; and how can casting a critical *legal* eye over the interaction between human rights and immigration law offer new insights into the uncomfortable relationship between the two in the UK media?

As is established across this volume, hostile reporting of human rights is a feature across a number of contexts in the UK media. In the second and third sections of this chapter, we explore why this hostility is so potent when those human rights are attached to non-citizens, that is, immigrants, and their permission to enter and reside in the UK. We first identify a perception of 'dual foreignness' in immigration-based human rights cases, which intensifies negative reporting, particularly in the right-wing press. Despite being a longstanding component of the UK's international obligations and an integrated part of the domestic legal landscape, the press continues to represent human rights as being imposed from 'outside', from 'Europe', and as failing to represent or respect 'British values'. When applied for the benefit of a person who is also considered to be 'outside' and 'un-British', we argue that this combination of overlapping spheres of 'otherness' makes for particularly toxic press coverage.

The second reason for the heightened hostility in the reporting of immigration and human rights cases is the legal anatomy of such cases, which we argue is structurally skewed towards negative reporting. Human rights are used as a way of challenging the state's immigration decisions to protect the interests of the appellant. This framework immediately creates an 'us and them' divide, through which the state's attempts to protect British values and British people, as represented through the media, are pitched against the threat of the migrant trying to secure protection for her human rights. In this way, upholding a human rights appeal is seen as damaging to the UK in a zero-sum game created by the division. In addition, restricting appeals to human rights grounds, and limiting the circumstances in which those human rights appeals can be successful, excludes most day-to-day cases and shifts focus to the more exceptional and unusual cases. Thus, the legal construction of these cases feeds into the extreme negativity with which they are presented by the UK media.

In our final section, we observe that these two issues do not seem to be reproduced in the local press. There is a difference between the subject matter reported in local and national news, but this notwithstanding we identify more positive treatment in the local reporting on immigrants due to closer observation of press standards and a much closer eye on the impact of what is written on community cohesion in the local area. However, it is interesting to note that whilst this can be seen to address some of the problems we see in the reporting on immigrants found at national level, it does nothing to touch the portrayal of human rights. The positive stories about immigrants are not presented through a human rights lens, and the human rights aspects of their stories are not discussed. Rather, in trying to present migrants as 'like us' and people to be celebrated, local news removes their need for human rights in the same way 'we' do not rely on human rights.

The failure of human rights as a grassroots project, that is, the failure to communicate and convince people of the banality of human rights as existing in the background of normal life not as wiggle room in exceptional circumstances, is well attested. We argue that this is played out in the positive reporting of immigrants in the local press, where human rights are noticeably absent, as well as in the negative national press which presents the 'dual foreignness' of human rights and immigrants as a problem, spurred on by the legal anatomy of these cases. Human rights, despite the legal role they have often played in improving the lives of immigrants to the UK, do nothing to alleviate their harsh treatment in the UK news media.

Bibliography

Arendt, H., *The Origins of Totalitarianism* (Harcourt, Brace and Jovanovich 1968 [1951]).

Balabanova, E., 'Human Rights and Public Debate: The Media as a Scapegoat?' in M. Farrell, E. Drywood and E. Hughes (eds), *Human Rights in the Media: Fear and Fetish* (Routledge 2019).

Balabanova, E., *The Media and Human Rights: The Cosmopolitan Promise* (Routledge 2015)

Balch, A. and E. Balabanova, 'Ethics, Politics and Migration: Public Debates on the Free Movement of Romanians and Bulgarians in the UK, 2006–2013' (2016) 36(1) *Politics* 19–35.

Banya, M., 'Human Rights for Whom? A Closer Look at Elitism and Women's Rights in Africa' (*Open Democracy*, 2 December 2013) available online at: www.opendemocracy.net/openglobalrights/moiyattu-banya/human-rights-for-whom-closer-look-at-elitism-and-women's-rights-in-a (accessed 10 July 2018).

Bedau, H., '"Anarchical Fallacies": Bentham's Attack on Human Rights' (2000) 22(1) *Human Rights Quarterly* 261.

Bell, C., 'Human Rights and the Struggle for Change: A Study in Self-Critical Legal Thought' in Dickson *et al.* (eds), *Examining Critical Perspectives on Human Rights* (CUP 2016)

Benhabib, S., *The Rights of Others: Aliens, Residents and Citizens* (CUP 2004).

Bennett, S. J. ter Wal, A. Lipiński, M. Fabiszak and M. Krzyżanowski, 'The Representation of Third-Country Nationals in European News Discourse' (2013) 7(3) *Journalism Practice* 248–265.

Boomgaarden, H. G. and R. Vliegenthart, 'Explaining the rise of anti-immigrant parties: The role of new media content' (2007) 26 *Electoral Studies* 404–417.

Campbell, D., '"Catgate" and the Challenge to Parliamentary Sovereignty in Immigration Law' [2015] *Public Law* 426.

Cisneros, J. D., 'Contaminated Communities: The Metaphor of "Immigrant as Pollutant" in Media Representations of Immigration' (2008) 11(4) *Rhetoric and Public Affairs* 569–602.

Costello, C., *The Human Rights of Migrants and Refugees in European Law* (OUP 2006).

Duffy, B. and T. Frere-Smith, *Perceptions and Reality: Public Attitudes to Immigration* (Ipsos MORI Social Research Institute January 2014).

Dworkin, R., *Taking Rights Seriously* (Harvard University Press 1977).

Farrell, M. and E. Hughes, 'Magna Carta and the Invention of British Rights' in M. Farrell, E. Drywood and E. Hughes (eds), *Human Rights in the Media: Fear and Fetish* (Routledge 2019).

M. Gordon, 'Instrumentalism in Human Rights and the Media: Locking Out Democratic Scepticism?' in in M. Farrell, E. Drywood and E. Hughes (eds), *Human Rights in the Media: Fear and Fetish* (Routledge 2019).

Finney, N., 'The Challenge of Reporting Refugees and Asylum Seekers: ICAR Report on Regional Media Events Organised by the PressWise Refugees, Asylum Seekers and the Media (RAM) Project' (ICAR 2003).

Greenslade, R., 'Seeking Scapegoats: The coverage of asylum in the UK press', *Asylum and Migration Working Paper 5* (Institute for Public Policy Research May 2005).

Harvey, C., 'Refugees and Human Rights: the Future of International Protection in the United Kingdom' (2015) 6 *European Human Rights Law Review* 603.

Hathaway, J. and M. Foster, *The Law of Refugee Status* (CUP 2014).

Kaye, R., "Blaming the Victim: An analysis of press representation of refugees and asylum-seekers in the United Kingdom in the 1990s" in R. King and N. Wood (eds), *Media and Migration: Constructions of Mobility and Difference* (Routledge 2001), 53–70.

Kennedy, D., *The Dark Sides of Virtue: Reassessing International Humanitarianism* (Princeton University Press 2004).

Mutua, M., 'The Ideology of Human Rights' (1996) 36 *Virginia Journal of International Law* 589.

Mead, D., '"They offer you a feature on stockings and suspenders next to a call for stiffer penalties for sex offenders": do we learn more about the media than about human rights from tabloid coverage of human rights stories?' in M. Farrell, E. Drywood and E. Hughes (eds), *Human Rights in the Media: Fear and Fetish* (Routledge 2019).

Mead, D., '"You Couldn't Make It Up": Some Narratives of the Media's Coverage of Human Rights' in K. Ziegler, E. Wicks and L. Hodson (eds.), *The UK and European Human Rights: A Strained Relationship* (Hart 2015).

Moreno-Lax, V., *Accessing Asylum in Europe: Extraterritorial Border Controls and Refugee Rights under EU Law* (OUP 2017).

McCloskey, B., 'Third-Country Refugees: the Dublin Regulation/Article 8 ECHR Interface and Judicial Remedies' (2017) 29(4) *International Journal of Refugee Law* 641.

Moyn, S., 'Human Rights Are Superficial' (*Humanity Journal*, 10 June 2014) available online at: http://humanityjournal.org/blog/human-rights-are-superficial/ (accessed 12 July 2018).

Murray, C., 'Monstering Strasbourg over Prisoner Voting Rights' in M. Farrell, E. Drywood and E. Hughes (eds), *Human Rights in the Media: Fear and Fetish* (Routledge 2019).

National Union on Journalists, *Fair Play: Refugees and Asylum Seekers in Scotland: A Guide for Journalists* (Oxfam revised 2007).

Ofcom, 'News Consumption in the UK: 2016' (29 June 2017) available online at: www.ofcom.org.uk/__data/assets/pdf_file/0016/103570/news-consumption-uk-2016.pdf (accessed 12 July 2018).

Philo, G., E. Briant and P. Donald, *Bad News for Refugees* (Pluto Press 2013).

Pedersen, O. and C. Murray 'Examining Critical Perspectives on Human Rights: An Introduction' in R. Dickson *et al.* (eds), *Examining Critical Perspectives on Human Rights* (CUP 2016).

Pliatzky, L., 'Quangos and Agencies' (1992) 70 *Public Administration* 555.

Reynolds, S., 'It's Not Me, It's You: Examining the Print Media's Approach to 'Europe' in Brexit Britain' in M. Farrell, E. Drywood and E. Hughes (eds), *Human Rights in the Media: Fear and Fetish* (Routledge 2019).

Ron, J., D. Crow and S. Golden, 'The Struggle for a Truly Grassroots Human Rights Movement' (*Open Global Rights*, 18 June 2013) available online at: www.openglobalrights.org/struggle-for-truly-grassroots-human-rights-move/ (accessed 12 July 2018).

Royston, T. and C. O'Brien, 'Court of Appeal Declares That Tribunals Must Apply Any Secondary Legislation That Breaches Human Rights' (2018) 25(2) *Journal of Social Welfare and Family Law* D49.

Schemer, C., 'The Influence of News Media on Stereotypic Attitudes towards Immigrants in a Political Campaign' (2012) 62(5) *Journal of Communication* 739–757.

Shulka, N. (ed), *The Good Immigrant* (Unbound 2016).

Stabac, Z., K. Thorbjørnsrud and A. Todal Jenssesn, 'News Consumption and Public Opposition to Immigration Across Countries' in T. Aalberg and J. Curran (eds), *How Media Inform Democracy: A Comparative Approach* (Routledge 2012) 176–188.

Threadgold, T., 'The Media and Migration in the United Kingdom, 1999 to 2009' (Migration Policy Institute 2009).

Walgrave, S. and K. de Swert, 'The making of the (issues of the) Vlaams Blok: the media and the success of the Belgian extreme-right party' (2004) 21(4) *Political Communication* 479–500.

Wodak, R., '"Us" and "them": inclusion and exclusion – discrimination via discourse' in G. Delanty, R. Wodak and P. Jones (eds), *Identity, Belonging and Migration* (Liverpool University Press 2008) 54–77.

6 Trial by media

The fair trial jurisprudence of the European Court of Human Rights in the UK press

*Yvonne McDermott**

Introduction

Article 6 of the European Convention of Human Rights, on the right to a fair trial, is the most heavily litigated provision before the European Court of Human Rights.[1] While only an estimated 1.8% of cases taken against the United Kingdom are successful, Article 6 violations comprise approximately 30% of those successful cases.[2] This chapter analyses print media coverage of Article 6 cases against the United Kingdom. It finds that, apart from a select handful of cases, this jurisprudence has been given surprisingly little media attention. The absence of media scrutiny, even in those cases where the European Court's ruling had the potential to bring about profound changes to longstanding criminal procedure and evidence rules in the United Kingdom, is notable.

This chapter also raises a distinct but related argument on media coverage of the European Court of Human Rights, which is that the fairness deficit in the Court's own procedures receives little or no media attention in the United Kingdom. This is particularly noteworthy in light of the less-justified criticisms frequently levelled against the Court in press coverage in the United Kingdom.

Media reportage of the UK's leading ECtHR fair trial cases

Claimants have taken cases against the United Kingdom on alleged breaches of their Article 6 rights to, *inter alia*, access to a lawyer, examine witnesses, the presumption of innocence, and equality of arms. A number of these cases have

* I would like to thank Md. Zubair Kasem Khan for research assistance on an earlier draft.

1 P Roberts, 'Does Article 6 of the European Convention on Human Rights Require Reasoned Verdicts in Criminal Trials?' (2011) 11 *Human Rights Law Review* 213, 214; Ryan Goss, *Criminal Fair Trial Rights* (Oxford: Hart, 2016).

2 A Donald, J Gordon, and P Leach, *The UK and the European Court of Human Rights*, Equality and Human Rights Commission, Research Report 83, 2012, available online at: www.equalityhumanrights.com/sites/default/files/83._european_court_of_human_rights.pdf, vii-viii.

reached the status of leading cases in the European Court's jurisprudence.[3] In preparing this chapter, a thorough search of UK news databases was carried out to determine the extent to which the UK print media reported on the key cases set out below, and whether any patterns in reporting could be identified.[4]

Presumption of innocence

The claimant in *Allen v. the United Kingdom*[5] was a mother who had been convicted of manslaughter for the death of her baby son in an alleged case of 'shaken baby syndrome'. On appeal, her conviction was quashed on the grounds that the medical evidence relied upon was unsafe.[6] By this time, Lorraine Allen had spent three years in prison. Her claim for compensation for this miscarriage of justice was denied, and she took her case to Strasbourg, claiming that the decision denying her compensation violated her right to the presumption of innocence.

Allen's claim came at an important time for the UK's criminal justice system in cases of miscarriages of justice – just two years before the Grand Chamber

3 Reasonable minds may differ on what constitutes a 'leading case'. For the purposes of this chapter, a case taken against the United Kingdom was classified as 'leading' if it (a) featured in the Council of Europe's, *Guide on Article 6: Right to a fair trial (criminal limb)*, 2014, available online at https://rm.coe.int/1680304c4e; (b) was discussed in the chapter on Article 6 in the leading textbook on the law of the European Convention on Human Rights (D Harris, M O'Boyle, E Bates, and C Buckley, *Harris, O'Boyle, and Warbrick Law of the European Convention on Human Rights* (3rd edn., Oxford: Oxford University Press, 2014), and (c) was heard before the Grand Chamber of the Court pursuant to Article 30 or 43 of the Convention. The only case discussed in this chapter that does not meet all three criteria is *Ibrahim and Others v. the United Kingdom*, as the Grand Chamber delivered its judgment in September 2016, the case did not, at the time of writing, yet feature in a great deal of formal guidance or academic commentary on Article 6. Nevertheless, for reasons that will become apparent, the decision is notable both in its content and in relation to the media attention it received, thus justifying its inclusion. Similarly, *Othman (Abu Qatada) v. the United Kingdom* was not a Grand Chamber decision, but was significant in both its development of the law and its coverage in the media, which necessitates its analysis.

4 To carry out this analysis, the *Nexis* (part of the *Lexis Nexis* database) was used. *Nexis* indexes all major newspapers from around the world. It also includes regional papers. To limit the search to UK media, 'UK publications' was selected from the drop-down menu on 'Sources'. Generally, no custom date range was selected, save in the cases where a search for stories from 'all available dates' revealed a large range of unrelated stories (e.g. where claimants had a common name, or, where they had gone on to feature extensively in the media for unrelated reasons) – where that was the case, a custom date of one month before and eleven months after the ECtHR judgment was chosen. Searches were carried out, first, on the full name of the claimant (or each claimant, where a case had more than one claimant); second, on the surname of the claimant with the connector 'w/p' (within the same paragraph as) 'Strasbourg', 'Europe', or 'European'. Where the above two searches did not give rise to more than 50 search results, a keyword search of relevant keywords (e.g. 'hearsay' for *Al-Khawaja and Tahery*) within the same paragraph as 'European' or 'Strasbourg' within a defined date range of a month before and two months after the date of the decision was undertaken, to ensure that no relevant stories had been missed.

5 *Allen v. the United Kingdom* (application no. 25424/09), 12 July 2013.

6 *R v. Harris* [2005] EWCA Crim 1980, 21 July 2005.

issued its judgment, the UK Supreme Court had, by the narrowest of majorities, held that wrongfully convicted persons did not need to prove their innocence to avail of compensation.[7] The Grand Chamber's decision was also significant in the development of the Court's case law on Article 6 insofar as it established the applicability of Article 6(2) of the Convention to post-conviction proceedings, where there is an established link between the concluded criminal proceedings and subsequent proceedings.[8] The Court ruled in favour of the UK, finding that the language used by the courts in assessing whether a miscarriage of justice had occurred did not suggest that Allen had been treated in a manner inconsistent with her innocence, nor that her acquittal had been undermined.[9]

One might expect that Lorraine Allen's case had all of the elements of a newsworthy story – a mother, falsely accused of killing her child and imprisoned for three years before her conviction was overturned, seeks restitution for her wrongful conviction, only to be denied justice at every turn. The case also had the potential to impact upon domestic practice on compensation for those whose convictions had been overturned. Yet, only *The Guardian* reported on the potential impact of the case before Strasbourg issued its ruling.[10] After the judgment, the story was covered only by *The Guardian*,[11] *The Independent*,[12] and *The Sun*, which provided a brief (175-word) summary.[13]

The absence of media coverage of the *Allen* case is interesting. A cynical view might be that the intense media scrutiny arises only on cases where the United Kingdom has lost, and that a case like this, where the claimant was unsuccessful, is of lesser interest to news outlets. On the other hand, one could imagine how the story could have been told as being one where a deserving claimant was unsuccessful, compared to successful claimants like *Abu Qatada* (who had been deported to Jordan a week before the *Allen* ruling, to much fanfare).[14] For reasons known only to the media outlets themselves, that angle was not taken.

It could be that the *Allen* case received less coverage than one might expect because, three days before the Grand Chamber's ruling in the case, the United

7 *R (Adams) v. Secretary of State for Justice; In Re MacDermott and McCartney* [2011] UKSC 18, 11 May 2011.
8 *Allen*, n 5, para. 104.
9 *Allen*, n 5, para. 134.
10 J Robins, 'Guilt, non-guilt and innocence: what will Strasbourg decide?', *The Guardian*, 21 November 2012. The case was also reported by *BBC Derby*, Allen's local BBC station, as 'Lorraine Allen compensation battle heads to Europe' on 14 November 2012.
11 O Bowcott, 'Freed woman loses compensation fight', *The Guardian*, 13 July 2013.
12 'Lorraine Allen: Mother wrongly jailed for killing son in 'shaken baby' case loses Human Rights compensation bid', *The Independent,* 12 July 2013.
13 'Mum's failed compo bid', *Sunday Sun*, 14 July 2013. The case was also reported on again by BBC Derby ('Wrongly jailed mum Lorraine Allen loses compensation bid', 12 July 2013) and in *The Times Law Reports:* 'Presumption of innocence intact', *The Times*, 30 July 2013.
14 E.g. 'Britain finally deports Abu Qatada to Jordan after decade long saga', *The Telegraph*, 7 July 2013; James Slack, 'Qatada 'to be booted out by Sunday': At last! Britain deals with hate preacher as farcical bid to deport him finally nears its conclusion', *Daily Mail*, 2 July 2013.

Kingdom had lost a highly newsworthy case on whole life sentences.[15] In *Vinter, Bamber and Moore v. the United Kingdom*, the Strasbourg court ruled that mandatory life sentences with no possibility of parole were a breach of Article 3 of the Convention.[16] Perhaps unsurprisingly, the majority of press media in the UK reacted with outrage at this ruling, telling readers that the decision by 'meddling European judges'[17] put the 'government on a collision course with Strasbourg'.[18] The comments of Conservative MP Priti Patel, that 'it is a disgrace that Europe can over-rule the decisions made by courts in this country', were widely reported.[19] It could be surmised that the judgment in *Allen* did not fit neatly with this narrative, and this may explain in part why the case received hardly any coverage. The *Vinter, Bamber and Moore* story continued to run after the judgment was handed down on 9 July 2013, perhaps eclipsing the *Allen* judgment on 12 July 2013.[20]

Disclosure/equality of arms

A handful of Grand Chamber decisions relating to the UK have considered the prosecution's failure to disclose relevant material to the defence. The materiality of the evidence to the case appears to be the most significant factor in determining whether non-disclosure will be found to have breached Article 6. For example, no breach was found in *Jasper v. the United Kingdom*, where the undisclosed material played no part in the prosecution's case.[21] On the other hand, the claimants were successful in the case of *Rowe and Davis*, where the prosecution failed to inform the trial judge that a key witness was a paid informer.[22]

The ECtHR's judgments in *Jasper* and *Rowe and Davis* were both handed down in 2000. The decision in *Jasper* was only reported in a *Times Law Report*

15 *Vinter and ors v. the United Kingdom* (application nos. 66069/09 and 130/10 and 3896/10), 9 July 2013.

16 *Ibid.*, para. 30.

17 J Doyle, J Slack and J Tozer, 'What about the victims' rights? Meddling European judges rule that even Britain's most evil killers have human right to seek freedom', *Daily Mail*, 9 July 2013.

18 M Chorley, 'Dozens of Britain's worst killers set to launch bids for freedom after European Court of Human Rights rules we DON'T have the right lock them up for life', *Daily Mail*, 9 July 2013

19 *Ibid.*; T McTague, 'UK's most notorious murderers given chance of freedom after "whole life" sentences ruled against human rights', *The Mirror*, 9 July 2013.

20 Some later stories included: J Young, 'Let's have a UK Bill of Rights to replace crazy European laws', *Express Online*, 14 July 2013; P Murray, 'Instead of freeing them, make their time tougher', *Scottish Express*, 14 July 2013; D Lawson, 'Yes, Bamber can be rehabilitated. But he must stay inside', *Sunday Times*, 14 July 2013; 'What about the rights of those they murdered?', *The Daily Telegraph*, 11 July 2013; J Armstrong, 'These people should be hanged, not freed: Murder Victims' Relatives Slam Euro Ruling on Lifers', *Daily Mirror*, 11 July 2013.

21 *Jasper v. the United Kingdom* (application no. 27052/95), 16 February 2000.

22 *Rowe and Davis v. the United Kingdom* (application no. 28901/95), 16 February 2000.

on the European Court's decision, and one story from *The Express* on both the *Jasper* and *Rowe and Davis* cases, which warned that 'Britain could be forced to change the way crucial facts are kept hidden during criminal court cases because of fears that secrecy is leading to grave miscarriages of justice.'[23] The tone of the piece does not seem critical of the European Court, nor is there any suggestion of (as we have seen in the reportage on later cases) Strasbourg judges 'overruling' British judges or courts. As with the *Allen* case, discussed above, we might wonder whether the lack of coverage of *Jasper* is in some way related to the fact that the claimant was unsuccessful.

The *Rowe and Davis* ECtHR decision received somewhat more media attention, possibly because their appeal before the Court of Appeal was pending at the time of the Strasbourg judgment in their case. It is also clear from the range of media stories at the time that momentum was building towards the belief that the applicants had been wrongly convicted. Rowe and Davis were two of the so-called 'M25 Three', convicted in 1990 of a series of brutal robberies and a murder that took place on a single night. Victims had testified that the gang was comprised of two white men and one black man, but all three convicted men were black.[24] The key witness was a suspect who testified on the promise that he would not be prosecuted for his own involvement in the crimes, and had received a £10,300 reward for testifying.[25] In February 2000, the ECtHR had held that their rights had been violated by the failure to disclose this fact to the trial judge.[26] In July 2000, the Court of Appeal ruled that their conviction was unsafe and freed the three men.[27]

Rowe and Davis v. the United Kingdom was covered – albeit briefly in some instances – by most of the major news outlets.[28] The *Daily Mail*, in a 92-word section, noted the success of the claim and that the judgment was likely to have a bearing on the upcoming appeal.[29] Similar-length pieces featured in *The Sun*,[30] *Evening Standard*,[31] and *The Mirror*,[32] with more detailed stories in

23 D Taylor, 'Don't be so secret, M'Lud', *The Express*, 21 October 1999.
24 R Verkaik, 'European judges say "M25 Gang" denied a fair trial', *The Independent*, 17 February 2000.
25 C Dyer, 'European court says M25 pair denied fair trial', *The Guardian*, 17 February 2000.
26 *Rowe and Davis*, n 22.
27 *R v. Davis and Others* [2000] EWCA Crim 109, 17 July 2000.
28 As Raphael Rowe is now a successful journalist, a search of his name gave rise to over 300 results. Results were thus limited to the year 2000, which revealed 50 results, of which many were coverage of the Court of Appeal's overturning of his conviction in July 2000. There were ten stories featuring either claimant's name from January to May 2000, which included a Times Law Report and a letter from Rowe himself to *The Guardian*, sent from prison.
29 'European court rules for "M25 Three"', *Daily Mail*, 17 February 2000.
30 'Court backs "M25 Three"', *The Sun*, 17 February 2000.
31 J Sturgis, 'M25 "killers" denied a fair trial, Euro court rules', *Evening Standard*, 16 February 2000.
32 S Greenhill, 'Court victory for M25 Trio', *The Mirror*, 17 February 2000.

The Independent[33] and *The Guardian*.[34] None of these articles criticized the European Court for siding with (at that time) convicted criminals or for overstepping its authority – indeed, a sympathetic view of the claimants' wrongful conviction case is apparent, even before the Court of Appeal's ruling on the matter.

Like *Rowe and Davis*, a breach of Article 6 was also found in *Edwards and Lewis v. the United Kingdom*, where evidence of entrapment, which would have led to the collapse of the trial, was withheld from both defendants, who were convicted of possessing drugs and counterfeit currency respectively, at trial.[35] This case was clearly of great significance to policing in the UK, insofar as it had the potential to impact upon the use of undercover police officers as *agents provocateurs*. It was also notable as a case where claimants with less-than-wholesome professional activities successfully secured compensation from Strasbourg. It is quite remarkable that the case received next to no media coverage, aside from a mention in the *Times Law Reports*.[36] This seems to go against the theory, expressed above in relation to *Allen* and *Jasper*, that cases where the UK has lost attract greater media coverage. One might imagine that these individuals' successful claims would have been rather more newsworthy, but it is difficult to say with certainty why the story was not picked up by the UK media. It might be that other events, such as the US presidential election that was ongoing at the time,[37] called for more column inches than the reporting of this case from the European Court of Human Rights.

Unavailable witnesses and hearsay

The case of *Al-Khawaja and Tahery v. the United Kingdom* has undoubtedly been one of the most notable ECtHR fair trial cases against the UK, and it has been scrutinised extensively in the academic literature.[38] Al-Khawaja was a doctor convicted of the sexual assault of two patients, one of whom testified in his

33 R Verkaik, 'European judges say "M25 Gang" denied a fair trial', *The Independent*, 17 February 2000.

34 C Dyer, 'European court says M25 pair denied fair trial', *The Guardian*, 17 February 2000.

35 *Edwards and Lewis v. the United Kingdom* (application nos. 39647/98 and 40461/98), 27 October 2004.

36 'Non-disclosure of evidence made trial unfair', 3 November 2004. A thorough search on *Nexis* of the defendants' names, keywords from the case, and time-limited search on their surnames and the words 'European' or 'Strasbourg' from 2004 revealed no further results, apart from a *Bristol Post* story on Martin John Edwards' original conviction.

37 George W. Bush defeated John Kerry in the election, held on 2 November 2004.

38 M Redmayne, 'Hearsay and Human Rights: Al-Khawaja in the Grand Chamber' (2012) 75 *Modern Law Review* 865; C Gearty, 'Al-Khawaja and Tahery v United Kingdom', *UK Constitutional Law Association*, 9 January 2012, available online at https://ukconstitutionallaw.org/2012/01/09/conor-gearty-al-khawaja-and-tahery-v-united-kingdom/; Marny Requa, 'Absent witnesses and the UK Supreme Court: judicial deference as judicial dialogue?' (2010) 14 *The International Journal of Evidence & Proof* 208; Laura Hoyano, 'What is balanced on the scales of justice? In search of the essence of the right to a fair trial' (2014) 1 *Criminal Law Review* 4.

trial. The other patient had committed suicide after making her statement to the police. This statement was admitted as evidence in the trial, with a warning to the jury that they should treat her evidence with caution, in light of the fact that she had not testified in court or been cross-examined. Two of the deceased victim's friends also testified as to what she had told them of the incident before her suicide. Al-Khawaja was convicted on the basis of this evidence, and the Court of Appeal denied his appeal.[39]

Tahery was alleged to have stabbed a victim during a gang fight. A key eyewitnesses refused to give testimony in court because he claimed to be too scared to do so. Instead, his written statement was read out, with a warning given to the jury similar to the warning given to the jury in *Al-Khawaja*. On the basis of this evidence, Tahery was convicted of wounding with intent, and the Court of Appeal denied leave to appeal.[40]

As both cases considered issues of hearsay and unavailable witnesses, the *Al-Khawaja* and *Tahery* complaints were joined as a single case in Strasbourg. In January 2009, the ECtHR found a breach of Article 6, insofar as the convictions were based 'solely or to a decisive extent' on the testimony of witnesses whom the accused had not been given the opportunity to examine.[41]

Al-Khawaja and Tahery had the potential to bring about significant changes to the rules of evidence in England and Wales, in particular the long-standing principles on the admissibility of hearsay evidence and the significance of jury cautions. Remarkably, however, the ECtHR's 2009 judgment received relatively little attention, compared to other cases such as *Abu Qatada*[42] and *Vinter, Bamber and Moore*.[43] Only *The Mirror* covered the decision, while it seemed to slip under the radar of other publications.[44] Sue Carroll described the decision, which awarded Al-Khawaja £5,000 compensation, as a 'slap in the face' for 'British justice'.[45] Carroll criticized 'the unelected judges in Strasbourg' who 'ignored' the fact that one of the victims was deceased and could not have been cross-examined;[46] of course, this aspect of the case was in fact at the heart of the Court's ruling, and was discussed at length in the 2009 decision.[47] This clear misrepresentation of the ECtHR's ruling is interesting; it could be attributed to the complexity of the issue (and perhaps the author's reliance on a summary or press release from the Court, rather than reading the judgment itself), or to an

39 *R v. Al-Khawaja* [2005] EWCA Crim 2697, 3 November 2005.

40 *R v Tahery* [2006] EWCA Crim 529.

41 *Al-Khawaja and Tahery v. the United Kingdom* (application nos. 26766/05 and 22228/06), 20 January 2009.

42 See below, 167.

43 See above, 160.

44 E Stretch, 'Doc's blood money', *The Mirror*, 10 February 2009; S Carroll, 'When rights are wrong', *The Mirror*, 10 February 2009.

45 S Carroll, 'When rights are wrong', *The Mirror*, 10 February 2009.

46 *Ibid.*

47 *Al-Khawaja and Tahery*, n 41.

editorial line that better fitted this depiction of the judgment than the judgment's rather complex reality. Also interesting is *The Mirror*'s clear incensement at the compensation received by Al-Khawaja, but not by Tahery in the same case. There is no clear explanation for this difference in treatment.

Despite its lack of coverage in the media, it is fair to say that the ECtHR's decision in *Al-Khawaja and Tahery* caused quite some consternation in legal circles. Lord Hoffmann, in a public lecture delivered in March 2009, deemed it 'quite extraordinary that on a question which had received so much consideration in the Law Commission and Parliament, the Strasbourg court should have taken it upon themselves to say that they [the Law Commission and Parliament] were wrong.'[48] The UK Supreme Court agreed; when a case with similar facts, *R v. Horncastle*, came before it in December 2009, the Court declined to follow Strasbourg's 'solely or to a decisive extent' test.[49] It found that:

> There will … be rare occasions where this court has concerns as to whether a decision of the Strasbourg Court sufficiently appreciates or accommodates particular aspects of our domestic process. In such circumstances it is open to this court to decline to follow the Strasbourg decision, giving reasons for adopting this course.[50]

Horncastle had the potential to lead to something of a quagmire, by allowing the Supreme Court to cherry pick which ECtHR decisions it wished to comply with and which decisions it saw fit to disregard on the grounds of a difference of opinion, and this in turn raised concerns about legal certainty. Legally, the dictum in *Horncastle* was correct; UK courts are merely required to 'take into account' Strasbourg jurisprudence. However, in practice before then, the courts had shown a great deference to principles established in ECtHR jurisprudence.

As it happened, the Grand Chamber later diluted the importance of the 'sole or decisive' rule in its decision on *Al-Khawaja and Tahery*.[51] It found that even where a statement is the sole or decisive evidence against a defendant, its admission would not be fatal to Article 6.[52] Instead, this was an important factor that would have to be weighed up and assessed against other factors, such as the existence of procedural safeguards to protect the rights of the accused.[53] In the light of sufficient counterbalancing factors in Al-Khawaja's case,[54] which were absent

48 Lord Hoffmann, 'The Universality of Human Rights', Judicial Studies Board Annual Lecture 19 March 2009, 19.

49 *R v. Horncastle and ors*, [2009] UKSC 14, 9 December 2009.

50 *Ibid.*, para. 11.

51 *Al-Khawaja and Tahery v. the United Kingdom* (application nos. 26766/05 and 22228/06), 15 December 2011.

52 *Ibid.*, para. 147.

53 *Ibid.*

54 Although these have been criticized, given that the existence of more evidence against the accused was included as a 'counterbalancing factor' – see, e.g. Hoyano, n 38.

in Tahery's case, the Grand Chamber upheld the finding of a violation against Tahery but found no violation of Article 6 in relation to Al-Khawaja.[55]

In spite of the initial lack of coverage of the ECtHR's 2009 ruling in *Al-Khawaja*, coverage of the story began to gain momentum with the Supreme Court's decision in *Horncastle* and judges' public criticisms of the case. In February 2011 – more than two years after the Strasbourg judgment – *The Times* reported that the Lord Chief Justice and several Supreme Court judges had publicly criticized the decision.[56] Jon Ungoed-Thomas, writing for the *Sunday Times*, took a much stronger line, reporting it as 'The European court creeping into every area of our lives; Strasbourg's judges are making federal law that undermines British courts and aids criminals'.[57] Ungoed-Thomas noted the Supreme Court's ruling in *Horncastle*, as well as the Law Lords' public criticisms, before incorporating criticism of unrelated cases, such as *Lautsi v Italy*, the ECtHR's controversial decision on the display of crucifixes in Italian schools.[58] As the Grand Chamber's decision approached in late 2011, its potential implications were noted in *The Guardian*,[59] *Daily Mail*,[60] and *The Daily Telegraph*.[61]

As noted above, the Grand Chamber ultimately held that Tahery's rights had been breached but Al-Khawaja's had not, and it found that convictions based solely or to a decisive extent on hearsay evidence would not always be a breach of Article 6. The media could have taken one of two possible angles on the Grand Chamber's decision. The first would have been to report that the ECtHR had backed down, following criticism from the UK government and the Supreme Court, and nuanced its understanding of English criminal procedure. The second possible angle could have emphasized that Ali Tahery, an Iranian national convicted of stabbing another person, was awarded £15,000 compensation for a breach of his rights.[62]

---

55 *Al-Khawaja and Tahery*, n 51.

56 F Gibb, 'Judges warn of new clash with Europe over human rights; Ministers fight ruling against hearsay evidence', *The Times*, 22 February 2011.

57 Jon Ungoed-Thomas, 'The European court creeping into every area of our lives; Strasbourg's judges are making federal law that undermines British courts and aids criminals', *Sunday Times*, 13 February 2011.

58 *Lautsi v. Italy* (application no. 30814/06), 18 March 2011.

59 J Rozenberg, 'Strasbourg's ruling on hearsay evidence could change its relationship with UK', *The Guardian*, 12 December 2011.

60 S Doughty, 'British judges could be told to ignore our laws', *Daily Mail*, 16 November 2011 (discussing the Lord Chief Justice's remarks to the Parliamentary Joint Committee on Human Rights).

61 M Riddell, 'The battle between Parliament and the judges has only just begun; The conflict over human rights will test our constitution to breaking point', *The Daily Telegraph*, 31 May 2011 (discussing both decisions handed down by 'barmy judges' in the UK on the basis of human rights, and the upcoming Grand Chamber decision in *Al-Khawaja and Tahery*, where 'Strasbourg is likely to stand firm, thus unleashing the wrath of British judges')

62 Tahery's conviction was later overturned in the Court of Appeal: *R v. Tahery* [2013] EWCA Crim 1053.

It is notable that only the *Daily Mail*, *Guardian*, *Times*, *Telegraph* and *Independent* actually reported on the Grand Chamber judgment, with the majority taking the first angle on the story, noting the UK's triumph in Strasbourg and that the ECtHR had heeded objections from British judges.[63] Only *The Telegraph* took the second approach, with its headline 'Gangster wins human rights pay out but UK still scores victory'.[64] Coverage in the *Daily Mail*, given its usual vociferous standpoint on the ECtHR, was notably muted. *MailOnline* reported that 'European human rights judges yesterday backed down in the face of protests from Britain by ruling hearsay evidence can be allowed in criminal trials', but noted, 'The judgment had a sting in the tail, however – with the court ruling an Iranian guilty of a knife attack who was convicted using hearsay evidence must be paid £15,000 in costs and compensation.'[65] By the time the print version of the story was released, the judgment was reframed as a 'rare victory' for the United Kingdom, but mention of Tahery's compensation was no longer a 'sting in the tail'; instead, the decision was reported as follows:

> An earlier judgment by Europe in the same two cases ruled that convictions based on statements from absent witnesses who could not be cross-examined were a breach of human rights law.
>
> But the Grand Chamber said each case should be considered on its merits. As a result, there will now be no blanket ban on the use of hearsay evidence, defined as 'a statement not made in oral evidence'.
>
> The judges then ruled that the conviction of a London-based Iranian for a knife attack did breach his human rights, and ordered him to be paid £15,000 in costs and compensation. But they decided that the conviction of Imad Al-Khawaja, a consultant at Brighton General Hospital, for indecently assaulting two women patients was fair.[66]

The absence of attention given to this decision was notable, particularly in light of the fact that, despite Strasbourg's retreat from its previous position, Tahery was still awarded compensation. In addition, given the coverage in the lead-up to the Grand Chamber's decision, and the reportage on domestic judges' criticisms of the ECtHR's 2009 judgment, the silence by the same news outlets when that

63 O Bowcott, 'Europe backs UK's use of hearsay evidence in court: Ruling avoids clash with Britain's top judges', *The Guardian*, 15 December 2011; Joshua Rozenberg, 'At last, Strasbourg heeds our Supreme Court', *The Guardian*, 15 December 2011; Lewis Smith, 'Hearsay is not a breach of human rights says EU (sic)', *The Independent*, 15 December 2011; Frances Gibb, 'British courts triumph in battle with Europe', *The Times*, 15 December 2011; James Slack, 'UK wins in European human rights court', *Daily Mail*, 16 December 2011.

64 T Whitehead, 'Gangster wins human rights pay out but UK still scores victory', *The Telegraph*, 15 December 2011.

65 J Slack, 'UK WINS in European human rights court as judge rules hearsay evidence can be used in criminal trials', *MailOnline*, 15 December 2011, available online at www.dailymail.co.uk/news/article-2074781/UK-WINS-European-human-rights-court-judge-rules-hearsay-evidence-used-criminal-trials.html

66 J Slack, 'UK wins in European human rights court', *Daily Mail*, 16 December 2011.

judgment was partially overturned is remarkable. It is safe to assume that the decision would have received a lot more coverage had the Court ruled against the United Kingdom again.

Extradition to face an unfair trial

In the well-known case of *Soering v. the United Kingdom*, which concerned a breach of Article 3 of the ECHR, the Court noted that a case could arise in relation to 'an extradition decision in circumstances where the fugitive has suffered or risks suffering a flagrant denial of a fair trial in the requesting country'.[67] Despite allegations of extradition to face an unfair trial arising under Article 6 in the intervening two decades,[68] the first case where extradition was found to give rise to a violation of Article 6 was *Othman (Abu Qatada) v. the United Kingdom* in 2012.[69] Abu Qatada, a radical preacher who had gained some notoriety in the UK, was sought by Jordan to face a retrial for terrorist offences. The ECtHR found that there was a real risk of the use of evidence obtained by torture being used in the Jordanian case, and that, therefore, unless assurances could be obtained from Jordan that the torture evidence would not be used, deportation would give rise to a breach of Article 6.[70] Ultimately, the United Kingdom and Jordan signed a memorandum of understanding confirming that torture evidence would not be used,[71] and Abu Qatada was extradited in 2013.[72] He was acquitted by a Jordanian court in 2014.[73]

Observers of media coverage of the ECtHR will be unsurprised to learn that the decision in *Abu Qatada* received a great deal more coverage than any of the other aforementioned fair trial cases. A search of 'Abu Qatada' and 'European Court', limited to just UK news sources, revealed more than Nexis's limit of 3000 results. 'Abu Qatada' and 'Strasbourg' gave rise to over 2000 UK news stories. The vast majority of these stories were critical of the ECtHR's ruling – even those news outlets that are typically defensive of the Court took a critical view. For example, Simon Jenkins, writing for *The Guardian*, argued that '[t]he fair trial article is so vague it could plausibly be invoked against any justice system. The EC[t]HR is bogged down in empire-building and is a mess.'[74]

In comparison to other notable cases, such as *Al-Khawaja and Tahery*, the explosion of media interest in the ECtHR's ruling in *Abu Qatada* is quite striking.

67 *Soering v. the United Kingdom* (application no. 14038/88), 7 July 1989, para. 113.

68 *Mamatkulov and Askarov v. Turkey* (application nos. 46827/99 and 46951/99), 31 March 2009, paras. 90–91; *Al-Saadoon and Mufdhi v. the United Kingdom* (application no. 61498/08), 2 March 2010, para. 149; *Ahorugeze v. Sweden* (application no. 37075/09), 27 October 2011, para. 115

69 *Othman (Abu Qatada) v. the United Kingdom* (application no. 8139/09), 17 January 2012.

70 *Ibid.*

71 'Abu Qatada case: UK agrees assistance treaty with Jordan', *BBC News*, 24 April 2013.

72 'Abu Qatada deported from UK to stand trial in Jordan', *BBC News*, 7 July 2013.

73 'Abu Qatada cleared of terror charges', *BBC News*, 24 September 2014.

74 S Jenkins, 'Deport Abu Qatada: or if not, give him the law's full protection', *The Guardian*, 7 February 2012.

It could be linked to the fact that Abu Qatada already had a public reputation as a hate preacher before he took his case to Strasbourg, and there was clearly a groundswell of public opinion in favour of his deportation. Another factor in the widespread reporting of this case may be that the facts were easier to understand and convey to the public than the rather complex issues of evidence law arising in *Al-Khawaja and Tahery*. Lastly, the UK's defeat, and the much-publicised insistence of the then-Home Secretary, Theresa May, that he should be deported as a matter of urgency,[75] surely added to the newsworthiness of the case.

Freedom from self-incrimination and the right to legal advice

In 1996, the Grand Chamber of the ECtHR handed down its decision in *Saunders v. the United Kingdom.*[76] The applicant, a former chief executive at the Guinness company, complained that statements made by him under compulsion to Government inspectors appointed under the Companies Acts were later used against him in his criminal trial for conspiracy, false accounting and theft, of which he was convicted.[77] The Grand Chamber found a violation, dismissing the Government's argument that the complexity of fraud cases and the public interest in trying such cases could justify a departure from established due process principles.[78]

By contrast to the huge number of results for other cases discussed above, a search for 'Ernest Saunders' and 'Strasbourg' gave rise to just 50 results, some of which related to a later successful ECtHR case taken by Gerald Ronson, Jack Lyons and Anthony Parnes, who had also worked as executives in Guinness with Saunders and were convicted in similar circumstances. The *Saunders* case occasionally pops up in later articles as an example of purportedly ridiculous ECtHR decisions, such as an article by retired High Court judge Oliver Popplewell for *The Sunday Times*, entitled 'You can have too many human rights', which reported the decision thus:

> In the Guinness trial, Ernest Saunders was charged with dishonesty. He was required to give evidence at a Department of Trade inquiry. This he did. When he was subsequently tried by a jury and convicted of dishonesty, he rushed off to Strasbourg and claimed that it was unfair that the evidence, which he had given on his oath at the inquiry, should have been put before the jury. The European court had no difficulty in deciding that it was unfair for that to happen. Strasbourg, with its different procedures and different standards of justice, is a pretty poor venue for the final resolution of cases under the Human Rights Act.[79]

75 '"Unacceptable" UK can't deport Abu Qatada – Theresa May', *BBC News*, 7 February 2012.
76 *Saunders v. the United Kingdom* (application no. 19187/91), 17 December 1996.
77 *Ibid.*, paras. 18; 33–34; 57.
78 *Ibid.*, para. 74
79 Oliver Popplewell, 'You can have too many human rights', *Sunday Times*, 29 August 2004.

Thus, we can see *Saunders* as an early source for the media's derision of Strasbourg's case law on Article 6. The above article bears many of the hallmarks of later reporting on successful cases against the UK in the ECtHR: a less-than-accurate statement of the law (the ECtHR is not a 'venue for the final resolution of cases under the [UK's] Human Rights Act'), and an apparent disbelief that the European Court should find in favour of a high-profile convicted person.

Another 1996 decision on the right to freedom from self-incrimination was *Murray v. the United Kingdom*, which concerned a suspected IRA terrorist who was denied access to a lawyer and refused to answer questions in the police station or on trial. Adverse inferences were drawn from his silence and he was convicted.[80] The Strasbourg court held that it was not unfair to draw adverse inferences from silence,[81] but that the claimant's rights had been violated when he was denied access to a lawyer.[82]

In advance of the ECtHR's 1995 judgment in *Murray*, *The Guardian* and *The Times* featured lengthy pieces on the consequences that the case would have for the right to silence in England and Wales.[83] Perhaps surprisingly, the Grand Chamber's later judgment in 1996, finding that John Murray had suffered a breach of his right to access to a lawyer, received much less attention from these same sources.[84]

The Mirror and *The Evening Standard* wrote short pieces criticizing the Grand Chamber's judgment,[85] with the latter describing the decision as causing 'fresh embarrassment [to the UK government] at the hands of European judges'.[86] While the ECtHR declined to award Murray compensation, opting instead to award him £15,000 for costs alone,[87] this fact was somewhat obscured in the media coverage of the case. *The Times* reported the story under the headline 'Republican wins £15,000 from human rights court',[88] relegating mention of Murray's rejected claim for compensation to halfway down the article, while the *Mirror's* headline was, 'IRA case man wins £15,000'.[89] By contrast, *The Independent* lead

80 *Murray v. the United Kingdom* (application no. 18731/91), 8 February 1996.
81 *Ibid.*, para. 57.
82 *Ibid.*, para. 70.
83 E Rees, 'Guilt by Inference: Ending the right to silence means a major tilt in the scales of justice', *The Guardian*, 11 April 1995; G Slapper, 'Silence rebuke could cause louder outcry', *The Times*, 20 June 1995.
84 No report from *The Guardian* could be found on *Nexis*, while *The Times* reported it in a short (526-word) piece: R Ford, 'Republican wins £15,000 from human rights court', *The Times*, 9 February 1996.
85 'IRA case man wins £15,000', *Daily Mirror*, 9 February 1996; David Shaw, 'New Euro blow on IRA "human rights"', *Evening Standard*, 8 February 1996.
86 *Ibid.*
87 *Murray v. the United Kingdom*, n 80.
88 R Ford, 'Republican wins £15,000 from human rights court', *The Times*, 9 February 1996
89 'IRA case man wins £15,000', *Daily Mirror*, 9 February 1996.

with 'EU (sic) court deals new blow on terror case', and noted in the second paragraph that:

> The court in Strasbourg denied John Murray – convicted of an IRA kidnapping five years ago – any compensation, but ordered that the Government pays pounds 15,000 of his legal costs. It will now have to amend its legislation, which in Northern Ireland enables terrorist suspects to be interviewed by police for 48 hours without access to lawyers.[90]

The *Daily Mail* did not report the case at the time of the Grand Chamber's ruling, but in 1998, when legislative changes were made to ensure that adverse inferences could only be drawn from an accused's silence when his or her lawyer was present during questioning, the paper was scathing.[91] It reported that 'Europe has forced Britain to retreat on tough laws limiting a criminal's right to silence' and that the change 'underlines the growing superiority of European law over Westminster'.[92]

The *Murray* judgment signalled the start of a series of highly publicized and criticized ECtHR decisions involving breaches of the right to a fair trial where the claimant was a terrorist or suspected terrorist. The narrative of out-of-touch 'EU' judges granting compensation to evil wrongdoers and overriding the will of Parliament is a familiar one, which arises in later cases. Nevertheless, the case clearly received much less coverage than contemporary cases involving terrorist suspects or convicts, including *Abu Qatada* (discussed above) and, more recently, the case of *Ibrahim and others v. the United Kingdom*.[93]

In its decision in *Ibrahim and others*, handed down in 2016, the Grand Chamber dismissed the claims of three of the four applicants, who were suspects in the London bombing attacks of July 2005.[94] The Grand Chamber found that there had been compelling and urgent reasons to temporarily deny the three access to a lawyer in police custody.[95] The case of the fourth applicant, Ismail Abdurahman, was somewhat different, in that he had initially been called in for questioning as a witness, but it later became apparent that he had assisted one of the bombers. The Court found that at this point, he should have been cautioned and offered legal advice.[96] Instead, the police continued to question him, and he was later charged with, and subsequently convicted of, assisting the

---

90 H Mills, 'EU court deals new blow on terror case', *The Independent*, 9 February 1996.

91 S Doughty, 'Judges force retreat over right to silence', *Daily Mail*, 2 December 1998.

92 *Ibid.*

93 *Ibrahim and others v. the United Kingdom* (applications nos. 50541/08, 50571/08, 50573/08 and 40351/09), 13 September 2016.

94 *Ibid.*

95 *Ibid.*, paras. 275–279.

96 *Ibid.*, paras. 298–300.

bomber and failing to disclose information.[97] The Grand Chamber concluded that the overall fairness of proceedings under Article 6 had been jeopardized by the police's actions.[98]

While the Grand Chamber found that Abdurahman's Article 6 rights had been breached, it declined to award him compensation, and instead made an order solely for his legal fees.[99] This nuance in outcome appears to have been missed in media coverage of the case. *The Sun* ran with the headline, 'WHAT ABOUT OUR HUMAN RIGHTS? European court orders UK to pay convicted terrorist £13,000 over "human rights violations" ',[100] while *The Evening Standard*,[101] *Daily Mail*,[102] and *The Sun*[103] featured similar stories. Even *The Independent* and *The Guardian*, which have traditionally taken a less sensationalist view of ECtHR decisions, reported the costs awarded to Abdurahman in their headlines, relegating the defeat of his three co-applicants to further down in their articles.[104] Whether this reflects a broader change in approach by these outlets remains to be seen; what is undeniable is the increased news coverage of such cases, with 156 news stories revealed in a search of Ismail Abdurahman's name.

Making sense of UK print media's relative lack of reporting on the right to a fair trial

The above analysis showed a large amount of discrepancy between the amount of coverage given to fair trial cases against the UK in the European Court of Human Rights. Whilst some cases received a great deal of critique in the UK press, others were barely reported, or were reported relatively uncritically, despite their legal significance. In what Colm O'Cinneide has dubbed the 'war of examples' on human rights, where particular judgments are seized upon and critiqued

97 *Ibid.*, paras. 153–173.
98 *Ibid.*, para. 311.
99 *Ibrahim and others v. the United Kingdom*, n 93.
100 'WHAT ABOUT OUR HUMAN RIGHTS? European court orders UK to pay convicted terrorist £13,000 over "human rights violations" ', *The Sun*, 14 September 2016.
101 H Al-Othman, 'Government ordered to pay £13,000 to convicted terrorist in human rights ruling', *Evening Standard*, 14 September 2016.
102 I Drury, 'EU judges order UK to pay terrorist who helped the failed July 21 bombers £13,600 "because his human rights were breached" ', *Daily Mail*, 14 September 2016.
103 K Brady, 'European judges have told Britain to pay thousands of Pounds to a terrorist who helped the failed July 21 bombers - because, poor thing, his human rights were breached', *The Sun*, 18 September 2016.
104 L Dearden, 'European court orders UK to pay convicted terrorist £13,000 over 'human rights violations' following London plot; Ismail Abdurahman hid one of the men who attempted to bomb London on 21 July 2005', *The Independent*, 13 September 2016; Owen Bowcott, 'Failed London bombers' accomplice awarded €16,000 legal costs; European court of human rights rules Ismail Abdurahman's right to fair trial over his role in 21/7 failed attacks was violated', *The Guardian*, 13 September 2016.

without discussing the wider picture,[105] the choice of examples is unpredictable. However, a number of themes and trends can be identified in this reporting (or lack thereof).

First, whilst there is no definitive chronological pattern in how Article 6 cases have been reported, many of the key cases that were released after 2010 received more coverage than the earlier cases analysed above. In particular, the decisions in *Abu Qatada* (2012) and *Ibrahim* (2016) garnered significant media attention. However, *Allen* (2013) received limited media treatment, while some earlier cases, namely *Murray* (1996) were the subject of quite extensive reporting. As noted above, the European Court's judgment in *Allen* was issued at approximately the same time as its much-reported decision on whole life sentences, which seems to have eclipsed it. Whilst coverage of *Murray* was rather critical of Strasbourg's growing influence over the UK's criminal justice processes, it is a truism that the harshest and most extensive media critique generally attaches to later decisions, particularly *Abu Qatada*, and *Ibrahim*. Decisions issued in the intervening period tended to be sparsely reported, and the newspaper articles that were written about those decisions were generally uncritical of the ECtHR – we saw this theme emerge with the reporting of *Jasper* (2000); *Rowe and Davis* (2000), and *Edwards and Lewis* (2004). Whilst *Saunders* (1996) was not widely reported at the time of the judgment, it has been noted in later journalistic critique as an example of Strasbourg's folly.[106] The first *Al-Khawaja and Tahery* ECtHR decision was reported only in *The Mirror*, albeit with highly critical commentary on the Court's decision.[107]

A second theme emerging from the divergent reporting patterns is the significance of the claimant's background to the amount of attention their case will attract. As a general rule, where the papers (and perhaps by analogy, their readers) view claimants in an unsympathetic light, they can be expected to dedicate more column inches to reporting those cases. This is particularly true where the claimant is an alleged terrorist. This is a trend that began with the *Murray* case in the 1990s, and one that has gained much more momentum in the intervening years, as evidenced by coverage of the *Abu Qatada* and *Ibrahim and others* cases.[108] Much of the coverage of *Al-Khawaja and Tahery* focused on Al-Khawaja's convictions for sexually assaulting his patients; the media apparently viewed these crimes as more abhorrent than other crimes, such as Tahery's conviction for stabbing a person in a street fight, or the convictions of *Rowe and Davis* for murder, robberies, and assault. It is notable, however, that Tahery, Rowe and Davis subsequently had their convictions quashed by the Court of Appeal, and the papers may well have had their doubts as to the safety of those convictions at the time that all three successfully took their cases against the UK in Strasbourg.

105 C O'Cinnéide, Democracy, Rights, and the Constitution: New Directions in the Human Rights Era' (2004) 57 *Current Legal Problems* 175.

106 See above, n 79.

107 See above, n 45.

108 See above, 167.

A third theme to be adduced from the above is that cases where the claimant was unsuccessful were, generally speaking, less likely to receive media attention, regardless of their significance for either domestic or international human rights law. For example, the cases of *Allen* and *Jasper* received very little media coverage, where the UK successfully defended itself against both claims. It is impossible to say with any certainty that the cases might have received greater coverage had the claimants succeeded in their claims; indeed, a number of successful claims (such as *Edwards and Lewis*) received little or no media attention, despite the potential significance of those claims for how policing is carried out in the UK.

Perhaps the most surprising aspect of the above analysis was the comparative dearth of reports on the *Al-Khawaja and Tahery* case; it was only really when British judges began to publicly criticise the decision that the media recognised it as a viable story, and even then, coverage was quite limited. Perhaps terrorist suspects and convicts are seen as a more odious class of claimants for the UK media and public at large, but this does not explain the media storms surrounding such issues as prisoner voting[109] and whole-life sentences,[110] where the claimants were convicted of non-terror offences. It may be that fair trial cases are perceived as too complex for the public to understand, or that issues such as the hearsay rule and equality of arms are less exciting and more difficult to sensationalise than cases on prisoner voting and sentencing. Alternatively, it could be argued that some media outlets wish to portray the ECHR as a 'villains' charter'[111] that predominantly serves terrorists and not the general public, and that coverage of a wider range of fair trial cases would muddy the waters of that narrative.

The last theme that can be noted is that the UK media struggles to distinguish between the award of legal costs by the ECtHR and the award of compensation. In a number of cases discussed above, the European Court only awarded the successful claimants their legal costs, and declined to award additional compensation for the breach of their rights.[112] Nevertheless, these awards of costs were described in terms that suggested the claimants had been awarded compensation.[113] This failure to distinguish between the award of legal costs and compensation is not unique to press coverage of ECtHR case law; similar trends in

---

109 Searches of 'John Hirst' and 'voting' revealed 484 results on *Nexis*, while 'prisoner voting' and 'Strasbourg' gave rise to 411 hits. By comparison, 'hearsay' and 'Strasbourg' resulted in fewer than 50 hits on *Nexis*.

110 See above, 160.

111 A term used by Lieve Gies, 'A Villains' Charter? The Press and the Human Rights Act' (2011) 7(2) *Crime, Media, Culture* 167–183, in relation to the depiction of the UK Human Rights Act. See further, L Gies, 'Human Rights, the British Press and the Deserving Claimant', in K S Ziegler *et al.* (eds), *The UK and European Human Rights: A Strained Relationship?* (Oxford: Hart, 2015) 473.

112 E.g. *Murray v. the United Kingdom*, n 80; *Ibrahim and others v. the United Kingdom*, n 93.

113 See above, n 64; n 88–89; n 100–104.

reporting of legal aid as though it were money handed to criminals is common in relation to domestic criminal trials.[114]

The ECtHR's procedural deficit and the lack of media analysis thereof

Some of the more commonplace media criticisms of the European Court of Human Rights have been ably analysed and critiqued both in this volume,[115] and elsewhere in the academic literature. The Court is commonly criticised for being too activist, despite its fairly cautious approach in reality.[116] ECtHR judges are criticised for being 'unelected',[117] even though they are, in fact, elected.[118] The impression of claimants' high success rates has been grossly inflated,[119] and the facts behind some of the most widely reported cases reveal a more nuanced reality than the extreme picture painted in some newspaper articles.[120]

In the context of these less justified criticisms, a remarkable aspect of the media's treatment of the European Court of Human Rights has been the lack of focus on the Court's own procedures, and some of the more questionable aspects of procedure before the Court. For example, the length of time (over five years in some cases) that a case takes to get before the Court has been suggested to be in contravention of the right to a speedy trial.[121] This is due, in no small part, to the

114 As seen, for example, in the reports on the legal aid granted to the 'black cab rapist' John Worboys: James Mills, 'Rage at Rapist's Aid: Rape victims angered over 'unjust' legal aid bill for John Worboys', *The Sun*, 22 February 2018; Rory Tingle, 'Revealed: John Worboys has received £166,000 in legal aid since his arrest a decade ago but MoJ refuses to say how much black cab rapist's parole appeal has cost taxpayers', *Daily Mail*, 21 February 2018.

115 See further in this volume, C R G Murray, 'Monstering Strasbourg over Prisoner Voting Rights' Chapter 4 and D Mead, '"They offer you a feature on stockings and suspenders next to a call for stiffer penalties for sex offenders": Do we learn more about the media than about human rights from tabloid coverage of human rights stories?' Chapter 1.

116 See further, e.g., S Lambrecht, 'HRA Watch: Reform, Repeal, Replace? Criticism of the European Court of Human Rights: A UK Phenomenon?' *UK Constitutional Law Blog*, 27 July 2015; T Lock: 'HRA Watch: Reform, Repeal, Replace? Legal Implications of Human Rights Reform in the UK', *UK Constitutional Law Blog*, 15 May 2015; J Henley, 'Why is the European court of human rights hated by the UK right?', *The Guardian*, 22 December 2013.

117 E.g. J Chapman, 'Day we stood up to Europe: In an unprecedented move, MPs reject European court's ruling that prisoners must get the vote', *Daily Mail*, 11 February 2011 ('the time has come for Britain to tell unelected Strasbourg judges that they have overstepped their authority'); J Slack, 'Unelected euro judges are bringing terror to the streets of Britain', *Daily Mail*, 18 January 2012

118 Article 22, European Convention on Human Rights.

119 Donald *et al.*, n 2.

120 See, for example, in this volume, on immigration: E Drywood and H Gray, 'Demonising Immigrants: How a Human Rights Narrative Has Contributed to Negative Portrayals of Immigrants in the UK Media' Chapter 5.

121 I Cameron, 'The Court and the Member States: Procedural Aspects', in G Ulfstein *et al.* (eds), *Constituting Europe: The European Court of Human Rights in a National, European and Global Context* (Cambridge: Cambridge University Press, 2013), 25.

Court's ever-increasing caseload; its 2017 Annual Report noted that there were 26,000 outstanding cases, 6,000 of which were classified as 'non-repetitive priority cases'.[122] Yet, this fact is not mentioned amongst the above-mentioned media criticisms, which apparently prefer to paint the Court as a behemoth, stamping on the sovereignty of Member States with startling efficiency.

In an attempt to clear its backlog, the ECtHR introduced a new system of 'summary procedures' in 2015.[123] Ironically, as an institution that seeks to defend the right to a fair trial, the Court has found itself under fire from critics who believe that these expedited proceedings have jeopardised the right to a reasoned judgment before the Court itself.[124] Concerns have also been raised on judicial independence before the Court,[125] and on the lack of access to a lawyer for claimants before the Court.[126] Yet, these criticisms have received little or no media attention.[127]

Conclusion

This chapter analysed the manner in which key cases from the European Court of Human Rights on the right to a fair trial were reported in the British media. It found the level of such coverage to be mixed and rather unpredictable. Whilst one could almost guarantee that a terrorist suspect's successful claim against the UK under Article 6 of the Convention will be widely critiqued in the press, other cases that had the potential for more profound legal consequences often received little attention. This was particularly striking in examining the absence of coverage of *Al-Khawaja and Tahery*, arguably the most significant and widely discussed Article 6 case of the early twenty-first century. It was not until British judges began to publicly criticise the ECtHR's ruling that the press picked up on the importance of that decision and began reporting it, in some cases several years after the original Strasbourg judgment. Furthermore, press reporting on

---

122 European Court of Human Rights, *Annual Report 2017*, available online at www.echr.coe.int/Documents/Annual_report_2017_ENG.pdf, 8.

123 Council of Europe, *Report on the Implementation of the Revised Rule on the Lodging of New Applications*, February 2015, available online at: www.echr.coe.int/Documents/Report_Rule_47_ENG.pdf

124 J Gerards, 'Inadmissibility Decisions of the European Court of Human Rights: A Critique of the Lack of Reasoning' (2014) 14 *Human Rights Law Review* 148; Lize Glas, 'Changes in the Procedural Practice of the European Court of Human Rights: Consequences for the Convention System and Lessons to be Drawn' (2014) 14 *Human Rights Law Review* 671.

125 K Dzehtsiarou and D Coffey, 'Legitimacy and Independence of International Tribunals' (2014) 37 *Hastings International and Comparative Law Review* 269.

126 G Dikov, 'The Ones that Lost: Russian Cases Rejected at the European Court', *Open Democracy*, 7 December 2009, available online at www.opendemocracy.net/od-russia/grigory-dikov/ones-that-lost-russian-cases-rejected-at-european-court; J Gerards and L Glas, 'Access to Justice in the European Convention on Human Rights System' (2017) 35 *Netherlands Quarterly of Human Rights* 11.

127 Cf. E Metcalfe, 'Time for the UK supreme court to think again on hearsay', *The Guardian*, 15 December 2011, debunking these criticisms.

early significant cases, even where the claimant was successful in their case against the UK, was noticeably less critical in the earlier cases discussed (such as *Rowe and Davis* and *Edwards and Lewis*) than it was in later cases (such as *Ibrahim and others*). Perhaps paradoxically, given the intense scrutiny on some aspects of the European Court's operations (some of which, as discussed in Part III, are less founded in reality), the Court's own fairness deficit received next to no media attention.

It remains to be seen whether press coverage of Article 6 case law will continue in the trajectory noted above, and whether some of the emergent themes noted in Part II above will become stronger in years to come. What is clear from the above analysis is that the common themes in media coverage of other areas of human rights, as identified elsewhere in this volume, are also apparent in reports on the ECtHR's fair trial cases. These themes include the strong rhetorical opposition to the Court's divergence from the UK Parliament's views, outrage at the success of 'undeserving' claimants in Strasbourg, and, at times, less-than-accurate reporting on the Court's actual judgment or the outcome of the case. These trends seem unlikely to abate any time soon.

Bibliography

Cameron, Iain, 'The Court and the Member States: Procedural Aspects', in Geir Ulfstein *et al.* (eds), *Constituting Europe: The European Court of Human Rights in a National, European and Global Context* (Cambridge: Cambridge University Press, 2013), 25.

Council of Europe, *Report on the Implementation of the Revised Rule on the Lodging of New Applications*, February 2015, available online at: www.echr.coe.int/Documents/Report_Rule_47_ENG.pdf

Donald, Alice, Jane Gordon and Philip Leach, *The UK and the European Court of Human Rights*, Equality and Human Rights Commission, Research Report 83, 2012, available online at: www.equalityhumanrights.com/sites/default/files/83._european_court_of_human_rights.pdf

Drywood, Eleanor and Harriet Gray, 'Demonising Immigrants: How a Human Rights Narrative Has Contributed to Negative Portrayals of Immigrants in the UK Media', in Farrell, M., Drywood, E. and Hughes, E. (eds), *Human Rights in the Media: Fear and Fetish* (Abingdon: Routledge, 2019).

Dzehtsiarou, Kanstantsin and Donal Coffey, 'Legitimacy and Independence of International Tribunals' (2014) 37 *Hastings International and Comparative Law Review* 269.

Gerards, Janneke, 'Inadmissibility Decisions of the European Court of Human Rights: A Critique of the Lack of Reasoning' (2014) 14 *Human Rights Law Review* 148.

Gerards, Janneke and Lize Glas, 'Access to Justice in the European Convention on Human Rights System' (2017) 35 *Netherlands Quarterly of Human Rights* 11.

Gies, Lieve, 'A Villains' Charter? The Press and the Human Rights Act' (2011) 7(2) *Crime, Media, Culture* 167

Gies, Lieve, 'Human Rights, the British Press and the Deserving Claimant', in Katja S Ziegler *et al.* (eds), *The UK and European Human Rights: A Strained Relationship?* (Oxford: Hart, 2015) 473.

Glas, Lize, 'Changes in the Procedural Practice of the European Court of Human Rights: Consequences for the Convention System and Lessons to be Drawn' (2014) 14 *Human Rights Law Review* 671.

Goss, Ryan, *Criminal Fair Trial Rights* (Oxford: Hart, 2016).

Harris, David, Michael O'Boyle, Edward Bates and Carla Buckley, *Harris, O'Boyle, and Warbrick Law of the European Convention on Human Rights* (3rd edn., Oxford: Oxford University Press, 2014).

Hoyano, Laura, 'What is balanced on the scales of justice? In search of the essence of the right to a fair trial' (2014) 1 *Criminal Law Review* 4.

Mead, David, '"They offer you a feature on stockings and suspenders next to a call for stiffer penalties for sex offenders": Do we learn more about the media than about human rights from tabloid coverage of human rights stories?' in Farrell, M., Drywood, E. and Hughes, E. (eds), *Human Rights in the Media: Fear and Fetish* (Abingdon: Routledge, 2019).

Murray, C. R. G., 'Monstering Strasbourg over Prisoner Voting Rights' in Farrell, M., Drywood, E. and Hughes, E. (eds), *Human Rights in the Media: Fear and Fetish* (Abingdon: Routledge, 2018)

O'Cinneide, Colm, 'Democracy, Rights, and the Constitution: New Directions in the Human Rights Era' (2004) 57 *Current Legal Problems* 175

Redmayne, Mike, 'Hearsay and Human Rights: Al-Khawaja in the Grand Chamber' (2012) 75 *Modern Law Review* 865

Requa, Marny, 'Absent witnesses and the UK Supreme Court: judicial deference as judicial dialogue?' (2010) 14 *The International Journal of Evidence & Proof* 208

Roberts, Paul, 'Does Article 6 of the European Convention on Human Rights Require Reasoned Verdicts in Criminal Trials?' (2011) 11 *Human Rights Law Review* 213

Part III

In-depth

7 Human rights and public debate

The media as scapegoat?

Ekaterina Balabanova

Introduction

Is the media guilty of 'monstering' human rights as the barrister Adam Wagner suggested in 2014?[1] Even non-lawyers would probably agree that there are serious problems in the way human rights are portrayed in the media: the case for the prosecution appears rather strong. There are plenty of examples of misreporting, misrepresenting and misunderstanding human rights in the media. Wagner himself identifies a wide range – from straightforward (and quite common) mistakes such as confusing EU and human rights law,[2] to more misleading 'facts' about the costs of human rights court cases,[3] or stories about the creation of 'new' human rights that already exist.[4] Many of these stories draw heavily on myths originating from different primary sources – about 'the illegal immigrant who cannot be deported because, and I am not making this up, he had a pet cat',[5] the 'Euro judges [who] go against the UK in 3 out of 5 cases',[6] or the prisoners' human rights claims costing the UK £500,000 per week in legal aid.[7]

1 A. Wagner, 'The Monstering of Human Rights' (19 September 2014) https://adam1cor.files.wordpress.com/2014/09/the-monstering-of-human-rights-adam-wagner-2014.pdf (accessed 7 April 2017).

2 A. Wagner, 'No, The Sun, the Human Rights Act is not the EU' (UK Human Rights Blog, 10 February 2013) https://ukhumanrightsblog.com/2013/02/10/no-the-sun-the-human-rights-act-is-not-the-eu/ (accessed 18 July 2018).

3 A. Wagner, 'More press nonsense, this time on human rights damages' (UK Human Rights Blog, 12 October 2013) available online at: https://ukhumanrightsblog.com/2013/10/12/more-press-nonsense-this-time-on-human-rights-damages/ (accessed 18 July 2018).

4 A. Wagner, 'Times on the legal naughty step for bizarre "right to marry" headline splash' (UK Human Rights Blog, 29 December 2013) available online at: https://ukhumanrightsblog.com/2013/12/29/times-on-the-legal-naughty-step-for-bizarre-right-to-marry-headline-splash/ (accessed 18 July 2018).

5 T. May quoted in D. Casciani, 'The case of the cat deportation tale', *BBC* (London, 6 October 2011) www.bbc.co.uk/news/uk-politics-15171980 (accessed 7 April 2017).

6 C. Woodhouse, 'Euro judges go against UK in 3 out of 5 cases', *The Sun* (London, 24 August 2014) available online at: www.thesun.co.uk/archives/politics/1053158/euro-judges-go-against-uk-in-3-out-of-5-cases/ (accessed 7 April 2017).

7 J. Doyle, '£500,000 a week in legal aid for prisoners' human rights claims: YOU pay for them to seek easier life or early release', *Daily Mail* (London, 30 December 2012) available

Those who have been well educated about human rights, or perhaps others who have the time and inclination to look beyond the headlines and consult more reliable sources, have the capacity to ignore this kind of 'fake news' about human rights. They may even go to the trouble of contacting the publisher and gaining a retraction or correction, but this is clearly insufficient when faced with the sheer volume and pace with which such material is produced. A more sensible way to address the problem might be to develop a deeper understanding of why the media persistently propagates certain ideas about human rights, and trace this to deeper systemic and structural issues.

As the European Court of Human Rights has confirmed through its jurisprudence, the media is fundamental to protecting and upholding human rights through a range of democratic duties.[8] How do these functions relate to broader questions around media-state relations? How can concepts and theories from the field of media studies help explain why the media often fails to perform its duties regarding human rights?

This chapter explains how media principles, dynamics, choices and priorities impact on effective coverage of human rights. In one sense, this chapter's aim is to defend the indefensible: to provide an explanation for why the media behaves the way it does over human rights. However, by placing media coverage of human rights issues in the context of the 'state of the art' in knowledge and research on media-state relations, analysis can move beyond simplistic or reductive accounts and avoid name-calling. The chapter will argue that in the laudable and understandable quest for greater quality or truth in the public debate, we are in danger of scapegoating the media. One need only consider the ways in which authoritarian regimes rely on such tactics to realize the risks this poses. The rest of the introduction outlines the key patterns and challenges around human rights and the media before the subsequent sections look in detail at concepts and theories from media studies.

It should be noted first of all that there has been a shift from 'very little coverage of human rights' observed in relation to the 1980s[9] to media becoming much 'more receptive to human rights issues today than at any time in the modern history of the media' in the early 2000s.[10] Human rights are seen as more

---

online at: www.dailymail.co.uk/news/article-2255065/500-000-legal-aid-week-prisoners-human-rights-claims-YOU-pay-seek-easier-life-early-release.html (accessed 7 April 2017). See also, in this volume, C. R. G. Murray, 'Monstering Strasbourg over Prisoner Voting Rights', Chapter 4, and E. Drywood and H. Gray, 'Demonising Immigrants: How a Human Rights Narrative Has Contributed to Negative Portrayals of Immigrants in the UK Media' Chapter 5.

8 P. Coe, 'Redefining "media" using a "media-as-a-constitutional-component" concept: an evaluation of the need for the European Court of Human Rights to alter its understanding of "media" within a new media landscape' (2007) 37(1) *Legal Studies* 25.

9 J. Ovsiovitch, 'News coverage of human rights' (1993) 46 *Political Research Quarterly* 671, 685.

10 International Council on Human Rights Policy (ICHRP), *Journalism, Media and the Challenge of Human Rights Reporting* (ICHRP 2002) 32.

newsworthy not only when violated, but also when the institutions and the mechanisms for their promotion and protection are discussed.[11] However, this increased frequency and salience of the topic in the media has not gone hand in hand with accuracy, knowledge and understanding of the issues being reported. While during the Cold War coverage was criticized for incompleteness of information,[12] inconsistency,[13] bias[14] and racial prejudice,[15] the shortcomings identified in the post-Cold War era have pointed towards a knowledge gap, selective representation, poor quality of reporting and failure to act as a check on state power.[16] Worryingly these latter challenges were already recognized as present in 2002 by the International Council on Human Rights Policy[17] and then identified again in 2012 by Internews in its toolkit for reporting on human rights issues – *Speak Up, Speak Out* – suggesting that they are deep and persistent. The evidence indicates that there is an 'inadequate understanding', even 'ignorance' about what human rights are, how they are created, promoted, protected and enforced and what the role of national governments is in this process.[18] There is a 'superficial grasp of the institutional apparatus of human rights and this lack of knowledge applies not only to journalists, but also to many politicians and other actors in civil society'.[19]

These challenges around accuracy, knowledge and understanding raise questions about the ability of the media to perform as a 'watchdog' or a 'fourth estate' holding governments to account. They also relate to the multifaceted nature of the concept of human rights – the term covers a considerable range of different rights that have developed over time and are prioritised differently by the various state and non-state actors involved in the international human rights regime. As the 'rights that one has simply because one is human'[20] international

---

11 *Ibid.*

12 Ovsiovitch (n 9).

13 V. Berry and A. McChesney, 'Human rights and foreign policy-making' in T. O. Matthews and C. Pratt (eds), *Human Rights in Canadian Foreign Policy* (McGill-Queen's University Press 1988).

14 M. Reisman, 'Reporting the facts as they are not known: Media responsibility in concealed human rights violations' (1984) 78 *American Journal of International Law* 650; E. Herman and N. Chomsky, *Manufacturing Consent: The Political Economy of the Mass Media* (Vintage 1988).

15 Robinson, cited in Ovsiovitch (n 9) 672.

16 L. Bennett, R. G. Lawrence and S. Livingston, 'None dare call it torture: Indexing and the limits of press independence in the Abu Ghraib scandal' (2006) 563(3) *Journal of Communication* 467; W. Cole, 'No news is good news: Human rights coverage in the American print media, 1980–2000' (2010) 9(3) *Journal of Human Rights* 303; ICHRP (n 10); Internews, *Speak Up, Speak Out: A Toolkit for Reporting on Human Rights Issues* (Internews 2012); H. Ramos, J. Ron and O. Thoms, 'Shaping the Northern media's human rights coverage, 1986–2000' (2007) 44(4) *Journal of Peace Research* 385.

17 ICHRP (n 10).

18 Internews (n 16).

19 ICHRP (n 10) 19.

20 J. Donnelly, *International Human Rights. Dilemmas in World Politics* (4th edn, Westview Press 2013) 19.

human rights have at their core the dignity, equality and the worth of the individual. The Universal Declaration of Human Rights (UDHR) provides the most authoritative and commonly referred to list of human rights – contained in 30 articles encompassing a range of political and civil, as well as economic, social and cultural rights. This notwithstanding, human rights tend to be seen as a minimalist framework[21] and a representation of a social practice 'founded on a particular conception of "being human", implemented by particular kinds of mechanisms'.[22] Despite the fact that Article 5 of the Vienna Declaration from the 1993 World Conference on Human Rights reaffirmed that 'all human rights are universal, indivisible and interdependent and interrelated', the evidence suggests that human rights in the West are understood to be mainly about civil and political rights, whereas the importance or abuses of economic, social and cultural rights are largely ignored.[23] The US is a good example here: the language of civil and political rights appears to be more resonant with the state and the public there[24] and the country has refused to ratify the International Covenant on Economic, Social and Cultural Rights (ICESCR) having ratified, albeit slowly, the International Covenant on Civil and Political Rights (ICCPR). This selectivity also applies to the perception of where the main challenges to human rights might be taking place. One general tendency is to see human rights violations as occurring abroad, as something that happens outside the country.[25] In the US, for example, the language of human rights is normally only deployed when the topic is foreign. Civil or constitutional rights, such as non-discrimination or the right to free speech, are not explicitly considered to be human rights in the domestic context by the US public or the US government.

Likewise, in the UK, human rights problems have traditionally been seen as 'foreign' issues, but in the twenty-first century there has been a shift towards a greater receptiveness regarding the application of human rights perspectives to domestic issues. This is largely as a result of the 'rights brought home'[26] process, which means that a human rights framework applies explicitly through UK domestic legislation, specifically the 1998 Human Rights Act (HRA). However, this domestication of human rights ideas in the UK context never enjoyed full political support and can be linked to a backlash among the right-wing press and numerous campaigns blaming the HRA and its use within the legal system for, among other things, a loss of national sovereignty.

---

21 T. Weiss, *The United Nations and Changing World Politics* (Westview Press 2009).

22 J. Donnelly, *Universal Human Rights in Theory and Practice* (3rd edn, Cornell University Press 2013).

23 ICHRP (n 10); Ramos *et al.* (n 16).

24 S. Brandle, *Television News and Human Rights in the US & UK: The Violations Will Not Be Televised* (Routledge 2016).

25 *Ibid*; ICHRP (n 10).

26 J. Petley, 'What rights? Whose responsibilities?' (2009) 43 Soundings 77, 78.

Another important shortcoming when the issue of human rights is raised in media output is the lack of historical, political, social and local context and the failure to provide in-depth and detailed analysis.[27] Finally, the media are also seen as sometimes perpetrating human rights abuses themselves, such as invading privacy, perpetuating bias and stereotypes or deepening existing conflicts or even inciting violence, murder and genocide, as in Rwanda, Somalia and the Former Yugoslavia.[28] As Schimmel puts it, 'the media facilitates, often inadvertently and unconsciously, the efforts of governments engaged in human rights abuses to deny and cover up their actions, and shield them from public knowledge and scrutiny'.[29]

The rest of the chapter is organized in three parts. Part one discusses and problematizes understandings of what the media is – and what it is not – by deconstructing well-known metaphors that seek to explain the normative role of media in liberal democracies. Part two introduces key concepts and methodologies from communications and media scholarship in order to examine and assess explanations for the media's sub-optimal performance when it comes to human rights. Part three brings the discussion forward to the contemporary debate, asking whether the rise of social media has fundamentally shifted the media-human rights nexus and what challenges this presents for our understanding of what 'the media' does, and is for.

Pet or predator? Media and metaphor

Any judgment and assessment of how the media treats human rights is dependent upon a set of normative assumptions about the role of media – real and ideal. The debate about the role of media in democratic societies is ongoing and longstanding. Does the media act as a 'watchdog' – an independent check on the power of the state, reporting about government misconduct and exposing abuses of public authority? Or does it behave more like a lapdog – 'the hired guns of particular political or commercial interests' collaborating with politicians, totally submissive to authority and lacking independent power?[30] If it is the latter, it would seem natural that the media would ignore, dismiss or purposefully misrepresent human rights – it would be oblivious to all interests apart from those of powerful elites, framing its stories accordingly.[31]

Another popular metaphor of the media as something controlled, tamed, is that of the guard-dog: 'a sentry not for the community as a whole, but for those particular groups who have the power and influence to create and control their

27 ICHRP (n 10); Internews (n 16).

28 Internews (n 16); M. Frohardt and J. Temin, *Use and Abuse of Media in Vulnerable* Societies (United States Institute of Peace 2003).

29 N. Schimmel, 'Media accountability to investigate human rights violations' (2009) 21 *Peace Review: A Journal of Social Justice* 442, 444.

30 J. Street, *Mass Media, Politics and Democracy* (2nd edn, Palgrave Macmillan 2011) 186.

31 G. Donohue, P. Tichenor and C. Olien, 'A guard dog perspective on the role of media' (1995) 45(2) *Journal of Communication* 115.

own security systems'.[32] What about the journalists – do they see themselves as bloodhounds hunting for news or as missionaries?[33] Or perhaps the media is neither a watchdog, lapdog, guard-dog, or bloodhound but instead an independent force: a wolf (or pack of wolves), driven by base instincts. Alternatively, the media may be seen as merely another establishment actor within an interlinking oligarchic system: fully integrated and unquestioning of the overarching power structures but sometimes acting in its own interests and directly opposing other economic and political powers; sometimes joining forces with them?[34]

Normatively, the role of the media in democratic societies is generally assumed to be functional: informing the public about the issues of the day in an objective manner, aiming to be neutral and detached to the extent that this is possible. While partisanship in political journalism and output from commentators holding political allegiances is permitted and expected, it should be somewhat separated and not presented as objective reporting.[35] Referring to the media's role as a source of information on the basis of which reasoned and rational choices can be made on the important issues facing the society Anderson argues that:

> high-quality, independent news journalism which provides accurate and thoughtful information and analysis about current events is crucial to the creation of an enlightened citizenry that is able to participate meaningfully in society and politics.[36]

The metaphor of the watchdog adds to this democratic ideal the role of 'fourth estate', where there is an expectation that media oversees public life, providing critical scrutiny of the activities of powerful elites – political, business, etc.[37] The origins of the term itself can be traced back to the late-eighteenth/mid-nineteenth century and its first use is associated with the names of Edmund Burke and Thomas Carlyle, who both referred to the political power of the press alongside that of the other three estates – the Lords, the Church and the Commons. They believed that the power of the press arose from its ability to give or withhold publicity and from its informative capacity. The fourth estate was thought to have the potential to draw attention to abuses by any one of the other three estates thus truly linking the public with those in power. This function is

32 *Ibid*, 116.

33 R. Köcher, 'Bloodhounds or missionaries: Role definitions of German and British journalists' (1986) 1(1) *European Journal of Communication* 27.

34 B. Cohen, *The Press and Foreign Policy* (Princeton University Press 1963); H. Gans, *Deciding What's News: A Study of CBS Evening News, NBC Nightly News, Newsweek and Time* (Pantheon Books 1979); T. Gitlin, *The Whole World Is Watching* (University of California Press 1980).

35 B. McNair, *News and Journalism in the UK* (5th edn, Routledge 2009).

36 P. Anderson, 'Challenges for journalism', in P. J. Anderson and G. Ward (eds) *The Future of Journalism in the Advanced Democracies* (Ashgate 2007) 51–72, 65.

37 McNair (n 35); B. McNair, *An Introduction to Political Communication* (5th edn, Routledge 2011).

supported by another of the media's main roles – to provide a platform for public political discourse ('public sphere'), facilitating the formation of public opinion and feeding that opinion back to the public.[38] In the words of Poster,[39] 'the media is the public sphere'. As such, it should act as a 'public forum' maintaining public debate in order to resolve societal disputes and arrive at public consensus, in addition to informing authorities about potentially crucial issues.[40] McNair also talks about media acting as a mediator/representative – mediating between the citizen and the politician and representing citizens before power making sure that the voice of the public is heard in the democratic process.[41] This particular function of representing the people to authority is considered to be an essential element of the media's role as, by representing individuals' divergent needs and views, the media can inform political elites about disputes that can afterwards be addressed within existing political structures.[42] A final key dimension to the media's role in democracy is its advocacy capacity – both on behalf of the people and particular interests or political positions. This goes back to pluralistic ideas where the media can be partisan, take sides in political debates and seek to persuade people of a specific viewpoint. However, it is believed that in order to maintain appearance of objective reporting and factual accuracy, a separation of fact and opinion, as well as distinction between public and private media, are necessary[43].

Whether contemporary media indeed performs these roles continues to be contested with criticism over agenda, content and style. Prominent in these critiques are accusations that the media fails to perform its watchdog role in relation to questions of pluralism and objectivity because it is dominated by powerful interests that crowd out alternative perspectives. According to Herman and Chomsky, instead of providing democratic scrutiny or maintaining the accountability of political elites, the media is managed to manipulate or 'manufacture consent' in the general population, producing and sustaining 'necessary illusions' for the state.[44] They see the media as more of a pair of virtual reality goggles than any kind of trained pet, arguing that the 'media operate[s] on the basis of a set of ideological premises, depend[s] heavily and uncritically on elite information sources and participate[s] in propaganda campaigns helpful to elite interests'.[45] The public do not receive 'news', instead, they are subjected to information that has passed through a series of filters: ownership, sources, advertising, ideology and flak. These influence what is published and make sure that the only news that exists is that already deemed appropriate by powerful interests.

---

38 J. Habermas, *The Structural Transformation of the Public Sphere* (Polity Press 1989).

39 M. Poster, 'Cyberdemocracy: internet and the public sphere', in D. Porter (ed.) *Internet Culture* (Routledge 1997) 201–218, 217.

40 J. Curran, *Media and Power* (Routledge 2002).

41 McNair (n 35); McNair (n 37).

42 Curran (n 40).

43 McNair (n 35); McNair (n 37).

44 Herman and Chomsky (n 14); N. Chomsky, *Necessary Illusions: Thought Control in Democratic Societies* (South End Press 1989).

45 E. Herman, 'The Propaganda model: A retrospective' (Against All Reason 9 December 2003).

Furthermore, changing patterns of news consumption mean that there are enormous competitive pressures on the media – falling numbers of journalists and the collapse of local newspapers are just one indicator of this phenomenon – leading some to suggest that lowering journalistic standards threaten democracy.[46] This is through processes of 'dumbing down',[47] the rise of 'tabloidisation'[48] and the growing tendency for media to simplify in order to appeal to 'the lowest common denominator'.[49] News has become 'spectacle'.[50] Anderson and Ward argue that this has serious implications when it comes to delivering the 'informational needs of a democracy'.[51] They make the distinction between 'soft news' – associated with the concepts of infotainment, entertainment, tabloidisation and popularisation – and 'hard news' – understood as 'journalism that can be recognised as having the primary intent to inform and encourage reflection, debate and action on political, social and economic issues'.[52] This is about balance, rather than claiming that one kind of news should completely dominate. However, the authors themselves acknowledge that it is not so easy to distinguish between the two categories of news stories and news cases may be difficult to categorise, indicative of ongoing blurring of genres and styles.

Finally, analysis of news content tends to conclude that there has been a significant fall in investigative journalism and a growing dependence on public relations material, partly because commercial pressures mean less time for due diligence and fact-checking, compromising the fourth estate.[53] As Lewis *et al.* put it:

> many of the elements of rigorous, independent journalism are inevitably depleted when reporters are obliged to produce more stories in less time.... In short, profits are increasingly being won at the cost of journalistic integrity, autonomy and quality. [54]

This fall in the number of foreign correspondents and local reporters arguably limits the information that can be communicated about global human rights issues, and makes it more likely that chronic violations go unreported.[55]

46 McNair (n 35).
47 B. Franklin. *Newszak and News Media* (1997).
48 McNair (n 35).
49 M. Temple, 'Dumbing down is good for you' (2006) 1(2) *British Politics* 257, 259.
50 E. Louw, *The Media and Political Process* (2nd edn, Sage 2010).
51 P. Anderson and G. Ward, *The Future of Journalism in the Advanced Democracies* (Ashgate 2007) 67.
52 *Ibid*, 8.
53 N. Davies, *Flat Earth News* (Vintage 2008); J. Lewis, A. Williams and B. Franklin, 'A compromised fourth estate? UK newspapers journalism, public relations and news sources' (2008) 9(1) *Journalism Studies* 1; J. Lewis, A. Williams and B. Franklin, 'Four rumours and an explanation: a political economic account of journalists' changing newsgathering and reporting practices' (2008) 2(1) *Journalism Practice* 27.
54 J. Lewis *et al.* (n 53) 42.
55 S. Caliendo, M. Gibney and A. Payne, ''All the news that's fit to print?' *New York Times* coverage of human rights violations' (1999) 4 *Harvard International Journal of Press/Politics*

In light of the most prominent weaknesses in media coverage of human rights issues identified in the introduction, it is clear that there are justifiable concerns about the way the media informs about human rights, acts as a watchdog in cases of human rights violations, provides a platform for debate and advocacy and represents the full range of opinions on human rights issues of the day. No doubt this is problematic since it is widely acknowledged that, in the field of human rights, the media has the capacity (and has indeed been able) to communicate information about human rights, human rights abuses, provide a platform for civil society, promote tolerance, and keep an eye on governments.[56]

As other chapters in this volume illustrate, there is plentiful evidence of inaccuracy or imprecision in the reporting of legal judgments, misunderstandings in the media about relevant legislation and courts, such as the Human Rights Act (HRA 1998) or the European Convention on Human Rights (ECHR 1950) and the European Court of Human Rights (ECtHR). The rest of this chapter moves beyond a balance-book approach, instead incorporating concepts and theories from media studies to encompass a wider range of concerns that are equally valid when evaluating media coverage of human rights, including problems of balance, focus, selection and salience.[57] The importance of such assessments only grows as human rights issues become more visible in the media.[58]

Concepts and theories from media studies

What are the key factors that help explain media behaviour when it comes to coverage of human rights? What follows here is an examination of some of the key concepts and methodologies from communication and media scholarship. Research on the role of news values, agenda-setting, framing and the communication of suffering can help make sense of the media's sub-optimal performance when it comes to human rights.

News values

The question of newsworthiness is referred to in media analysis as 'news values', or those criteria that explain why some phenomena are designated as worthwhile

48; H. Sandvig, 'The mass media and the United Nations in a human rights dilemma' in A. Eide, A. Skogly and S. Skogly (eds) *Human Rights and the Media* (Norwegian Institute of Human Rights 1988).

56 C. Apodaca, 'The whole world could be watching: human rights and the media' (2007) 6(2) *Journal of Human Rights* 147; T. Hammarberg, 'Foreword: Media freedom in Europe' in H. R. Writings (ed) *Human Rights and a Changing Media Landscape* (Council of Europe Publishing 2011) 7–20; E. McPherson, 'How editors choose which human rights news to cover: a case study of Mexican newspapers' in T. A. Borer (ed) *Media, Mobilisation, and Human Rights: Mediating Suffering* (Zed Books 2012) 96–121; J. Metzl, 'Information technology and human rights' (1996) 18(4) Human Rights Quarterly 705; J. R. Pruce, 'The spectacle of suffering and humanitarian intervention in Somalia' in T. A. Borer (ed.) *Media, Mobilisation, and Human Rights: Mediating Suffering* (Zed Books 2012) 216–239.

57 Internews (n 16); ICHRP (n 10).

58 Ramos *et al.* (n 16); Cole (n 16); ICHRP (n 10).

for news coverage, and others are not – how the media filters 'the news'.[59] As Palmer suggests, news values work as 'a system of criteria which are used to make decisions about the inclusion and exclusion of material' that 'transcend individual judgments, although of course they are to be found embodied in every news judgment made by particular journalists'.[60] The scholarship on news values helps our understanding of why there is a disproportionate focus on certain types of 'crisis' or 'disaster', for example if the destruction is either graphic or large-scale, if there are victims with whom the audience will identify, or if there can be a local/ national angle. Other criteria include events or stories that are extreme, include a dramatic component, involve 'elite' nations or communities among many others. This selectivity is also path-dependent because, as McPherson points out, norms of newsworthiness become established and become aligned with the values of the news outlet itself. This means that the more it 'fits' the 'journalistic, economic, and political aims relative to other bits of information, the more likely it is to be published'.[61]

The problem for those seeking an accurate and balanced portrayal of human rights issues, is that many important human rights issues are unlikely to fit these criteria neatly. As a result, there are many important human rights issues that remain undocumented and unexplored. Moreover, there is a pattern to this: there seems to be a trend for less visible and more long-term issues to be down-played, for individualism to be portrayed as 'natural', and more civic or collective values to be interpreted as 'marginal'.[62] To take just one example, while the denial of human rights for those detained in Guantanamo Bay has managed to maintain some attention in Western media up until today,[63] delivering on criteria such as dramatism, involvement of elite nations and visibility, among others, there has been less consistency when it comes to problems of human rights abuses affecting poorer people in less developed places like Darfur or Democratic Republic of the Congo, where the ongoing complex conflicts have struggled for visibility and Western attention. Another example might be the opportunity to focus on

---

59 J. Galtung and M. Ruge, 'The structure of foreign news: the presentation of the Congo, Cuba and Cyprus crises in four Norwegian newspapers' (1965) 2 *Journal of Peace Research* 64; T. Harcup and D. O'Neil, 'What is news? Galtung and Ruge revisited' (2001) 2(2) *Journalism Studies* 261; D. O'Neill and T. Harcup. 'News values and selectivity' in K. Wahl-Jorgensen and T. Hanitzsch (eds) *The Handbook of Journalism Studies* (Routledge 2009) 161–174.

60 J. Palmer, *Spinning into Control: News Values and Source Strategies* (Leicester University Press 2000) 45.

61 McPherson (n 56), 96.

62 R. McChesney, *Rich Media, Poor Democracy: Communications Politics in Dubious Times* (The New Press 2000) 49–50, 110.

63 T. Miles, 'Torture still being carried out at Guantanamo Bay despite US denials, says UN investigator', *The Independent* (London, 14 December 2017) available online at: www.independent.co.uk/news/world/americas/torture-guantanamo-bay-detention-centre-9-11-conspirator-un-human-rights-investigation-pentagon-a8109231.html (accessed 15 December 2017).

human rights when the media covered the 2008 Olympic Games in Beijing. The drama of the games overshadowed any systematic investigations by journalists of human rights violations in China. Research into what gets into the news is fairly clear: there is a very uneven coverage of humanitarian crises, and this is particularly notable when it comes to certain regions or countries that wield less power on the international stage. A good example is Western coverage of countries in Africa[64] where human rights issues can sometimes be underplayed while the region is stereotypically framed as dark, distant, dangerous and disease-ridden.[65]

The concept of 'news values' is helpful to explain which events are more likely to make the news and which will not. While it may not be able to offer a complete explanation of news composition, it also offers an insight into how a story is treated once selected.[66] It could be argued that, by selecting and shaping news, the media does not reflect the world, it forms specific representations of it. These media representations 'reduce, shrink, condense and select/repeat aspects of intricate social relations in order to represent them as fixed, natural, obvious and ready to consume'.[67] According to Curran and Seaton,[68] news values are instruments journalists use to 'translate untidy reality into neat stories with beginnings, middles and denouements' and by doing this they tend to 'reinforce conventional opinions and established authority'. In other words, the concept of news values underlines the way in which news selection is not based exclusively on intrinsic qualities of news events, but also takes into account external factors, psychology of news decisions and ideology.[69]

This brings the discussion to questions of ideology. If news values have such an influence on news selection, and they are not 'a set of neutral, routine practices', then it is a small step to argue they form part of an 'ideological structure' that privileges the perspectives of the powerful elites in society.[70] Herman and Chomsky's manufacturing consent/propaganda model discussed earlier suggests

---

64 V. Hawkins, *The Silence of the UN Security Council: Conflict and Peace Enforcement in the 1990s* (European Press Academic Publishing 2004).

65 L. Beattie, D. Miller, E. Miller and G. Philo, 'The media and Africa: images of disaster and rebellion' in G. Philo (ed.) *Message Received* (Longman 1999); G. Myers, T. Klak and T. Koehl, 'The inscription of difference: news coverage of the conflicts in Rwanda and Bosnia' (1996) 15(1) *Political Geography* 21.

66 D. McQuail, *McQuail's Mass Communication Theory* (Sage 2000); J. Hartley, *Understanding News* (Methuen 1982); J. Palmer (n 60).

67 N. Ndlela, 'The African paradigm: The coverage of the Zimbabwean crisis in the Norwegian media' (2005) 2 *Westminster Papers in Communication and Culture* 71.

68 J. Curran and J. Seaton, *Power Without Responsibility. The Press, Broadcasting and New Media in Britain* (Routledge 2003) 336.

69 J. Staab, 'The role of news factors in news selection: A theoretical reconsideration' (1990) 5 European Journal of Communication 423; W. Donsbach, 'Psychology of news decisions: Factors behind journalists' professional behaviour' (2004) 5(2) *Journalism* 131; J. Westerstahl and F. Johansson, 'Foreign news; News values and ideologies', (1994) 9 *European Journal of Communication* 71.

70 S. Hall, 'The determinations of news photographs' in S. Cohen and J. Young (eds) *The Manufacture of News: Deviance, Social Problems and the Mass Media* (Constable 1973) 226–243, 235.

that through the 'selection of topics' (as one of a number of ways) the media acts to 'inculcate and defend the economic, social, and political agenda of privileged groups that dominate the domestic society and the state'.[71] This directly contradicts the notion of independent watchdog and gives more support to the 'lapdog' or 'guard-dog' interpretations of media behaviour. The evidence suggests that with some nuances this is particularly prominent with regard to foreign policy and the foreign policy establishment.[72] The question of ideology links with ideas of bias, just as the concept of news values itself does. In McQuail's analysis the 'ideological bias' is one of a possible four types that feature in the media – 'partisan', 'propaganda' and 'unwitting' being the other three. [73] The distinction is made along the lines of explicitness and intention. Ingrained routines about what is news and what makes a story newsworthy relate to unwitting bias; ideologies are more about assumptions regarding events or behaviour or how the world works.

Agenda-setting and framing

One of the reasons why biased, selective or skewed media coverage of human rights is of such concern is because of the presumed power of the media to set the agenda in public debates. What does research tell us about how this works and the extent to which the media possesses this power? In its most basic formulation, an agenda-setting function refers to the way in which media, by focusing on some issues rather than others, is able to influence the public debate such that only these issues receive political attention.[74] The greater the quantity of coverage, the more it is perceived to be an important topic. This is different from the suggestion that the media can change the way we think, the argument is instead that the media is able to tell its readers 'what to think about'.[75] An important question is whether this is a power wielded for strategic aims, or whether it is instead a 'by-product' of news values and the exigencies of the production process.[76] This has mixed implications for human rights. Studies have established that an increase in the language of human rights in the media is 'at least partially responsible for the increased awareness of, and support for, human rights found in the US public'.[77] However, with respect to the media's apparent failure to provide balanced

71 Herman and Chomsky (n 14), 298.

72 D. Hallin, *The Uncensored War: The Media and Vietnam* (University of California Press 1986); Bennett *et al.* (n 16).

73 D. McQuail, *Media Performance* (Sage 1992).

74 K. Lang and G. E. Lang. 'The mass media and voting' in B. Berelson and M. Janowitz (eds) *Reader in Public Opinion and Communication* (Free Press 1966) 455–472; M. McCombs and D. Shaw, 'The agenda-setting function of mass media' (1972) 36(2) *Public Opinion Quarterly* 176.

75 Cohen (n 34) 13.

76 M. McCombs, *Setting the Agenda: The Mass Media and Public Opinion* (Polity Press 2004), 19.

77 K. J. Pritchard, 'Human rights: a decent respect for public opinion' (1991) 13 *Human Rights Quarterly* 123, 138.

information about the full spectrum of human rights, this risks many falling off the political agenda or receiving inadequate attention from political elites.[78]

Establishing the way in which this process works requires more than measurement of the mere quantity of coverage an issue receives. 'Second-level' analysis is needed to assess how, why and with what effects certain interpretations of a topic become more prevalent. A common way to discuss this is through the concept of 'frames' – identifying devices used in constructing the news that 'organize everyday reality'[79] by providing 'meaning to an unfolding strip of events'.[80] Frames help make sense of reality, but they also inevitably promote 'particular definitions and interpretations of political issues'.[81] They can be formally defined as 'persistent patterns of cognition, interpretation, and presentation, of selection, emphasis and exclusion by which symbol handlers routinely organize discourse'.[82] However, in discursive terminology, frames include certain ideas and arguments, and exclude others, in order to provide a coherent, persuasive and convincing account of an issue or topic.[83] They are relevant to human rights because they 'define problems', 'diagnose causes', 'make moral judgments', and 'suggest remedies'.[84] Taken together agenda-setting and framing point to the fact that the media decides what human rights to cover and which issues or aspects of a story to highlight and which to ignore. These decisions imply a level of power over what we know and do not know about human rights and the possibility to affect how the public view different issues.[85]

Communicating suffering

There are a number of techniques that media use to gain attention and get a reaction from audiences, including using graphic or disturbing images or language and connecting stories with celebrities. These are designed to divide opinions. While shock tactics may have a short-term dividend, some of these techniques bring risks in terms of reinforcing discriminatory or nationalist sentiments.[86]

---

78 Caliendo (n 55).

79 G. Tuchman, *Making News: A Study in the Social Construction of Reality* (Free Press 1978) 193.

80 W. Gamson and A. Modigliani, 'The changing course of affirmative action' in R. Braungart and M. Braungart (eds) *Research in Political Sociology* (Jai Press 1987) 137–177, 143.

81 D. Shah, M. Watts, D. Domke and D. P. Fan, 'News framing and cueing of issue regimes: explaining Clinton's public approval in spite of scandal' (2002) 66 *Public Opinion Quarterly* 339.

82 Gitlin (n 34) 7.

83 Z. Pan and G. Kosicki, 'Framing analysis: An approach to news discourse' (1993) 10(1) *Political Communication* 55.

84 R. Entman, 'Framing: Toward a clarification of a fractured paradigm' (1993) 43(4) *Journal of Communication* 51.

85 P. Brewer and K. Gross, 'Values, framing and citizens' thoughts about policy issues: effects on content and quantity' (2005) 26(6) *Political Psychology* 929.

86 T. Borer. "Fresh, wet tears': shock media and human rights awareness campaigns', in T. Borer (ed.) *Media, Mobilisation, and Human Rights: Mediating Suffering* (Zed Books 2012a) 143–180.

Simplistic, reductive framings of suffering often depend on one-dimensional representations of 'the other', and raise concerns over 'disaster pornography'.[87]

Certain human rights issues are intimately connected to celebrities – e.g. Angelina Jolie and refugees[88] or George Clooney and Darfur[89] – but the results of these endorsements and campaigns are open to debate. Some argue that celebrities help to bring greater level of public and political attention,[90] others complain that their involvement can bring confusion, ignorance and turn many people off.[91] They can be effective when working together with experts and NGOs.[92] However, they also tend to simplify everything into a Manichean good vs. evil where 'nuance is inevitably lost'[93] and genuinely radical or challenging voices that critique structural issues are muted.[94]

Some have claimed that the increasing ease with which we can see images of human rights abuses from the other side of the world has not led to greater levels of empathy, rather it has created 'compassion fatigue'[95] where we are 'so used to the spectacle of dreadful events, misery or suffering that we stop noticing them.... We are bored.... It leads to the conclusion that this is just the way things are and nothing can be done that will make a difference'.[96] The media is implicated because of patterns of repetitive and predictable framing, reducing details to those that will 'sell', such that compassion fatigue is a result of formulaic content.[97]

The expanded ability to witness global events and the images of suffering in real time creates a mixture of curiosity, guilt and repulsion, but an absence of the traditional sense of solidarity. Lili Chouliaraki[98] argues that the ability to (virtually) experience the conditions of distant others 'invites contemplation on our

87 R. Omaar and A. Waal, 'Disaster pornography from Somalia' (1993) 61 *Media and Values* 13.
88 UNHCR, 'Special Envoy Angelina Jolie' (n.d.) available online at: www.unhcr.org/uk/special-envoy-angelina-jolie.html (accessed 20 December 2017).
89 M. Shearlaw, 'What happened to Darfur after George Clooney came to town?' (2014) Guardian, 11 December available online at: www.theguardian.com/world/2014/dec/11/-sp-george-cloony-darfur-what-next (accessed 20 December 2017).
90 L. Dittrich, 'The celebrity shall save you' (2009) *Esquire* 118; P. Valley, 'From A-lister to aid worker: Does celebrity diplomacy really work?' *Independent* 17 January 2009.
91 D. Haynes, 'The Celebritization of Human Trafficking' (2014) 653(1) *The Annals of the American Academy of Political and Social Science* 25.
92 A. Cooper and J. Turcotte, 'Celebrity diplomats as mobilisers? Celebrities and activism in a hypermediated time', in T. A. Borer (ed) *Media, Mobilisation, and Human Rights: Mediating Suffering*. (Zed Books 2012) 181–204, 201.
93 H. Dieter and R. Kumar, 'The downside of celebrity diplomacy: The neglected complexity of development' (2008) 14(3) *Global Governance* 259, 260.
94 Valley (n 89).
95 S. Moeller, *Compassion Fatigue: How the Media Sell Disease, Famine, War and Death* (Routledge 1999).
96 K. Tester, *Compassion, Morality and the Media* (Open University Press 2001) 13.
97 Moeller (n 94) 32.
98 L. Chouliaraki, *The Ironic Spectator. Solidarity in the Age of Post-Humanitarianism* (Polity 2013) 2.

own condition … a move from an ethics of *pity* to an ethics of *irony*'. The West has become an 'ironic spectator … an impure or ambivalent figure that stands, at once, as skeptical towards any moral appeal of solidary action and, yet, open to doing something about those who suffer'.[99]

Taken together the concepts of news values, agenda-setting and framing alongside the principles guiding the communication of suffering go a long way in shedding light over the media's approach to the reporting of the variety of human rights issues. The next section examines in greater detail the implications of new communications technologies for human rights, in particular the explosion of social media usage in the twenty-first century.

Social media and human rights

Over the last ten years social media has been regularly connected with major events or political shifts that have a strong human rights dimension, often attributed with a causal or influential role. Any analysis of the role of the media in whatever political or social context has to take into account the changing communications landscape, not least because of changing patterns of news consumption. A report by Pew Research in 2016 about patterns in the US claimed that twice as many adults (38%) got their news online compared with print (20%) with mobile devices the preferred method and with the trend even more pronounced for younger adults.[100] Research carried out in the UK found 41% of adults used the internet to get their news, with the number reading newspapers falling rapidly and making print the least popular medium overall.[101]

Apart from the impact this has in economic terms on the traditional news media, a great majority of scholarly work on the media is in danger of becoming outdated because of this new phenomenon that barely existed in the late 1990s. Social networking sites grew alongside the expansion of the internet but really only exploded in the early 2000s with the launch of many of the names that are still familiar such as LinkedIn, Facebook – and, of course, many others that are fading into history such as Myspace. Writing in 2018 the increasing ubiquity of 'fourth screen' technologies has not only acted as a catalyst to this earlier phenomenon with the spread of newer, easier to use, social networking technologies. It has also enabled what appears to be another progression – this time towards video sharing/streaming and virtual/augmented reality. To what extent has – or will – this change the media-human rights nexus?

There are a growing number of examples or cases which one could cite when answering this question. A non-exhaustive list might include: Iran's elections in 2009 where social media was thought to lead to increased global scrutiny about

99 *Ibid*., 3.
100 A. Mitchell, J. Gottfried, M. Barthel and E. Shearer, 'The Modern News Consumer: News Attitudes and Practices in the Digital Era' (2016) Pew Research Centre.
101 Ofcom, 'News Consumption in the UK: Research Report' (Ofcom 2015).

protests and their demands for democratic rights; the Indignados and Occupy movements which were dependent upon social media; Europe's migration crisis where the pictures of Alan Kurdi, who died crossing the Mediterranean in 2015, appeared to spark a political shift towards a more human-rights focus across the continent; the Syrian conflict, where a single Twitter account of Bana al-Abed (run by her mother Fatemah) and picture of a young boy injured by a bomb (Omran Daqneesh) became integral to Western debates about the human impacts of war. Social media has been attributed with helping to respond to crises such as the 2010 Haitian earthquake and generating a focus on the human rights implications, or helping to fuel protests against the human rights abuses of authoritarian regimes, for example in Egypt's Tahrir square in 2011, or helping raise awareness of specific events or tragedies that contravene human rights norms, such as the use of chemical weapons in Syria in 2013.

Will the impacts of social media lead to an increase in the recognition and protection of human rights worldwide? In many ways, how we understand the significance of new forms of media follows a pattern common to the advent of any other novel technology. At first there is a great deal of hype about transformative potential, then normally a realisation that this might have been exaggerated before the true meaning and significance slowly becomes apparent. This is what IT consultancy Gartner has referred to as the 'hype cycle' where an 'Innovation Trigger' leads to a 'Peak of Inflated Expectations' followed by a 'Trough of Disillusionment' before a 'Slope of Enlightenment' eventually results in a kind of plateau (until the next new technology arrives).[102] The rest of this section considers, in the context of the media-human rights nexus, the key inventions in the field of new communication technologies and social media platforms. It considers their impact on human rights, highlighting the most optimistic expectations, which often emerged in reactions to particular examples or cases. It contrasts these with more critical analyses and asks whether (or when) we have reached the lowest point in terms of disillusionment, and whether (or when) academics and analysts can embark on an upward slope towards a more realistic and enlightened assessment.

New technology offers interesting avenues and opportunities for new modes of resistance and protest by 'freedom technologists',[103] and some believe it can usher in greater equality of access to information in the political debate. The capacity for an individual or a small organisation to release large amounts of data into the public domain (e.g. Edward Snowdon, or WikiLeaks) is a phenomenon which has prompted some to claim that 'dominant articulations of power' can be undermined or challenged.[104] Thus authoritarian states who do not recognise

102 Available online at: www.gartner.com/technology/research/methodologies/hype-cycle.jsp

103 J. Postill, 'Freedom technologists and the new protest movements: A theory of protest formulas' (2014) 20(4) *Convergence: The International Journal of Research into New Media Technologies* 402.

104 B. Brevini, A. Hintz and P. McCurdy (eds) *Beyond WikiLeaks: Implications for the Future of Communications, Journalism and Society* (Palgrave Macmillan 2013) 4.

or protect human rights can be challenged through the media via an 'ethic of transparency'.[105] But this is not a one-sided affair: it is an arms-race where states readily dispense with human rights considerations to expand and extend security through cyber-surveillance.[106] While the language of human rights has become the language of moral critique in the international sphere,[107] it has also been appropriated by extremist, nihilist and anti-liberal forces who will use social networks to spread fear and hate.[108]

For every Bill Gates claiming that new communications technology will change the world, there are sceptics who point to the rise of 'slacktivism' and argue that social networks are no substitute for organised, hierarchical activism.[109] Or, as Evgeny Morozov[110] argued in *The Net Delusion*, social media might be more suited to oppression than freedom, and cyberspace looks like somewhere more characterised by a Hobbesian state of hate and division than any kind of global utopian society. It is certainly the case that the most optimistic hopes raised in the mid-1990s that the internet would promote a wave of democratisation and global understanding were somewhat crushed with the re-emergence of old structural inequalities online.[111]

Assumptions about the disruptive potential of new hardware and software platforms are linked to the supposed anti-establishment ethos[112] of the entrepreneurs and organisations that created them, leading to expectations about new forms of political activism.[113] Yet, in 2016 and 2017 that disruption was driven by populist political forces harnessing social media – quite a contrast to the earlier hopes that the technology could usher in a new democratic age based on international solidarity and human rights. 'Fake news' spread by social network platforms was blamed for spreading violent extremism, and changing election results (e.g. the EU referendum of 2016 and Donald Trump's election to president of the US in the same year). Likewise, the OECD has warned that global interconnectedness and social media have acted to expose, rather than close, gaps in cross-cultural

105 J. Assange, 'State and Terrorist Conspiracies' and 'Conspiracy as Governance' (2006) available online at: http://cryptome.org/0002/ja-conspiracies.pdf (accessed 17 May 2017).

106 Z. Bauman, D. Bigo, P. Esteves, E. Guild, V. Jabri, D. Lyon and R. B. J. Walker, 'After Snowden: Rethinking the Impact of Surveillance' (2014) 8(2) *International Political Sociology* 121.

107 C. Beitz, *The Idea of Human Rights* (Oxford University Press 2009).

108 C. Galloway, 'Media jihad: What PR can learn in Islamic State's public relations masterclass' (2016) *Public Relations Review*.

109 M. Gladwell, 'Small change: Why the revolution will not be tweeted', *The New Yorker* (New York) 4 October 2010, available online at: www.newyorker.com/magazine/2010/10/04/small-change-malcolm-gladwell (accessed 8 April 2017).

110 E. Morozov, *The Net Delusion: The Dark Side of Internet Freedom* (Public Affairs Books 2011).

111 J. Curran, N. Fenton and D. Freedman, *Misunderstanding the Internet* (Routledge 2012) 179.

112 F. Turner, *From Counterculture to Cyberculture* (2006).

113 E.g. P. Gerbaudo, *Tweets and the Streets: Social Media and Contemporary Activism* (Pluto Press 2012).

understanding and demanded these be closed through education to ensure shared respect for human dignity.[114]

These developments challenge assumed positive impacts relating to enhanced global information flows. Will they really erode borders and improve transparency? Can new technologies encourage a more inclusive public sphere through reduced barriers to engagement or new opportunities for dialogue and exchange? In one sense, these contemporary questions regarding the impact of social media echo the discussions prompted by the rise of 'electric media' in the mid-twentieth century, for example Marshall McLuhan's claim that 'the globe is no more than a village. Electric speed bringing all social and political functions together in a sudden implosion has heightened human awareness of responsibility to an intense degree'.[115] In other ways, the debate is very different in the twenty-first century, with the exciting democratising potential of new platforms that allow individuals to become creators, producers, broadcasters, or 'citizen journalists'.

A key moment that demonstrated the power of content produced by non-professionals was in the scandal around Abu Ghraib, where personal digital photos taken by soldiers were shared worldwide, symbolising forever the torture and abuse of prisoners by the US army.[116] Social media of footage of the death of protestor Neda Agha-Soltan in 2009 fuelled global condemnation of the Iranian government crackdown on protests in 2009.[117] In the period following the uprisings in parts of North Africa and the Middle East often referred to as the 'Arab Spring' scholars pondered whether new technologies were 'reconfiguring the cosmopolitanising potential of reporting'[118] and citizen journalists were generating 'new solidarity' and 'new authenticity'. But are citizen journalists and new media technologies replacing or rejuvenating the media's role as public watchdog?

It certainly seems to be the case that social media use is positively correlated with political engagement,[119] but has it qualitatively altered – deepened or widened – that engagement? Much of the research on citizen journalism has been on potential shifts in power relations in terms of the media industry, and in the ways in which 'user-generated' content has become embedded in news production processes.[120] However, the deeply personal nature of the content of citizen journalists makes the question of authenticity absolutely essential. For example,

114 OECD, 'Global Competency for an Inclusive World' (2017) Programme for International Student Assessment.

115 M. McLuhan, *Understanding Media* (Mentor 1964) 5.

116 Bennett *et al.* (n 16).

117 S. Joseph, 'Social media, political change and human rights' (2012) 35 *Boston College International and Comparative Law Review* 145, 148.

118 L. Chouliaraki and B. Blaagaard, 'Introduction' (2013) 14(2) *Journalism Studies* 150, 150.

119 M. Xenosa, A. Vromenb and B. Loaderc, 'The great equalizer? Patterns of social media use and youth political engagement in three advanced democracies' (2014) 17(2) *Information, Communication & Society* 151.

120 N. Usher, 'The Appropriation/Amplification Model of Citizen Journalism' (2017) 11(2–3) *Journalism Practice* 247.

user-generated content about the experience of being gay in a homophobic authoritarian state can be a powerful weapon for human rights advocates. The impact of campaigns can be dramatically reduced if the individual turns out to be an imposter. One example of this was when Amina Arrat, otherwise known as the 'Gay Girl in Damascus' turned out to be Tom McMaster, a student from Scotland.[121] It is also why there has been endless debate and scrutiny of the authenticity of Bana al-Abed's Twitter account.[122] While the transformative potential of social media is clearly considerable, it is an enormous task to assess any human rights 'dividend'. Aside from the populist and authoritarian uses described here, we must add the phenomena around 'trolling' and the racist, anti-immigrant, homophobic and anti-democratic nature of much of the material on social media. Together these issues mean that social media represent a range of serious threats to human rights. The response of governments and the new global corporate giants of Facebook, Twitter and others to these challenges in terms of regulation will determine the longer-term human rights impacts of new communications technologies.

Conclusions

Knowing about and understanding human rights is essential for their effective protection and enforcement. One need only consider the media systems of countries perceived to be gross violators, such as North Korea, Syria or Eritrea, to see the correlation between a functioning and healthy media, and the protection of human rights. From one perspective, the media plays a crucial role in providing a source of information that is then part of public debate, and the basis upon which rational choices can be made by policymakers, and by the voters whom they represent. As Walter Lippmann pointed out, people rely on the media to gain political knowledge because they are unlikely to gain it from personal experience. He argued that 'the world that [people] have to deal with politically is out of reach, out of sight, out of mind' and so we become dependent upon the media.[123] Of course, this dependence means that the media has the potential to 'wield significant influence over citizens' perceptions, opinions and behaviours'.[124] However, 'the news' is not a straightforward digest of daily events – there are constraints regarding what is perceived by journalists and editors to be newsworthy. News organisations are also businesses, and the commercial pressure

121 D. Kenner, 'Straight Guy in Scotland' (2011) *Foreign Policy*.

122 R. Gladstone, M. Specia and S. Ember, 'Girl Posting to Twitter From Aleppo Gains Sympathy, but Doubts Follow' *New York Times*, (7 December 2016) available online at: www.nytimes.com/2016/12/07/world/middleeast/aleppo-twitter-girl-syria.html?_r=0 (accessed 18 April 2017).

123 W. Lippman, *Public Opinion* (Free Press 1922) 18.

124 R. Entman, J. Matthes and L. Pellicano, 'Nature, sources and effects of news framing', in K. Wahl-Jorgensen and T. Hanitzsch (eds) *The Handbook of Journalism Studies* (Routledge 2009) 175–190, 179.

to attract and maintain an audience means that the most topical or controversial issues are the ones that will be selected for coverage. There is a clear preference for certain types of articles: those that are simple, are accompanied by a powerful image, and tell what could be predicted as a compelling story. This is good and bad news for coverage of human rights. It means that only those human rights that accord with the values and factors that influence the coverage of all news more generally will be covered.

This chapter began with the observation that while the media is central to the constitutional safeguarding of human rights in liberal democracies, it is increasingly accused of helping to destroy the very idea of human rights. The concepts of agenda-setting and framing help understand the ways in which media make decisions about what to cover and which issues to highlight. This is potentially very significant in the context of human rights, where these choices can determine the types of rights, and rights-holders that get political attention. As Pasackow claims: '[m]ore than simply reporting, media outlets have the power to indirectly determine emergency responses and disaster priorities.'[125] The ways in which human rights are framed in the media will not only put forward certain interpretations of their power, scope and relevance, but also strengthen or undermine their legitimacy in the public debate. Research suggests that repetition of frames is very powerful in silencing alternative perspectives, particularly if they are tailored to fit with already held assumptions of specific audiences.[126]

When trying to explain what the media is and what it does when it comes to human rights there is a strong tendency to resort to metaphor – from watchdog, to lapdog, to wolves and other monsters. This betrays a desire to simplify, presenting the complex, amorphous and expanding array of communication systems we now refer to as the media. How can the idea of human rights be sustained and nourished in this context? How can the general public be encouraged to sympathize with others and recognize their human rights, particularly those in other countries? The evidence presented here helps to explain and understand the complex ways the media impacts upon the idea of human rights. Prominent in this story is the power of nationalism, which remains a strong force and is often the framework through which media make sense of global events, meaning that human rights are for citizens only: the rights of non-citizens are systematically overlooked.[127] The advent of new global media technologies inevitably raise hopes of a world where human rights are widely recognized and respected, but

---

125 Cited in T. Borer. 'Introduction: Willful ignorance – news production, audience reception and responses to suffering', in T. Borer (ed.) *Media, Mobilisation and Human Rights: Mediating Suffering*. (Zed Books 2012) 1–41, 21–22.

126 D. Chong, 'Framing strategies for economic and social rights in the United States' in T. A. Borer (ed.) *Media, Mobilisation and Human Rights: Mediating Suffering* (Zed Books 2012) 122–142.

127 M. Kyriakidou, 'Imagining ourselves beyond the nation? Exploring cosmopolitanism in relation to media coverage of distant suffering' (2009) 9(3) *Studies in Ethnicity and Nationalism* 481.

these cosmopolitan desires are met with a gap or deficit[128] between the potential and the reality of media systems that remain resolutely human institutions, complete with their deficiencies, bias and vulnerability to powerful interests.

Bibliography

C. Apodaca, 'The whole world could be watching: human rights and the media' (2007) 6(2) *Journal of Human Rights* 147.

P. Anderson, 'Challenges for journalism', in P. J. Anderson and G. Ward (eds) *The Future of Journalism in the Advanced Democracies* (Ashgate 2007) 51–72.

P. Anderson and G. Ward, *The Future of Journalism in the Advanced Democracies* (Ashgate 2007).

J. Assange, 'State and Terrorist Conspiracies' and 'Conspiracy as Governance' (2006) available online at: http://cryptome.org/0002/ja-conspiracies.pdf (accessed 17 May 2017).

E. Balabanova, *The Media and Human Rights: The Cosmopolitan Promise.* (Routledge 2014)

Z. Bauman, D. Bigo, P. Esteves, E. Guild, V. Jabri, D. Lyon and R. B. J. Walker, 'After Snowden: Rethinking the Impact of Surveillance' (2014) 8(2) *International Political Sociology* 121

L. Beattie, D. Miller, E. Miller and G. Philo, 'The media and Africa: images of disaster and rebellion' in G. Philo (ed.) *Message Received* (Longman 1999).

C. Beitz, *The Idea of Human Rights* (Oxford University Press 2009).

L. Bennett, R. G. Lawrence and S. Livingston, 'None dare call it torture: Indexing and the limits of press independence in the Abu Ghraib scandal' (2006) 563(3) *Journal of Communication* 467.

V. Berry and A. McChesney, 'Human rights and foreign policy-making' in T. O. Matthews and C. Pratt (eds), *Human Rights in Canadian Foreign Policy* (McGill-Queen's University Press 1988).

T. Borer. 'Introduction: Willful ignorance – news production, audience reception and responses to suffering', in T. Borer (ed) *Media, Mobilisation and Human Rights: Mediating Suffering.* (Zed Books 2012) 1–41.

T. Borer. '"Fresh, wet tears": shock media and human rights awareness campaigns', in T. Borer (ed.) *Media, Mobilisation, and Human Rights: Mediating Suffering* (Zed Books 2012) 143–180.

S. Brandle, *Television News and Human Rights in the US & UK: The Violations Will Not Be Televised* (Routledge 2016).

B. Brevini, A. Hintz and P. McCurdy (eds) *Beyond WikiLeaks: Implications for the Future of Communications, Journalism and Society* (Palgrave Macmillan 2013).

P. Brewer and K. Gross, 'Values, framing and citizens' thoughts about policy issues: effects on content and quantity' (2005) 26(6) *Political Psychology* 929.

S. Caliendo, M. Gibney and A. Payne, ''All the news that's fit to print?' *New York Times* coverage of human rights violations' (1999) 4 *Harvard International Journal of Press/Politics* 48.

128 E. Balabanova, *The Media and Human Rights: The Cosmopolitan Promise* (Routledge 2014).

D. Casciani, 'The case of the cat deportation tale', *BBC* (London, 6 October 2011) available online at: www.bbc.co.uk/news/uk-politics-15171980 (accessed 7 April 2017).

D. Chong, 'Framing strategies for economic and social rights in the United States' in T. A. Borer (ed.) *Media, Mobilisation and Human Rights: Mediating Suffering* (Zed Books 2012) 122–142.

L. Chouliaraki, *The Ironic Spectator. Solidarity in the Age of Post-Humanitarianism* (Polity 2013).

L. Chouliaraki and B. Blaagaard, 'Introduction' (2013) 14(2) *Journalism Studies* 150.

P. Coe, 'Redefining 'media' using a 'media-as-a-constitutional-component' concept: an evaluation of the need for the European Court of Human Rights to alter its understanding of 'media' within a new media landscape' (2007) 37(1) *Legal Studies* 25.

B. Cohen, *The Press and Foreign Policy* (Princeton University Press 1963).

W. Cole, 'No news is good news: Human rights coverage in the American print media, 1980–2000' (2010) 9(3) *Journal of Human Rights* 303.

Cooper and J. Turcotte, 'Celebrity diplomats as mobilisers? Celebrities and activism in a hypermediated time', in T. A. Borer (ed.) *Media, Mobilisation, and Human Rights: Mediating Suffering* (Zed Books 2012) 181–204.

J. Curran, *Media and Power* (Routledge 2002).

J. Curran, N. Fenton and D. Freedman, *Misunderstanding the Internet* (Routledge 2012).

J. Curran and J. Seaton, *Power Without Responsibility. The Press, Broadcasting and New Media in Britain* (Routledge 2003).

N. Chomsky, *Necessary Illusions: Thought Control in Democratic Societies* (South End Press 1989).

N. Davies, *Flat Earth News* (Vintage 2008).

H. Dieter and R. Kumar, 'The downside of celebrity diplomacy: The neglected complexity of development' (2008) 14(3) *Global Governance* 259.

L. Dittrich, 'The celebrity shall save you' (2009) *Esquire* 118.

J. Donnelly, *International Human Rights. Dilemmas in World Politics* (4th edn, Westview Press 2013).

J. Donnelly, *Universal Human Rights in Theory and Practice* (3rd edn, Cornell University Press 2013).

G. Donohue, P. Tichenor and C. Olien, 'A guard dog perspective on the role of media' (1995) 45(2) *Journal of Communication* 115.

W. Donsbach, 'Psychology of news decisions: Factors behind journalists' professional behaviour' (2004) 5(2) *Journalism* 131.

J. Doyle, '£500,000 a week in legal aid for prisoners' human rights claims: YOU pay for them to seek easier life or early release', *Daily Mail* (London, 30 December 2012) available online at: www.dailymail.co.uk/news/article-2255065/500-000-legal-aid-week-prisoners-human-rights-claims-YOU-pay-seek-easier-life-early-release.html (accessed 7 April 2017).

R. Entman, 'Framing: Toward a clarification of a fractured paradigm' (1993) 43(4) *Journal of Communication* 51.

R. Entman, J. Matthes and L. Pellicano, 'Nature, sources and effects of news framing', in K. Wahl-Jorgensen and T. Hanitzsch (eds) *The Handbook of Journalism Studies* (Routledge 2009) 175–190.

B. Franklin. *Newszak and News Media* (Arnold 1997).

M. Frohardt and J. Temin, *Use and Abuse of Media in Vulnerable* Societies (United States Institute of Peace 2003).

A.Galloway, 'Media jihad: What PR can learn in Islamic State's public relations masterclass' (2016) *Public Relations Review.*

J. Galtung and M. Ruge, 'The structure of foreign news: the presentation of the Congo, Cuba and Cyprus crises in four Norwegian newspapers' (1965) 2 *Journal of Peace Research* 64.

W. Gamson and A. Modigliani, 'The changing course of affirmative action' in R. Braungart and M. Braungart (eds) *Research in Political Sociology* (Jai Press 1987) 137–177.

H. Gans, *Deciding What's News: A Study of CBS Evening News, NBC Nightly News, Newsweek and Time* (Pantheon Books 1979).

P. Gerbaudo, *Tweets and the Streets: Social Media and Contemporary Activism* (Pluto Press 2012).

T. Gitlin, *The Whole World Is Watching* (University of California Press 1980).

M. Gladwell, 'Small change: Why the revolution will not be tweeted', *The New Yorker* (New York, 4 October 2010) available online at: www.newyorker.com/magazine/2010/10/04/small-change-malcolm-gladwell (accessed 8 April 2017).

R. Gladstone, M. Specia and S. Ember, 'Girl Posting to Twitter From Aleppo Gains Sympathy, but Doubts Follow' *New York Times* (7th December 2016) available online at: www.nytimes.com/2016/12/07/world/middleeast/aleppo-twitter-girl-syria.html?_r=0 (accessed 18 April 2017).

J. Habermas, *The Structural Transformation of the Public Sphere* (Polity Press 1989)

S. Hall, 'The determinations of news photographs' in S. Cohen and J. Young (eds) *The Manufacture of News: Deviance, Social Problems and the Mass Media* (Constable 1973) 226–243.

A.Hallin, *The Uncensored War: The Media and Vietnam* (University of California Press 1986).

T. Hammarberg, 'Foreword: Media freedom in Europe' in H. R. Writings (ed.) *Human Rights and a Changing Media Landscape* (Council of Europe Publishing 2011) 7–20.

T. Harcup and D. O'Neil, 'What is news? Galtung and Ruge revisited' (2001) 2(2) *Journalism Studies* 261.

J. Hartley, *Understanding News* (Methuen 1982).

E. Herman, 'The Propaganda model: A retrospective' (Against All Reason, 9 December 2003).

V. Hawkins, *The Silence of the UN Security Council: Conflict and Peace Enforcement in the 1990s* (European Press Academic Publishing 2004).

D. Haynes, 'The Celebritization of Human Trafficking' (2014) 653(1) *The Annals of the American Academy of Political and Social Science* 25.

International Council on Human Rights Policy (ICHRP), *Journalism, Media and the Challenge of Human Rights Reporting* (ICHRP 2002).

Internews, *Speak Up, Speak Out: A Toolkit for Reporting on Human Rights Issues* (Internews 2012).

S. Joseph, 'Social media, political change and human rights' (2012) 35 *Boston College International and Comparative Law Review* 145.

D. Kenner, 'Straight Guy in Scotland' (2011) *Foreign Policy.*

R. Köcher, 'Bloodhounds or missionaries: Role definitions of German and British journalists' (1986) 1(1) *European Journal of Communication* 27.

M. Kyriakidou, 'Imagining ourselves beyond the nation? Exploring cosmopolitanism in relation to media coverage of distant suffering' (2009) 9(3) *Studies in Ethnicity and Nationalism* 481.

K. Lang and G. E. Lang. 'The mass media and voting' in B. Berelson and M. Janowitz (eds) *Reader in Public Opinion and Communication* (Free Press 1966) 455–472.

J. Lewis, A. Williams and B. Franklin, 'A compromised fourth estate? UK newspapers journalism, public relations and news sources' (2008) 9(1) *Journalism Studies.*

J. Lewis, A. Williams and B. Franklin, 'Four rumours and an explanation: a political economic account of journalists' changing newsgathering and reporting practices' (2008) 2(1) *Journalism Practice* 27.

W. Lippman, *Public Opinion* (Free Press 1922).

E. Louw, *The Media and Political Process* (2nd edn, Sage 2010).

R. McChesney, *Rich Media, Poor Democracy: Communications Politics in Dubious Times* (The New Press 2000).

M. McCombs, *Setting the Agenda: The Mass Media and Public Opinion* (Polity Press 2004).

M. McCombs and D. Shaw, 'The agenda-setting function of mass media' (1972) 36(2) *Public Opinion Quarterly* 176.

M. McLuhan, *Understanding Media* (Mentor 1964).

B. McNair, *An Introduction to Political Communication* (5th edn, Routledge 2011).

B. McNair, *News and Journalism in the UK* (5th edn, Routledge 2009).

E. McPherson, 'How editors choose which human rights news to cover: a case study of Mexican newspapers' in T. A. Borer (ed) *Media, Mobilisation, and Human Rights: Mediating Suffering* (Zed Books 2012) 96–121.

D. McQuail, *Media Performance* (Sage 1992).

D. McQuail, *McQuail's Mass Communication Theory* (Sage 2000).

T. Miles, 'Torture still being carried out at Guantanamo Bay despite US denials, says UN investigator', *The Independent* (London, 14 December 2017) available online at: www.independent.co.uk/news/world/americas/torture-guantanamo-bay-detention-centre-9-11-conspirator-un-human-rights-investigation-pentagon-a8109231.html (accessed 15 December 2017).

J. Metzl, 'Information technology and human rights' (1996) 18(4) *Human Rights Qu*arterly 705.

A. Mitchell, J. Gottfried, M. Barthel and E. Shearer, 'The Modern News Consumer: News Attitudes and Practices in the Digital Era' (Pew Research Centre 2016).

S. Moeller, *Compassion Fatigue: How the Media Sell Disease, Famine, War and Death* (Routledge 1999).

E. Morozov, *The Net Delusion: The Dark Side of Internet Freedom* (Public Affairs Books 2011).

A.Myers, T. Klak and T. Koehl, 'The inscription of difference: news coverage of the conflicts in Rwanda and Bosnia' (1996) 15(1) *Political Geography* 21.

N. Ndlela, 'The African paradigm: The coverage of the Zimbabwean crisis in the Norwegian media' (2005) 2 *Westminster Papers in Communication and Culture* 71.

OECD, 'Global Competency for an Inclusive World' (2017) Programme for International Student Assessment.

Ofcom, 'News Consumption in the UK: Research Report' (Ofcom 2015).

R. Omaar and A. Waal, 'Disaster pornography from Somalia' (1993) 61 *Media and Values* 13.

D. O'Neill and T. Harcup. 'News values and selectivity' in K. Wahl-Jorgensen and T. Hanitzsch (eds) *The Handbook of Journalism Studies* (Routledge 2009) 161–174.

J. Ovsiovitch, 'News coverage of human rights' (1993) 46 *Political Research Quarterly* 671.

J. Palmer, *Spinning into Control: News Values and Source Strategies* (Leicester University Press 2000).

Z. Pan and G. Kosicki, 'Framing analysis: An approach to news discourse' (1993) 10(1) *Political Communication* 55.

J. Petley, 'What rights? Whose responsibilities?' (2009) 43 Soundings-London-Lawrence and Wishart 77.

M. Poster, 'Cyberdemocracy: internet and the public sphere', in D. Porter (ed) *Internet Culture.* (Routledge 1997) 201–218.

J. Postill, 'Freedom technologists and the new protest movements: A theory of protest formulas' (2014) 20(4) *Convergence: The International Journal of Research into New Media Technologies* 402.

K. J. Pritchard, 'Human rights: a decent respect for public opinion' (1991) 13 *Human Rights Quarterly* 123.

J. R. Pruce, 'The spectacle of suffering and humanitarian intervention in Somalia' in T. A. Borer (ed.) *Media, Mobilisation, and Human Rights: Mediating Suffering* (Zed Books 2012) 216–239.

J. Ron and O. Thoms, 'Shaping the Northern media's human rights coverage, 1986–2000' (2007) 44(4) *Journal of Peace Research* 385.

H. Sandvig, 'The mass media and the United Nations in a human rights dilemma' in A. Eide, A. Skogly and S. Skogly (eds) *Human Rights and the Media* (Norwegian Institute of Human Rights 1988).

N. Schimmel, 'Media accountability to investigate human rights violations' (2009) 21 *Peace Review: A Journal of Social Justice* 442.

D. Shah, M. Watts, D. Domke and D. P. Fan, 'News framing and cueing of issue regimes: explaining Clinton's public approval in spite of scandal' (2002) 66 *Public Opinion Quarterly* 339.

M. Shearlaw, 'What happened to Darfur after George Clooney came to town?' (2014) Guardian, 11 December available online at: www.theguardian.com/world/2014/dec/11/-sp-george-cloony-darfur-what-next (accessed 20 December 2017).

J. Staab, 'The role of news factors in news selection: A theoretical reconsideration' (1990) 5 *European Journal of Communication* 423.

J. Street, *Mass Media, Politics and Democracy* (2nd edn, Palgrave Macmillan 2011).

M. Temple, 'Dumbing down is good for you' (2006), 1(2) *British Politics* 257.

K. Tester, *Compassion, Morality and the Media* (Open University Press 2001).

G. Tuchman, *Making News: A Study in the Social Construction of Reality* (Free Press 1978).

F. Turner, *From Counterculture to Cyberculture* (2006).

UNHCR, 'Special Envoy Angelina Jolie' (n.d.) available online at: www.unhcr.org/uk/special-envoy-angelina-jolie.html (accessed 20 December 2017).

N. Usher, 'The Appropriation/Amplification Model of Citizen Journalism' (2017) 11(2–3) *Journalism Practice* 247.

P. Valley, 'From A-lister to aid worker: Does celebrity diplomacy really work?' (2009) *Independent* 17 January

A. Wagner, 'The Monstering of Human Rights' (19 September 2014) available online at: https://adam1cor.files.wordpress.com/2014/09/the-monstering-of-human-rights-adam-wagner-2014.pdf (accessed 7 April 2017).

A. Wagner, 'More press nonsense, this time on human rights damages' (UK Human Rights Blog, 12 October 2013) available online at: https://ukhumanrightsblog.com/2013/10/12/more-press-nonsense-this-time-on-human-rights-damages/ (accessed 18 July 2018).

A. Wagner, 'No, The Sun, the Human Rights Act is not the EU' (UK Human Rights Blog, 10 February 2013) available online at: https://ukhumanrightsblog.com/2013/02/10/no-the-sun-the-human-rights-act-is-not-the-eu/ (accessed 18 July 2018).

A. Wagner, 'Times on the legal naughty step for bizarre 'right to marry' headline splash' (UK Human Rights Blog, 29 December 2013) available online at: https://ukhumanrightsblog.com/2013/12/29/times-on-the-legal-naughty-step-for-bizarre-right-to-marry-headline-splash/ (accessed 18 July 2018).

T. Weiss, *The United Nations and Changing World Politics* (Westview Press 2009).

J. Westerstahl and F. Johansson, 'Foreign news; News values and ideologies', (1994) 9 *European Journal of Communication* 71.

C. Woodhouse, 'Euro judges go against UK in 3 out of 5 cases', *The Sun* (London, 24 August 2014) available online at: www.thesun.co.uk/archives/politics/1053158/euro-judges-go-against-uk-in-3-out-of-5-cases/ (accessed 7 April 2017).

M. Xenosa, A. Vromenb and B. Loaderc, 'The great equalizer? Patterns of social media use and youth political engagement in three advanced democracies' (2014) 17(2) *Information, Communication & Society* 151.

8 Careful what you wish for

Press criticism of the legal protection of human rights

Jacob Rowbottom

Introduction

Other chapters in this volume have commented on the negative coverage of the Human Rights Act and the European Convention on Human Rights (ECHR) in certain sections of the media. This chapter, however, provides a reminder that there is one area where newspapers are not so critical of the ECHR and seem to favour judicial protection – the field of media freedom. Many of the usual complaints about the protection of fundamental rights tend to be put to one side when media freedom is at stake. To examine this, the chapter will first look at two of the key objections commonly advanced against the judicial protection of human rights in certain sections of the media: that foreign judges impose their views on the UK and that judges take on an activist and creative role. These criticisms do not simply query the merits of the particular decision, but also question the legitimacy of the domestic and Strasbourg court to make such decisions.

This chapter will show how various newspapers have relied on the human rights laws that they have subjected to intense criticism. A number of judicial decisions have liberalised media laws including contempt of court, the protection of sources and defamation law. However, the decisions that have bolstered press freedom have not been attacked as judicial activism or as an imposition by 'foreign judges'. The willingness of various newspapers to rely on the judicial protection of press freedom maybe suggests that readers should question whether the media are really as opposed to rights protection as is sometimes suggested. The apparent double standards allow us to cast a sceptical eye over both the criticisms of the court and the arguments made for press freedom. The criticisms targeted at the court are largely motivated by disagreement with the outcomes of a case. The hostility towards rights protection shown by parts of the media and the willingness to rely on that protection shows the collision of the ideological agenda pursued in the editorial departments and the interests of the media institution itself. The fact that the criticism of the courts serves an ideological agenda or that the championing of press freedom serves the self-interest of the industry does not mean that the arguments advanced in the newspapers are without merit. The tension, however, makes transparent a more ambivalent attitude of the press towards rights protection, which may not be apparent at first sight, reminding us not to take the assertions in the newspapers at face value.

That certain newspapers abandon the criticisms of human rights protection when press freedom is at stake is unsurprising. However, the position should not be immediately dismissed as self-serving hypocrisy. After looking at the various decisions that have strengthened press freedom, the chapter will consider whether the seeming contradiction can be explained by treating press freedom as a special type of right to which the usual criticisms of the courts do not apply. To examine this argument, it is important to understand the concept of press freedom commonly advanced in newspapers and by representatives of the press. The newspapers typically rely on an instrumental understanding of media freedom, in which journalists perform a vital democratic function and hold the powerful to account. While powerful, that argument need not point to the strong protection of press freedom sought by the press and is consistent with the more qualified accounts of the rights held by the media.

Before looking at these issues in further detail, I should add a note of caution. The views I refer to are not shared by all sections of the press at all times. I will attribute a position to 'the press', by which I mean only those sections of the press that campaign against rights protection. Even among the titles that are critical of rights protection, the position of a single newspaper may not be consistent over time and the editorial slant can vary with personnel and events. There is a danger of presenting a caricature of what 'the press' advocates. However, there are a number of newspapers that at various points have called for withdrawal from the ECHR and the repeal of the Human Rights Act 1998, which will provide the central focus for the attitude of 'the press' in this chapter.

Criticism of rights protection

This section presents the general thrust of the main arguments against the legal protection of human rights that have been made repeatedly in the pages of several newspapers. In particular, two strands of argument will be considered: that the human rights ruling are made by 'foreign' courts and unelected judges. After considering each of these criticisms, the discussion will then show how newspapers have relied on these very features of human rights law when their own interests are at stake. Newspapers have gone to the courts both at home and in Strasbourg, sometimes calling for expansive interpretations of media freedom and freedom of expression to be taken, and sometimes asking the courts to challenge the will of the legislature. In looking at these issues, the discussion will reveal the tension in which the press utilise the institutions and procedures of which they are normally so critical.

Foreign judges deciding UK cases

A common criticism of the European Convention on Human Rights relates to the right to petition the Strasbourg Court to claim that the UK failed to protect fundamental rights. The criticism runs that the right to petition allows foreign judges to override decisions made at the national level. The point can be seen in the media coverage of certain deportation decisions. For example, in a 2013 editorial, *The Sun* complained that Abu Qatada could not be 'kicked out' of the country because 'the foreign judges of the European Court of Human Rights overruled our own court'.[1] *The Daily Express* wrote in an editorial on deportation issues that 'Britain is not an Independent Nation' because 'foreign judges in Strasbourg are able to dictate decisions in the interests of foreign criminals that are prejudicial to the well-being of the British people and the British Government just lamely accepts them'.[2] The thrust of the criticism is that the power to govern ourselves is being surrendered to foreign judges.

More generally, some editorials argue that human rights decisions should rest with domestic judges, rather than those in Strasbourg. For example, a 2014 editorial in *The Sun* argued that the ECtHR thinks 'Britain is a routine abuser of human rights' and that the 'buck should stop with our judges' rather than those in Strasbourg.[3] Demands are also made for a rebalancing between the ECtHR and the UK, so that the Strasbourg Court provides greater leeway to the domestic authorities. Along these lines, a *Times* editorial wrote that 'Too much power that belongs in a sovereign parliament has drained elsewhere, in particular to the European Court of Human Rights'.[4] While recognising the importance of human rights, the editorial warned against an 'excessively strict interpretation of human rights' and preferred a scheme for rights protection where it would be 'the British parliament that would adjudicate rather than a distant court in Strasbourg'.[5] The central criticism advanced in certain parts of the press is that foreign judges should not determine questions of rights protection for the UK, and that the institutions should be changed to give greater weight to the domestic authorities.

The point is not only about the judges being 'foreign'. The coverage sometimes questions the quality of the judges sitting on the European Court of Human Rights. The criticism runs that the judges appointed to the Court, who 'are routinely overturning the decisions of parliament and Britain's highest courts', have limited experience and are appointed on a political basis.[6] A similar line of attack runs that some of those judges come from countries that have a limited history of human rights protection.[7] The result is that the 'unelected and in many cases

1 Editorial, 'Qatada Saga' *The Sun* (19 April 2013).

2 Editorial, 'A Reminder that Britain is not an Independent Nation' *The Daily Express* (3 May 2013).

3 Editorial, 'Wrongly judged' *The Sun* (24 August 2014). See further, in this volume, D Mead, "They offer you a feature on stockings and suspenders next to a call for stiffer penalties for sex offenders": do we learn more about the media than about human rights from tabloid coverage of human rights stories? Chapter 1.

4 Editorial, 'Good Judgment' *The Times* (3 October 2014).

5 *Ibid.* See further, in this volume, S Reynolds, 'It's Not Me, It's You: Examining the Print Media's Approach to 'Europe' in Brexit Britain' chapter 2.

6 J Ungoed-Thomas and J Follain, 'Judges with little experience on £150,000 a year' *The Sunday Times* (13 February 2011).

7 J Willey and M Hickley, 'In some of their own countries, justice is nothing more than a sick joke, with executions, torture and corruption the norm ... and yet they sit in judgment on OUR law' *The Daily Mail* (29 May 2002).

unqualified' judges in Strasbourg have 'given human rights a bad name'.[8] The line of argument continues that the Strasbourg Court has over-reached its remit and become 'supra-national lawmakers, accountable to nobody for their whims'.[9] The general thrust of the criticism is not simply with the outcomes of the decision, but with defects at the heart of the institution.

The merits of these various criticisms are the subject of debate and this is not the place to resolve those issues. Instead, the point to be made here is that British newspapers have relied on the Strasbourg Court – the very institution that is attacked as a foreign imposition on the UK – to protect press freedom. In such cases, the newspapers have gone to the 'foreign judges' precisely because the national authorities have failed to provide sufficient protection to the rights of the newspapers. As a consequence, the names of British newspapers can be found in several of the landmark decisions in Strasbourg that have defined Article 10.

One of the most celebrated landmarks in the early Article 10 jurisprudence was the decision in *Sunday Times v UK*, in which the Strasbourg judges provided a catalyst for reform of the domestic laws on contempt of court.[10] The case arose out of *The Sunday Times*' campaign for justice for the victims of the drug Thalidomide.[11] By the early 1970s, the company that had produced Thalidomide was in the process of negotiating a settlement with a group of victims that had initiated claims in negligence. Incensed by the pressure being applied to the victims' families to accept a relatively low sum in settlement for the claims,[12] *The Sunday Times* published an article in 1972 arguing that the company had a moral obligation to make a more generous payment to the claimants. When the newspaper proposed to publish a further article criticising the testing and marketing of Thalidomide, the Attorney General obtained an injunction restraining publication on the grounds that it would be a contempt of court.

While the Court of Appeal accepted the newspaper's appeal, the initial decision to grant the injunction was restored by the House of Lords.[13] At the heart of the Lords' reasoning was a concern that legal disputes should not be 'prejudged' in the national press, and that the *Sunday Times* article threatened to do just that by implying the negligence of the company. Lord Reid spoke of the dangers of 'trial by media', which would generate 'disrespect for the processes of the law' and would be unfavourable to 'unpopular people and unpopular causes'.[14] Lord Diplock went further by stating that the article that had already been published about the litigation, as well as the proposed article, amounted to a contempt.[15]

8 T Kavanagh, 'Laws gave criminals a soft option' *The Sun* (3 October 2014).
9 'Comment', *The Daily Mail*, 4 September 2013
10 *Sunday Times v UK* (1979) 2 EHRR 245.
11 The campaign started in 1967, when the *Sunday Times* published a number of articles about the victims of Thalidomide.
12 See H Evans, *My Paper Chase* (Little Brown 2009) 325.
13 *Attorney General v Sunday Times* [1974] AC 273.
14 *Ibid.* at 300.
15 *Ibid.* at 312.

To Lord Diplock, holding a litigant up to 'public obloquy' could hinder access to the courts and usurp the function of the court.[16] He thought that if the law failed to offer adequate protection to the victims, then the press should direct their efforts towards Parliament rather than 'vilifying individual litigants'.[17] As a result of this holding, *The Sunday Times* was unable to publish its full investigation into the testing and marketing of Thalidomide until the injunction was finally discharged in 1976. The investigations conducted by *The Sunday Times* about Thalidomide are rightly regarded as a highlight in the history of British campaigning journalism. However, the episode showed how limited the protection afforded to freedom of expression was in the domestic law.

The newspaper, however, did not leave the matter there and took the case to the European Court of Human Rights, which found that the injunction violated Article 10. Whatever the risks of trial by media, the Strasbourg Court thought no such risk was posed by the article in question, which was 'couched in moderate terms' and presented the other sides of the story. The European Court stated that 'courts cannot operate in a vacuum' and, while the courts are the final arbiter of legal disputes, 'this does not mean that there can be no prior discussion of disputes elsewhere'. While the domestic courts had treated the issue as the balancing of two competing public interests, the Strasbourg Court stated that Article 10 requires that priority be given to freedom of expression. The Court thereby provided a strict interpretation of the right, stating that competing interests are to be 'narrowly interpreted' and providing less leeway to the domestic authorities. The Strasbourg Court found that the *Sunday Times*, proposed article was on a matter of 'undisputed public concern' in discussing the 'question of where responsibility for a tragedy of this kind actually lies', and the role of the press was not limited to discussing the general principles away from specific cases. In this celebrated case, a panel of 'foreign' judges explained why the domestic court had failed to comply with the ECHR – the very thing that some newspapers complain about. Nonetheless, the case is regarded as a landmark. It helped to establish key principles in the Article 10 jurisprudence. It also had effects in relation to the domestic law, prompting the legislative reform of contempt of court law.

In another landmark decision, *Goodwin v UK*, the Strasbourg Court ruled that the domestic courts failed to give adequate protection to journalists' sources.[18] A journalist at a specialist publication received confidential information about a company's business plan and planned to publish an article based on that information. The company obtained an injunction to restrain publication of the story. However, the company went further and sought a court order requiring the journalist to disclose the identity of the confidential source. Under the domestic law, s.10 of the Contempt of Court Act 1981 provides that a person is not in contempt of court for refusing to disclose a source of a story for publication unless

16 *Ibid.* at 313.

17 *Ibid.*

18 *Goodwin v UK* (1996) 22 EHRR 123, 1 B.H.R.C. 81.

it is necessary for the prevention of crime and disorder, for national security or in the interests of justice. Despite this protection, the domestic court ordered the journalist to disclose the source, finding that it was necessary in the interests of justice to enable the company take measures to secure the return of any leaked documents and preventing further dissemination of the information.[19] The decision was upheld in the House of Lords, with Lord Bridge describing the question for the court as 'weighing one public interest against another' and referring to the process as a 'balancing exercise'.[20] He concluded his ruling with the statement that '[f]reedom of speech is itself a right which is dependent on the rule of law for its protection and it is paradoxical that a serious challenge to the rule of law should be mounted by responsible journalists'.[21]

Lord Bridge's decision was criticised in some newspapers, with *The Times* writing that the protection of sources was being 'eroded' and that freedom of expression was seen in the UK 'merely as the residual freedom to impart information and ideas if it is not restricted by law'.[22] *The Guardian* wrote that '[o]nly the English judiciary with their narrow and restrictive approach to free speech could have ruled in favour of commerce'.[23] *The Guardian* has not been part of the media attack on the Strasbourg Court and *The Times* has been more moderate than some of the other titles. However, it is interesting to note that those newspapers seem to suggest the domestic courts were failing to provide robust protection for human rights.

The journalist took the claim to the Strasbourg Court which ruled that disclosure was not necessary to protect the interests of justice.[24] The injunction restricting publication already provided sufficient protection by preventing the further dissemination of the business plan. Consequently, 'the threat of damage to the company had thus already been neutralised by the injunction', which thereby rendered the disclosure order redundant.[25] The interests of the company in preventing dissemination of the information outside of the press and in unmasking a disloyal employee were not sufficient to outweigh the interest in press freedom.[26] In coming to this conclusion, the Court did not challenge the framework being used by the domestic court or the types of consideration being taken into account, but instead disagreed on the weighting assigned to the different factors on the facts of the case.

After the decision in *Goodwin* in Strasbourg, *The Times* ran an article commenting that it was a 'good judgment from the Strasbourg court', welcoming the decision at a time when 'pan-European institutions are not popular with everyone in Britain'.[27] The feature invited readers to contrast Lord Bridge's domestic

19 *X Ltd v Morgan-Grampian* [1991] 1 AC 1 at 44–45.
20 *Ibid.* at 43.
21 *Ibid.* at 49.
22 Editorial, 'Freedom of Expression' *The Times* (9 April 1990).
23 Editorial, 'Next stop Strasbourg' *The Guardian* (11 April 1990).
24 *Goodwin v UK* (1996) 22 EHRR 123
25 *Ibid.* at [42].
26 *Ibid.* at [45].
27 Editorial 'Our Fretful Relations' *The Times* (28 March 1996).

ruling with the Strasbourg judge's 'commonsense judgment'.[28] The coverage of the domestic court and subsequent Strasbourg Court rulings seemed to suggest that the British judiciary was hopelessly out of touch with modern democratic values and had something to learn from their European counterparts. Not everyone was pleased by the decision and the government at the time argued that the decision was wrongly decided and made calls to reform the Strasbourg Court.[29]

These are not the only Strasbourg rulings that the press benefitted from prior to the Human Rights Act 1998. The Strasbourg Court made rulings on a variety of issues relating to freedom of expression that has paved the way for the liberalisation of media laws in the UK and elsewhere. In particular, the Strasbourg Court has ruled that large libel damages are a disproportionate interference with Article 10.[30] The Court has stressed that wide latitude should be granted to statements of opinion, and that public figures are expected to tolerate more criticism and scrutiny than a private individual.[31] An interim injunction that continued to restrain the publication of *Spycatcher* in the UK after the title was freely available in other countries was found to violate Article 10.[32] The Strasbourg Court has also held that hate speech laws should not inhibit a journalist informing the public of certain extreme views that are held in society.[33] The 'foreign' judges have taken the lead in several areas protecting certain aspects of freedom of expression. In some of these cases, the Court pointed out ways that the domestic law was deficient and the rulings have chipped away at the various restrictions on press freedom. More generally, these cases have cumulatively influenced the attitude of the domestic court in relation to press freedom.

It might be argued that prior to the Human Rights Act 1998, the press had no alternative but to go to Strasbourg. The domestic judges recognised the principle of freedom of expression and freedom of the press, but did not have the legal tools to offer sufficient protection. However, since the Human Rights Act 1998 came into force, new powers have been granted to the domestic courts to protect rights directly. Nonetheless, the press has still gone to Strasbourg to secure greater protection for press freedom and has continued to ask 'foreign' judges to challenge the decisions of the domestic courts. For example, in *Interbrew*, Sedley LJ ordered a journalist to disclose the identity of a source that had leaked information about a possible takeover bid.[34] While the court order was not enforced, the case was taken to the Strasbourg Court. Again, the UK was found to be in

28 Though the article did go on to criticise the Court's decision to award damages for mental anguish.

29 The calls were made following *Goodwin* and a number of other decisions finding the UK to be in violation of the Convention. See, P Wynn Davies, 'Human Rights, British Wrongs' *The Independent* (28 November 1996).

30 *Tolstoy Miloslavsky v United Kingdom* (1995) 20 EHRR 442.

31 *Lingens v Austria* (1986) 8 EHRR 407

32 *The Observer v United Kingdom* (1991) 14 EHRR 153.

33 *Jersild v Denmark* (1995) 19 EHRR 1.

34 *Interbrew SA v Financial Times LTD* [2002] E.M.L.R. 24

violation of Article 10.[35] Like *Goodwin*, the Court did not challenge the framework applied by the domestic court, but concluded that the reasons for ordering disclosure were not sufficiently pressing.

In another notable post-HRA application, the *Daily Mirror* took the UK to Strasbourg following Naomi Campbell's successful privacy action in relation to an article about her treatment at Narcotic Anonymous.[36] The Court found that an order for the newspaper to pay Campbell's success fees under a conditional fee agreement was a disproportionate interference with Article 10. A journalist is also relying on Article 10 after failing to secure access to documents under the Freedom of Information Act 2000 relating to inquiries conducted by the Charity Commission. While the Supreme Court rejected the journalist's claim in *Kennedy*, the case is (at the time of writing) being taken Strasbourg to argue for an expansive interpretation of Article 10 to include freedom of information rights.[37]

The discussion so far shows that there has been a significant history of the British press using the Strasbourg Court to secure the protection of press rights. Some of those decisions have been landmarks in developing the Article 10 jurisprudence. More broadly, the decisions have also promoted a more positive protection of the media in the UK, providing an environment that has seen a liberalisation in certain areas of law. The Strasbourg rulings have also led to a movement away from the traditional British approach whereby the rights of the media are 'neither more nor less than that of the general public'.[38] Instead, the domestic courts have followed the Strasbourg jurisprudence to find that journalists 'are accorded a special position' under Article 10.[39] 'Foreign' judges may be finding against British institutions, but for the most part these rulings were welcomed by the press. This observation does not answer the criticisms of the Strasbourg Court advanced in the press. However, the reliance on the ECHR by the press stands in stark contrast to the editorial attack on the legitimacy of the institutions in certain newspapers.

Unelected judges

The second line of attack that is sometimes advanced against the legal protection of fundamental rights is that the decisions come from an unelected branch of government. This is frequently mixed in with the attack on the Strasbourg Court, with some newspapers making a point against foreign *and* unelected judges. However, the attack based on the unelected judges and undemocratic nature of judicial decisions has been made in relation to the domestic courts too. The point is made both when the courts challenge decisions made by democratically accountable branches of government, and when the court develops the law.

---

35 *Financial Times v UK* (2010) 50 EHRR 46

36 *Mirror Group Newspapers v UK* (2011) 53 EHRR 5.

37 See *Kennedy v Charity Commission* [2014] UKSC 20. The application has been communicated to the ECtHR, listed as *Times and Kennedy v UK* (App. No 64367/14, 17/03/2015).

38 *Attorney General v Guardian Newspapers Ltd (No 2)* [1990] 1 AC 109 at 183.

39 *In re Guardian News and Media and others* [2013] EWCA Crim 2367 at 56.

The line of attack can be seen in the response by certain sections of the media to the growth of privacy laws. Following a number of decisions developing the law of misuse of private information, most notably *Mosley*,[40] Paul Dacre, of *The Daily Mail*, complained that the development lacks an explicit democratic sanction: 'This law is not coming from Parliament – no, that would smack of democracy – but from the arrogant and amoral judgements – words I use very deliberately – of one man.'[41] The comments were made in 2008 and were targeted at Sir David Eady who, as the then Judge in Charge of the Jury List, was, in practice, the lead media law judge in England and Wales. While Eady J had a considerable role in shaping the emerging law, the growth of the protection of private information was not the project of one judge acting alone. The development was the result of the House of Lords' decision in *Campbell v MGN*[42] and other significant privacy rulings in the lower courts.[43] Aside from the criticism of Sir David Eady, the central point in Dacre's attack was the development of privacy law being undemocratic. Similar points continue to be made. In an article reviewing privacy injunctions, a reporter for *The Sun* wrote: 'The UK courts have created a privacy law to mask the stealthy wealthy but without asking Parliament.'[44] Of course, the development did receive statutory sanction through the enactment of the Human Rights Act 1998, though the terms of the Act left it to the courts to flesh out the scope and level of protection for privacy. The central force of the criticism is that expansion of the law has come from an unelected branch.

The point is made not only in relation to privacy, but permeates discussion of the courts in some parts of the press. Newspapers and their columnists draw attention to the unelected status of the judges when criticising a controversial judicial decision. For example, a Supreme Court ruling that the indefinite notification requirements for sex offenders without review are disproportionate was criticised as 'a ruling by unelected judges'.[45] In a criticism of immigration policies, one newspaper columnist wrote that to 'regain control over our borders we would first need to regain control over those unelected judges'.[46] To consider this further, it is worth unpacking the attack on unelected judges to different components. First is the argument that the judges are being overly creative in developing

40 *Mosley v. News Group Newspapers* [2008] EWHC 1777 (QB).

41 Paul Dacre, Speech to the Society of Editors Conference in Bristol (November 2008).

42 *Campbell v MGN* [2004] UKHL 22.

43 See *McKennitt v Ash* [2006] EWCA Civ 1714.

44 T Wells, 'Unexpected items in the gagging area' *The Sun* (6 May 2016).

45 I Drury, 'Using Human Rights Law, Of Course' *The Daily Mail* (22 March 2016). Discussing the effects of *R. (on the application of F) v Secretary of State for the Home Department* [2010] UKSC 17, [2011] 1 AC 331.

46 C Brooker, 'We can't control our borders until we control those judges' *The Daily Telegraph* (9 November 2014). The article was subsequently amended to include a correction that Article 8 was not solely responsible for the immigration policies complained of. On the portrayal of immigrants in the media more broadly, see, in this volume, E Drywood and H Gray, 'Demonising Immigrants: How a Human Rights Narrative Has Contributed to Negative Portrayals of Immigrants in the UK Media' Chapter 5.

the common law and Convention rights, in a way that takes them beyond their proper function. A second element of the criticism is that in interpreting legislation, invalidating executive decisions or making declarations of incompatibility, the unelected court is challenging the democratic will.

There is nothing wrong with arguments about the proper balance of power between the courts and the democratically accountable branches of government. The debate is one that is prominent in constitutional law, between legal constitutionalists and political constitutionalists.[47] While the former champion the role of the courts in protecting fundamental rights, the latter see legal rights as touching on contested political matters that are better left to the legislature and executive. By focusing on the unelected nature of judiciary, the press could be seen to be taking a political constitutionalist's position. Nonetheless, newspapers have relied on the unelected judges to protect press freedom and called upon them to act creatively, in developing the common law, challenging the legislature and interpreting the ECHR.

In developing the common law, the courts took piecemeal steps to liberalise defamation law prior to the Defamation Act 2013. In the 1993 decision in *Derbyshire CC v Times Newspapers*, the House of Lords ruled that local authorities cannot bring claims in defamation, relying on the common law right to freedom of expression.[48] The decision was a considerable breakthrough in protecting the criticism of public bodies. The decision was welcomed by *The Times* as a move towards stronger protection for the right to freedom of expression, which is 'commonplace in most democracies and indeed forms part of the European Convention on Human Rights which Britain has signed'.[49]

Several years later in *Reynolds v Times Newspapers*, the lawyers for *The Times* asked the courts to change defamation law to provide a blanket good faith defence for all political expression. While the House of Lords rejected *The Times'* argument for a blanket defence, they nonetheless recognised a new form of qualified privilege to protect responsible publications on matters of public interest.[50] That was a major development in the courts and the level of creativity can be compared to that shown in developing privacy law. The decision received a mixed reception from those newspapers that covered the case, with some commenting that the responsible journalism test was too uncertain. The criticism, however, suggests that the courts were not radical enough and does not condemn the judges for being too creative.[51] When the House of Lords reaffirmed the liberalising intent

47 For discussion of political constitutionalism, see the essays in the special edition 'Political Constitutions', 14 *German Law Journal* No. 12 (2013).

48 *Derbyshire CC v Times Newspapers* [1993] AC 534.

49 Editorial, 'A Lead From the Lords' *The Times* (19 February 1993).

50 *Reynolds v Times Newspapers* [2001] 2 AC 127.

51 A Brett, 'A show of words' *The Times* (9 November 1999); Guardian Media Section, 'Ditch these libel laws' *The Guardian* (1 November 1999); Editorial, 'Libel remains a lottery' *The Guardian* (29 October 1999).

of *Reynolds*, nearly seven years later in *Jameel*,[52] the newspapers were less ambivalent and *The Times* stated that the ruling was 'an important victory not only for the British press but for the vital democratic principle of free expression'.[53]

The criticism of judicial creativity is found not only with the common law, but extends to the interpretation of the ECHR. The privacy cases are sometimes criticised for going beyond the text of Article 8 of the ECHR and treating the Convention as a living instrument.[54] However, that has not stopped newspapers arguing that the court should follow the more creative interpretations of Article 10; for example, a *Times*' journalist once asked the courts to recognise freedom of information as a fundamental right.[55] While there is momentum towards such a position in the Strasbourg jurisprudence, it is a step that clearly goes against the past decisions of the ECtHR and stretches the text of the Convention. In bringing such a claim, some newspapers are effectively calling for the Convention to be treated as a 'living instrument'.

The media have relied on human rights principles to challenge statutory measures enacted by Parliament. In 2015, the Investigatory Powers Tribunal heard a claim from News Group Newspapers and journalists from *The Sun* in relation to the use of Regulation of Investigatory Powers Act 2000 to authorise police to access their communications data that might have revealed a journalist's source.[56] Burton J found that the statute did not provide adequate protection for journalists, as it lacked a process for prior authorisation of the data request before an independent body. In coming to this conclusion, Burton J referred to a range of cases on the protection of journalists' sources, including the leading authorities from the European Court of Human Rights. The decision criticised the statutory scheme for failing to meet the standards in the Article 10 jurisprudence. Unsurprisingly, the tribunal was not criticised in the tabloid press as an example of a judge overstepping the mark, relying on foreign rulings or challenging the will of the legislature. Instead, *The Sun* reported that that tribunal 'slammed the Government for failing to give enough protection to journalists' sources in law' as required under the ECHR.[57] An editorial on the same day argued that the police had been 'spurred on by the Leveson Inquiry's war on the Press' and welcomed the tribunal's ruling that 'our rights were breached'.[58] Far from denouncing the

52 *Jameel v Wall Street Journal* [2006] UKHL 44, [2007] AC 359.

53 Editorial, 'The Public Interest' *The Times* (12 October 2006).

54 Comment, 'After 60 years, bring back Britain's rights' *The Daily Mail* (4 September 2013).

55 *Kennedy v Charity Commission* [2014] UKSC 20. While *The Times* described the decision as a 'victory', the rejection of the Article 10 argument was '[n]ot a good day' for 'the cause of greater openness in public affairs', see Editorial, 'A Supreme Court's ruling is a surprise victory for open Justice and the right to know' *The Times* (27 March 2014).

56 *News Group Newspapers v Commissioner of the Police of the Metropolis* [2015] UKIPTrib 14_176-H, [2016] 2 All ER 483. Burton J also found one of the four authorisations not to be necessary or proportionate.

57 'As Court Rules Met Officers Acted Illegally In Sun Plebgate Probe ...' *The Sun* (18 December 2015).

58 Editorial, 'Cops Shamed' *The Sun* (18 December 2015).

ruling as a challenge to the legislative will or gutting powers to fight crime and terrorism, the Tribunal's ruling was welcomed for checking the other branches of government.

The cases discussed above are just examples, of which there are more in other areas of law. For instance, the press have relied on Article 10 to support claims to limit or remove reporting restrictions on court cases,[59] although, in that area, the courts have tended to give greater emphasis to domestic common law principles.[60] Some newspapers have gone a step further in calling for measures that could give more power to the courts. For example, some titles have advocated a British Bill of Rights. While it is not clear what that would entail, it is likely to mean that domestic courts will retain significant powers to curb the democratically accountable part of government. The hope of some newspapers may be that a domestic bill would protect only those rights which fit with their agenda. Along such lines, some representatives of the media have gone further and called for a UK version of the US Constitution's First Amendment that prohibits laws that abridge freedom of speech. If such a provision were introduced, it would grant even stronger power to the courts to challenge the will of the legislature. That proposal is therefore for a step towards a more legal constitution, which stands in stark contrast to the complaints advanced against the courts.

While some newspapers are strongly critical of unelected judges in some areas, the same titles do not show much trust for politicians when press freedom is at stake. That much was evident in the protests by some newspapers following the Leveson Report's proposals for a statutory body to recognise a new regulator for the press. The criticisms of the proposal showed a high level of mistrust for politicians, fearing that a body accrediting a regulator would open the door to political meddling and censorship. Of course, making a stand for press freedom in the course of political debate is not inconsistent with the criticisms against the court. A political constitutionalist would argue that the appropriate place for constitutional debate is within the political branches.[61] There is also good reason why the press may prefer Parliament as the final arbiter of rights protection, as the newspaper companies have considerable political lobbying power. The tension with the criticism of the courts arises when the newspaper threatens to make a legal challenge if their position does not prevail in the political branches. Along these lines, some representatives from the newspaper industry have threatened to challenge the new system of press self-regulation in the courts by relying on Article 10, and have expressed a willingness to go to Strasbourg if necessary.[62]

---

59 *Guardian News and Media Ltd, Re HM Treasury v Ahmed* [2010] UKSC 1.

60 *Guardian News and Media Ltd v City of Westminster Magistrates' Court* [2012] EWCA Civ 420

61 See, in this volume, M Gordon, 'Instrumentalism in Human Rights and the Media: Locking Out Democratic Scepticism?' Chapter 10.

62 L O'Carroll, 'Tory and Leveson plans for exemplary privacy damages "may be unlawful"' *The Guardian* (21 February 2013).

So far, the discussion has shown that certain sections of the press have attacked the legitimacy of the courts in human rights cases on account of the foreign judges in Strasbourg and the unelected judges both in Strasbourg and the domestic courts. Nonetheless the legitimacy of these courts is not called into question when the human right in question is media freedom. Conversely, sections of the press champion the legitimacy of the legislature to strike the right balance with certain rights, but attack the legitimacy of Parliament to interfere with press freedom.

This seeming tension may simply reflect the differing priorities of the editorial and legal departments within the media institution. The former may have a view on the role of the judiciary and Parliament, while the legal department is simply charged with serving the interests of the media institution. However, that takes us only so far, as the position outlined in the editorial content is not consistent on these issues and does not criticise rulings in favour of press freedom as undemocratic. However, to simply argue that the press is inconsistent would be to take a cheap shot. We would not expect newspaper to be consistent, and the same criticism could be made of many commentators. Those parts of the press that do criticise the legal protection of human rights do not have a coherent constitutional theory, and nor should we expect them to. This inconsistency might, however, lead us to take a sceptical view both of the attack on human rights protection and of the arguments for more robust protection of press freedom. Does the press really think human rights protection is undemocratic and foreign? At the very least the press should be careful what it wishes for, as if the status of the court to protect human rights issues is undermined, that will also impact on the legal protection of press freedom.

None of this is to suggest that the courts have acted consistently as champions of press freedom. That much is clear from the various cases that have gone to Strasbourg as a result of the limited protection from the domestic courts. There have been numerous cases where the courts have given limited weight to press freedom and made disappointing decisions. In the domestic court, the protection of journalists' sources and government secrecy provide two such examples.[63] While the courts took some steps to liberalise defamation law, there were still many decisions where the courts took a very restrictive approach to expression rights.[64] The disappointing decisions provide one possible explanation for the disenchantment with the HRA among some newspapers; another reason is that other Convention rights can restrict the activities of the press, and Article 10(2)

---

63 For example, see *Interbrew SA v Financial Times LTD* [2002] E.M.L.R. 24 and *Shayler* [2002] UKHL 11, [2003] 1 AC 247 for widely criticised domestic decisions.

64 For example, in *Jameel v Wall Street Journal* [2006] UKHL 44, [2007] AC 359, which is regarded as a liberal ruling in relation to *Reynolds*, a majority of the House of Lords rejected an argument that a company should show damage to bring an action in defamation. The position was later changed in the Defamation Act 2013. For discussion see M Amos, 'What Has Human Rights Law Done for the Media?' in M Amos, J Harrison and L Woods (eds), *Freedom of Expression and the Media* (Leiden, Martinus Nijhoff 2012) 207

provides a framework permitting such restrictions.[65] The most obvious example is privacy law, as the Article 8 rights have led to new restrictions that were not present prior to the Human Rights Act 1998. That is not the only Convention right that can curb the press. Others include rights against ill treatment,[66] fair trial rights and the protection of reputation. The individual decisions that restrict the media can be criticised without arguing that judges lack the legitimacy to deal with such questions. However, the line of argument advanced in certain parts of the media goes beyond the criticism of specific rulings. The position in some parts of the press seems to be to demand the near-absolute protection of the media, while arguing that other rights should be left to the legislature. The next section will consider whether a case can be made for such special protection for media rights.

An exceptional approach to press freedom

The position of the press could be defended from charges of inconsistency if the different treatment of press freedom was justified in principle. Such an argument would have to reframe the position in certain newspapers away from a simplistic attack on foreign and unelected judges. Instead a more subtle argument could be advanced along the lines that the problem lies with the judicial protection of certain types of human rights, but not others. In particular, the argument would have to explain why press freedom falls into a category of rights that is more appropriate for judicial protection. Such an explanation can be advanced along the lines that speech and media rights have a special place in the political constitution, as these are the very rights that secure the wellbeing of the democratic system. While certain questions are best left to Parliament as an elected and accountable body, this only makes sense if members of the public have the information and communications necessary to hold government to account and make informed decisions.

Such a line of argument would be consistent with the general arguments for press freedom advanced in many newspapers. In particular, editorials trumpet the role of the press in a democracy exposing abuses of power and holding government to account. For example, in the aftermath of the Leveson Report, a *Daily Mail* editorial stated that:

> A true liberal would understand that, in a democracy, it is a key function of the free Press to hold politicians and public figures to account and, where it exists, expose corruption and incompetence. It was, after all, a free Press which revealed the criminal abuse of expenses by MPs.[67]

The MPs' expenses scandal is the example most frequently relied on in recent years. Other recent examples include the Edward Snowden disclosures about the security

65 *Ibid.*, 199–203.
66 *A v BBC* [2014] UKSC 25, relying on Article 3.
67 'Comment', *The Daily Mail* (27 February 2013).

services and the Panama Papers about tax avoidance.[68] The Thalidomide scandal reported by *The Times* provides another example, sometimes held up as a British equivalent to Watergate, as a landmark for serious journalism. The role of the media in holding government to account is often referred to as the 'watchdog' function.

There are several reasons why this 'watchdog' argument has proved to be so attractive to the media industry.[69] First, it provides a powerful and intuitive argument that justifies the freedoms of the press as a type of public service. The press claims its freedoms are important not for its own self-interest, but for the sake of the public and democracy in general. Framing the argument in that way provides a way to legitimate the powers of the press. The argument does not rest on an unrealistic account of democracy. The press does not claim to be educating the public or turning them into ideal deliberators. Instead, the press can serve its function by acting on behalf of the public and sounding the alarm in the event of potential misconduct. The argument also helps to distinguish press freedom from freedom of speech, as under the watchdog argument the press claim to be acting as specialist scrutiny body acting in the public interest.[70] Accordingly, the argument can be used to claim special rights and privileges that are normally unavailable to individual speakers.

That account of press freedom that is often advanced in newspaper columns is widely shared. The Leveson Report – criticised by many newspapers as a foe of press freedom for by putting forward proposals for a new system of press regulation – took a similar stance, stating that the press is an institution that can perform many functions not normally expected of an individual speaker. One of the functions identified in the Report is for the press to act 'as a check on political and other holders of power'.[71] The point has often been recognised in both the domestic courts and the Strasbourg Court, referring to the role of the media acting as a 'public watchdog'.[72]

Despite this agreement on the justification for press freedom, the interpretation of what the watchdog argument requires is radically different. The courts in the UK and Europe have found that press freedom warrants the strongest protection only when the newspaper acts responsibly (fulfilling certain standards in newsgathering) and when covering subject matter regarded as in the public interest.[73] The view taken in the courts is generally that sensational reporting about

68 Both stories were based on confidential information leaked to the press, see L Harding, *The Snowden Files* (Guardian Books, 2014) and J Garside, H Watt and D Pegg 'The Panama Papers: how the world's rich and famous hide their money offshore' *The Guardian* (3 April 2016).

69 This section draws on the argument in J Rowbottom 'Leveson, press freedom and the watchdogs' (2013) 21 *Renewal* 57.

70 R Dworkin, *A Matter of Principle* (Oxford, Clarendon Press 1985) 386.

71 Lord Justice Leveson, *An Inquiry into the Culture, Practices and Ethics of the Press: Report* (HC 780, 2012) 64.

72 See *Axel Springer v Germany* [2012] E.M.L.R. 15, (2012) 55 EHRR 6 at 79.

73 *Ibid.* at 93.

the lives of celebrities has little to do with the democratic functions. Under this methodology, the domestic court and the ECtHR looks at whether the restriction is going to interfere with the watchdog function, and assess the proportionality of the measure. For this reason, the courts have been more willing to impose limits on intrusive reporting that has little relation to political discussion.

By contrast, the sections of the press that are most critical of human rights protection tend to reject the balancing of press freedom with other rights and interests. The newspapers argue that any interference with the prerogatives of an editor threatens press freedom. The public interest, on this view, is not something to be factored into a balancing exercise. Instead, the argument runs that the public interest has a constant presence in all press activity and should normally trump other rights. This can be seen in the arguments that any article that helps a newspaper to remain profitable is in the public interest.[74] The view is also apparent from the response to the Supreme Court's decision to uphold a privacy injunction in *PJS*.[75] *The Sun* argued that it was not for the court – 'old duffer judges' – to decide where the public interest lies, but for the public.[76] The newspaper stated that the danger lies in judges imposing their 'snooty prejudices about tabloid stories they find "prurient".'[77] The newspapers might use the language of public service to justify their freedoms, but their stance is that the press should be free to decide when a story is in the public interest. Taking such a view is to prioritise media freedom over other competing rights. It is ultimately the media making the call of where the public interest lies, subject only to the constraints of the market.

The constant presence of a public interest in all press activity, including the celebrity gossip stories, reflects an understanding of press freedom that emphasises the structural independence of the press from government, rather than on the content published in each instance. Implicit in the statements from the press is a separation of powers style argument, that we should be concerned whenever government seeks to interfere with the functioning of the media.[78] On this view, limiting stories that have little public interest content should be cause for alarm. Such controls could be seen as the thin end of the wedge, and could soon be used to suppress or chill stories that have a genuine public interest. Alternatively, if the government is free to enact measures restricting the ability of the media to report stories that are profitable but not in the public interest, that power could be used as leverage over the media entities.

The instrumental case for freedom of expression is not really a typical human rights argument and does not provide firm ground for press freedom as a trump.

74 The courts have on occasion accepted arguments along such lines. See *ETK v News Group Newspapers* [2011] EWCA Civ 439, [2011] 1 W.L.R. 1827 at 13.

75 *PJS v News Group Newspapers Ltd* [2016] UKSC 26; [2016] 2 W.L.R. 1253.

76 T Wells, 'The day free speech drowned in a padding pool of olive oil' *The Sun* (20 May 2016).

77 Editorial, 'Court's snobs reign Supreme' *The Sun* (20 May 2016).

78 For the classic statement of the separation of powers argument, see P Stewart, 'Or of the Press' (1975) 26 *Hastings Law Journal* 631.

Taking an instrumental justification has invited the sort of balancing and conditions that certain sections of the press object to. Press freedom is primarily about the rights of an institution, and its justification lies primarily in protecting the interests of the audience. For this reason, Ronald Dworkin commented that the instrumental justifications provides for a 'policy for free speech' that seeks to 'secure some general benefit to the community as a whole'.[79] Once this step is taken, Dworkin warned, it invites arguments that the rights of the press 'must be balanced against other private and social interests in the community'.[80] In addition to balancing, the argument implies that media freedom only warrants strong protection when it is performing one of its democratic functions. That is reflected in the Leveson Report's acceptance that press freedom is 'largely understood as an instrumental good, to be valued, promoted and protected to the extent that it is with the result that it is thereby enabled to flourish commercially as a sector and to serve its important democratic functions'.[81] Under that view, the functions that are assigned to the media help to define the limits of the right.

The arguments advanced in the press coverage tend to stress the watchdog function as the pre-eminent role of the press. However, the instrumental justification of the press serving a democracy is not limited to the watchdog function and the court has tended to see that function as one role among several performed by the media. In particular, the courts have also emphasised the role of the press in providing information and ideas to the public, and also to provide a forum for discussion. These other functions may not warrant such robust protection for press independence, and may even warrant some state intervention. For example, regulations promoting accurate content in the media can serve the functions of the media in ensuring the public is well informed.

The watchdog argument is powerful and provides a strong reason for caution in relation to government interventions into media freedom. The discussion has shown that the press and courts seem to share an instrumental understanding of press freedom, but have different views on what that means. The argument advanced in some sections of the press seeks to rely on the instrumental justification to construct a libertarian model for freedom of expression. Such a case can be made, but it faces an uphill struggle in arguing that the interests of a democracy are best served by prioritising the interests of the press. That view focuses only on government as a source of danger and fails to accommodate the problems posed by the power of the press in a democracy. While the press plays a vital role in a democracy, that does not mean its work should be free from external checks, including some legal controls. The law of privacy can be seen as a response to concerns about media power and an attempt to impose a limit on the source

79 R Dworkin *A Matter of Principle* (Oxford, Clarendon Press 1985) 385–386.

80 *Ibid.*

81 Lord Justice Leveson, *An Inquiry into the Culture, Practices and Ethics of the Press: Report*, (HC 780, 2012) 63.

of that power.[82] This also explains why the analogy with the separation of powers does not make a convincing case for the type of freedom demanded by the press. The separation of powers does not demand complete independence and an absence of any legal constraint, but simply requires that one branch of government does not dominate another. Furthermore, a model of press freedom that is based on structural separation does not sit easily with the close relations between the press and government that is often practised.[83]

The discussion has shown how certain sections of the press are critical of the courts in relation to human rights protection, but have been the beneficiaries of human rights protection at both the domestic and European level. Despite the critical commentary about the courts and demands for rights considerations to be balanced by Parliament, newspapers have sometimes called for the near absolute protection for press freedom. The arguments advanced by the press often tend towards overstatement and are often self-serving. This is to be expected, as a detailed and careful argument is unlikely to mobilise public opinion. This section has explored whether this position can be explained through an understanding of press freedom as an instrumental right justified through its service to democracy. Along these lines, the reason why Parliament is trusted to balance various rights and interests is because it is democratically accountable. The argument then runs that this mechanism of accountability itself depends on press freedom. This provides a compelling case for press freedom that is not present in all human rights claims. The difficulty with that argument is that such an instrumental justification does not point to an absolute right of media freedom and is unlikely to offer the level of protection demanded by some parts of the press.[84] The instrumental approach looks at the general benefits of press freedom and allows limits on that freedom to be imposed when those benefits are outweighed by other rights and interests. This explains why the courts, while sharing the language of democratic watchdogs, often disappoint the press, especially when it comes to privacy rulings.

Conclusion

Among some quarters of the press, there has been considerable hostility to the legal protection of fundamental human rights. The two lines of argument commonly raised are that human rights principles are the product of a foreign court and that the judicial protection of fundamental rights is undemocratic. Both arguments are defensible. The point of this chapter has not been to challenge the merits of those views, but rather to contrast that position with the newspapers' reliance on legal human rights protection in relation to press freedom. Far from

---

82 J Rowbottom, 'A Landmark at a Turning Point: Campbell and the use of privacy law to constrain media power' (2015) 7 *Journal of Media Law* 170.

83 J Rowbottom, 'Politicians, the press and lobbying' (2013) 5 *Journal of Media Law* 253.

84 See J Rowbottom (n 69) on the difference between the strong and weak forms of the watchdog argument.

challenging the legitimacy of the courts to intervene in such matters, newspapers have often celebrated the judicial victories.

This is no surprise. Whatever one's ideological commitments, media institutions will use whatever resources they have to advance their own cause and interests. Nor should we expect various newspapers to have a coherent constitutional theory. Whatever its view of the appropriate balance of power between the branches of government, the primary concern is the protection of press freedom. What is of interest is that some sections of the press push a far-reaching account of the right to press freedom that is suspicious of both the courts and legislature. It is a vision that stresses the independence of the press from other branches of government. The vision appears to be demanding and its full implications have not been fleshed out.

The instrumental argument for press freedom serving British democracy advanced in some parts of the media does not put the right on such a secure footing. While it is possible to argue that democracy requires absolute protection of the press, the watchdog function does not offer as strong an argument for protecting the press where its actions are deemed to be harmful to the public or individuals. The newspapers are holders of significant power themselves and require some accountability mechanisms. The press may have good reason to oppose certain restrictions, but sometimes the commentators over-play press freedom arguments. What is important is the focus on specific proposals and decisions, to consider the impact on media freedom. This often requires a close look at the detail, at the more subtle effects and does not lend itself to powerful headlines.

Bibliography

M Amos, 'What Has Human Rights Law Done for the Media?' in M Amos, J Harrison and L Woods (eds), *Freedom of Expression and the Media* (Leiden, Martinus Nijhoff 2012).

R Dworkin, *A Matter of Principle* (Oxford, Clarendon Press 1985).

H Evans, *My Paper Chase* (Little Brown 2009).

L Harding, *The Snowden Files* (Guardian Books 2014).

Lord Justice Leveson, *An Inquiry into the Culture, Practices and Ethics of the Press: Report* (HC 780, 2012).

J Rowbottom, 'A Landmark at a Turning Point: Campbell and the use of privacy law to constrain media power' (2015) 7 *Journal of Media Law* 170.

J Rowbottom, 'Leveson, press freedom and the watchdogs' (2013) 21 *Renewal* 57.

J Rowbottom, 'Politicians, the press and lobbying' (2013) 5 *Journal of Media Law* 253.

P Stewart, 'Or of the Press' (1975) 26 *Hastings Law Journal* 631.

Part IV

Op-Eds

9 Arguing the case for human rights in Brexit Britain

Colm O'Cinnéide

Introduction

UK human rights law is controversial. In particular, the central role played by the Human Rights Act 1998 (HRA) and its associated case-law in protecting rights through law has attracted sharp media and political criticism – not least because of the way in which the HRA has ensured that the jurisprudence of the European Court of Human Rights (hereafter 'the Strasbourg Court') has come to exert a substantial influence over the development of UK law.[1] This symbiotic relationship between the HRA and the European Convention on Human Rights (ECHR) case-law has been the focus of plenty of media hostility.[2] It has also generated academic and political demands for the law to be reformed, with a view to diluting the influence of the Strasbourg Court over UK law and replacing it with more 'home-grown' standards that allegedly better reflect the UK's constitutional traditions of judicial deference to political and administrative decision-making.[3] In response, human rights experts and civil society advocates who value the role played by the HRA/ECHR in British public life have sprung to the defence of the existing state of UK human rights law.[4] This debate has

1 For an overview (with apologies for the self-citation in the first footnote of this piece), see C. O'Cinnéide, 'Human Rights and the UK Constitution', in D. Oliver, J. Jowell and C. O'Cinnéide (eds), *The Changing Constitution* (OUP, 2015) 67–103.

2 See, in this volume, D. Mead, ' "They offer you a feature on stockings and suspenders next to a call for stiffer penalties for sex offenders": do we learn more about the media than about human rights from tabloid coverage of human rights stories?' Chapter 1 and S. Reynolds, 'It's Not Me, It's You: Examining the Print Media's Approach to "Europe" in Brexit Britain' Chapter 2.

3 See, for example, M. Pinto-Duschinsky, *Bring Rights Back Home: Making human rights compatible with parliamentary democracy in the UK* (Policy Exchange, 2011); Conservative Party, *Protecting Human Rights in the UK*, 3 October 2014, available online at: www.conservatives.com/~/media/Files/Downloadable%20Files/HUMAN_RIGHTS.pdfN. Malcolm, *Human Rights and Political Wrongs* (Judicial Power Project, 2017), available online at: http://judicialpowerproject.org.uk/human-rights-and-political-wrongs-a-new-approach-to-human-rights-law/

4 See, for example, the material published by RightsInfo, available online at: www.rightsinfo.org; the 'Save the Human Rights Act' campaign launched by Liberty, available online at:

rumbled on with varying degrees of intensity since the late 2000s, increasing or decreasing in intensity and volume depending on background events. At the time of writing, it is relatively quiescent: for now, it has been obscured by the complexity of the great Brexit imbroglio. However, the issue has not gone away: the HRA/ECHR's impact on UK law is likely to continue to be a sore spot for a long time to come.

Given that Brexit seems to have induced a partial lull in this debate, it makes sense to try and take stock, and to assess the current state of play. It is also a good time to look at some of the arguments being made by both sides to the debate, with a view to identifying some of their relative strengths and weaknesses and assessing how they may develop in the future. Thus far, clear battle lines have been established between the two sides of the HRA/ECHR controversy – but changes in circumstances may require changes in battle formation, and a critical analysis of the argumentative terrain may help shed some light on how this clash of legal ideas may evolve.

In what follows, particular attention is paid to how defenders of the legal status quo – i.e. the experts and advocates who support retaining the HRA as it currently stands, and by extension the ECHR's current influence over British law – have responded to media and political attacks on UK human rights law.[5] There is plenty of excellent analysis in this book and elsewhere of the criticism directed at the HRA/ECHR, and of the hostile media coverage directed at UK human rights law more generally. However, the strengths and weaknesses of the countercase put forward by supporters of the status quo have attracted less commentary. This chapter aims to rectify this. It sets out in particular to examine how human rights experts[6] and advocates have engaged with the media and political attacks

---

www.libertyhumanrights.org.uk/campaigning/save-our-human-rights-act-0; the campaigning material produced by Act for the Act, available online at: http://actfortheact.uk/; the support work undertaken by the Thomas Paine Initiative, summarised at http://global-dialogue.eu/projects/thomas-paine-initiative/; C. O'Cinnéide, *Human Rights and the UK Constitution* (British Academy, 2012); M. Amos, 'The Value of the European Court of Human Rights to the United Kingdom" (2017) 28(3) *European Journal of International* Law 763–785; D. Grieve MP, 'Why Human Rights Should Matter to Conservatives', speech to the UCL Constitutional Unit 3 December 2014, available online at: www.dominicgrieve.org.uk/news/why-human-rights-should-matter-conservatives

5 To reflect the way in which the HRA and ECHR are often intertwined in public debate, and the manner in which criticism of one of these legal instruments is often linked to criticism of the other, the term 'HRA/ECHR' will be used throughout this chapter.

6 The phrase 'human rights experts' is used here as a shorthand to denote commentators who claim to have particular expertise in the design and functioning of human rights law broadly defined: its use is not meant to imply that all commentators with expertise in this field support retention of the HRA/ECHR in their current form. The phrase 'human rights advocates' is used here to denote campaigners who are focused on making political arguments in favour of retention of the HRA/ECHR, as distinct from arguments that are rooted in claims of particular expertise. However, the distinction between 'expert' and 'advocate' in this context, as elsewhere, is blurred.

on the HRA/ECHR, and to critically assess the coherence of the argumentation they have deployed in response to these attacks.

In so doing, this chapter draws upon published academic and advocate commentary on the HRA/ECHR debate. It also takes account of mainstream and social media discussions, as well as public debates in which the author has participated or at which the author has been present during the period 2005–2017. The aim of this analysis is not to probe specific lines of academic argumentation as such: indeed, it is striking how little has been written in academic journals specifically on the HRA/ECHR controversy. Instead, the focus of this chapter is on wider patterns of expert/advocate responses to the media and political attacks on the HRA/ECHR, which often are not framed in academic terms but rather are targeted at a wider audience with a view to building up public support for the existing state of UK human rights law. Particular attention is paid to certain key arguments which crop up repeatedly across this pattern of responses: it is these recurring elements of the public defence of the HRA/ECHR whose cogency and impact are analysed in what follows.

In assessing the strength and weaknesses of these particular arguments, the main yardstick will be their efficacy as rhetorical moves designed to gain popular and/or elite support for the HRA/ECHR, or at least to contest hostile criticism of existing UK human rights law. In other words, they will not be assessed by reference to some Platonic idea of ideal legal argumentation, or to the extent to which they adhere to a Habermasian ideal speech situation. Instead, a narrowly focused variant of the 'critical realist' approach proposed by Raymond Geuss is utilised, whereby the cogency of these arguments will be assessed by their skilfulness in opening up ways of bringing about a desired end point (in this case, retention of something approximating to the current legal status quo in relation to the HRA/ECHR) while being responsive to the surrounding political, social and legal environment.[7] In this regard, the extent to which such arguments adhere to the traditional logical virtues of consistency, inter-subjective coherence and meaningful engagement with counter-claims will be taken into account – on the assumption that such rational forms of argumentation qualify as effective examples of what Simone Chambers describes as 'deliberative rhetoric', by engaging 'citizens' practical judgment and as such [treating their] audience as autonomous deliberators deserving of respect', and thus are likely to find at least some substantive purchase in the public sphere.[8] However, some consideration will also be given to their effectiveness as what Chambers refers to as 'plebiscitary rhetoric', i.e. speech deployed instrumentally just to win an argument, generally by means

7 Geuss has described a 'skill' in the political sense as 'an ability to act in a flexible way that is responsive to features of the given environment with the result that action or interaction is enhanced': see R. Geuss, *Philosophy and Real Politics* (Princeton University Press, 2008) 15–16.

8 This may be optimistic – but it is an assumption on which all academic speech, for example, is predicated. For the classic analysis of the role of rational, inter-subjective argumentation within a functioning public sphere, see J. Habermas, *The Structural Transformation of the Public Sphere* (Cambridge, MA: MIT Press, 1989; orig. 1962).

of invoking an emotional or identitarian response, which may not necessarily conform to the ideals of democratic deliberation theory but which still can be highly effective in winning hearts and minds in charged public debates.[9] The background political context is also taken into account in this analysis, in particular the potential impact of Brexit on this debate going forward.

The first part of this chapter surveys the development of the HRA/ECHR debate over the last few years, with particular attention being paid to how (i) media narratives have helped to construct a climate of political hostility vis-à-vis the HRA/ECHR and (ii) the way in which human rights experts and advocates have tried to challenge these narratives. The second part analyses the strengths and weaknesses of some specific positions that supporters of the HRA/ECHR have adopted in response to media and political criticisms of their provisions, and discusses how some of these pro-HRA/ECHR argumentative stances can be better tailored to take in to account the current political context.

The current state of the human rights law debate

Changing times: the media and political assault on the HRA/ECHR

Things have changed since the HRA became law in 2000, incorporating ECHR rights into UK law as part of the New Labour constitutional reform package. Back then, while there was a degree of opposition to the HRA from academics wedded to particular political constitutionalist positions, media and political criticism of the Act was muted. Since then, some of its most prominent academic critics have become partially reconciled to the HRA[10] – but media and political criticism has grown and grown. In 2005, the then Prime Minister, Tony Blair MP, speculated that it might be necessary to 'change the rules of the game' and amend the HRA to deal with the threat of terrorism.[11] Subsequently, in 2006, David Cameron MP as Leader of the Opposition suggested that the HRA should be replaced with a new and improved (if vaguely outlined) British Bill of Rights.[12] General commitments to this effect were included in the Tory general election manifestos of 2010 and 2015 – while the calls for the UK to leave the ECHR system of rights protection, once marginal, have acquired some heavyweight support.[13]

9 S. Chambers, 'Has Deliberative Democracy Abandoned Mass Democracy?' 37(3) (2009) *Political Theory* 323–350.

10 See, for example, A. Tomkins, 'What's Left of the Political Constitution?' (2013) 14(12) *German L.J.* 2275–2292.

11 Simon Jeffrey, 'The Rules of the Game Are Changing', *The Guardian* (5 August 2005), available online at: www.theguardian.com/uk/2005/aug/05/july7.uksecurity5

12 D. Cameron, 'Balancing Freedom and Security – A modern British Bill of Rights', Centre for Policy Studies, 26 June 2006, available online at: https://conservative-speeches.sayit.mysociety.org/speech/600031

13 For example, Theresa May MP, then Home Secretary, suggested that the UK should consider leaving the ECHR system in the run-up to the Brexit referendum: see T. May,

Various factors have played a role in this shift, including the post-9/11 embrace of the 'War on Terror' narrative, the hostile reaction to the *Hirst v UK (No 2)* judgment on prisoner voting rights by the Strasbourg Court,[14] and growing Eurosceptic concerns about the role played by the ECHR in shaping UK law. However, one factor that has loomed large has been the way in which the HRA/ECHR have been repeatedly targeted for criticism by certain media outlets in the UK, which has in turn fuelled political disenchantment with UK human rights law in general. The manner in which this media reporting has established a narrative to the effect that UK human rights law has taken a bad turn is widely acknowledged to have been crucial in shifting perceptions of the HRA/ECHR over the last decade: it has affirmed and lent new energy to long-established currents of thought within British public life which are inherently uncomfortable with the type of legal mechanisms for protecting human rights established by the HRA/ECHR, and generated pressure for politicians to be seen to be responding to the alleged deficiencies of existing law in this regard.[15]

The way this media narrative has developed has been controversial. British media outlets that adhere to a right-wing editorial line regularly report or comment on human rights cases in a way that angers many lawyers, academics and others working in the field, on account of what they see as (i) the selective manner in which particular cases are highlighted and others ignored; (ii) the inaccurate manner in which legal issues relevant to reported cases are set out; and (iii) the distorted manner in which the background legal and political context to such cases is described.[16] Human rights experts and advocates have been particularly critical of how this media reporting has often zeroed in on a few cases featuring terrorism suspects, rule-breaking migrants and other unpopular minorities. Furthermore, they have rolled their eyes relentlessly in response to reporting which mixes up the ECHR and EU law, glosses over the basic principles of separation of powers, or otherwise fails to give casual readers an adequate account of the legal/political context against which these cases play out. For these critics, these trends add up to a biased pattern of media coverage – which, since the UK's vote to leave the EU in the June 2016 referendum, has been amplified by the turbocharged 'friend/enemy' populist rhetoric that certain media outlets have adopted when reporting on legal and political developments relevant to Brexit.[17]

'Speech on Brexit', 25 April 2016, available online at: www.conservativehome.com/parliament/2016/04/theresa-mays-speech-on-brexit-full-text.html (last accessed 29 May 2016).

14 (2006) 42 EHRR 41.

15 A researcher associated with a prominent think tank associated with the Conservative party commented to the author at a public event in 2012 that 'the papers have put human rights reform on the agenda: the people want action, and so things have to change'.

16 See, in this volume, for example, E Drywood and H Gray, Demonising Immigrants: How a Human Rights Narrative Has Contributed to Negative Portrayals of Immigrants in the UK Media' Chapter 5; Y McDermott, Trial by Media: The Fair Trial Jurisprudence of the European Court of Human Rights in the UK Press, Chapter 6.

17 See, for example, 'Enemies of the People', *Daily Mail* (3 November 2016), referring to the Divisional Court judgment in *Miller v Secretary of State for Exiting the EU* [2016] EWHC 2768 (Admin).

At the time of writing, it is thus common for human rights experts and advocates to refer to the existence of a 'hostile' media landscape, and to lament how such coverage has created a toxic environment around the HRA/ECHR and soured popular attitudes towards human rights more generally.[18] It seems also to have encouraged a shift in attitudes among political opinion-formers, by stirring up hitherto largely quiescent concerns about the powers conferred on unelected judges by the HRA/ECHR and, in particular, the influence exerted by the case-law of the Strasbourg Court over UK law.

Certain strands of British political thought have always been unfavourably disposed towards judicial rights review. Perhaps reflecting the historical influence of Bentham,[19] and certainly shaped by the UK's political constitutionalist tradition and the central role accorded to parliamentary supremacy in its scheme of values, they share a strong sceptical orientation towards human rights law and its reliance on legal mechanisms to secure individual rights protection. More specifically, politicians, legal experts and others influenced by this tradition of rights scepticism tend to regard legal mechanisms such as the HRA or ECHR as being (i) unduly indeterminate, in the sense that the open-ended and abstract character of its rules undermines legal certainty; (ii) open to ideological capture, by virtue of this inherent indeterminacy; and (iii) undemocratic, in that it erodes the authority of democratically accountable bodies while giving too much power to the judiciary and legal elites more generally. These are familiar – indeed, perennial – points of criticism directed at human rights law. However, in the eyes of its defenders, distorted media reporting has given fresh fuel to these concerns, and given them a political salience that is not justified in the specific case of the HRA or ECHR.[20]

Furthermore, it would also appear that the media's fast and loose attitude towards the reporting of human rights cases also influences political commentary on the HRA/ECHR – perhaps best exemplified by Theresa May's widely derided 'cat' speech in 2011.[21] The hostile media narrative seems to have not alone stirred up old conceptual objections to the expansion of human rights law, but also made it fair game for robust and sometimes scattergun political attacks.

The media attacks on the HRA/ECHR have thus interacted with certain deeply embedded strands of rights scepticism to generate the toxic political environment that has surrounded the HRA/ECHR in recent years. They have also helped to ensure that human rights law has become a particular target of the increasingly assertive nationalistic right of British politics – not least thanks to how such media attacks have often presented human rights law as being too

18 For an excellent and balanced overview of public attitudes towards human rights, see A. Donald and E. Mottershaw, *Identifying Human Rights Stories: A Scoping Study* (Middlesex University/Thomas Paine Initiative, 2014).

19 See D. Dyzenhaus, 'The Left and the Question of Law' (2004) 17 *Canadian Journal of Law and Jurisprudence* 7.

20 See, in this volume, David Mead's examination of how distorted media reporting works, D. Mead, Chapter 1.

21 'Theresa May Under Fire Over Deportation Cat Claim', *BBC News* (4 October 2011), available online at: www.bbc.co.uk/news/uk-politics-15160326

protective of prisoners, migrants and other politically marginalised groups, while simultaneously framing it as an elitist 'European' project which has served as a Trojan Horse for campaigning left-wing lawyers to take control of the evolution of the UK's legal order. It has thus framed existing UK human rights law as a perfect target for the hard Eurosceptic element of the British political spectrum, as well as its anti-immigration wing – while discouraging other elements of the political classes from standing up for its virtues.[22]

The push-back: how supporters of the HRA/ECHR have responded to this assault

Attempts have been made to counter this hostile, rights-sceptic media narrative and its spill-over into political discourse. Human rights experts often can be found defending human rights law in print, social media and TV/radio. Academic studies have analysed patterns of bias in media reporting of the HRA/ECHR[23] – which have been backed up by the findings of parliamentary inquiries: for example, the Joint Committee on Human Rights has criticised the existence of a 'wide discrepancy' between some of the media coverage of various aspects of the jurisprudence of the European Court of Human Rights and the established facts of the situation.[24] NGOs have launched campaigns to defend the HRA and other aspects of UK human rights law,[25] while politicians have spoken in its defence.[26]

This push-back seems to have had some impact. Polling surveys suggest that popular views of human rights law are now quite mixed, with sizeable elements of the electorate being broadly supportive of the status quo or at least disinclined to view reform of the HRA as a priority.[27] It is common now for inaccurate or slanted reporting of human rights decisions to attract copious criticism on social media, as do political attacks on human rights law more generally. Most of the UK's leading political parties have affirmed their commitment to the existing

22 Criticism has been directed towards the Labour Party for failing to defend the HRA with sufficient enthusiasm. For example, Conor Gearty has commented that '[t]he Human Rights Act has never been supported by government, even by the Blair administration which secured its enactment': see C. Gearty, 'The Human Rights Act Should Not Be Repealed', *U.K. Const. L. Blog*, 17 Sept 2016, available online at: https://ukconstitutionallaw.org/

23 See, for example, A. Donald, J. Gordon and P. Leach, *The UK and the European Court of Human Rights*, Equality and Human Rights Commission Research Report No. 83 (London: EHRC, 2012).

24 JCHR, Session 2014–5, HL Paper 130/HC 1088, 7th Report, *Human Rights Judgments*, 11 March 2016, para 2.8.

25 See the RightsInfo, Liberty and Act for the Act campaigns referenced in n 4 above.

26 See, for example, the speech by Dominic Grieve MP cited at n 4.

27 'Poll Shows Little Support for Abolition of Human Rights Act' *Daily Mail* (8 November 2015), available online at: www.dailymail.co.uk/wires/pa/article-3308783/Poll-shows-little-support-abolition-Human-Rights-Act.html See also e.g. Equality and Diversity Forum, *Public Attitudes to Human Rights* (London: EDF, 2012); K. Kaur-Ballagan, S. Castell, K. Brough and H. Friemert, *Public Perceptions of Human Rights* (Manchester: Equality and Human Rights Commission, 2009).

legal framework, which also has been defended by high-profile Conservative politicians.[28] The legal profession has been generally supportive of the HRA and other elements of the existing law, as has civil society in general.[29]

Indeed, at the time of writing, this mobilisation in defence of existing UK human rights law (perhaps in tandem with the energy-draining impact of Brexit) seems to have deterred political moves to alter the status quo – in the short term, at least. Despite her expressed hostility towards the ECHR, the Prime Minister, Theresa May MP, has accepted that there is no majority support in the current House of Commons for repeal of the HRA and/or ECHR repudiation.[30] Furthermore, political and media attacks on UK human rights law appear to have tailed off to some degree over the last few years – while human rights defenders have gone on the offence over the potential negative impact of Brexit on existing levels of rights protection, with the parliamentary opposition to the EU (Withdrawal) Bill particularly focusing on the Bill's failure to carry over the EU Charter of Fundamental Rights into UK law post-Brexit.[31] The devolution dimension to the human rights debate has also come to the fore in these debates, which in turn has highlighted the complexity of the issues at stake and the way in which both expert and political opinion in the devolved regions tends to be broadly supportive of the existing status quo.[32]

Where the debate stands now

In general, the push-back against the 'anti-rights' narrative seems to have complicated the debate around UK human rights law, and generated a degree of

28 Tim Ross, 'Tories at War Over Plan to Scrap the Human Rights Act' *Daily Telegraph* (23 May 2015), available online at: www.telegraph.co.uk/news/politics/queens-speech/11626477/Tories-at-war-over-plan-to-scrap-Human-Rights-Act.html

29 See the declaration of support for the HRA by more than 130 civil society organisations, arranged by Liberty in 2016 – available online at: www.libertyhumanrights.org.uk/campaigning/save-our-human-rights-act/pledge-save-our-human-rights-act

30 See the report by Adam Wagner, 'Theresa May Will NOT Try To Take UK Out Of European Convention on Human Rights', *RightsInfo*, 30 June 2016, available online at: https://rightsinfo.org/breaking-theresa-may-will-not-try-leave-european-convention-human-rights/

31 Rowena Mason 'Brexit: Starmer to force vote on UK's adoption of EU charter of rights' *The Guardian* (2 January 2018), available online at: www.theguardian.com/politics/2018/jan/02/brexit-keir-starmer-to-force-vote-on-uks-adoption-of-eu-charter-of-rights

32 See M. Elliott, 'Could the Devolved Nations Block Repeal of the Human Rights Act?', *Public Law for Everyone blog* (5 December 2015), available online at: http://publiclawforeveryone.com/2015/05/12/could-the-devolved-nations-block-repeal-of-the-human-rights-act-and-the-enactment-of-a-new-bill-of-rights/ C. Harvey, 'HRA Watch: Reform, Repeal, Replace? Rights in a Fractured Union', *UK Const. L. Blog* (1 June 2015), available online at: http://ukconstitutionallaw.org. The Commission on a Bill of Rights, which reported in 2012 on the desirability of introducing a new UK Bill of Rights, concluded that there was little support in the devolved nations for repeal of the HRA and that there was 'little, if any, criticism of the Strasbourg Court, of the European label of the Convention, or of human rights generally in Scotland, Wales or Northern Ireland'. See Commission on a Bill of Rights, *A UK Bill of Rights? The Choice Before Us*, Volume 1, Chapter 9 (2012) 163.

popular and political support for the status quo. This is despite the gloomy attitude of many human rights experts, who continue to lament how the political/media dice are stacked against them. Indeed, the argument could be made that political support for the HRA/ECHR in the UK has remained strikingly robust, notwithstanding the media attacks on their functioning and the considerable political appetite for change that exists within the Conservative party at least. Brexit also acts as a disincentive for change: not only does it suck up government energy, but HRA repeal or ECHR withdrawal will risk further alienating other European states and generating new tensions in respect of the devolved settlement.[33]

Having said that, it is clear that UK human rights law is still politically controversial – and will remain so for a long time to come. Rights scepticism is likely to remain a default position for much of the UK's media commentariat. On the political level, Theresa May as Prime Minister has indicated that she intends to have a manifesto commitment to repeal the HRA and withdraw from the ECHR included in the Conservative manifesto for the 2020 general election.[34] Furthermore, in a comparatively new development, Policy Exchange, a think tank associated with the Conservative Party, have begun to sponsor research produced by academics critical of the extent to which existing human rights law allows courts to interfere with what they consider to be political decisions.[35] This research is likely to provide a platform for a more sustained intellectual assault on the HRA/ECHR than has been seen in recent times, given that it is adding some critical academic voices to a debate from which they have largely been absent for the last decade or more: as such, it may over time add more substance to the sound and fury of the 'anti-rights' media and political narrative that has become a persistent feature of UK public life.

The struggle to shape the public and political perception of human rights law therefore goes on, and is likely to persist for an extended period of time. As such, supporters of the HRA/ECHR need to be ready for a long game: they need to make the political, moral and prudential case for retention of the existing human rights framework over and over again, if they are to have any real hope of averting or diluting the hostility it currently attracts.

Post-Brexit Britain may seem like a poor environment in which to be defending the HRA/ECHR in this way, given how existing bonds with Europe will have been weakened. However, the impact of Brexit on the human rights debate may actually prove to be quite complex. Perhaps counter-intuitively, it may

33 See P. Goodman, 'Remaining in the ECHR is a cost of leaving the EU', 30 October 2017, *Conservative Home Blog*, available online at: www.conservativehome.com/thetorydiary/2017/10/remaining-in-the-echr-is-the-price-for-leaving-the-eu.html

34 *Daily Telegraph*, 'Theresa May to fight 2020 election on plans to take Britain out of European Convention on Human Rights after Brexit is completed', 28 December 2016, available online at: www.telegraph.co.uk/news/2016/12/28/theresa-may-fight-2020-election-plans-take-britain-european/

35 See the website of the Judicial Power Project, hosted by Policy Exchange: http://judicialpowerproject.org.uk/

actually increase support for the HRA/ECHR – or at least serve as a counsel of caution before embarking on any substantive reforms to the status quo. After the UK leaves the EU, the importance of the ECHR and the Council of Europe more generally as an institutional framework linking the UK to Europe may become more apparent – and Europhiles may be all the more motivated to defend both the Convention and the HRA, having lost the Brexit referendum. The importance of the HRA/ECHR as a set of legal safeguards against abuse of state powers may also become more apparent in the post-Brexit era. So too may the risk of causing serious constitutional damage to the devolution architecture, not least as it relates to Northern Ireland.[36]

Furthermore, there is clear evidence that public opinion is not hostile to the idea of legally enforceable rights in the abstract.[37] Indeed, quite the contrary: considerable support exists for such rights protection to exist in UK law.[38] Instead, the problem is that a perception exists that the HRA/ECHR gives disproportionate protection to less than fully deserving minority groups, that their provisions are not relevant to the daily life of 'ordinary' citizens, and that this is the product of European diktat rather than the 'native' tradition of rights protection. As Donald and Mottershaw put it:

> According to the research, people often hold inconsistent and complex views about human rights. A person's reaction to 'human rights' may in fact be driven by their reaction to other themes which they see as associated with human rights, such as Europe, criminality, immigration and perceived unfairness. People tend to become more positive when exposed to messages that: make human rights feel relevant to them; connect with tradition; emphasise fairness; and increase their understanding of how human rights laws work in practice.[39]

As a result, supporters of the HRA/ECHR need to show the general public why the HRA/ECHR is relevant to them – by, as Donald and Mottershaw again have argued, encouraging 'more balanced and well-informed discussion about the HRA' and bringing 'more systematically into the public domain human rights stories that concern everyday scenarios … and that reflect the impact of human rights standards and principles both inside and outside the courts'.[40] There would appear to be a general audience out there willing to hear this message, notwithstanding the hostility of substantial parts of the UK media. Similarly, despite the existence of significant strands of rights-sceptic thought within UK public life,

36 See Harvey (n 32 above).

37 See Donald and Mottershaw (n 18 above) 3–5.

38 This may explain why opponents of the HRA/ECHR have focused on replacing the HRA with another legal rights instrument, rather than going back to a pre-1998/HRA enactment situation where no enforceable charter of rights existed in UK law.

39 Donald and Mottershaw (n 18 above) 5.

40 *Ibid.*

plenty of politicians remain very supportive of the HRA/ECHR, as shown by the persistent political resistance to attempts to change the law in this regard.

As such, supporters of the HRA/ECHR have everything to play for in the years ahead. But, having said that, some strategic thinking is required. Certain traps need to be avoided if the arguments in favour of retaining the HRA/ECHR are going to maintain their traction in the current fraught political landscape. Furthermore, avoiding these traps may require a departure from some of the standard approaches used by human rights experts and advocates up to now to 'sell' the HRA/ECHR. There is a real need for such rights enthusiasts to think critically about their approach to preserving the status quo, and to take account of the background political context against which their campaigning will play out.

Examining the strengths and weaknesses of pro-HRA/ ECHR arguments

How supporters of the HRA/ECHR have made their case

In pushing back against media and political criticism of the HRA/ECHR, human rights experts and advocates have made particular use of certain distinct lines of argumentation to make their case in favour of the status quo. To start with, they have often challenged the hostile media narrative about human rights law, by highlighting what they see as biased or inaccurate reporting or commentary. Second, they have attempted to defend the HRA/ECHR by invoking the special status and authority of human rights law as a mode of legal regulation, pointing to the way it gives effect to international standards, the idealism of its normative foundations, and its importance in securing individual rights. Third, they have identified positive benefits that the HRA/ECHR have brought about, which might be imperilled if the existing legal framework were altered. Fourth, they have identified flaws in reform proposals, highlighting various legal issues and undesirable side-effects that might be generated by proposed changes to UK human rights law.[41]

These different strands of argumentation are usually intertwined together in expert commentary and advocacy work directed towards defending the HRA/ ECHR. The aim of such commentary is usually to make a positive case for retention of the existing legal framework, while challenging the desirability of proposed reforms. A variety of different modes of presentation have been used to get these arguments across to politicians, policy-makers and the general public, including op-ed pieces in national newspapers,[42] set-piece speeches,[43] blog

41 These four strands are present in all the advocacy material and the academic papers referenced in n 4 above.

42 See, for example, F. Klug, 'The Human Rights Act is a British Bill of Rights', *The Guardian* (13 December 2012) available online at: www.theguardian.com/commentisfree/2012/ dec/13/human-rights-act-british-bill-rights J. Parkinson, 'The Human Rights Act Helps us Hold Power to Account: We Must Defend It' *The Guardian* (26 July 2016).

43 Grieve (above n 4).

posts,[44] academic publications,[45] poster campaigns,[46] online campaigns,[47] and social media videos.[48]

Interestingly, it is possible to detect a shift in how these arguments have been presented over time. When reform or repeal of the HRA initially began to be talked about as a real possibility in the late 2000s and early 2010s, pro-HRA/ECHR arguments were primarily articulated through academic commentary, op-eds pieces and set-piece speeches. In other words, they were designed to influence the policy debate within Westminster, Whitehall and the political parties, rather than public opinion more generally. That has changed: the campaigns launched by NGOs such as Act for the Act in recent years have been much more targeted at a general audience.

This makes sense, as a strategy. In line with Donald and Mottershaw's arguments cited above, human rights experts and advocates need to engage with wider public debate about the HRA/ECHR, rather than operating on the assumption that the strength of their case will inevitably be respected within elite policy-making processes. It is not enough to win arguments in the corridors of political and legal power: there also needs to be serious engagement with the wider public debate.[49]

Expanding the reach and impact of pro-HRA/ECHR arguments

Having said that, making the case for the HRA/ECHR does (as noted above) involve pushing against a media headwind, as well as taking on a deeply entrenched culture of rights scepticism in Westminster and Whitehall in particular – in a political context where pan-European standards such as the ECHR are very exposed to Eurosceptic critique.[50] Furthermore, in a media and political culture increas-

44 See, for example, T. Lock: 'HRA Watch: Reform, Repeal, Replace? Legal Implications of Human Rights Reform in the UK', *U.K. Const. L. Blog* (15 May 2015), available online at: http://ukconstitutionallaw.org C. Gearty, 'The Human Rights Act Should Not Be Repealed', *U.K. Const. L. Blog* (17 Sept 2016), available online at: https://ukconstitutionallaw.org/

45 O'Cinnéide (n 4 above); C. Gearty, *On Fantasy Island: Britain, Strasbourg and Human Rights* (CUP, 2016).

46 Act for the Act placed a number of very striking posters across the London tune network in 2016: the posters can be viewed at http://actfortheact.uk/.

47 Ibid. See also Liberty's 'Save Our HRA' campaign, at: www.libertyhumanrights.org.uk/campaigning/save-our-human-rights-act-0.

48 A video sketch presented by Patrick Stewart on the theme of 'What has the HRA ever done for us?' can be viewed at www.youtube.com/watch?v=ptfmAY6M6aA Since being uploaded to that site on 25 April 2016, it has attracted 913,899 views at the time of writing (April 2017).

49 It is worth noting here that elite satisfaction with the status quo proved insufficient to prevent the popular vote for Brexit in 2016.

50 Advocacy for the HRA/ECHR also rubs up against a culture of what is described as 'rights complacency', whereby the assumption is often made that existing levels of rights protection in the UK need little if any revision on account of the inherent health of British political

ingly characterised by exaggerated rhetoric, distorted factual claims, and concerns about the generation of click bait-orientated 'fake news', it can be very difficult for subtle analysis of the impact of existing law to find an audience, or to change minds.

As a consequence, in engaging with wider public debate about human rights law, supporters of the HRA/ECHR will inevitably have to make their arguments in different registers: they will have to appeal to policy makers through the type of expert-elite, evidence-based argumentation that resonates in those circles, but also set out to win hearts and minds more generally across the wider population through the use of more varied types of rhetorical appeal. Again, more recent advocacy work in support of the HRA/ECHR has gone down this route, with for example Act for the Act emphasising the human stories of individuals and families who have been protected by the HRA or used it to challenge patently unfair treatment by public authorities – but arguably much more of this is required.[51]

Furthermore, supporters of the HRA/ECHR need to consider how much to engage with criticism of UK human rights law on a constructive basis –and when to treat some of these arguments with dismissive scorn. There has arguably been an unfortunate tendency for human rights experts and advocates to be too dismissive of anti-HRA/ECHR arguments, especially in deliberative contexts where respect for competing points of view is expected: a problem compounded in this context by the fact that the arguments made by the 'other side' often have real force, and need to be taken very seriously (as discussed further below). However, scornful dismissal is a useful rhetorical tool to deploy in public debates – even if its use often qualifies as dubious 'plebiscitary' rhetoric rather than the more ideal 'deliberative' approach, to use Chambers' above-mentioned classification.

Enhancing the substance of pro-HRA/ECHR arguments

Taking these considerations about audience, register and tone into account, it is worth now returning to the four main lines of argumentation advanced in favour of the HRA/ECHR as outlined above, namely (i) 'setting the record straight' by challenging the hostile media narrative about human rights law; (ii) highlighting the special status and authority of human rights law and its roots in idealistic international standards; (iii) setting out the positive benefits of the HRA/ECHR; and (iv) highlighting flaws in reform proposals. How effectively have supporters of the HRA/ECHR developed and communicated these lines of argumentation – and how potent are they in winning hearts and minds, as well as influencing policy makers?

---

and legal culture. For a discussion of how the ECHR case-law disturbed this culture of complacency to some degree, and how the HRA was introduced during a period when that culture was being subject to an unusually sustained level of self-criticism, see O'Cinnéide (n 1 above).

51 See Donald and Mottershaw (above n 18).

The simple answer is to say that all four strands of argumentation have appeal. They respectively (a) challenge the hostile anti-HRA/ECHR media narrative; (b) highlight the pedigree of existing human rights law and why it has developed the way it has; (c) give reasons to value the contribution of the HRA/ECHR to the UK's legal system; and (d) call into question the merits of alternative modes of structuring rights protection in the UK. Good arguments can in general be invoked in support of each of these strands, and they can be 'pitched' in both expert-elite and popular terms. Indeed, their strength can be shown by the way in which attempts to do away with the HRA/ECHR, or at least to substantially alter the human rights status quo, have struggled to move forward. The 'push-back' discussed above has been effective: indeed, it has arguably crystallised active support for the HRA/ECHR that was lacking at the outset of this current controversy.[52]

However, within some of these strands, there are argumentative threads which are weak and/or lacking in impact – either on the basis that they are limited in appeal to policy-makers, often on account of how they fail to engage properly with some of the better arguments on the 'other side', or because they are lacking in resonance and impact. These weaknesses are particularly prevalent in the first two strands – more specifically when human rights experts and advocates demand fairer coverage for human rights law, or when they place particular emphasis on the special status and authority of human rights law to justify the particular set of institutional arrangements represented by the HRA/ECHR.

Challenging the hostile media narrative

Turning to the first strand, the issue of media fairness, it obviously makes sense for supporters of the current status quo to keep challenging anti-HRA/ECHR media spin, as well as political attacks on human rights law that lean on this pattern of distorted reporting for support. MPs, civil servants, opinion formers and the public at large need to hear that the picture they are given about the functioning of UK human rights law in much of the media is distorted. As already discussed, this type of push-back has already helped to complicate the debate about the HRA/ECHR – and it will continue to play an important role in the future, if the anti-HRA/ECHR media narrative is to be prevented from becoming established as received truth.

However, human rights experts and advocates need to recognise that appeals for fair press coverage of the functioning of human rights law may have limited impact. Ideologically slanted reporting has been a feature of mass media since

52 For an example of this, note the way in which the Labour Party in opposition has committed itself to a much more explicit pro-HRA stance than it did when in government: e.g. see The *Today Programme*, 'Keir Starmer: Call to change Human Rights Act "a diversion"', *BBC News* (7 June 2017), available online at: www.bbc.co.uk/news/av/election-2017-40184841/keir-starmer-call-to-change-human-rights-act-a-diversion

its inception: the 'fake news' phenomenon may be amplified in our current era due to the influence of social media, but it has plenty of historical antecedents. Expecting all media reporting to be scrupulously balanced when it comes to human rights law, or to faithfully adhere to what human rights experts would regard as an 'objective' standard of reporting in this context, is a fools' game. Coverage of human rights law is inevitably going to be influenced to some degree by the background assumptions of journalists, editors and commentators – not to mention their desire to attract online 'hits', and ultimately to sell their output to a specific audience.

Similarly, it is questionable whether media reporting of human rights law can be as precise, accurate and nuanced as some experts would like. In common with any specialised and developed field of activity, legal issues can be complex, detailed and play out against a background context that can be difficult to comprehend without subject-specific training. Expecting media reporting to grasp the subtle nuances of a particular human rights judgment, and to faithfully reflect all its complexity and wider impact, is unduly optimistic. Media reporting of the law always takes shortcuts, and aims to paint in broad and accessible colours rather than achieve an elevated degree of realism: trying to change this trend when it comes to human rights law threatens to be another fools' errand.[53]

Furthermore, the expectation that sometimes exists in human rights circles that media commentators should faithfully reflect the expert understanding of legal developments in this field is also unrealistic. As Onora O'Neill has argued, we live in a culture characterised by a high levels of mistrust – of authority, expertise and status.[54] The value of trust has been undermined, and replaced with a commitment to scepticism, critique and questioning. Expecting this social shift to be suspended, or reversed, when it comes to human rights expertise is optimistic, to put it mildly.

This is not to say that human rights experts do not have a special claim to authority in this context: their understanding of how human rights law is formed, developed and interpreted deserves to be accorded particular weight in analysis of legal developments in this field, as is true for any other expert. Nor is it to suggest that human rights experts and advocates should not challenge distorted media reporting or poorly reasoned media/political commentary: this has to be an essential element of any pro-HRA/ECHR campaign, if such distorted analysis is not to be accepted as received truth by the public at large. But there is a need here for realism and lowered expectations as to how successful such appeals for fairer reporting/commentary can be. In an era where the media is expected to challenge authority, and to second-guess the status quo, defenders of existing

53 For more on this, see E. Heinze, 'The Reality and Hyper-reality of Human Rights: Public Consciousness and the Mass Media', in *Examining Critical Perspectives on Human Rights: The End of an Era?*, R. Dickenson *et al.*, eds., Cambridge University Press (2012), 193–216.

54 O. O'Neill, *A Question of Trust?* BBC Reith Lectures (CUP, 2002).

human rights law need to recognise that their claims of special expertise will not always count as a trump card.

Not so clever: appealing to the special status and authority of human rights law

Appeals to other forms of authority can also struggle to gain traction in current media/political conditions. This includes when that appeal is made to the authority of human rights law, under the second strand of pro-HRA/ECHR argumentation – which is perhaps the weakest element in the otherwise reasonably robust line of defences erected by supporters of the existing human rights status quo.

Supporters of the HRA/ECHR like to emphasise how the UK is bound under international law to comply with the requirements of the ECHR, including the obligation set out in Article 46 of the Convention to give effect to judgments of the Strasbourg Court. They are also fond of highlighting the background framework of international human rights law in general, including both Council of Europe and UN/international law standards, which UK law is supposed to reflect and uphold. These legal obligations are frequently invoked in debates about reform of UK human rights law, with the argument being made that the legal status quo is justified on the basis that it gives tangible effect to these obligations within domestic law.[55]

However, this line of argument assumes that compliance with such international standards is generally assumed to be a good thing, and that the authority of international human rights law, and associated institutions such as the Strasbourg Court, is widely acknowledged. Rights experts and advocates should not presume that others share their view of the sacrosanct nature of international human rights law – and that the media and/or general public will defer to its authority.

In this respect, it is notable that the media and political campaign against the HRA/ECHR has consistently emphasised both (i) the 'foreignness' of both the ECHR and the Strasbourg Court; and (ii) the 'undemocratic' character of human rights law in general. These lines of attack call the legitimacy of international rights standards into question, by casting a doubt over their democratic *bona fides*.[56] As such, this makes it more difficult to rely upon these international standards to justify existing UK law. When senior politicians like the Prime Minister openly express support for leaving the ECHR, and the Tory policy paper on human rights law reform puts it on the table as a possibility, it is a clear sign that the authority of human rights instruments is not a given. Furthermore, this line of attack is not only generated by politicians and media commentators: the authority claims of

55 This tendency was particularly pronounced in the early years of the HRA/'British Bill of Rights' debate: for a random example, see Justice, 'A British Bill of Rights – a model for the 21st century' (2009) available online at: https://justice.org.uk/british-bill-rights-model-21st-century/

56 See, for example, the arguments set out in Pinto-Duschinsky, *Bring Rights Back Home* (n 3 above).

international human rights law have also been contested by certain strands of legal scholarship, usually on the basis that they lack a firm foundation in the direct exercise of democratic decision-making.[57] But human rights experts and advocates all too frequently rely on this authority claim in defending the HRA/ECHR, without justifying this reliance: they assume what they are increasingly being asked to prove, namely the legitimacy of the standards on which the existing law is built.[58]

Human rights experts and advocates can also be quick to assume that the inherent idealism of international human rights law, and the aims and objectives of its founding progenitors, can be invoked to good effect when it comes to defending the HRA/ECHR. This explains why the noble aspirations underpinning the ECHR are frequently cited in debates about the future of UK human rights law: implicitly, the argument is being made that the idealistic ambitions of human rights law give it a unique status and authority, which should insulate it against divisive or half-baked reform proposals.

However, yet again, this authority claim is vulnerable. The originating idealism of human rights law is not seriously contested – but its contemporary expression in HRA/ECHR case-law is. Hostile political comments directed against existing UK human rights law often argue that it has departed from the original aims of the ECHR, which are understood to involve the protection of a minimal core of fundamental rights against Nazi-style abuses – in contrast to the much more extensive protection afforded to a variety of rights under current HRA/ECHR jurisprudence.[59] In other words, existing human rights law is attacked on the basis that it has outgrown its purpose, and departed from its underlying ideals. Much of the distorted media commentary also picks up on this theme: it regularly frames the outcome of human rights cases as representing a betrayal or distortion of the true purpose of such laws.[60] As such, appeals to the special status of human rights law are a double-edged sword: it can be invoked to argue both for and against existing UK human rights law.

57 See, for example, J. Rubenfeld, 'Unilateralism and Constitutionalism' (2004) 79 *N.Y.U. L. Rev.* 1971; A. Buchanan and R. Powell, 'Constitutional Democracy and the Rule of International Law: Are They Compatible?' (2008) 16(3) *Journal of Political Philosophy* 326–349.

58 For more on this, see C. O'Cinnéide, 'Saying "No" to Strasbourg: When Are National Parliaments Justified in Refusing to Give Effect to Judgments of International Human Rights Courts?', in M. Saul, G. Ulfstein and A. Follesdal, *The International Human Rights Judiciary and National Parliaments: Europe and Beyond* (OUP, 2017).

59 See, for example, 'Tories vow to bring back 'common sense' with human rights overhaul' *Daily Telegraph* (2 October 2014); T. Stanley, 'Scrapping the Human Rights Act won't abolish human rights. It will repatriate them', *The Telegraph* (1 June 2015), available online at: www.telegraph.co.uk/news/general-election-2015/politics-blog/11641836/Scrapping-the-Human-Rights-Act-wont-abolish-human-rights.-It-will-repatriate-them.html

60 See, for example, the comment by the Daily Mail's columnist Sebastian Shakespeare to the effect that the 'the ECHR has gone so far beyond its founding brief that it has become a serious threat to democracy': Sebastian Shakespeare, 'Human rights and an affront to justice' *Mail Online* (7 October 2013), available online at: www.dailymail.co.uk/debate/article-2449247/Human-rights-affront-justice.html

Similar issues arise with a related line of argument also advanced by human rights experts/advocates in support of the HRA/ECHR – namely the way in which the rights protective function of human rights law is invoked as justification for treating it as a privileged form of legal regulation, which deserves to be subject to some sort of non-retrogression principle whereby compelling reasons are necessary before any roll-back of its provisions is justified. This line of argumentation has featured particularly strongly in the related debate over whether the EU Charter of Fundamental Rights should remain part of UK law post-Brexit. Charter enthusiasts have argued that the additional protection it confers upon individual rights should as a matter of principle not be rolled back, as this would constitute a retrogressive step[61] – despite the relatively limited scope of application of the Charter, the under-developed state of the CJEU's Charter jurisprudence, and the unwieldly list of rights protected by this particular human rights instrument. However, similar non-retrogression arguments have also featured heavily in the HRA/ECHR debate: as with the Charter, some supporters of the status quo like to argue that there should in principle be no rolling-back of established individual rights protection.[62]

But, yet again, this claim is very vulnerable to attack. It assumes that existing rights protection should be sealed off from political attack and/or revisionist critiques, and that any roll-back of such protection must be inherently problematic. But courts interpreting human rights instruments do not always arrive at correct conclusions, as any legal scholar will tell you – and the scope of legal rights protection has fluctuated with time, political developments and evolving understandings of the normative content of rights. Furthermore, different states protect rights in different ways, reflecting their different constitutional, legal and political cultures, and institutional mechanisms for rights protections are regularly adjusted to reflect changes in this background context. One can be a strong supporter of human rights in general, but not necessarily agree with how rights have been interpreted or applied in a particular set of cases – or with the particular institutional mechanism that is used to ensure their protection at a particular point in time. Arguing that existing legal rights protection should be presumptively insulated against change can therefore sound like a form of special pleading. It also, of course, is exposed to the charge of being anti-democratic – in the sense that it denies decision-making room to electorally accountable politicians, by trying to seal off established areas of human rights law from external political intervention.

Another vulnerable aspect of pro-HRA/ECHR argumentation is the way in which rights experts/advocates sometimes respond to criticism of human rights law by invoking technical aspects of legal doctrine to justify its integrity. Thus, for example, it is common for defenders of the ECHR to point to the existence

61 See, for example, J. Cooper, 'We Need to Keep the EU Charter of Fundamental Rights' *The Times* (19 July 2017).

62 See, for example, Parkinson (n 42 above).

of the Strasbourg Court's margin of appreciation doctrine as a reason why the Court should not be viewed as interfering too much with national sovereignty: the existence of the doctrine is cited as evidence that the ECHR system already accommodates concerns about supranational overreach. Similarly, supporters of the HRA/ECHR regularly refer to how UK courts and the Strasbourg Court engage in dialogue with each other as an example of the two-way nature of the UK/ECHR relationship.[63] The proportionality test that looms large throughout much of human rights law is also regularly cited as an example of how the courts take the public interest into account in adjudicating rights cases, rather than focusing on individual entitlements at the expense of the common good. But all these doctrinal-based lines of argument presume that the overall structure of human rights law is legitimate – which many of its critics deny. For them, no amount of nuanced judicial decision-making will compensate for what they see as the inherently undemocratic nature of the HRA/ECHR as currently constituted.[64]

Furthermore, the application of these doctrinal tests – for example, deciding whether to apply the margin of appreciation, or to deem the objective justification test to be satisfied – inevitably involves value judgments. Therefore, when supporters of the HRA/ECHR cite the existence of these tests to reassure those concerned about judicial overreach, they are effectively arguing that judges should be trusted to get these value judgments right. But, for many critics of human rights law, judges should not be given the authority to be making those judgments in the first place: for them, the very existence of open-ended legal doctrines such as the margin of appreciation is inherently problematic. Furthermore, appeals to doctrine will not appease critics who think that doctrine is regularly misapplied, or that the relevant court lacks competency, or is institutionally predisposed towards deciding cases in a particular way – and both media and political commentary on the HRA/ECHR has regularly called the competency and integrity of the Strasbourg Court in particular into question.[65] These attacks are usually under-reasoned, and at times seem based on little more than casual prejudice about the inadequacy of foreign judges: but this distrust is not going to be easy to overcome by invitations to trust doctrine.

In general, such appeals to doctrine are unlikely to have much resonance beyond the ranks of true believers: neither confirmed heretics, nor undecided agnostics, are likely to be won over by reassurances that the legal structure of the HRA/ECHR is well-designed, when their scepticism relates to how it functions in practice. The same is true for any pro-HRA/ECHR arguments that frame the operation of human rights law as a straightforward application of well-established

63 See, for example, Philippe Sands's point that '[r]ather than Strasbourg being a problem, there is now considerable evidence that judgments in the UK courts influence decisions taken in Strasbourg', in P. Sands, 'This British bill of rights could end the UK', *The Guardian* (14 May 2015), available online at: www.theguardian.com/commentisfree/2015/may/14/british-bill-rights-could-end-uk

64 O'Cinnéide (n 58 above).

65 See, for example, Malcolm (n. 3 above) Stanley (n 60 above).

legal norms: this will not satisfy anyone concerned about the case-law outcomes of this process, or the value choices that underpin them.

The range of arguments made in favour of the HRA/ECHR that are based on appeals to the special status of human rights law, or to the design of its doctrinal structure, are therefore vulnerable: they are exposed to a number of counter-claims, and often rely on appeals to authority that lack resonance in the current political climate. This is not to say that such arguments cannot be deployed to good effect in a rhetorical sense, as part of wider battles to win the hearts and minds of the public. Indeed, some of the most high profile advocacy campaigns launched by civil society groups in support of existing UK human rights law have placed considerable emphasis on the special status of human rights law, the importance of the interests it protects, and the significance of the bridge the HRA/ECHR establishes between domestic and international law.[66] Such arguments certainly have a strong emotional appeal, tapping as they do into the post-1945 idealistic foundations of contemporary human rights thought. They also serve to frame opponents of the HRA/ECHR as working to undermine the special status of human rights law and the values it strives to promote – which has considerable utility as a form of 'plebiscitary rhetoric' to use Chambers's classification, i.e. speech deployed instrumentally to win an argument, usually by invoking an emotional or identitarian response.[67] However, as 'deliberative rhetoric', such arguments struggle to engage head-on with key claims being made by the other side – and hence are arguably limited in effect.

Rising to the challenge: highlighting the positive benefits of the HRA/ECHR – and the negative consequences of reform proposals

In contrast, the two remaining strands of pro-HRA/ECHR argumentation – namely attempts to set out the positive benefits of the HRA/ECHR, and to identify flaws in reform proposals – go straight to the heart of the current debate. When human rights experts and advocates give substantive reasons as to why the HRA and ECHR have enhanced UK law – by, for example, showing how the impact of these legal instruments has enhanced the capacity of the British legal system to do justice, and given 'deserving' individuals legal remedies that would not otherwise have been available to them – they are making a tangible, clearly defined, positive case for existing human rights law that is not dependant on abstract appeals to special authority. As such, this line of argumentation helps

66 This is particularly true of the campaigns launched by RightsInfo and Liberty: see, n 4 above.

67 The widely-viewed video sketch narrated by Patrick Stewart, discussed above at n 48, would be an example of this tendency: it lists the rights protected by the HRA and suggests that its repeal would entail a loss of these rights, when those arguing for reform would argue that HRA repeal will merely result in those rights being protected in a different way. The sketch therefore does not really engage with the anti-HRA/ECHR case – but would appear to be a highly effective rhetorical tool in mobilising support behind the HRA.

both policy-makers and the general public understand what 'added value' the HRA and ECHR have brought to the British legal system, and why repealing the HRA and/or withdrawing from the ECHR would deprive UK law of a useful tool for doing justice. On the flip side, highlighting the problems that exist with the reform proposals that have been put forward by various commentators in this context, including the various Bill of Rights schemes that have periodically surfaced over the last decade or so, serves to draw attention to the complexities and negative side-effects of changing the status quo – especially as regards the devolution settlement. It also puts the onus on critics of the HRA/ECHR to come up with workable proposals for a new human rights law – which, thus far, they have struggled to do.

Taken together, these two strands of argumentation thus reinforce each other: the positive case for the HRA/ECHR is complemented and thrown into starker relief by negative criticism of proposed alternative proposals. They allow supporters of the HRA/ECHR to 'get on the front foot', to use a cricket metaphor, and to take the initiative in the debate. They also are strands of argumentation that can have some impact on both policy-makers and the general public. When human rights experts and advocates explain why the HRA and ECHR taken together enhance the capacity of British law to 'do right' by individuals in need and otherwise improve the functioning of the justice system, they are giving expert-elite policy-makers concrete reasons for retaining the status quo. They are also establishing a narrative that has potential appeal to the general public, by demonstrating how the HRA/ECHR can make a positive impact on individual lives. In contrast, identifying the weaknesses of reform proposals will inevitably caution policy-makers against rushing to embrace them – and may help educate the public more generally about the comparative benefits of the existing framework of UK human rights law.

Human rights experts have provided plenty of critical analysis of the weaknesses of the various reform proposals that have been put forward over the last decade – including in particular the Conservative proposals for a new Bill of Rights published in 2014.[68] However, they have been surprisingly slow to start making a positive case for the HRA/ECHR based upon its tangible impact on the UK's legal system – as distinct from appealing to the status and authority of human rights law, as discussed above. In his attack on the HRA/ECHR written in 2011, Pinto-Duschinsky rightly noted the absence in the academic literature on human rights law of much in the way of substantive justification for the relationship established between the HRA and the ECHR.[69] However, recent literature has begun to remedy this flaw.[70] But more is needed: the case for the

68 See, for example, A. Young, 'HRA Howlers: The Conservative Party and Reform of the Human Rights Act 1998', *U.K. Const. L. Blog* (7 October 2014), available online at: http://ukconstitutionallaw.org

69 Pinto-Duschinsky (n 3 above).

70 See, for example, M. Amos, 'The Value of the European Court of Human Rights to the United Kingdom' (2017) 28(3) *European Journal of International Law* 763–785.

HRA/ECHR requires that experts start showing in detail how these conjoined legal instruments enhance the functioning, legitimacy and integrity of the UK's legal system more generally.[71]

Interestingly, human rights advocates have been quicker off the mark in this regard. Campaigns in support of the HRA/ECHR, such as those run by Act for the Act, RightsInfo and Liberty, have increasingly focused on showing how the HRA in particular has helped individuals achieve justice. As such, they are helping to show the positive benefits of the Act – and thereby attempting to give effect to Donald and Mottershaw's argument that '[p]eople tend to become more positive when exposed to messages that: make human rights feel relevant to them; connect with tradition; emphasise fairness; and increase their understanding of how human rights laws work in practice'.[72] Such campaigning could be accused of glossing over the complexity of human rights law. It could also be accused of 'soft soaping' the law, by presenting it as organically linked to established constitutional traditions and of benefit to all members of society rather than as something disruptive and challenging which primarily benefits marginalised groups such as criminal suspects, prisoners and assorted minorities of different stripes. However, it has considerable value as a form of 'plebiscitary rhetoric', not least by how it lends an emotional and identitarian dimension to the pro-HRA/ECHR case that other supportive arguments lack – and it rests on a sufficiently 'deliberative' basis to stand up to intellectual challenge.[73] As a result, it is exactly this type of argumentative strategy that defenders of the HRA/ECHR will need to deploy in the years of debate about the state of UK human rights law that doubtless lie before us.

Conclusion

With Brexit dominating the political agenda, the human rights debate is currently on stand-still. However, it is likely to flare up again in the not too distant future. When it does, Brexit may affect this debate in unexpected ways. It has the potential to act as a rallying point for both sides, but may also (perhaps counter-intuitively) lessen enthusiasm for repeal of the HRA or withdrawal from the ECHR system in Westminster and Whitehall. Having said that, the HRA and ECHR remain vulnerable – and their supporters need to set about winning hearts and minds across the general public and not just within the ranks of the expert-elite. As such, they need to think about their argumentative strategy and focus on arguments that 'sell' the HRA/ECHR rather than appealing to status, authority

71 For more on this point, see C. O'Cinnéide, 'Rights Under Pressure' (2017) *EHRLR*, 43–48.

72 Donald and Mottenshaw (n 18 above).

73 See Amos (n 71 above); O'Cinnéide (n 72 above). See also in general the arguments made by Tom Hickman as to the continuities that exist between the common law and the operation of the HRA/ECHR, in T. Hickman, *Public Law After the Human Rights Act* (Hart, 2010).

and expertise. There are signs that this lesson is beginning to sink in – but there is a long road ahead.

Bibliography

M. Amos, 'The Value of the European Court of Human Rights to the United Kingdom" (2017) 28(3) *European Journal of International Law* 763–785.

A. Buchanan and R. Powell, 'Constitutional Democracy and the Rule of International Law: Are They Compatible?' (2008) 16(3) *Journal of Political Philosophy* 326–349.

S. Chambers, 'Has Deliberative Democracy Abandoned Mass Democracy?' 37(3) (2009) *Political Theory* 323–350.

A. Donald and E. Mottershaw, *Identifying Human Rights Stories: A Scoping Study* (Middlesex University/Thomas Paine Initiative, 2014).

A. Donald, J. Gordon and P. Leach, *The UK and the European Court of Human Rights*, Equality and Human Rights Commission Research Report No. 83 (London: EHRC, 2012).

D. Dyzenhaus, 'The Left and the Question of Law' (2004) 17 *Canadian Journal of Law and Jurisprudence* 7.

Equality and Diversity Forum, *Public Attitudes to Human Rights* (London: EDF, 2012).

C. Gearty, *On Fantasy Island: Britain, Strasbourg and Human Rights* (CUP, 2016).

R. Geuss, *Philosophy and Real Politics* (Princeton University Press, 2008).

J. Habermas, *The Structural Transformation of the Public Sphere* (Cambridge, MA: MIT Press, 1989; orig. 1962).

E. Heinze, 'The Reality and Hyper-reality of Human Rights: Public Consciousness and the Mass Media', in *Examining Critical Perspectives on Human Rights: The End of an Era?*, R. Dickenson *et al.*, eds, (Cambridge University Press, 2012).

T. Hickman, *Public Law After the Human Rights Act* (Hart, 2010).

K. Kaur-Ballagan, S. Castell, K. Brough and H. Friemert, *Public Perceptions of Human Rights* (Manchester: Equality and Human Rights Commission, 2009).

N. Malcolm, *Human Rights and Political Wrongs* (Policy Exchange/Judicial Power Project, 2017).

C. O'Cinnéide, *Human Rights and the UK Constitution* (British Academy, 2012).

C. O'Cinnéide, 'Human Rights and the UK Constitution', in D. Oliver, J. Jowell, C. O'Cinnéide (eds), *The Changing Constitution* (OUP, 2015) 67–103.

C. O'Cinnéide, 'Saying "No" to Strasbourg: When Are National Parliaments Justified in Refusing to Give Effect to Judgments of International Human Rights Courts?', in M. Saul, G. Ulfstein and A. Follesdal, *The International Human Rights Judiciary and National Parliaments: Europe and Beyond* (OUP, 2017).

O. O'Neill, *A Question of Trust?* BBC Reith Lectures (CUP, 2002).

M. Pinto-Duschinsky, *Bring Rights Back Home: Making human rights compatible with parliamentary democracy in the UK* (Policy Exchange, 2011).

J. Rubenfeld, 'Unilateralism and Constitutionalism' (2004) 79 *N.Y.U. L. Rev.* 1971.

A. Tomkins, 'What's Left of the Political Constitution?' (2013) 14(12) *German L.J.* 2275–2292.

10 Instrumentalism in human rights and the media

Locking out democratic scepticism?

Michael Gordon

Introduction

Public debates about human rights – as filtered through the lens of the media – have a seemingly binary character. The 'Bad Press' distorts and rejects rights claims, whereas the 'Good Press' embraces the architecture and value commitments which underpin modern human rights law. Yet, in framing debates about rights in this way, the inherently political nature of both positions (and any others which might be imagined between these caricatured extremes) is readily overlooked. This paper reflects on the implications of characterising argument about the contemporary salience of human rights in this way. It suggests that human rights claims are instrumentalised, by press both 'Bad' and 'Good', but for different ends.

This should not be surprising, however, for it is in the very nature of the legal human rights discourse that rights claims become instrumentalised in a paradigm which is oriented to the (in)justice of outcomes. This outcome orientation of modern human rights law, and the use and representation of rights claims in (and by) the modern media, may distract our attention from thinking about the means by which political decisions are (and ought to be) taken. One particular consequence is that little space is left for public debate to be influenced by democratic scepticism about human rights law. It may be unreasonable – perhaps even impossible – to expect that democratic critiques of modern human rights law could be translated for use in the media. Nevertheless, the reflection of the instrumental nature of human rights law in debates about media reporting has the potential to lock in this outcome-oriented paradigm, and lock out sceptical perspectives on the systemic difficulties with legal structures established for the protection of human rights.

This chapter first explores the architecture of the debate about media representations of legal human rights, and the way in which discussion is framed in binary terms. The chapter then moves on to consider the implications of the instrumentalism which prompts a focus on the ends, rather than the means, of human rights law in public debate. Finally, the chapter concludes by reflecting on the consequences of framing media debate about human rights law in these terms, and considers whether this is simply further evidence that, in furiously debating the use and abuse of rights claims by the modern press, we are having the wrong argument, about the wrong problem.

The architecture of debate about media representations of legal human rights

The legal protection of human rights in the UK was transformed by the enactment of the Human Rights Act 1998 (HRA). This legislation provided overarching protection for the core rights set out in the European Convention of Human Rights (ECHR), to which the UK had been a signatory as a matter of international law since 1950.[1] For some, it was the 'cornerstone' of the UK's new constitution.[2] While such claims as to the constitutional centrality of the HRA 1998 are misplaced, not least given live questions about the likelihood that this legislation will endure,[3] the impact of the domestication of human rights has been significant. It has changed the form and nature of much constitutional argument, and prompted an (ongoing) recalibration of the relationships between the courts, the government, and Parliament. And this has been the UK's part of a broader 'rights revolution', with human rights discourse becoming the dominant language of social justice across the modern world, and in western liberal democracies in particular.[4]

The modern prominence of human rights – both in the UK constitution, and as the primary language of international political argument – has inevitably been reflected in the attention given to the subject in the media. As many other chapters of this collection demonstrate, many of the issues tackled in the language of human rights are intensely controversial, ranging from torture and detention without trial, to immigration and asylum, to LGBT discrimination, and abortion.[5] As complex, contentious moral-political issues, they are, for a number of reasons,

---

1 On the Human Rights Act 1998 generally see, for example, K D Ewing, 'The Human Rights Act and Parliamentary Democracy' (1999) 62 *Modern Law Review* 79; C Gearty, *Principles of Human Rights Adjudication* (Oxford, Oxford University Press, 2004); A Kavanagh, *Constitutional Review under the UK Human Rights Act* (Cambridge, Cambridge University Press, 2009); A L Young, *Parliamentary Sovereignty and the Human Rights Act* (Oxford, Hart Publishing, 2009).

2 V Bogdanor, 'Our New Constitution' (2004) 120 *Law Quarterly Review* 242, 259. See also V Bogdanor, *The New British Constitution* (Oxford, Hart Publishing, 2009).

3 See the (ongoing) debates – within the Conservative Party in particular – about whether the Human Rights Act should be replaced with a British Bill of Rights; see, for example, the report of the Commission on a Bill of Rights, *A UK Bill of Rights? The Choice Before Us* (December 2012). For an overview, see House of Commons Library, 'A British Bill of Rights?', *Briefing Paper 7193* (18 May 2016)

4 See, for example, S Moyn, *The Last Utopia* (Harvard, Harvard University Press, 2010).

5 See, for example, in this volume, C R G Murray, 'Monstering Strasbourg over Prisoner Voting Rights' Chapter 4; E Drywood and H Gray, 'Demonising Immigrants: How a Human Rights Narrative Has Contributed to Negative Portrayals of Immigrants in the UK Media', Chapter 5 and Y McDermott, 'Trial by Media: The Fair Trial Jurisprudence of the European Court of Human Rights in the UK Press' Chapter 6.

also liable to be simplified, or even flatly misrepresented, in media reporting. The focus of this chapter, however, is on a different topic – rather than considering the extent to which human rights issues are accurately or inaccurately represented in media reporting, why this might occur, the existence of good or bad faith, or the implications, this chapter aims to consider the structure of debates about human rights, as manifested in the media.

Why adopt a focus on the structure of debate about human rights? Discussion concerning the fair and accurate representation of human rights issues, arguments, cases and claims in the media is undoubtedly important. Yet there are also structural issues which deserve sustained attention, and are often underappreciated. Human rights do not simply provide a basis for asking discrete questions of law and morality, they also offer a specific way of organising and channelling challenges to the use of public power. The systemic dimensions of human rights law as a means of public accountability are also crucial, because challenges to official decisions or policies on human rights grounds do not occur in isolation, but within a broader scheme. This broader scheme has both institutional and conceptual components: in relation to the institutional, rights claims are developed in specified courts, by specialised advocates, and resolved by the judiciary; in relation to the conceptual, the relevant actors must question whether a right has been engaged, where there has been interference with that right, and whether any identifiable interference can be justified as legitimate or proportionate.[6] This standard legal scheme provides a degree of uniformity to the evaluation of human rights claims, and the operation of this general system can be as significant as the substantive issues concerning the content of any specific right in shaping how a particular question or case is resolved.

As human rights structures become an ever more prominent means through which the exercise of public power can be challenged, the public representation of these claims becomes of parallel importance. A crucial part of accountability in a democratic state is that this occurs openly, and is therefore something which citizens can have access to, and potentially become engaged in. The media must therefore play a significant role in publicising the means by which official actors are challenged and held responsible for policy choices, to avoid the processes of governmental accountability becoming merely an exercise in intra-elite intrigue. Yet that the media have an important constitutional function is well established; the press gallery was long ago described as the ‘Fourth Estate’ by Carlyle, which was ‘more important far’ than the other three estates in Parliament, the House of Commons, House of Lords and the Crown.[7] The modern media of the information age may be much more complex, yet the essential idea that it has a

6 For an example in the European Court of Human Rights, see *Al-Jedda v United Kingdom* (Application No. 27021/08) (2011) 53 E.H.R.R. 23; for influential discussion of the approach of the courts in the UK, see *Huang v Secretary of State for the Home Department* [2007] UKHL 11; [2007] 2 A.C. 167.

7 T Carlyle, *On Heroes, Hero-Worship and the Heroic in History* (1840), Lecture V.

key role in the effective operation of the accountability processes of a system of government remains clear. The media may now be crucial in setting the political agenda, investigating specific instances of governmental failure, generating or amplifying public pressure on office holders, cultivating sentiment around key policy decisions, and many other things besides. There can be little doubt that the activities of the media must be accommodated within any account of the operation of a system of government, for they will play a significant role in shaping how power is used within (and sometimes outside of) the formal rules of the political order.[8]

Media representations of accountability claims made within the legal human rights framework are therefore of clear significance and, as such, deserving of critical scrutiny. Perhaps the key feature of public debates about rights – as filtered through the lens of the media – is that they have an ostensibly binary character. This is particularly the case when we focus on the press, which unlike television and radio broadcasters, are not subject to requirements of reporting with 'due accuracy' and presenting issues with 'due impartiality' as imposed by legislation,[9] and enforced by Ofcom, the UK's communications regulator.[10] The binary nature of the debate is framed around the existence of, and differences between, a 'Bad Press' and a 'Good Press'. The 'Bad Press' distorts the meaning of fundamental human rights provisions, and their applicability in the UK in particular, in support of a hostile right wing political agenda lacking in compassion for anyone who is foreign, different, or perhaps especially in the current climate, European.[11] The paradigmatic example of a newspaper exhibiting this hostility to human rights claims is generally seen as the *Daily Mail*.[12] This representation of rights is largely underpinned by a distinction between the deserving and undeserving; there are groups or individuals who do not deserve the legal protection of their human rights, a claim which appears to challenge the ostensible universality of these fundamental claims. In contrast, we have the 'Good Press' – with the

8 See, for example, the recognition by Woodhouse of the significant influence of the contemporary media over the application of the constitutional conventions concerning the responsibility of government ministers: 'Most cases of resignation in the last 50 years owe something to the media'; 'a sustained campaign by the media against a minister may be sufficient to bring him or her down'; D Woodhouse, 'UK Ministerial Responsibility in 2002' (2004) *Public Administration* 1–19, 16.

9 Communications Act 2003, ss. 319–320.

10 See *The Ofcom Broadcasting Code* (April 2017), available online at: www.ofcom.org.uk/__data/assets/pdf_file/0005/100103/broadcast-code-april-2017.pdf

11 See further, in this volume, S Reynolds, 'It's Not Me, It's You: Examining the Print Media's Approach to 'Europe' in Brexit Britain' Chapter 2 and E Drywood and H Gray, 'Demonising Immigrants: How a Human Rights Narrative Has Contributed to Negative Portrayals of Immigrants in the UK Media' Chapter 5.

12 See, for example, 'Travellers use "human rights" to stop police "spying on them 24/7" then immediately dump and set fire to 70 TONS of rubbish on private land', *Daily Mail* (5 April 2017), available online at: www.dailymail.co.uk/news/article-4382730/Travellers-use-human-rights-stop-police-watching-them.html

Guardian perhaps standing as the exemplar of this tradition.[13] The 'Good Press' accepts the universality of rights, and the substantive values of liberty and equality which are seen to underpin rights to live, associate, express opinions, be free from torture and unjustified punishments, and others. And in so doing the 'Good Press' demonstrates compassion for the very groups or individuals demonised by the 'Bad Press', and extols the virtues of having a system by which rights claims can be promoted.

This account of the framing of debate about human rights law around a diametrically opposed 'Bad' and 'Good' press is obviously, to some extent, a caricature of what is in reality a more varied landscape. Yet, while a simplification in some respects, in other respects it feels as if much public debate about media representations of human rights is structured in exactly this way: those on the side of virtue understand and respect human rights, whereas those focused on the pursuit of grubby self-interest regard universal rights as an exclusive luxury at best, and a dangerous indulgence at worst. It also works in combination with a second binary distinction. The 'Good' and 'Bad' press approaches to human rights are themselves underpinned by a binary conception of legality – or perhaps of the idea of the rule of law. This binary conception of the rule of law posits the legality of a particular state of affairs as a matter of absolute judgment – either something is definitively lawful or it is not. While this is no doubt an accurate representation of the outcome of nearly any specific legal case, it masks the real complexity of the contested moral, political, and policy dimensions of an assessment of human rights compatibility that is inherent in such adjudication. The ensuing lack of nuance as to the operation of legal systems for the enforcement of human rights reinforces the basic division between a 'Good' and 'Bad' press – the result of a rights claim becomes a clear-cut matter of legal fact, and something to be praised or lamented, depending only on the vantage point occupied.

These binary approaches seem to structure a great deal of thought and debate about legal human rights. But what is lost in this is the political aspect of human rights law, which is suppressed by the binary conception of legality which constitutes the terrain on which both the 'Good Press' and 'Bad Press' engage alike. For to embrace the language and significance of human rights to establish and sustain claims for social goods or entitlements, fair treatment or respect, is to make a political choice, and to engage in political discourse via the medium of rights, rather than ascend to a higher level of enlightenment, and operate above the fray. While human rights law may present itself as based on unquestionable premises around which there is little or no room for debate, there is no objective argument from reason which can establish the natural or fundamental character of either the particular human rights identified in a legal scheme of protection,

13 See, for example, 'New human rights to protect against "mind hacking" and brain data theft proposed', *The Guardian* (26 April 2017), available online at: www.theguardian.com/science/2017/apr/26/new-human-rights-to-protect-against-mind-hacking-and-brain-data-theft-proposed.

or justify as uncontentious the ways in which these basic rights are fleshed out and applied in specific contexts.[14] Of course, there is immense rhetorical power in the idea of rights inherent to all people – whether in a particular context, or in systemic terms – as human rights becomes a catch-all, stock phrase for the pursuit of justice, fairness, liberty, equality, autonomy, well-being and much else besides. But such rights must be contingent and political, rather than 'trumps' which bypass the existence of differing perspectives on how we should organise our societies.[15]

Against this backdrop, it becomes evident that the position adopted by the 'Good Press' on human rights is no less political than that adopted by the 'Bad Press'. It may be, in substance, a politics which many instinctively prefer, especially within the legal professions and academia, given the primacy, perhaps even reverence, afforded to human rights law – but it is still a politics. It is to use rights – to instrumentalise human rights instruments, language, provisions[16] – just as the 'Bad Press' does. The difference here is one of ends, not means. Yet this media instrumentalism concerning human rights is also a reflection of the nature of human rights law itself. The claim of human rights law to circumvent politics through its grounding in universal values – based on a simplistic, binary conception of the rule of law – is an impossibility, and may raise a range of difficulties, which will be explored in the next section.

Ends, means and human rights as instruments

Once the instrumentalism of human rights law is recognised, we can see more clearly the difficulties with the structure of debates about media representations of rights. The instrumental nature of human rights law means both the 'Good Press' and 'Bad Press' are caught in a paradigm which is crucially oriented to outcomes. Human rights language is used to establish or bolster claims for desirable social goods, with legal processes for rights protection the mechanism by which these claims might be vindicated: the fundamental human right to X must be understood to require the provision of entitlement Y (or the removal of constraint Z), and the courts must use the powers at their disposal to ensure that this is recognised by law.[17] This is an enterprise which is focused on the outcomes

14 See, for example, Bentham's famous account of rights as 'nonsense on stilts'; J Bentham, *Rights, Representation, and Reform: Nonsense upon Stilts and Other Writings on the French Revolution* in P Schofield, C Pease-Watkin, and C Blamires (eds), *The Collected Works of Jeremy Bentham* (Oxford, Oxford University Press, 2002). For influential discussion of these ideas in a more recent context, see J A G Griffith, 'The Political Constitution' (1979) 42 *Modern Law Review* 1.

15 For the contrary view, arguing in favour of 'rights as trumps', see R Dworkin, *Taking Rights Seriously* (London, Duckworth, 2nd edn 1978).

16 On 'rights-instrumentalism', see J Waldron, *Law and Disagreement* (Oxford, Clarendon Press, 1999) 252–254.

17 The formal powers available to the courts to give effect to the determined requirements of human rights law will vary depending on the system of protection in place; under the

of social decision-making. The ends are inevitably prioritised over the means of reaching a decision about the distribution of social goods or individual entitlements, because it is the ends that are being legally measured as to their compatibility (or incompatibility) against the benchmark which the premises of human rights law provide.

Now this is not to argue that ends do not matter. And, as such, we are of course fully entitled to take a side in criticising and challenging the particular instrumentalisation of rights by the 'Bad Press', where that has the effect of fostering hostility and social division, or stigmatising vulnerable people or groups. Instead, it is to recognise that to do so is to engage in an enterprise that is political as well as legal, and that we are not here above the fray, challenging prejudice with objective legal facts derived from the unquestionable premises of human rights law. And once the inevitably political character of human rights argument is acknowledged – even within the confines of legal structures for the protection of such rights – it also becomes clear that a focus on only the outcomes which flow from such systems will be inadequate. While it is certainly the case that the ends of human rights processes matter, they do not matter exclusively – we cannot, in other words, become entirely drawn into a debate which is solely about ends, and forget entirely about means. For the process by which social ends are determined, and how those ends are distributed, matters too. This is especially the case in a state committed to democratic ideals, which are premised on the political equality of citizens. Political equality must be delivered through the means as well as the ends of collective decision-making, and so the manner in which decisions are made must matter at least as much as the substantive quality of the decisions reached.

When we recognise the importance of considering the means of decision-making, as well as the ends of the process, the contemporary institutions, structures, and discourse of human rights law (but also the politics and morality inevitably underpinning the human rights project) can be found lacking in a number of ways. Human rights law positions itself to frame, constrain, and limit substantive political possibilities.[18] But given the human rights project must be a political enterprise, in reality the effect is to alter, perhaps even warp, the politics

---

Human Rights Act 1998, the courts should interpret legislation in a way that is rights compatible 'so far as it is possible to do so' (s.3), or might otherwise at their discretion make a declaration of incompatibility which does not affect the legal validity of primary legislation (s.4). The actions of public authorities which violate human rights, and were not mandated by primary legislation, should be struck down as unlawful (s.6). The Human Rights Act has been described as one example of the 'new commonwealth models' of rights protection, which withhold full powers to invalidate legislation from courts, yet are still effective in embedding a legal human rights culture; see S Gardbaum, *The New Commonwealth Model of Constitutionalism: Theory and Practice* (Cambridge, Cambridge University Press, 2013).

18 See, for example, M Loughlin, *Sword and Scales: An Examination of the Relationship between Law and Politics* (Oxford, Hart Publishing, 2000); M Loughlin, *The Idea of Public Law* (Oxford, Oxford University Press, 2003) Chapter 7.

which must inherently be the basis for any society.[19] Human rights discourse privileges individualism above all, with its ultimate representative the rights-bearer defending their entitlements against the state.[20] It fractures issues, considering them in isolation from other related matters, and in only the partial context that the individual-state dynamic makes possible. Even when claims are brought in groups, arguments develop by drawing fine distinctions between atomised individuals, serving ultimately to sub-categorise any collective. The legalism which accompanies the conversion of human rights discourse into human rights law narrows further the terms of argument.[21] It establishes the supremacy of an elite level practice, conducted in a language which is doubly problematic, in that it is vague while ostensibly accessible, but this accessibility is actually illusory. This leads to engagement through terms of art which can be disorienting when it subverts the meaning of otherwise understandable concepts.[22] The primacy given to individual rights by the legal institutionalisation of mechanisms for human rights protection has the potential to subjugate other important principles of justice, like collectivism and shared responsibility, while capturing others, like equality and non-discrimination, and imposing definitions of them in formal rather than substantive terms. And, finally, there may also be a range of concerns as to the forum which human rights law promotes as the crucible in which claims must be raised and vindicated: the fact that such claims must be developed in the courtroom, subject to the strictures of legal argument, and decided by members of the judiciary, who are generally isolated and removed from political accountability by design, while unrepresentative of the population at large.[23] Ultimately, the decision to task the judiciary with the legal protection of human rights can be seen to empower non-democratic actors with some of the most sensitive and important decisions that stand to be taken in a society.[24] Even where the power to make such

19 See, for example, Gordon Silverstein, *Law's Allure: How Law Shapes, Constrains, Saves, and Kills Politics* (Cambridge, Cambridge University Press, 2009).

20 See, for example, K Marx, 'On the Jewish Question' (1844), republished in D McLellan, *Karl Marx: Selected Writings* (Oxford, Oxford University Press, 2nd edn 2000).

21 See, for example, J N Shklar, *Legalism* (Cambridge, MA: Harvard University Press, 1964); MA Glendon, *Rights Talk: The Impoverishment of Political Discourse* (New York, Free Press, 1991).

22 See, for example, the discussion of the distortion of the 'right to liberty and security', focusing on Art 5 of the ECHR, in KD Ewing and JC Tham, 'The Continuing Futility of the Human Rights Act' [2008] *Public Law* 668. A similar critique might apply to the intensely fluid 'right to private and family life' recognised by Art 8 of the ECHR.

23 This is certainly the case in the UK, where (as of May 2017) there had only been one woman ever appointed to the UK's highest court (whether in the form of the House of Lords or the Supreme Court), no female judge ever appointed as the Lord Chief Justice or one of the Heads of Division, and lamentable representation of judges who are female or from black or minority ethnic groups across the senior judiciary. See the Judicial Diversity Statistics (July 2016) at available online at: www.judiciary.gov.uk/about-the-judiciary/who-are-the-judiciary/diversity/judicial-diversity-statistics-2016/

24 See, for example, Waldron, n 15; J Waldron, 'The Core of the Case Against Judicial Review' (2006) 115 *Yale Law Journal* 1346.

decisions definitively is not passed to the judges – as in the UK, under the Human Rights Act 1998 – there are still many reasons for concern about the impact of human rights law on the democratic practices of a state founded, formally at least, on the political equality of citizens.

These deficiencies with the processes and structures of human rights decision-making – and no doubt others that might be identified – are not reflected, and indeed are barely even recognised, in media representations of human rights law. Even where structural issues have been critical in the context of a particular human rights case, they are explored only in a cursory fashion – and, crucially, on the terms established by the courts themselves. To take an example, the case of *R (Nicklinson) v Ministry of Justice*[25] concerned (among other claims) a challenge to the criminalisation of assisting another in committing suicide,[26] on the grounds that it violated the Article 8 ECHR right to private and family life of the disabled claimants who were physically incapable of ending their own lives without medical assistance. The judgment is an immensely complex one, given the Supreme Court essentially split three ways, with Lords Neuberger, Mance and Wilson holding that it would not be inappropriate for the courts to make a declaration that the law in this area was incompatible with human rights, but only at some future point. Lady Hale and Lord Kerr argued that the court could make such a declaration and should not wait; whereas Lords Sumption, Clarke, Reed, and Hughes determined that this was a sensitive matter of political judgment for Parliament, not for the judges. As such, there was a 5–4 majority in favour of the courts being entitled to issue a declaration of human rights incompatibility at some point, but a 7–2 majority against doing it at that time (for some because it would never be appropriate, for others only if Parliament failed to reconsider the matter).

This key constitutional question – who should decide, Parliament or the courts? – is in many ways a proxy through which the more elaborate kinds of human rights scepticism outlined above can be addressed. The media reporting of the Supreme Court decision acknowledged that the question of the division of responsibility between Parliament and the courts had been in issue, yet treated it as a matter which had essentially been resolved in this case, and by the court, rather than something which is ongoing, and about which non-judicial actors may take a different view. In the *Guardian*, for example, it was reported that the Supreme Court had 'ruled that judges do have the "constitutional authority" to intervene in the debate', but the focus was on the substantive finding, and there was no explanation of why it might be contentious for the legalisation of assisted dying to be a matter for judicial, rather than parliamentary, determination.[27]

25 [2014] UKSC 38; [2015] AC 657

26 Suicide Act 1961, s.2.

27 'Assisted suicide campaigners fail to get supreme court to overturn ban', *The Guardian* (25 June 2014), available online at: www.theguardian.com/society/2014/jun/25/assisted-suicide-ban-doctors-supreme-court

The same can be said of the reporting of the decision in the *Daily Mail* – there is little that can be gleaned as to why we might be sceptical about judicial claims to possess the authority to resolve this issue on human rights grounds, although it does provide further context about the dynamic between Parliament and the courts in reporting Lord Neuberger's view 'that if MPs and peers did not give serious consideration to legalising assisted suicide, there was a "real prospect" a future legal challenge would succeed.'[28] In the exemplars of the 'Good Press' and the 'Bad Press', as discussed above, we therefore find little in the reporting of a contentious human rights case that would provide insight into reasons for scepticism about the legal structures or processes of human rights law. Instead, despite the fact that some of these issues were under direct consideration by the Supreme Court, the human rights paradigm goes unchallenged in these media representations.

Of course, this is not to say that issues associated with the operation of the system of legal protection of human rights do not get aired in the press. On the contrary, both the *Guardian* and the *Daily Mail* have specific agendas concerning human rights law, which are made explicit in editorials related to the unending debates about repeal of the Human Rights Act 1998.[29] But whether defensive of, or hostile to, the human rights project, these issues are outlined in discrete pieces on the topic of potential legal reform – the reporting of the more regular use of legal human rights claims is therefore insulated from such considerations. Perhaps this is unsurprising because, as considered above, media representations of human rights reflect the outcome orientation of human rights law. However, the danger is that they then shape public debate in a way which locks in the binary framing of a 'Good' and 'Bad' press, responding to the 'Good' or 'Bad' ends of human rights decisions, with the means of human rights laws – the structures, processes, institutions, and discourse – relegated to a subsidiary matter.

This is especially regrettable when there is much about which to be sceptical in practice, as well as in principle. While some may believe we are in a new liberal era of judicial decision-making, longer term studies – both historical and

28 'European judges agree with British courts and throw out right-to-die case brought by paralysed ex-builder and widow of man who had locked-in syndrome', *Daily Mail* (16 July 2015), available online at: www.dailymail.co.uk/news/article-3163593/Paralysed-ex-builder-widow-man-locked-syndrome-lose-right-die-case-European-Court-Human-Rights.html#ixzz4gaZDHUdD This report is of the decision of the European Court of Human Rights, which also rejected the claims of *Nicklinson*, but it provides a summary of the Supreme Court's judgment from a year earlier. The *Daily Mail* website only carries Press Association reporting of the Supreme Court decision in June 2014.

29 See, for example, 'The Guardian view on scrapping the Human Rights Act' *The Guardian* (3 October 2014), available online at: www.theguardian.com/commentisfree/2014/oct/03/guardian-view-scrapping-human-rights-act-dangerous-jumble 'A nation imperilled by the Human Rights Act' *The Daily Mail* (1 August 2015), available online at: www.dailymail.co.uk/debate/article-3181945/DAILY-MAIL-COMMENT-nation-imperilled-Human-Rights-Act.html

contemporary – provide little to justify such complacency.[30] We see the false promise of human rights law – its rhetoric is of the delivery of universal social goods to all, yet the reality is that legal decision-making, even that concerning human rights, is at most based on gradualism, moderation, and leads inevitably to compromised outcomes. The results of the 'bedroom tax' litigation are instructive – there may have been headline success for the most vulnerable claimants, but the majority of the litigants, also in extremely disadvantageous circumstances, did not prevail, demonstrating that the application of human rights law can have a limited capacity to make a real impact on iniquitous government policies.[31] Similarly, the so-called 'workfare' litigation indicates that human rights law may only have an impact for select categories of claimants, leaving the vast majority of those affected by the (initially unlawful) withdrawal of jobseeker's allowance without any remedy.[32] There are also recent cases in which the justice of human rights outcomes may be very much disputed. For example, the Supreme Court decision that the use of police 'stop and search' powers did not discriminate against members of black and minority ethnic groups, but indeed were for their 'benefit'.[33] Or the decision of that court that it would be unlawful for the National Assembly for Wales to introduce a policy allowing for the NHS to boost its funding by charging the insurance companies of employers whose employees had required treatment for cancers and other medical conditions attributable to exposure to asbestos, because this would

30 See especially K D Ewing and C A Gearty, *Freedom Under Thatcher: Civil Liberties in Modern Britain* (Oxford, Clarendon Press, 1990); J A G Griffith, *The Politics of the Judiciary*, 5th edn (London, Fontana Press, 1997); K D Ewing and C A Gearty, *The Struggle for Civil Liberties: Political Freedom and the Rule of Law in Britain, 1914–1945* (Oxford, Oxford University Press, 2000); K D Ewing, *The Bonfire of the Liberties: New Labour, Human Rights and the Rule of Law* (Oxford, Oxford University Press, 2010).

31 *R (Carmichael and others) v Secretary of State for Work and Pensions* [2016] UKSC 58; [2016] 1 W.L.R. 4550.

32 *R (Reilly) v Secretary of State for Work and Pensions (No. 2)* [2016] EWCA Civ 413. In this challenge to the retrospective legislation which the government introduced in Parliament to legalise what had been the unlawful withdrawal of jobseekers allowance from people who had refused to undertake unpaid work, only those who had lodged appeals prior to the retrospective legislation would be eligible for any relief available on human rights grounds. This was estimated in the proceedings in the Court of Appeal as some 2,500 out of 250,000 people – approximately 1% of the unlawfully sanctioned benefit claimants.

33 *R (Roberts) v Commissioner of Police of the Metropolis* [2015] UKSC 79; [2016] 1 W.L.R. 210, [41]: 'Any random "suspicionless" power of stop and search carries with it the risk that it will be used in an arbitrary or discriminatory manner in individual cases. There are, however, great benefits to the public in such a power.... The purpose of this is to reduce the risk of serious violence where knives and other offensive weapons are used, especially that associated with gangs and large crowds. It must be borne in mind that many of these gangs are largely composed of young people from black and minority ethnic groups. While there is a concern that members of these groups should not be disproportionately targeted, it is members of these groups who will benefit most from the reduction in violence, serious injury and death that may result from the use of such powers'.

amount to a retrospective interference with their right to the peaceful enjoyment of property.[34]

Human rights law may also impact negatively upon the way in which future policy choices can be made and delivered. To take a high profile example, while successive UK governments have refused to implement the judgment of the European Court of Human Rights in *Hirst (No. 2)*,[35] which held that a 'blanket ban' on prisoner voting rights was incompatible with the right to free elections under Article 3 of Protocol 1 of the ECHR, all consideration has been of very modest changes to the availability of the franchise for prisoners.[36] The effect of this decision has been to box in the future policy spectrum, and make it essentially inconceivable for more radical solutions – such as the universal democratic enfranchisement of all serving prisoners, subject to no restrictions at all – to be promoted in the current political environment. Moreover, even when social policy choices are made which can be defended from human rights challenges constructed by powerful commercial interests, the delay to the implementation of legislative changes, which have been democratically determined and entirely lawful from the outset, is itself damaging to the public interest. This has been very visible in the succession of challenges engaging human rights claims by tobacco companies, alleging unjustified interference with their right to peaceful enjoyment of property, in response to increased regulation of their commercial activities through bans on advertising and restrictions on packaging.[37] Yet, so superficially attractive are the claims of universal human rights protected by law, that we even see the emergence of a narrative where human rights law draws credit almost magnetically, in comparison with a politics which is caricatured as obviously flawed. For example, attempts to portray the justice eventually obtained by campaigners for the 96 Liverpool supporters killed in the 1989 Hillsborough football disaster as a triumph of human rights law are especially difficult to accept.[38] The persistent and pervasive failures of the justice system

---

34 *Re Recovery of Medical Costs for Asbestos Diseases (Wales) Bill* [2015] UKSC 3; [2015] AC 1016.

35 *Hirst v United Kingdom (No 2)* (2005) 42 EHRR 849; considering this decision in the UK, see *R (Chester) v Secretary of State for Justice* [2013] UKSC 63, [2014] AC 271. See further, in this volume, C R G Murray, 'Monstering Strasbourg over Prisoner Voting Rights' Chapter 4.

36 See the report of the Joint Committee on the Draft Voting Eligibility (Prisoners) Bill established to consider the possibilities (HL Paper 103, HC 924, 18 December 2013). Even the very modest recommendations of the Committee have gone unimplemented.

37 See, for example, *Imperial Tobacco Ltd v Lord Advocate* [2012] UKSC 61; 2013 SC (UKSC) 153; *R (British American Tobacco UK Ltd) v Secretary of State for Health* [2016] EWCA Civ 1182, and the decision of the Supreme Court to refuse permission to appeal on 12 April 2017, available online at: www.supremecourt.uk/news/permission-to-appeal-decision-12-april-2017.html For discussion of this point, see C McCorkindale, 'The New Powers of the Judiciary in Scotland – Part I', *Judicial Power Project Blog* (29 April 2016), available online at: https://judicialpowerproject.org.uk/the-new-powers-of-the-judiciary-in-scotland/

38 See, for example, David Allen Green, 'Theresa May, Hillsborough, human rights law and the politics of superficiality', *The Financial Times* (27 April 2016), available online

over decades compounded the injustice perpetrated in the aftermath of Hillsborough, and was only undone by sustained political action by the families of the 96 supporters, with the crucial breakthrough in obtaining new coroner's inquests into the circumstances of the disaster delivered by the non-legal independent panel which reviewed and documented the official failings in a critical report.[39] And this is to say nothing of the difficulties presented by models based on even greater empowerment of the judiciary for the protection of fundamental rights, most influentially in the system pioneered in the United States of America,[40] but also across a range of democratic states.[41]

In such circumstances, a binary, simplified, outcome-oriented approach to human rights law can be seen to provide a fundamentally inadequate basis for public debate in this area. It is a matter for great regret that media representations reflect back this framing of human rights law, yet it is also understandable, given its deep rooting in the structures of legal rights protection. Yet perhaps an even greater cause for concern is that if human rights law continues to be represented in this way in the media, there is the potential for it to shape public discourse in a way which not only locks in this binary, ends-focused framing, but may simultaneously serve to lock out democratic scepticism about the processes of the legal systems of human rights protection. How far it may be possible to prevent the exclusion of such scepticism about the functioning of the structures and institutions of human rights law – if it is possible at all – will be considered in the next section.

---

at: http://blogs.ft.com/david-allen-green/2016/04/27/theresa-may-hillsborough-human-rights-law-and-the-politics-of-superficiality/

39 See *Hillsborough: The Report of the Hillsborough Independent Panel* (HC 581, 12 September 2012), at: available online at: http://hillsborough.independent.gov.uk/repository/report/HIP_report.pdf The judgment of the Divisional Court which quashed the original inquest was based on revelations made in the *Report of the Independent Panel* as to serious flaws concerning the imposition of a premature evidential cut-off point, claims about the use of alcohol by fans, evidence of the alteration of police statements, and existing safety concerns relating to the stadium; see *Attorney General v HM Coroner for South Yorkshire (West)* [2012] EWHC 3783 (Admin). The legal authority to quash the original inquest was provided by the Coroners Act 1988, s 13. The only mention of human rights law in the judgment is in the conclusion at [28], indicating that the new coroner would need to decide whether Art 2 ECHR was engaged when determining the format of the new inquests, and if so, to ensure that the format of the new inquests would be compatible with those requirements. Yet, in any event, it would already be clear that the new inquests would inevitably need to be structured in such a way as to consider the material revealed by the Independent Panel, so as to avoid the serious flaws which caused the original inquest to be quashed.

40 See, for example, G N Rosenberg, *The Hollow Hope: Can Courts Bring About Social Change?* (London, University of Chicago Press, 1991); M Tushnet, *Taking the Constitution Away from the Courts* (Princeton, Princeton University Press, 1999); J Decker, *The Other Rights Revolution: Conservative Lawyers and the Remaking of American Government* (New York, Oxford University Press, 2016); A Berman, *Give Us the Ballot: The Modern Struggle for Voting Rights in American* (New York, Picador, 2016).

41 See, for example,J Bakan, *Just Words: Constitutional Rights and Social Wrongs* (Toronto, University of Toronto Press, 1997); R Hirschl, *Towards Juristocracy: The Origins and Consequences of New Constitutionalism* (Cambridge MA, Harvard University Press, 2004).

Locking out democratic scepticism about human rights

The previous section identified a range of reasons for scepticism about the operation of human rights law in a democratic society. Human rights law empowers non-democratic (legal) actors,[42] can legalise the operation of politics, entrench individualism at the expense of collectivism, capture and narrow the terms of moral argument, while failing to fulfil its hollow promises about the ability of such legal mechanisms to establish a just state of affairs in a community. Yet these grounds for scepticism are not reflected in debate about media representations of human rights law, which is framed around binary ideas of a 'Good' and 'Bad' press, and a conception of the rule of law which promotes absolute ideas of legality. This paper has suggested that this may not be surprising, for the instrumentalism associated with such representations of human rights law originates at the very heart of the legal structures for the protection of human rights. The outcome orientation of human rights law – with a focus on the legality of the ends of policy, rather than the means by which policy decisions are reached – is reflected both in the representation of human rights in the media, and in the debate about the quality or veracity of those representations.

But there is a further concern which has the potential to flow from this position. There is a danger that the inevitable reflection of the instrumental nature of legal human rights in media representations becomes more than simply a reflection. If public discourse is influenced so as to shift away conclusively from the idea that fundamental rights are instruments, to a conception of legality which is absolute, singular, and laden with morality, there is a risk that the real character of human rights law becomes concealed, and an outcome-focused understanding potentially becomes locked in. If debates about human rights continue to be framed in binary terms, oriented to the ends of legal processes rather than the nature of those processes themselves, this may leave even less space for legitimate critique of human rights instrumentalism than exists at present. And if media representations serve to reinforce and entrench this vision of human rights law further and further, as the dominance of this outcome focused paradigm becomes locked in, the potential for critique of the means, structures, and systems of this form of legal protection could become locked out. Ultimately, and paradoxically, the instrumentalisation of law through human rights therefore has the potential to disguise the fact that the law itself is an instrument, the tool of political, social and economic actors, rather some inherent repository of benevolent values.

How, then, might we respond to this position? Can the press ('Good', 'Bad' or indifferent) respond in ways which meet this objection? Can instrumentalism be avoided, whether by the media or other actors engaged in public debate about the use and utility of systems for the legal protection of human rights? Is

42 For discussion of the idea of judges as non-democratic actors, see M Gordon, *Parliamentary Sovereignty in the UK Constitution: Process, Politics and Democracy* (Oxford, Hart Publishing, 2015) 141–142.

it inevitable that democratic scepticism will be locked out in the way considered above? There are no easy answers to these questions, and the difficulty for the media is clear: whatever we may think of the desirability of a legal culture framed around the concept of human rights, it exists, is increasingly significant, and cannot be ignored by the press. Nor is it necessarily the responsibility of the media to challenge the outcome-oriented paradigm which human rights law establishes. How could it anyway be done, even assuming the very best of faith? Given the necessary substantive specificity and temporal focus of most media reporting – as so obviously signalled in the very idea of 'current affairs' – it seems unimaginable that deeper systemic scepticism could be readily and, perhaps crucially, consistently acknowledged as one part of a standard written or video journalistic piece. Yet if this is the case, the representation of human rights law as being concerned with an ongoing series of individual matters may unavoidably reinforce the outcome focused paradigm, and preclude public engagement with structural issues.

If it is, therefore, difficult to anticipate how this kind of scepticism about human rights law can be manifested regularly in the media, perhaps it is as much as we can do to try to be aware of the instrumentalism of human rights and promote the need to be critical of the power structures such legal mechanisms create. It is also important that this should be done in a constructive fashion, which is not the way these concerns about judicial power are often voiced in the media. When scepticism is based on knee-jerk reactions rather than more considered reflection – such as hysterical claims, albeit not in a human rights context, about the judiciary as 'enemies of the people'[43] – this will only serve to polarise yet further an already binary debate, and diminish the potential for real democratic discussion about the best way to deliver democracy.

Moreover, when we engage in debate about human rights and their representation in the media, we may do well to qualify, to some extent, our criticism or praise for the use of rights claims by press outlets both 'Good' and 'Bad'. On either side (and the many steps in between), we see rights instrumentalism in support of political ends, and it is these political ends which also deserve to be challenged and scrutinised, over and above the deification or exploitation of the rights template in which they are presented. Just as the adequacy of the structures and mechanisms of human rights law cannot be presumed, and requires independent and sustained scrutiny, the outcomes of individual human rights cases should be recognised and assessed in terms of their distinct political character, rather than simply praised or condemned on the basis that they are the product of a system which is desirable or undesirable, depending on the caricature adopted.

43 This headline was in reaction to the decision of the Divisional Court in the *Miller* case, concerning the need for an Act of Parliament to authorise the government triggering Article 50 TEU, and commencing negotiation over withdrawal from the European Union. See 'Enemies of the people: Fury over "out of touch" judges who have "declared war on democracy" by defying 17.4m Brexit voters and who could trigger constitutional crisis', *Daily Mail* (3 November 2016) available online at: www.dailymail.co.uk/news/article-3903436/Enemies-people-Fury-touch-judges-defied-17-4m-Brexit-voters-trigger-constitutional-crisis.html

Such engagement with specific substantive problems from a human rights perspective does not mean that we move away from a position based on systemic scepticism; instead, it is to approach particular human rights problems in a way which is informed by that broader scepticism about the operation of such legal structures and institutions.

In contrast, some may respond that we should simply accept the human rights paradigm as unavoidable, and embrace its instrumentalism for pragmatic reasons. Perhaps the ease with which this debate about human rights law has become binary and focused on outcomes suggests that all that matters is that we achieve social justice, rather than how we do so. Indeed, there are good philosophical arguments that may be developed in support of this position which accommodate some of the scepticism about the transcendental claims of human rights law. Rorty, for example, rejects the argument that the nature or authority of human rights is grounded in an inherent, natural rationality common to all humans: 'no useful work seems to be done by insisting on a purportedly ahistorical human nature, there probably is no such nature, or at least nothing in that nature that is relevant to our moral choices'.[44] Yet 'human rights culture' may still have value when considered from the perspective of 'efficiency', if it assists us in determining 'how best to bring about the utopia sketched by the Enlightenment'.[45] That human rights are 'social constructions' rather than inalienable is irrelevant; instead what counts is whether they have 'utility'.[46]

Yet even if we accept that rights are far from philosophically unassailable trumps, there may be a number of objections to wielding such pragmatism in support of human rights law. First, the outcome-oriented nature of the human rights paradigm means that, in adopting it, we risk assuming that achieving progress (however that is defined) is always framed in these terms, and we simply need more rights, better rights, better judicial decision-making, better media representations. The possibility of democratic scepticism opens up debate about the credible potential of the structures and systems of human rights law, and raises issues which are problematic even when viewed pragmatically, in so far as they close our minds to constructing alternative institutional arrangements with even greater social value. If pragmatists like Rorty suggest that we 'look to the future rather than to eternity', and 'prefer new ideas about how to change things over stable criteria for determining the desirability of change',[47] there might be concern that the prevalence, even dominance, of human rights law as the mode and engine of progress could drive complacency about the 'end of history'.[48] And if the human rights project is simply an instrumental activity grounded in pragmatism, there would be no moral loss if it could be displaced by something better.

44 R Rorty, 'Human Rights, Rationality and Sentimentality' in *Truth and Progress: Philosophical Papers Vol. 3* (Cambridge, Cambridge University Press, 1998) 172.

45 *Ibid.* 172.

46 R Rorty, *Philosophy and Social Hope* (London, Penguin, 1999) 85–86.

47 Rorty, n 43, 174–175.

48 See F Fukuyama, *The End of History and the Last Man* (Harmondsworth, Penguin, 1992).

Second, Rorty acknowledges the existence of systemic issues with a human rights culture when recognising it may be 'revolting to think that our only hope for a decent society consists in softening the self-satisfied hearts of a leisure class'.[49] Yet he does not think moral progress is likely to 'burst up from below' rather than flow from 'condescension from the top'.[50] Yet whether this is the case or not, there are surely different considerations engaged if we act to institutionalise condescension from the top through legal mechanisms focused around judicial empowerment, as this may have other costs. In particular, there might be legitimate concerns that the non-democratic character of human rights mechanisms and institutions may actually interfere with the creation of the kind of human rights culture, based on inclusion and the minimisation of difference,[51] to which Rorty aspires.

It may ultimately be the case that the debate about media representations of human rights law is one which obscures far deeper questions about the means and utility of the legal systems and structures which have been established for the protection of ostensibly fundamental rights. Nor can we avoid these deeper questions by pragmatic appeals to embrace human rights instrumentalism. In that sense, we may currently be having the wrong debate about the wrong problems: one which occurs within the framework established by human rights law and the public representations of that phenomenon, rather than one which is open to contesting the foundations of the human rights project, especially on democratic grounds.

None of this is necessarily an argument against human rights law per se, nor is this a credible prospect in any event, despite some claims that human rights law faces its twilight.[52] Instead, the aim has been to identify inconsistencies in existing binary debates, and suggest that more nuance is required to understand fully the dynamics of media portrayals of legal human rights. We should be cautious in particular about adopting the absolutist conception of legality which underpins the archetypal characterisation of this debate, as between a 'Good' and 'Bad' press. For it throws a veil of unassailability over legal judgments, whether we view those results as desirable or obnoxious. And as the UK judiciary accrues greater power and influence in the constitution, legitimate scepticism of such claims to power is as important here as elsewhere. It may be an indictment of our present accountability processes to suggest that there are no alternatives to the judicial scrutiny of political action on human rights grounds, but the risk in choosing this path is that it excludes many others, now or in the future. Once democracy is positioned as something which is subject to human rights law, rather than something which should be understood necessarily to generate commitments to

49 Rorty, n 43, 182.
50 *Ibid.* 182.
51 Rorty, n 45, 84–85.
52 See, for example, E Posner, *The Twilight of Human Rights Law* (New York, Oxford University Press, 2014).

collective and individual rights, this conceptual switch will be difficult to reverse. This is especially the case if elites are persuaded to commit to the formal legal protection of human rights on the basis that it provides them with moral cover, contracts out a range of difficult decisions they would prefer to avoid to a potential judicial scapegoat, while broadly sustaining their social authority.[53]

How exactly we might alter the institutional arrangements associated with human rights protection has remained an open question in the UK for some time, and while no resolution appears imminent, any Bill of Rights is likely to replicate many of the core features of the Human Rights Act it would replace, as well as having been justified in exceptionalist and jingoistic terms.[54] The serious flaws of that debate do not vindicate the present arrangements,[55] and much more expansive thinking about democratic alternatives to human rights law is required. Yet this may be exactly the problem: the binary public debate about rights makes nuanced sceptical positions difficult, perhaps near impossible, to articulate, and accountability processes which would replace, rather than supplement, existing legalistic mechanisms become difficult, perhaps near impossible, to construct. The nature of rights discourse may, ironically, be the very thing that generates such impoverished debate about human rights and their place in the constitution. And while this is something we may try to acknowledge and understand, it is not something we can easily fix or break out of. So even if we are having the wrong argument about the wrong problem, the current public debate about human rights law is already framed in such a way as to make extremely challenging the shift from where we are now – arguing about rights-outcomes and their representation in simplistic binary terms – to where we might instead want to be going.

Conclusion

Considering the debate about human rights law and its representation in the media has the potential to give us important insights into deeper issues with (and within) our legal and political systems. This chapter has argued that, on all sides, the press should be understood to be using rights instrumentally because rights are, truly, an instrumental tool. In that sense, the debate about human rights and

53 See Hirschl, n 40.

54 See, for example, the language of the *Conservative Party Manifesto* (2015) 60: 'We have stopped prisoners from having the vote, and have deported suspected terrorists such as Abu Qatada, despite all the problems created by Labour's human rights laws. The next Conservative Government will scrap the Human Rights Act, and introduce a British Bill of Rights. This will break the formal link between British courts and the European Court of Human Rights, and make our own Supreme Court the ultimate arbiter of human rights matters in the UK.'

55 On other flaws in the Human Rights Act repeal debate, see A Tucker, 'The Anti-Democratic Turn in the Defense of the Human Rights Act' *UK Constitutional Law Association Blog* (6 July 2015), available online at: https://ukconstitutionallaw.org/2015/07/06/hra-watch-reform-repeal-replace-adam-tucker-the-anti-democratic-turn-in-the-defence-of-the-human-rights-act/

(or in) the media is simply one in which a more fundamental problem is manifested – the democratic political difficulties posed to a society which embraces the language and architecture of human rights as the basis for its core political morality. This problem is one which deserves real and sustained attention, yet the very nature of human rights law – which is ultimately focused on the ends, rather than the means, of political decision-making – frames the discourse about rights in ways which threaten to lock out discussion of the systemic, structural, institutional problems with the operation of legal human rights protection. While the displacement of democratic scepticism about the functioning of human rights law is far from inevitable, the prospect of an institutional realignment which moves us away from the current legal rights paradigm seems distant. It may be, then, that the value of democratic rights scepticism needs to be found in prompting fresh thinking about how to enhance accountability practices and processes which sit outside the architecture of human rights law, while also attempting to cultivate awareness of the false claims that such utopian legal frameworks ultimately propagate. In pursuing these goals, we will need to overcome the limitations of democratic scepticism if we are to challenge the limitations of human rights law.

Bibliography

J Bakan, *Just Words: Constitutional Rights and Social Wrongs* (Toronto, University of Toronto Press, 1997).

J Bentham, *Rights, Representation, and Reform: Nonsense upon Stilts and Other Writings on the French Revolution* in P Schofield, C Pease-Watkin, and C Blamires (eds), *The Collected Works of Jeremy Bentham* (Oxford, Oxford University Press, 2002).

A Berman, *Give Us the Ballot: The Modern Struggle for Voting Rights in American* (New York, Picador, 2016).

V Bogdanor, 'Our New Constitution' (2004) 120 *Law Quarterly Review* 242.

V Bogdanor, *The New British Constitution* (Oxford, Hart Publishing, 2009).

T Carlyle, *On Heroes, Hero-Worship and the Heroic in History* (1840).

J Decker, *The Other Rights Revolution: Conservative Lawyers and the Remaking of American Government* (New York, Oxford University Press, 2016).

R Dworkin, *Taking Rights Seriously* (London, Duckworth, 2nd edn 1978).

K D Ewing, 'The Human Rights Act and Parliamentary Democracy' (1999) 62 *Modern Law Review* 79.

K D Ewing, *The Bonfire of the Liberties: New Labour, Human Rights and the Rule of Law* (Oxford, Oxford University Press, 2010).

K D Ewing and C A Gearty, *Freedom Under Thatcher: Civil Liberties in Modern Britain* (Oxford, Clarendon Press, 1990).

K D Ewing and C A Gearty, *The Struggle for Civil Liberties: Political Freedom and the Rule of Law in Britain, 1914–1945* (Oxford, Oxford University Press, 2000).

K D Ewing and J C Tham, 'The Continuing Futility of the Human Rights Act' [2008] *Public Law* 668.

F Fukuyama, *The End of History and the Last Man* (Harmondsworth, Penguin, 1992).

S Gardbaum, *The New Commonwealth Model of Constitutionalism: Theory and Practice* (Cambridge, Cambridge University Press, 2013).

C Gearty, *Principles of Human Rights Adjudication* (Oxford, Oxford University Press, 2004).

M A Glendon, *Rights Talk: The Impoverishment of Political Discourse* (New York, Free Press, 1991).

M Gordon, *Parliamentary Sovereignty in the UK Constitution: Process, Politics and Democracy* (Oxford, Hart Publishing, 2015).

J A G Griffith, 'The Political Constitution' (1979) 42 *Modern Law Review* 1.

J A G Griffith, *The Politics of the Judiciary*, 5th edn (London, Fontana Press, 1997).

R Hirschl, *Towards Juristocracy: The Origins and Consequences of New Constitutionalism* (Cambridge MA, Harvard University Press, 2004).

A Kavanagh, *Constitutional Review under the UK Human Rights Act* (Cambridge, Cambridge University Press, 2009).

M Loughlin, *Sword and Scales: An Examination of the Relationship between Law and Politics* (Oxford, Hart Publishing, 2000).

M Loughlin, *The Idea of Public Law* (Oxford, Oxford University Press, 2003).

K Marx, 'On the Jewish Question' (1844), republished in D McLellan, *Karl Marx: Selected Writings* (Oxford, Oxford University Press, 2nd edn 2000).

S Moyn, *The Last Utopia* (Harvard, Harvard University Press, 2010).

E Posner, *The Twilight of Human Rights Law* (New York, Oxford University Press, 2014).

R Rorty, 'Human Rights, Rationality and Sentimentality' in *Truth and Progress: Philosophical Papers Vol. 3* (Cambridge, Cambridge University Press, 1998).

R Rorty, *Philosophy and Social Hope* (London, Penguin, 1999).

G N Rosenberg, *The Hollow Hope: Can Courts Bring About Social Change?* (London, University of Chicago Press, 1991).

J N Shklar, *Legalism* (Cambridge, Mass., Harvard University Press, 1964).

G Silverstein, *Law's Allure: How Law Shapes, Constrains, Saves, and Kills Politics* (Cambridge, Cambridge University Press, 2009).

M Tushnet, *Taking the Constitution Away from the Courts* (Princeton, Princeton University Press, 1999).

J Waldron, *Law and Disagreement* (Oxford, Clarendon Press, 1999).

J Waldron, 'The Core of the Case Against Judicial Review' (2006) 115 *Yale Law Journal* 1346.

D Woodhouse, 'UK Ministerial Responsibility in 2002' (2004) *Public Administration* 1–19.

A L Young, *Parliamentary Sovereignty and the Human Rights Act* (Oxford, Hart Publishing, 2009).

11 Magna Carta and the invention of 'British rights'

Michelle Farrell and Edel Hughes[1]

Introduction

Antipathy towards human rights, so evident in media coverage in the United Kingdom, revolves around the Human Rights Act 1998. As contributors to this volume have pointed out,[2] the Human Rights Act is 'hated' and described as, amongst other things, 'insidious',[3] a 'criminal's charter',[4] and, delightfully, the 'human wrongs act'.[5] Yet it is also commended, even fetishized as a 'direct descendant of that great Charter',[6] as inaugurating 'a human rights culture',[7] and as the root and branch of a 'human rights revolution'.[8] That the Act and the broader human rights 'project' is the subject of so much media commentary, both derisory and celebratory, perhaps arises in part from the UK's curious constitutional arrangements, which meant that, until the enactment of the Act, 'rights' were conceived of as residual liberties protected, for the most part, through the common law.[9] The UK has never had a constitutional 'bill of rights'. It did play

1 We would like to thank Thomas Beaumont, Eleanor Drywood and Rob Knox who provided useful suggestions, feedback and comments.

2 See, in this volume, for example, D Mead, '"They offer you a feature on stockings and suspenders next to a call for stiffer penalties for sex offenders": do we learn more about the media than about human rights from tabloid coverage of human rights stories?' Chapter 1 and L Gies, 'British human rights scepticism through the lens of European newspapers' Chapter 3.

3 Mead *ibid.* 31.

4 See, for example, G Wilson, 'Blair stung in to review of human rights law' *The Daily Telegraph* (15 May 2006) 4.

5 Editorial, 'The Human Wrongs Act' *The Express* (1 October 2013) 14.

6 T Farron, 'The Magna Carta enshrined our liberties – now we must fight for them again' *The Guardian* (15 June 2015) available online at: www.theguardian.com/commentisfree/2015/jun/15/magna-carta-800-years-human-rights-act

7 M O'Brien, HC Deb 21 October 1998 Col 1321–1322 available online at: https://publications.parliament.uk/pa/cm199798/cmhansrd/vo981021/debtext/81021-35.htm

8 C Dyer, 'So far so good' *The Guardian* (16 April 2002).

9 With the exception of statutes such as the Bill of Rights 1689 and the Magna Carta 1215, it is not until the latter half of the twentieth century that we see a proliferation of statutory protection of rights, prompted in many instances by the UK's membership of the European Union in 1973. See, for example, statutes that prohibit various forms of discrimination,

a leading role, though, in the drafting of the European Convention on Human Rights.[10] And, of course, the UK, under the post-war Labour government, ratified the Convention in 1951.[11] Having accepted the jurisdiction of the Court on ratification and the attendant right of individual petition in 1966,[12] the UK embraced the system as a whole and has since been subject to hundreds of rights claims litigated before the European Court of Human Rights. The European human rights system, then, was well known in the UK when Tony Blair's New Labour government set about 'bringing rights home'.[13] The coming into force of the Human Rights Act in 2000, did mean, however, that rights claims could be articulated domestically. It was arguably this development, along with huge changes in media communication and consumption, that captured media attention and, consequently, served to heighten public awareness of human rights. The decision to enact the Act was controversial from the outset.

Whilst debate, derisory and celebratory, tends to coalesce around the Human Rights Act, the real fault line of the Act is its relationship to the European system of human rights. The Human Rights Act gives further effect, in domestic law, to most of the provisions of the European Convention on Human Rights. As such, it, more or less, domesticates the European Convention. The Act is both clever and effective in its structural and substantive negotiation of the sovereignty of parliament in sections 3 and 4. However, whilst obviously constructed so as to meet the constitutional requirements of a sovereign parliament, by requiring that a 'court or tribunal determining a question which has arisen in connection with a Convention right ... take into account any judgment, decision, declaration or advisory opinion', the Act also anchors, to a considerable extent, the judgements and interpretations of the European Court of Human Rights in domestic law.

---

such as The Race Relations Act 1965, the Equal Pay Act 1970, and the Sex Discrimination Act 1975.

10 Sir David Maxwell Fyfe, a member of the Conservative party, was, according to Ed Bates, one of the 'founding fathers'. See E Bates, *The Evolution of the European Convention on Human Rights and Fundamental Freedoms* (Oxford University Press, 2010) 5. Marco Duranti describes him as a 'draftsman' who 'doggedly insist[ed] that a European human rights treaty not be modelled too strictly on the 1948 Universal Declaration of Human Rights.' See M Duranti, *The Conservative Human Rights Revolution: European Identity, Transnational Politics, and the Origins of the European Convention* (Oxford University Press, 2017) 4. Duranti traces the conservative origins of the European Convention, putting paid to the idea that this was some kind of left initiative.

11 The UK was the first to ratify. A W B Simpson, *Human Rights and the End of Empire: Britain and the Genesis of the European Convention* (OUP, 2001) 808.

12 On the background to the decision to accept the right of individual petition, see A Lester, 'U.K. acceptance of the Strasbourg jurisdiction: what really went on in Whitehall in 1965' (1998) Public Law 237.

13 P Boateng and J Straw, 'Bringing Rights Home: Labour's Plans to Incorporate the European Convention on Human Rights and Fundamental Freedoms in UK law' (1997) European Human Rights Law Review 71. This was initially published on 18 December 1996 as a Labour consultation document. J Straw, 'Bringing Rights Home' *The Guardian* (18 December 1996) 15; J Straw, 'Let's bring human rights home' *The Guardian* (26 October 2010).

It also, unquestionably, tethers the domestic system to the European one by effectively 'transplanting' the 'exact wording of each provision'.[14] This European character of the Human Rights Act seems to be the sore point.

Evidence abounds to demonstrate discomfort with the European, non-British, or apparently partisan, character of the Human Rights Act. This is illustrated, at times, in descriptions of the Act: Labour's Human Rights Act[15] and the European Human Rights Act.[16] The discomfort is most obvious, however, in the calls for a 'British Bill of Rights', the propounding of 'British values' and the demarcation of 'British rights'. These proposals are offered as a distinct contrast to the 'foreign', 'European', imposed character of the Human Rights Act. The underpinning rationale of the proposals is the innate existence of a British tradition of liberties and rights that renders European versions redundant or superfluous, ill-fitting or even unworthy. The British indigeneity of rights is not, however, only claimed by those who are anti-Human Rights Act or anti-European rights. With an apparently different intention, proponents of the Act also make these claims to ownership of the idea of rights: Paul Boateng and Jack Straw made this clear in their Labour vision for 'bringing rights *home*': 'it is time to *repatriate* British rights to British courts', they proclaimed.[17]

Magna Carta has become the underpinning touchstone for these claims to British exceptionalism. In this chapter, we examine how the tradition of British rights is invented, at least in part, via Magna Carta, in order to inculcate distaste for the European system and the Human Rights Act, in particular. Of course, Magna Carta is also used to ground support for the Act.[18] We make a number of interrelated observations on the role of Magna Carta in the repeal of the Human Rights Act debates. First, Magna Carta is central to the invention of the 'British rights' tradition. The idea of the 'invention of tradition',[19] as conceptualised by Eric Hobsbawn, provides a foil through which we can begin to understand how the Human Rights Act has been construed as anti-British, by many, and the

14 M Amos, 'Transplanting Human Rights Norms: The Case of the United Kingdom's Human Rights Act' (2013) *Human Rights Quarterly* 386, 390.

15 This description of the Act is fairly frequent across national newspapers. Writing in *The Guardian*, Francesca Klug critiqued the attribution of the Act to Labour. F Klug, 'Human rights don't belong to political parties' The Guardian (2 February 2010). It is most frequent in the *MailOnline*, *Daily Mail*, *Mail on Sunday* and *the Telegraph* with 'Labour's Act' generally a description to signal dissent.

16 This description has been used across national newspapers of every bent; it is most frequently used by *the Sun* and *the Express*. For further discussion of the media's approach to rights deemed European see, in this volume, S Reynolds, 'It's Not Me, It's You: Examining the Print Media's Approach to 'Europe' in Brexit Britain' Chapter 2 and on the 'foreignness' of rights see E Drywood and H Gray, 'Demonising Immigrants: How a Human Rights Narrative Has Contributed to Negative Portrayals of Immigrants in the UK Media' Chapter 5.

17 P Boateng and J Straw, 'Bringing Rights Home' (1997) (n 13 above) 71.

18 See Tim Farron's claim, for example (n 6 above).

19 E Hobsbawm, 'Inventing Traditions' in E Hobsbawm and T Ranger (eds), *The Invention of Tradition* (Cambridge University Press, 2012) 1.

very essence of British, by others. Samuel Moyn's concern for the 'myth of deep roots'[20] in human rights thinking dovetails neatly with Hobsbawm's 'invention of tradition' allowing us to think through the objective and the consequences of this turn to Magna Carta. Second, Magna Carta serves to suggest a glorious past and a more British future, whilst turning attention away from the present, the real. Yet, as a figment of an imagined rights past, Magna Carta cannot be the basis for an explanation of rights in the present nor can it explain the Human Rights Act.[21] The disdain for the Act and, equally, the fetishisation of the Act, filtered through an imagined history, crowd out the space for critical engagement with history and with rights. The media is central to the absorption, entrenchment and spread of the invented tradition of British rights and it is quite obvious that it is not the internationalists, who themselves argue that Britain is the natural home of rights, who have captured the media and public imagination.

Human rights, particularly as protected by the 1998 Act, are, arguably, neither the destructive force that some commentary would have us believe, nor a panacea for society's ills. Both poles actually aggrandize rights, personifying them whilst blurring our view of the state. There are many ways to think through rights in the United Kingdom's legal, political and social landscape. It is, as one example, possible to think critically or sceptically about rights, clearing the landscape and paving the way for alternative languages and strategies. Criticism and scepticism about rights is mainstream in contemporary academic research. And since the days of its initial promulgation,[22] the Human Rights Act has been regarded with scepticism within academic circles, particularly by political constitutionalists. However, the substantive grounds upon which such doubtful, sceptical, critical or dissenting approaches to rights rest rarely make media coverage.[23] It is also possible to think pragmatically or instrumentally about rights. In this vein, David Kennedy, a rights critic, invokes pragmatism as a remedy for what he terms the 'tendency towards idolatry' when we talk about human rights and human rights work.[24] Like criticism and scepticism, pragmaticism on rights is, though, entirely absent from media discussions of the Act. Polarity is the order of the day. Attention has been sucked so ideologically in to the form and the identity of human rights in the UK that substance and meaning are almost ignored. Getting

20 S Moyn, *The Last Utopia: Human Rights in History* (The Belknapp Press of Harvard University Press, 2010) 12.

21 This draws on Moyn's articulation of the problems with focusing on the origins of rights. S Moyn, *The Uses of History* (Verso, 2014) 12.

22 See, for example, T Campbell, K Ewing and A Tomkins (eds), *Sceptical Essays on Human Rights* (Oxford University Press, 2001).

23 See also, M Gordon, 'Instrumentalism in Human Rights and the Media: Locking out Democratic Scepticism?' Chapter 10.

24 See D Kennedy, 'The international human rights movement: part of the problem?' (2001) 3 HRLR 245, 246. See further, D Kennedy, 'Two Sides of the Coin: Human Rights Pragmatism and Idolatry' Keynote Address, Interdisciplinary Conference on Human Rights, London School of Economics (24 March 2006). Available online at: www.lse.ac.uk/humanRights/aboutUs/articlesAndTranscripts/Crossing_the_boundaries_David_Kennedy.pdf

to grips with how and why this polarity has come to dominate is instructive. The Human Rights Act is merely a surface over which internationalists, institutionalised rights 'favouring' New Labour and 'Runnymede Tories'[25] and 'little Britainers' are battling their respective ideologies. We argue that a key element in the production of these ideologies and the ensuing polarities has been the invented tradition of Magna Carta. In order to demonstrate our claims, we examine, first, some of the key features of the repeal debate. We then examine the role of Magna Carta in these debates and we show how media engagement with Magna Carta compares – ever so favourably – to engagement with the Human Rights Act. Third, we show how Magna Carta is invented as a tradition with the effect of erasing the possibility of real attention to contemporary rights in the UK.

The Human Rights Act: why the controversy?

Absent an entrenched constitution in the UK context, the Human Rights Act has been viewed by some commentators as a 'bill of rights', albeit a 'bill of rights with a difference'.[26] Its arrival though, has not been universally welcomed: writing some seven years after the Act came into force, Lord Justice Stephen Sedley noted:

> Instead of a comfortable bedding into our domestic law and culture of the elementary rights which we and the rest of Europe had signed up to in the aftermath of the Second World War, the Human Rights Act has become the scapegoat for half the things that go wrong in the state and civil society.[27]

The scapegoating of the Act, that Sedley refers to, often revolves around the contention that the Act is a 'villains' charter';[28] but more considered criticism generally centres on three issues: the issue of deference (the Act gives far too

25 See, M D'Ancona, 'The Human Rights Act spells peril for Cameron' *The Guardian* (18 May 2015) available online at: www.theguardian.com/commentisfree/2015/may/18/human-rights-act-david-cameron-runnymede-tories-slim-majority; P Coss, 'Presentism and the Myth of Magna Carta' (2017) 234 *Past and Present* 227, 232.

26 Francesca Klug maintains that the Human Rights Act qualifies for the description of a bill of rights for four main reasons: under section 3, all laws and regulations must be interpreted to comply with Convention rights 'so far as it is possible to do so'; courts themselves are required not to act incompatibly with the Human Rights Act; under section 19 ministers are required to 'give new legislation a human rights health check'; and because it 'goes much further than incorporating a human rights treaty into our law'. See F Klug, *A Magna Carta for All Humanity: Homing in on Human Rights* (Routledge: 2015) 260–261.

27 S Sedley, 'Bringing rights home: time to start a family?' (2008) 28.3 *Legal Studies* 327, 328. See also AWB Simpson (n 11 above) 1101, noting that '[i]t took until the new millennium before the European Convention was to be incorporated into domestic law in the United Kingdom.... But even after half a century there has been something slightly grudging about the process.'

28 For discussion of this portrayal in the media, see L Gies, 'A Villains' Charter? The Press and the Human Rights Act' (2001) 7(2) *Crime, Media, Culture* 167.

much power to the unelected and, therefore, undemocratic judiciary); the question of parliamentary sovereignty (which the Act purportedly usurps, in particular, as considered in its traditional Diceyan rendering); and the charge of supremacy (the Act requires British courts to punctiliously follow the judgments of the European Court).[29] Each of these criticisms are based to a certain extent on the way in which the Human Rights Act is constructed; the Act, for example, instructs the courts to interpret legislation in a way which is compatible with Convention rights (section 3) and leaves it open to the courts to issue declarations of incompatibility where they are unable to do so (section 4). Section 2, which states that domestic courts 'must take into account' judgments and decisions of the European Court, is frequently the source of greatest angst amongst those who claim that this constitutes a supranational court's unwarranted, and unwanted, interference in domestic affairs.[30] Section 2 is also an unwelcome reminder that the parentage of the Act lies in the European Convention, giving vent to the considerable ire currently directed towards all things 'European', as outlined particularly by both Stephanie Reynolds and Lieve Gies in this volume.[31] This is also perhaps reflective of a broader aversion to international law in the modern era.[32]

In a sense then, many of the criticisms of the Act tend to centre on the idea that Act has somehow undermined or contradicts the supremacy of Parliament. These criticisms largely disregard or seem ignorant of the fact that the 'fundamental premise of the Act is that Parliament is sovereign'.[33] Lord Hoffmann's oft-quoted passage from *ex parte Simms* confirms this contention by noting that the premise of parliamentary sovereignty means that 'Parliament can, if it chooses, legislate contrary to fundamental principles of human rights'[34] and the Human Rights Act does not change this. But, he continues:

> [T]he principle of legality means that Parliament must squarely confront what it is doing and accept the political cost ... the courts of the United

---

29 Conor Gearty refers to 'four large-scale myths' that abound in relation to the Act: 'that the law enacted in 1998 subverts British parliamentary sovereignty; that it hands power to the judges; that it transfers supremacy over UK rights law to the European Court of Human Rights in Strasbourg; and that the law is a charter for villains' and contends that each of these myths is false 'but in combination they have destabilized the measure to such an extent that repeal is now regarded by many as a desirable policy pathway' C Gearty, *On Fantasy Island: Britain, Europe, and Human Rights* (OUP 2016) 63.

30 See, for example, the comments of the then Secretary of State for Justice, Chris Grayling, in J Forsyth, 'Chris Grayling: 'I want to see our Supreme Court supreme again' *The Spectator*, 28 September 2013.

31 S Reynolds, 'It's not me, it's you: Examining the Print Media's Approach to "Europe" in Brexit Britain' Chapter 2; L Gies (n 2 above).

32 See generally B Bowring, *The Degradation of the International Legal Order? The Rehabilitation of Law and the Possibility of Politics* (Routledge-Cavendish, 2008).

33 T Bingham, 'The Human Rights Act: A View from the Bench' (2010) 6 *EHRLR* 568, 570.

34 *R v Secretary of State for the Home Department, ex parte Simms* [2000] 2 AC 115, 131.

> Kingdom, though acknowledging the sovereignty of Parliament, apply principles of constitutionality little different from those which exist in countries where the power of the legislature is expressly limited by a constitutional document.[35]

Although Lord Bingham described Lord Hoffmann's contribution to *ex parte Simms* as simply illustrative of a 'heightened sense of the judges' duty to respect and defend fundamental principles,'[36] it is perhaps not difficult to see how this may cause a certain degree of disquiet amongst those who claim that the Human Rights Act paves the way for judicial overreach. This was illustrated at the time of its coming into force by the argument that the Act would enable judges to 'make' rather than simply interpret the law,[37] a view with which some members of the judiciary at least would seem to concur.[38] At any rate, it is simply naïve to argue that the Human Rights Act only has impact at Parliament's command.

Magna Carta and the Human Rights Act: idolised and pilloried

The 800th anniversary of the signing of Magna Carta in 2015 witnessed a resurgence of interest in the Charter in political rhetoric, judicial speech-making, media attention and academic commentary. The Charter, as Robert Melton and James Hazell, writing in one of the scholarly outputs published to mark its anniversary, tell us, 'is revered by citizens and human rights activists all over the world. It has become a symbol for limited government and constitutionalism used by political theorists, constitutional drafters, political elites and even ordinary citizens to justify constraining political power.'[39] Despite all the fanfare surrounding its anniversary, however, the extent of its influence remains widely contested. Lawyers, it is asserted, tend to overstate its significance, whereas historians point to its numerous misreadings.[40] There is, as Christopher Greenwood has pointed out, 'real doubt about whether Magna Carta can properly be described as having

35 *Ibid.*

36 T Bingham, 'Governments and Judges: Friends or Enemies?' in T Bingham, *Lives of the Law: Selected Essays and Speeches 2000–2010* (OUP, 2011) 144–157, 155.

37 J Rozenberg, 'Rights Act shifts balance of power to judges' *The Telegraph* (2 October 2000).

38 M Bentham, 'Human Rights Act was an invitation to make law, says Britain's most senior judge' *Evening Standard* (30 January 2015), reporting comments made by then President of the Supreme Court, Lord Neuberger.

39 J Melton and R Hazell 'Magna Carta … Holy Grail?' in R Hazell and J Melton (eds), *Magna Carta and Its Modern Legacy* (CUP, 2015) 3.

40 See Lord Sumption. 'Magna Carta then and now', Address to the Friends of the British Library, 9 March 2015, discussing the difference in how the Magna Carta is portrayed by lawyers and historians, with the former holding that the charter is a major constitutional document and the latter more likely to highlight the misconceptions surrounding the charter. Available online at: www.supremecourt.uk/docs/speech-150309.pdf

had any serious impact on English law'.[41] Articles 39 and 40 of the Charter, frequently lauded as the earliest guarantors of rights such as habeas corpus and due process of law[42] did not in fact provide any such rights. As Greenwood notes in relation to Article 39:

> It is not about trial by jury, at least not as we know the jury today, which did not come into being in England until much later; nor did habeas corpus. The concept of 'lawful judgment of his peers' was a great deal more elastic then than we imagine hundreds of years later. Nor is it quite the bulwark against arbitrary arrest that it might appear. It says that no 'free man' (it did not apply to the serfs any more than the US Constitution originally applied to slaves) shall be penalised 'except by the law of the land'. It does not place limits on what laws might be enacted or for what forms of detention or punishment they might provide. Moreover, the king never had any intention of complying with the promises he made in Magna Carta.[43]

This has not, of course, prevented the judiciary, notably in the United States,[44] from invoking the Charter in discussions concerning trial by jury and due process rights.[45] Nor has it prevented the celebration of Magna Carta as the foundation of British liberty and even parliamentary democracy.

Leaving aside, for the moment, the debate as to the Charter's actual impact on the restraint of arbitrary power and on liberty, or, at an even further stretch, on rights protection, its main contribution may be seen to lie in the numerous misconceptions about this impact – the fact that it was 'as influential for what it was

---

41 C Greenwood, 'Magna Carta and the Development of Modern International Law' (2016) 49.3 *Israel Law Review* 435, 436.

42 Article 39 of the Magna Carta states: 'No free man shall be seized or imprisoned or stripped of his rights or possessions, or outlawed or exiled or deprived of his standing in any other way, nor will we proceed with force against him or send others to do so except by the lawful judgment of his peers or by the law of the land.' The text of Article 40 reads 'To no one will we sell, to no one deny or delay right or justice'.

43 C Greenwood (n 41 above) 436.

44 Between 1790 and 2014 the US Reports of the Supreme Court's decisions referred to the Magna Carta in more than 170 cases. See SJ Wermiel, 'Magna Carta in Supreme Court Jurisprudence' in D B Magraw, A Martinez and R E Brownell II (eds) *Magna Carta and the Rule of Law* (ABA Publishing, 2014) 111.

45 See, for example, *Glasser v United States*, 315 U.S. 60, 84 (1942) where Justice Frank Murphy noted that '[s]ince it was first recognized in Magna Carta, trial by jury has been a prized shield against oppression' or, perhaps an even greater stretch, Justice John Harlan in *Thompson v Utah*, 170 U.S. 343, 349 (1898) declaring that '[w]hen Magna Charta declared that no freeman should be deprived of life, etc., "but by the judgment of his peers or by the law of the land," it referred to a trial by twelve jurors.' It is generally agreed that the Magna Carta has been more influential in the US than in the UK, at least in terms of reliance on its principles in case-law. See, for example, J Fernández-Villaverde 'Magna Carta, the rule of law, and the limits on government' (2016) 47 *Int'l Rev of Law and Economics* 22–28.

widely *believed* to have said as for what it actually did',[46] with this perhaps being even truer in the US context than the UK one.[47] Lord Bingham, for example, discussing the remedy of habeas corpus, remarked that although the Charter:

> did not enshrine or establish a right for the unlawfully detained subject to apply for the issue of a writ of habeas corpus [...] however unhistorically, the judges appealed to the Charter when developing the remedy and it is doubtful whether, without this all but sacrosanct instrument to rely on, they could have acted as boldly as they did.[48]

Former Supreme Court President, Lord Neuberger, in a commemorative speech during the anniversary period, aired his agreement with Bingham that the myth might best be embraced:

> There can be little doubt that the 'lawyer's view' of Magna Carta is partly mythical. Of course, there is nothing wrong with myth. As the late Tom Bingham put it: 'The significance of Magna Carta lay not only in what it actually said but, perhaps to an even greater extent, in what later generations claimed and believed it had said. Sometimes the myth is more important that the actuality'.[49]

This 'unhistorical' approach adopted by the judiciary is arguably also reflected in the media engagement and in the understanding of the general public, who show a high level of awareness of the existence of Magna Carta but a low level of knowledge regarding its actual content or significance.[50]

Commemorating the Charter: condemning the Human Rights Act

A ceremony held on 12 June 2015 at Runnymede, the site of the signing of the Magna Carta by King John, commemorated its 800th anniversary. David Cameron, then Prime Minister, asserting the continuing relevance of the Charter, stated: '[w]hy do people set such store by Magna Carta? Because they look to

---

46 T Bingham (2011) (n 36 above) 6 (emphasis added).

47 G G George, 'UK Supreme Court Versus US Supreme Court: Modern Use of Magna Carta' in E Gibson-Morgan and A Chommeleux, 'The Rights and Aspirations of the Magna Carta' (Palgrave Macmillan, 2016) 57–59. See, however, M Dillon, 'Magna Carta and the United States Constitution: An Exercise in Building Fences' in DB Magraw (n 44 above) 81, making the interesting argument that the US Constitution was influenced neither by the 1215 Magna Carta nor the 1225 Magna Carta but rather by the "mythic" Magna Carta, 'largely created in the late sixteenth and early seventeenth century by the great common law jurist Sir Edward Coke, which was comingled with John Locke's social contract theory for transmission to Britain's American colonies by William Blackstone.'

48 T Bingham (2011) (n 36 above) 3–12, 6.

49 Lord Neuberger, 'Magna Carta and the Holy Grail' Lincoln's Inn (12 May 2015) available online at: www.supremecourt.uk/docs/speech-150512.pdf

50 See R Mortimore 'What Magna Carta Means to the Modern British Public' in Hazell and Melton (n 39 above) 56–76.

history. They see how the great charter shaped the world, for the best part of a millennium, helping to promote arguments for justice and for freedom'.[51] In the same speech, however, he goes on to essentially make the case for the Conservative Party proposals to repeal the Human Rights Act, arguing that the good name of rights has been 'distorted' and 'devalued':

> [i]t falls to us in this generation to restore the reputation of those rights and their critical underpinning of our legal system. It is our duty to safeguard the legacy, the idea, the momentous achievement of those barons. And there couldn't be a better time to reaffirm that commitment than an anniversary like this.[52]

This begs the question as to why the Charter is venerated to the point of overstating its impact and significance, yet the main modern legislation codifying rights and freedoms that are argued, questionably, to originate in this ancestral Charter are castigated in numerous quarters. The answer may lie in what Colin Murray has referred to as the 'weaponising' of Magna Carta whereby its 'place within the UK's ancient constitution' is established as 'a counterpoint to the incorporation' of the European Convention into UK law.[53] As Gies and Reynolds have both discussed in this volume, there is a certain hostility reserved for instructions seen to be emanating from Europe, the Brexit vote being an obvious illustration of this enmity.[54] Thus, for Cameron and others, whilst the Charter may not be perfect, it has the advantage of being *British*. As Jill Lepore points out in her interesting analysis of the significance of Magna Carta in the US context,

> [i]t would not be quite right to say that Magna Carta has withstood the ravages of time. It would be fairer to say that, like much else that is very old, it is on occasion taken out of the closet, dusted off, and put on display to answer a need. Such needs are generally political.[55]

---

51 'Magna Carta changed the world, David Cameron tells anniversary event' *BBC News*, 12 June 2015. Available online at: www.bbc.co.uk/news/uk-33126723

52 Quoted in C Davies, 'Magna Carta: leaders celebrate 800th anniversary of the Great Charter' *The Guardian*, 15 June 2015. Davies also notes that Amnesty International UK's head of policy and government affairs, Allan Hogarth, responded to the Prime Minister's speech by asserting that Cameron's use of the anniversary of Magna Carta to justify scrapping the Human Rights Act would 'have those 13th-century barons spinning in their highly-ornate, lead-lined coffins', noting that 'Any move to scrap the Act would be a real blow for human rights in this country and around the world'.

53 C Murray, 'The Magna Carta's tainted legacy: historic justifications for a British Bill of Rights and the case against the Human Rights Act' in Frederick Cowell (ed.), *Critically Examining the Case Against the 1998 Human Rights Act* (Routledge, 2018) 35–51, 35.

54 L Gies (n 2 above) and S Reynolds (n 31 above).

55 J Lepore, 'The Rule of History: Magna Carta, the Bill of Rights, and the hold of time' *The New Yorker* 20 April 2015. Available online at: www.newyorker.com/magazine/2015/04/20/the-rule-of-history

What could be more political than pitting it against the 'hated' Human Rights Act to suit the stated agenda of one section of the political establishment?

An examination of the portrayal of both Magna Carta and the Human Rights Act in UK national newspapers during the first six months of 2015 – a period covering the run-up to the commemoration of the 800th anniversary of the signing of Magna Carta in June 2015 – and also the general election of June 2015, where Conservative Party proposals to repeal the Human Rights Act 1998 featured as a manifesto commitment – is highly revealing.[56] A search for the phrase 'Magna Carta' returns 588 results, a search for 'Human Rights Act' 343 results, and a search for articles featuring both phrases 28 results. Articles concerning Magna Carta range from stories about commemorative two-pound coins,[57] to explainers of the Charter,[58] to its role in the creation of standard measures,[59] to more substantive pieces on its significance. What is striking about the coverage of the Charter is the overwhelmingly positive assessment it receives; it is variously described as the 'great document';[60] the 'key to democracy';[61] the 'British blueprint for a fairer world';[62] 'the most well-known and iconic legal document in existence';[63] and as being 'emblematic of a liberal tradition in English law-making that has influenced countries around the world'.[64] The only treatment of the Charter that could be considered as approaching critical comes from the *Telegraph's* reporting of Lord Sumption's description of Magna Carta as a 'turgid'

56 This search was carried out using the Lexis Library news service, with the search terms of 'Magna Carta' and 'Human Rights Act'. Articles were filtered to include only those where the search terms received 'major mentions' and were date limited to those appearing between 1 January 2015 and 30 June 2015.

57 H Perkins, 'New 2015 coins to honour our historic glories' *The Express* (1 January 2015) 27; 'Coins for 2015; All change, please' *The Daily Telegraph* (1 January 2015) 8; 'Magna Carta to feature on £2 coins' *The Times* (1 January 2015) 14.

58 K Maguire, 'Carta the unstoppable checks machine: 15 facts about Magna Carta ... the deal that's reined in kings for 800yrs' *Daily Mirror* (6 February 2015) 8; W Hartston, 'Top 10 Facts about the Magna Carta' *The Express* (16 June 2015); M Smith, 'What is Magna Carta? Why this 800-year-old piece of paper is still important: The Magna Carta turns 800 today – here's why it still matters in the 21st Century' *The Mirror* (15 June 2015).

59 J Stone, 'Beer Day Britain: How the Magna Carta created the humble pint: It's all to do with weights and measures' *The Independent* (15 June 2015).

60 M Harris, 'Ah, the irony of David Cameron invoking the memory of Magna Carta while dismantling our right to privacy: the challenges to our civil liberties are huge' *The Independent* (16 June 2015).

61 'The Key to Democracy' *The Sun* (16 June 2015) 15.

62 V Low, '800 years on and monarchy is still smiling; American lawyers pay tribute to Magna Carta, the British blueprint for a fairer world' *The Times* (16 June 2015) 7.

63 F Gibb, 'Lord Judge: we need vigilance over values of Magna Carta: On its 800th anniversary, the former lord chief Justice tells Frances Gibb why the great charter still resonates' *The Times* (12 February 2015) 58.

64 'The presumption of liberty prevails: The line of history that runs from Runnymede across eight centuries has determined what we have become as a nation' *The Telegraph* (15 June 2015).

document, much less significant in the development of rights than the French Revolution.[65]

Numerous pieces stress the continuing relevance of the Charter in an effort to demarcate a clear line of history between Magna Carta and our current rights protections. Dan Jones writes that Clauses 39 and 40:

> ... have been interpreted in the centuries that followed 1215 as setting out the basic liberties of an English subject.... These ideas are present in the Universal Declaration of Human Rights – described in 1946 by its champion Eleanor Roosevelt as 'a Magna Carta for all mankind'.[66]

There are also some cautionary articles on the dangers of disregarding or disrespecting the principles espoused in the Charter. In that regard, the 800th anniversary of the Charter is an:

> ... occasion to look back with pride at how our legal system has tried to control abuse of power, usually with great success. But it is also a reminder of the continuing need to protect the rule of law from politicians who do not understand its significance.[67]

Despite the lauding, in some quarters, of the Charter and the notion that its value lies partly in the fact that it is 'still relevant to everything from control orders to European integration',[68] many joined David Cameron in using the opportunity of the Magna Carta anniversary to contrast its provisions with the unsatisfactory nature of current rights guarantees.[69] *The Sun*, for example, claiming that the Charter 'came about because the people rose up and said they would not allow their rights to be crushed by a faceless body beyond their control' draws a parallel between the situation of 1215 with the contemporary one and calls for the Human Rights Act to be repealed: '[t]hat messy Act, alongside fudged rulings

---

65 D Barrett, 'Magna Carta: 'Turgid' document was eclipsed by the French, says top judge' *The Telegraph* (12 June 2015).

66 See D Jones, 'At the Heart of the Legend, the Charter' *The Sunday Telegraph* (4 January 2015) 7. The same edition also publishes a short piece linking the Magna Carta to the right to privacy, quoting the chairman of the Magna Carta 800th Committee who claimed that the document 'plays a vital role in the debate over government surveillance.' See 'Magna Carta has 'vital role in privacy debate'' *The Sunday Telegraph* (4 January 2015) 20.

67 D Pannick, 'Let us celebrate and protect Magna Carta's enduring relevance' *The Times* (19 February 2015) 56. See also, M Leftly, 'Law chief marks Magna Carta with fierce attack on Cameron' *The Independent on Sunday* (22 February 2015) 2, discussing the criticism of David Cameron and past governments for 'treating public law with contempt' by the chair of the Criminal Bar Association.

68 J Jones, 'Magna Carta exhibition is an 800-year-old lesson in people power' *The Guardian* 12 March 2015.

69 See D Martin, 'Human Rights Act has devalued Magna Carta, Says Cameron' *Daily Mail* 15 June 2015.

coming from Europe, stops Britain from making the best rules for Britons ... IN Britain. It has to go.'[70] The *Daily Mail* goes a step further and compares the judges of the European Court to King John (!):

> Like King John, the judges of the European Court of Human Rights are unelected. Like him, most are intellectually third-rate. But like him, too, they make up the law as they go along, seeking to exercise arbitrary power over peoples and parliaments.[71]

This, the broadside concludes, is a denial of the most basic democratic right to the rule of law that can only be remedied by repealing the Human Rights Act and enacting a British Bill of Rights.

In contrast to national newspapers' treatment of Magna Carta, the majority of the articles published during this period that feature discussion of some aspect of the Human Rights Act are negative in tone. These include a large number of articles about convicted terrorists who cannot be deported because of the Human Rights Act,[72] a seeming favourite topic of Human Rights Act detractors; as well as numerous articles on plans to scrap the Act, the vast majority of which are approving of the plan.[73] In fact, the only articles that could be deemed as portraying the 1998 Act in a positive light during this time period include an editorial in *The Guardian* on the right to protest,[74] an article on the launch of RightsInfo

70 'THE Sun SAYS Do it rights now' *The Sun* (15 June 2015) 6.

71 'Euro Judges Mock the Spirit of Magna Carta' *Daily Mail* (16 June 2015).

72 See, for example, R Mendick and T Ross, 'Convicted terror leader with link to Paris whom we cannot deport: Al-Qaeda fundraiser from Leicester connected to seiges (*sic*) in France, uses Human Rights Act to stay in Britain' *The Telegraph* (17 January 2015); J Lawton, 'Terrorist Mr Big we can't deport: Human Rights Farce' *Daily Star* (19 January 2017); 'Man linked to Paris horror to STAY in UK' *The Express* 19 January 2015, 8; H Gye, 'Terror leader fighting deportation because he claims he has a right to family life 'ran off with £40,000 of his British wife's money'' *Daily Mail* (26 January 2015); 'Fury as 'Human Rights' let 28 terrorists escape deportation' *The Express* (2 February 2015) 6; R Mendick, 'Jihadi John's friend cannot be deported from Britain: Anger as terrorism suspect linked to Jihadi John used Human Rights Act to stay in the UK' (28 February 2015).

73 See, for example, L Dearden, 'Ukip election policies: Slash foreign aid, bring back smoking in pubs, ditch Human Rights Act; 'Britishness', the NHS and immigration is pushed to the top of the agenda' *The Independent* (28 January 2015); L Williams, 'Scrap the Human Rights Act and keep TTIP: Here's what you voted for and will get with a Tory government, Britain' *The Independent* (8 May 2015); T McTague, 'Cameron brings back Michael Gove as justice secretary: Hard-line ally will scrap human rights act in bid to make British laws supreme over Strasbourg' *Daily Mail* (10 May 2015); J Slack and I Drury, 'Gove's first big job: Axe Labour's Hated Human Rights Act' *Daily Mail* (11 May 2015); A Pearson, 'Human Rights Act has done nothing for us' *The Daily Telegraph* (14 May 2015) 21.

74 'The Guardian view on the right to march: protest must be beyond price' *The Guardian* 10 February 2015.

in *The Times*,[75] a small number of articles warning against the plans to repeal the Act,[76] and some dealing specifically with SNP opposition to the repeal of the Act.[77]

The invention of 'British Rights'

First and foremost, for the repeal side, Magna Carta underpins the claims that European rights and the Human Rights Act are invasive and unsuitable to an environment with an existing rich tradition of home-grown liberties and rights. Murray writes wonderfully about the ways in which the 800th anniversary of Magna Carta was instrumentalised by the Conservative Government for its 'specific political ends'.[78] He remarks that 'the ultimate aim of Magna Carta rhetoric is to persuade the UK electorate that there is little role for international human rights law within the UK's governance order and, as a consequence to ease the UK out of the ECHR'.[79] The aim is also to invent, propagate and entrench a *British* rights tradition.

Recent invocation of Magna Carta for political ends is reminiscent of its instrumentalisation from the seventeenth century onwards.[80] Cameron has not underpinned his policy of repeal and replace in reference to the Charter through happenstance. The 800th anniversary was timely but Cameron had, prior to 2015, already invoked Magna Carta. In 2001, in the context of the debates on the Anti-Terrorism, Crime and Security Bill which would require derogation from Article 5 of the European Convention, he had made his stance on the impact of European Court case law and judicial overreach clear. Commenting on the need to derogate from article 5, to facilitate the indefinite detention of

75 F Gibb, 'Are human rights slipping down the political agenda?' *The Times* (23 April 2015).

76 R Beech, '13 basic rights you're going to lose under the new Conservative government' *The Mirror* 10 May 2015; 'Hands off our rights; The Tory plan to scrap the Human Rights Act takes our precious and hard-earned freedoms for granted.' *The Independent* 11 May 2015, 2; H McDonald, 'Scrapping Human Rights Act 'would breach Good Friday agreement' *The Guardian* 12 May 2015; A Travis, 'Tories' bid to scrap Human Rights Act looks simplistic and rushed' *The Guardian* 14 May 2015.

77 J Stone, 'The Scottish Government will try to stop the Tories repealing the Human Rights Act in Scotland; Nicola Sturgeon says the proposal is "appalling"' *The Independent* 12 May 2015; M Chorley, 'Sturgeon picks her first fight: SNP leader tells PM he can't scrap Human Rights Act in Scotland' *Daily Mail* 12 May 2015; B Riley-Smith, 'SNP planning to kill off Snoopers' Charter: Scottish Nationalists are hoping to use newfound parliamentary influence to block key Tory manifesto pledges' *The Telegraph* 12 May 2015; P Gilbride, 'Nicola Sturgeon will fight Tory bid to scrap the Human Rights Act' *Express* 13 May 2015; L Brooks, 'Scotland 'will not consent' to Tory plans to scrap Human Rights Act' *The Guardian* 13 May 2015.

78 C Murray (n 53 above) 35.

79 *Ibid.*, 36.

80 *Ibid.*

foreign nationals who could not otherwise be deported because of the principle of *non-refoulement*, Cameron stated:

> Surely we have to ask why we are in this mess in the first place … because of article 3 and the jurisprudence under article 3, the Home Secretary cannot deport those who are potentially a danger to this country. The limitation, however, is not caused by article 3 itself.… Nowhere does article 3 mention deportation. What has happened is that, over many years, jurisprudence has been developed that has prevented deportation. The problem, therefore, is jurisprudence under article 3, whereas the solution that we are being offered is derogation under article 5. It is a bit like having mumps but taking a treatment for measles. We are not treating the long-term problem. I profoundly believe that the long-term problem will get worse.[81]

In order to emphasise his disapproval at having to comply with the European Convention (by not returning people to a country where they would risk torture), he cited Magna Carta:

> The option of opting out and suspending habeas corpus is the wrong answer to the question. In many ways the Government had a choice between this country's ancient rights of habeas corpus and the right not be detained without trial; between Magna Carta and the ECHR.[82]

Cameron invokes Magna Carta, first, to decry the development of the principle of *non-refoulement*, and, in doing so, to argue that, absent this Convention requirement, the UK could get on with deporting non-nationals who pose a security threat. He invokes it, second, to lambast the evolutive interpretation of the European Convention, and, in so doing, to distinguish it as alien and foreign. He does this whilst emphasising the great tradition of British rights.

The British Bill of Rights, proposed by Cameron when he took over the Conservative party leadership in 2006, can be understood in the light of his established angst at the Human Rights Act and the European Convention. Repeating the word British over and over again, Cameron made it absolutely clear that the solution to the long-term 'foreign' problem was repeal. This use of Magna Carta recurred right through Cameron's leadership of the Conservative party:

> This is the country that wrote Magna Carta. The country that time and again has stood up for human rights, whether liberating Europe from fascism or leading the charge today against sexual violence in war.…We do not require instruction on this from judges in Strasbourg. So at long last … this country will have a new British Bill of Rights to be passed in our Parliament rooted

81 *Ibid.*, 39. Colin Murray's chapter drew our attention to this passage; for the Hansard discussion, see David Cameron, HC Debate, Vol 375 Col 145 (19 November 2001).

82 Murray *ibid.*, 39.

> in our values and as for Labour's Human Rights Act? We will scrap it, once and for all.[83]

Theresa May, with her longstanding distaste for the Human Rights Act, and armed with the 2015 manifesto promise to 'scrap the Act', assumed the Magna Carta rhetoric as Home Secretary and later with the party (and Government) leadership: '[H]uman rights were not invented in 1950 when the convention was drafted, or in 1998 when the convention was incorporated into our law.... This is Great Britain, the country of Magna Carta'.[84]

With Magna Carta and this invented tradition of rights, the past provides the model for reconstructing the unsatisfactory present with a return to British values and rights.[85] The rhetorical engagement of Magna Carta whilst inventing the tradition of rights and emphasising the foreignness of all things European also attempts to cement British identity in a time of insecurity about what exactly that means.[86] A top-down policy, essentially of rights-curtailing law reform, is sold to the 'British' public as a revolutionary endeavour – that 'momentous achievement'[87] where the 'people rose up'.[88]

But human rights are British!

On the other side of the debate, Magna Carta is also used to convince sceptics that European and international ideas of rights – contained in the Human Rights Act – are not alien, but British after all. In this vein, the Human Rights Act copper-fastens and enhances the nascent liberties of that Great Charter. It does so via the European Convention, which, after all, was 'British' in inspiration. This conception of the Human Rights Act manifests most obviously in Boateng and Straw's proposal to 'bring rights home'.[89] Discussing how the Labour government of the day came to accept the right of individual petition, Anthony Lester, a firm proponent of the Human Rights Act,[90] remarks that 'by virtue of the decision, Convention rights had crossed the English Channel to begin their entry in to our legal system. It would take a further 22 years for Parliament to bring those

83 D Cameron, 'Speech to the Conservative Party Conference' (1 October 2014) available online at: http://press.conservatives.com/post/98882674910/david-cameron-speech-to-conservative-party discussed in Judi Atkins, 'Re-Imagining Magna Carta: Myth, Metaphor and the Rhetoric of Britishness' (2016) 69 *Parliamentary Affairs* 603, 614.

84 T May, 'The United Kingdom, the European Union and our place in the World' (25 April 2016) cited in C Murray (n 53 above) 42.

85 See, E Hobsbawm, *On History* (Abacus, 1997) 34.

86 Atkin (n 83 above) 603 and 604.

87 See n 52 above and accompanying text.

88 See n 70 above and accompanying text.

89 See Boateng and Straw (1997) (above n 13).

90 See, for example, A Lester, *Five Ideas to Fight For: How Our Freedom is Under Threat and Why it Matters* (Oneworld Publications, 2016); A Lester, 'Human Rights must be protected against the abuse of power' *The Guardian* (16 May 2016); A Lester, 'The Utility of the Human Rights Act: A Reply to Keith Ewing' (2005) *Public Law* 249.

rights home'.[91] From Lester's perspective then, in line with the Baoteng and Straw approach, it was quite an organic process, albeit slow, from ratification of the Convention to the enactment of the Human Rights Act. The sense that this is organic is underscored by the suggestion that the rights were merely brought back where they had originated.[92]

Magna Carta provides a foundation at times for a history that is difficult to locate and for an idea that is otherwise slippery. The histories of human rights are contested; when historians, lawyers, journalists, human rights advocates and so on speak of rights as though they have an obvious established history, they are embracing what Moyn calls 'the myth of deep roots'. This serves to distract us from how we really got here, that is, the historical conditions that have led to and explain our present. It follows: 'If human rights are treated as inborn, or long in preparation, people will not confront the true reasons they have become so powerful today and examine whether those reasons are still pervasive.'[93] This uncritical acceptance of a deep history distracts from examination of the present or what is really going on, and it also legitimates that present as part of an evolutionary progression. It is no surprise then that Roosevelt could declare the Universal Declaration an 'international Magna Carta'[94] or that the British representative also compared the two documents.[95] In attempts to locate human rights historically, Magna Carta is invariably referenced.

RightsInfo, an online initiative, which aims to build knowledge and support for human rights in the UK, puts forward, quite baldly, this conception of history as a trajectory from Magna Carta to the present. Magna Carta is pinpointed as the origin of human rights, narratively,[96] and in an illustrated human rights timeline.[97] Klug discusses the history and the myths surrounding Magna Carta and presents the complexity of an historical analysis of the Charter in the light of the contemporary human rights movement. She engages Magna Carta, nevertheless,

91 See Lester 'UK Acceptance' (above n 12) 253.

92 Keith Ewing describes some of the tensions within the Labour party as regards proposals to incorporate the Convention. In contrast to Lester, he conveys the point that 'bringing rights home' was not the obvious next step for the Labour party even if it had been responsible for ratification and accepting the right of individual petition. Ewing remarks that giving effect to the Convention represented 'a fundamental shift in the position of the Labour Party which less than ten years [before] was still deeply suspicious about the contribution of the judges to civil liberties, and suspicious also of the idea that the courts should be in the driving seat on controversial political issues.' See, K Ewing, 'The Human Rights Act and Parliamentary Democracy' (1999) 62 *Modern Law Review* 80 and 98.

93 S Moyn, *The Last Utopia* (n 20 above) 12.

94 See n 10 above. See also, H Lauterpacht, 'The Universal Declaration of Human Rights' (1948) 25 *BYIL* 354 and F Klug (n 26 above) 9.

95 Lauterpacht *ibid.*, 371.

96 K Weller, 'Magna Carta: the Origin of Modern Human Rights' RightsInfo (3 April 2017) available online at: https://rightsinfo.org/magna-carta-rights-today/.

97 A Wagner, 'A brief history of how human Rights changed the world' RightsInfo (19 May 2015) available online at: https://rightsinfo.org/a-brief-history-of-how-human-rights-changed-the-world/.

as a reference point for human rights today and as part of a process which has led us to the present. She remarks:

> Whilst it would … be wildly historically inaccurate to bestow universal intentions on the multiple authors of the Charter, the principles established in the few clauses that remain on the statute book were nevertheless loosely enough phrased to allow for increasingly generous interpretations in the centuries that followed.… The drafters 'did not themselves envisage this continuous process of re-interpretation'.[98] Yet if they had been taken at their word and a narrow, literal meaning had been maintained throughout the centuries, the Magna Carta would never have become the inclusive, iconic document that still has resonance today. It would probably have had no more shelf life than any other medieval manuscript, let alone become the source of a major national celebration in 2015 to commemorate its 800th birthday.[99]

Dovetailing neatly with her sense of the Magna Carta as 'living instrument', Klug's investigation of the usages of Magna Carta is also teleological. Klug wants to defend the ethic of international human rights law as well as the Human Rights Act, instruments that she sees as the present manifestation of a process that has at least some of its roots in Magna Carta, and she does so by reading in to the past moves and evolutions that ally to the narrative. This rendering of Magna Carta is distinguishable in objective from that of Cameron with his 'British rights' or even the libertarian 'Runnymede Tories'. Klug harnesses Magna Carta to defend human rights and the Human Rights Act, not to destroy them in favour of 'British rights'. Tactically, however, defending human rights and the UK's rights identity with reference to a long rights tradition is only convincing if the alternative is not. In both cases, what we end up with is a distorted past and a distorted present. As Peter Coss writes: 'Validating the present by reference to the past inevitably risks distorting both the present and the past.'[100]

Inventing the newsworthy tradition

What we can see is that Magna Carta, in political rhetoric,[101] in the media, in academic work, and, particularly during the recent commemorations, in the judicial imagination,[102] is one of the key points of reference for the British tradition of

98 J C Holt, *Magna Carta* (Cambridge University Press, 1992) 14.

99 Klug (n 26 above) 260–261

100 Coss (n 25 above) 233.

101 The Conservative party is not alone in its use of Magna Carta. Judi Atkin's discussion of the political rhetoric around the Charter shows how it has been engaged also by the Labour party to justify constitutional reform and particularly by Gordon Brown to emphasise 'the British way'. Importantly, however, Atkin points out that Brown does not engage Magna Carta *against* European rights. Atkin (n 83 above) 607.

102 We refer here to involvement in, and speeches delivered at, various Magna Carta commemorative initiatives and events. Conor Gearty comments wryly upon this 'overflow of state

liberty. The myth and the myth-makers have, of course, been exposed:[103] 'Over the centuries, pride in England's unique liberty resulted in much myth about Magna Carta, and myth-makers could trace to it both bulwarks of English freedom, the common law and Parliament'.[104] Hobsbawm, writing about the duty of the historian 'to deconstruct political and or social myths dressed up as history', makes the point explicit:

> Every British child was once taught at school that the Magna Carta was the foundation of British liberties, but since McKechnie's monograph of 1914[105] every university student of British history has had to learn that the document extorted from King John by the Barons in 1215 was not intended to be a declaration of parliamentary supremacy and equal rights for free-born Englishmen, even though it came to be regarded as such in British political rhetoric much later.[106]

The 800th anniversary provided an opportunity for myth-making anew: as one example, at the behest of the Magna Carta Trust, there would be a 'Copy of Magna Carta for every UK primary school',[107] 'to teach children about freedom'.[108] Unable to fathom undoing the myth, or, more likely, just unwilling, some took the Commemoration as an opportunity to embrace it.[109]

Beyond the tradition of liberty, as we have seen, Magna Carta has become a reference point for the 'British rights' tradition. This is the *invention* of a tradition of rights, rights that are constructed as innate, and which have developed or evolved to reach, and explain, the present. 'Invented tradition', according to Hobsbawm, means:

> [A] set of practices, normally governed by overtly or tacitly accepted rules and of a ritual or symbolic nature, which seek to inculcate certain values and

organized joy' in his work examining the myths and fantasies of British exceptionalism. See Gearty (n 29 above) 34–36. See also Murray (n 53 above) 35–51 who discusses some of the judges' speeches.

103 Of course, there are counter arguments to the portrayal of Magna Carta as mythic by those who defend the use of Magna Carta through the ages. Richard Helmholz, for example, argues: 'In their commentaries on Magna Carta, Coke and Blackstone were performing a common legal task-interpreting an authoritative precedent to address a current issue.' See R H Helmholz, 'The Myth of Magna Carta Revisited' (2016) 94 *North Carolina Law Review* 1475, 1492.

104 R V Turner, *Magna Carta: Through the Ages* (Routledge, 2003) 3.

105 W S McKechnie, *Magna Carta: A Commentary on the Great Charter of King John* (2nd ed. Glasgow, J Maclehose and Sons, 1914).

106 E Hobsbawm, *On History* (no 85 above) 361.

107 J Burns, 'Copy of Magna Carta for every primary school' *BBC News* (21 April 2015).

108 A Singh, 'Magna Carta for every school to teach children about freedom' *The Daily Telegraph* (21 April 2015).

109 For an explicit example, see (above n 49) Neuberger's endorsement of the Bingham approach.

> norms of behaviour by repetition, which automatically implies continuity with the past. In fact, where possible, they normally attempt to establish continuity with a suitable historic past.[110]

Invented traditions, Hobsbawm explains, occur more frequently in response to rapid social transformation when old social patterns can no longer be addressed the 'old way'. Hobsbawm sees a surge in this invention of tradition, explicable by the rapid transformation which spans the past 200 years. In both the 'British Bill of Rights' proposals[111] and indeed in arguments in defence of human rights and the Human Rights Act, we can observe practices which seek to establish a continuity to Magna Carta, of course with different objectives. Hobsbawm provides some explanation for the use of the past in this way. He remarks:

> ... the past remains the most useful analytical tool for coping with constant change, but in a novel form. It turns in to the discovery of history as a process of directional change, of development or evolution. Change thus becomes its own legitimation, but it is thereby anchored to a transformed 'sense of the past'... In brief, what legitimates the present and explains it is not now the past as a set of reference points ... or even as duration ... but the past as a process of becoming the present.[112]

Traditions cannot be 'invented' if there is no way of propagating them and entrenching them. This, of course, is where the media is at its most powerful. It is hardly radical to remark that what we know about the world around us is 'largely attributable' to the media in its myriad forms.[113] The media, not exclusively of course, is crucial in the success of invented traditions. Eugenia Siapera summarises the mediation of invented traditions succinctly:

> Invented traditions must be replayed and disseminated regularly across the nation if they are to take hold. The media can become an important means by which such invented traditions are disseminated and replayed, eventually forming part of the nation's consciousness.[114]

Cameron roots his call to a 'modern British Bill of Rights' in a tradition of British values that asserts itself historically all the way back to Magna Carta.

110 E Hobsbawm, 'Inventing Traditions' (n 19 above) 1.

111 D Cameron, 'Balancing Freedom and Security: A Modern British Bill of Rights' (26 June 2006) available online at: https://conservative-speeches.sayit.mysociety.org/speech/600031

112 E Hobsbawm, *On History* (n 85 above) 23.

113 David Berg, 'Rhetoric, Reality and Mass Media' (1972) 58 *The Quarterly Journal of Speech* 255.

114 E Siapera, Cultural Diversity and Global Media: The Mediation of Difference (Wiley Blackwell, 2010) 21.

Repealing the 1998 Act is of no consequence because, even if copies of the Charter 'have faded ... its principles shine as brightly as ever'.[115] So the past becomes a process of explaining the present and of legitimising new directions. The challenges of contemporary society – the threat of terrorism, crime rates and insecurity – are, according to the Conservative narrative, all compounded in difficulty by the existence of the Human Rights Act; and it is not *even* British. British traditions, then, provide the answers. But something is needed to fill the gap once the Act is repealed. For one thing, rights-regarding Conservatives, the so-called 'Runnymede Tories', need to be placated. Thus, a 'British Bill of Rights'. The 800th anniversary of Magna Carta provided the legitimating reference point for inventing this new tradition and for commandeering this new direction.

On the other side of the debates, a similar instrumentalism of Magna Carta is at work. In an age where human rights are under attack and, at least in aca demic circles, under sustained critique, the past is engaged to convince. Human rights are the result of a progressive historical trajectory that began in Runnymede, evolved in London, was developed later in Rome, Geneva, New York and Strasbourg and returned home as the Human Rights Act. This entrenching of rights right through history seeks to legitimate the present. Human rights today has a simple story to tell, of progress, of inevitability. What is the value though in usurping the past as 'a vast preparation for the way things are, and the way people think, right now?'[116] Amongst other chasms of knowledge, this narration loses the sense of the past, elides power struggles and histories of struggles of all forms, it obfuscates how the powerful have instrumentalised rights language through the ages and it disguises the power-preserving nature of rights whether in supranational or domestic institutions. Defending rights by rooting them in history comes with risks. Moyn observes: 'if historians miss how different rights were in the past, they will fail even to recognize what it would take to explain rights in the present'.[117] Beyond the crudeness of reaching in to history to establish abstract roots for abstract entities, for those defending the Act, there are shortfalls in the 'human rights are not in fact alien' approach. First, success might depend on who can invent the more appealing or credible tradition. And our examination of Magna Carta in the media has not provided much evidence to suggest that the Act defenders are winning. Second, they miss the chance to defend the Act and rights on their own terms, that is, to explain how they actually improve our lot. Finally, they fail to engage with the very reasons for antipathy to the Act.[118]

115 D Cameron, 'British Values' Mail on Sunday (15 June 2014) available online at: www.dailymail.co.uk/debate/article-2658171/DAVID-CAMERON-British-values-arent-optional-theyre-vital-Thats-I-promote-EVERY-school-As-row-rages-Trojan-Horse-takeover-classrooms-Prime-Minister-delivers-uncompromising-pledge.html

116 Moyn, *The Uses of History* (n 21 above) xii.

117 *Ibid.*, 8.

118 For more on this, see Colm O'Cinnéide's chapter in this volume. C O'Cinnéide, 'Arguing the Case for Human Rights in Brexit Britain' Chapter 9.

Conclusion

Gearty asks, elegantly: 'How has the UK reached the point that it has, where invented versions of a golden past are being allowed to drive the country in an (to every sense) impoverished future.'[119] The answer lies, in part, in the success of the repeal side's 'invented tradition' of British rights rooted in Magna Carta. This version of the British rights tradition has been strategically invented in opposition to the alien, interfering and unacceptable European rights espoused in Strasbourg and domesticated through the Human Rights Act. The ruling elite, hell bent on repealing the Human Rights Act and fomenting opposition to Strasbourg, have deployed Magna Carta, strategically, to appease the libertarians and to disguise their rights-curtailing (if not, rights-eroding) intentions. The British Bill of Rights – homegrown rights rooted in the glorious tradition of Magna Carta – is the ideological endpoint of the repeal imagination.

It is the oppositional narrative at the heart of this invented tradition that invites so much media attention. The refrain of Britishness underpins this resistance to Europe and to human rights and it makes good headlines. It does not matter that this vision of the historical past is fictitious; the present condition of human rights is also irrelevant.

By locking horns with the repeal side on their own terms – the Britishness of rights and the value of the European human rights system – the Human Rights Act defenders have been tactically unconvincing and far from headline grabbing. The defenders need to up their game. At the very least, they need to expose the ideology at the heart of the repeal vision. They may also need to take a hard look at their own ideological persuasions. In this respect, the repealers and the defenders have a lot in common. The future is impoverished, not because the glorious present characterised by human rights protection is under threat, but because we are steeped in a mythical present rooted in 'invented traditions'.

Bibliography

M Amos, 'Transplanting Human Rights Norms: The Case of the United Kingdom's Human Rights Act' (2013) *Human Rights Quarterly* 386.

J Atkins, 'Re-Imagining Magna Carta: Myth, Metaphor and the Rhetoric of Britishness' (2016) 69 *Parliamentary Affairs* 603.

E Bates, *The Evolution of the European Convention on Human Rights and Fundamental Freedoms* (Oxford University Press, 2010).

D Berg, 'Rhetoric, Reality and Mass Media' (1972) 58 *The Quarterly Journal of Speech* 255.

T Bingham, 'The Human Rights Act: A View from the Bench' (2010) 6 *EHRLR* 568.

T Bingham, 'Governments and Judges: Friends or Enemies?' in T Bingham, *Lives of the Law: Selected Essays and Speeches 2000–2010* (OUP, 2011).

P Boateng and J Straw, 'Bringing Rights Home: Labour's Plans to Incorporate the European Convention on Human Rights and Fundamental Freedoms in UK law' (1997) *European Human Rights Law Review* 71.

119 C Gearty, xiii.

B Bowring, *The Degradation of the International Legal Order? The Rehabilitation of Law and the Possibility of Politics* (Routledge-Cavendish, 2008).

T Campbell, K Ewing and A Tomkins (eds), *Sceptical Essays on Human Rights* (Oxford University Press, 2001).

P Coss, 'Presentism and the Myth of Magna Carta' (2017) 234 *Past and Present* 227.

M Dillon, 'Magna Carta and the United States Constitution: An Exercise in Building Fences' in D B Magraw, A Martinez and R E Brownell II (eds) *Magna Carta and the Rule of Law* (ABA Publishing, 2014).

M Duranti, *The Conservative Human Rights Revolution: European Identity, Transnational Politics, and the Origins of the European Convention* (Oxford University Press, 2017).

K Ewing, 'The Human Rights Act and Parliamentary Democracy' (1999) 62 *Modern Law Review* 80.

J Fernández-Villaverde 'Magna Carta, the rule of law, and the limits on government' (2016) 47 *Int'l Rev of Law and Economics* 22.

C Gearty, *On Fantasy Island: Britain, Europe, and Human Rights* (OUP, 2016).

G G George, 'UK Supreme Court Versus US Supreme Court: Modern Use of Magna Carta' in E Gibson-Morgan and A Chommeleux, 'The Rights and Aspirations of the Magna Carta' (Palgrave Macmillan, 2016).

L Gies, 'A Villains' Charter? The Press and the Human Rights Act' (2001) 7(2) *Crime, Media, Culture* 167.

C Greenwood, 'Magna Carta and the Development of Modern International Law' (2016) 49 *Israel Law Review* 435.

R H Helmholz, 'The Myth of Magna Carta Revisited' (2016) 94 *North Carolina Law Review* 1475.

E Hobsbawm and T Ranger (eds), *The Invention of Tradition* (Cambridge University Press, 2012).

E Hobsbawm, *On History* (Abacus, 1997).

J C Holt, *Magna Carta* (Cambridge University Press, 1992)

D Kennedy, 'The international human rights movement: part of the problem?' (2001) 3 *HRLR* 245.

F Klug, *A Magna Carta for All Humanity: Homing in on Human Rights* (Routledge, 2015).

H Lauterpacht, 'The Universal Declaration of Human Rights' (1948) 25 *BYIL* 354.

A Lester, 'U.K. acceptance of the Strasbourg jurisdiction: what really went on in Whitehall in 1965' (1998) *Public Law* 237.

A Lester, 'The Utility of the Human Rights Act: A Reply to Keith Ewing' (2005) *Public Law* 249.

A Lester, *Five Ideas to Fight For: How Our Freedom is Under Threat and Why it Matters* (Oneworld Publications, 2016).

W S McKechnie, *Magna Carta: A Commentary on the Great Charter of King John* (2nd ed. Glasgow, J Maclehose and Sons, 1914).

J Melton and R Hazell 'Magna Carta … Holy Grail?' in R Hazell and J Melton (eds), *Magna Carta and Its Modern Legacy* (CUP, 2015).

R Mortimore 'What Magna Carta Means to the Modern British Public' in R Hazell and J Melton (eds), *Magna Carta and Its Modern Legacy* (CUP, 2015).

S Moyn, *The Last Utopia: Human Rights in History* (The Belknapp Press of Harvard University Press, 2010).

S Moyn, *The Uses of History* (Verso, 2014).

C Murray, 'The Magna Carta's tainted legacy: historic justifications for a British Bill of Rights and the case against the Human Rights Act' in Frederick Cowell (ed.), *Critically Examining the Case Against the 1998 Human Rights Act* (Routledge, 2018).

S Sedley, 'Bringing rights home: time to start a family?' (2008) 28.3 *Legal Studies* 327

E Siapera, *Cultural Diversity and Global Media: The Mediation of Difference* (Wiley Blackwell, 2010).

A W B Simpson, *Human Rights and the End of Empire: Britain and the Genesis of the European Convention* (OUP, 2001).

R V Turner, *Magna Carta: Through the Ages* (Routledge, 2003).

S J Wermiel, 'Magna Carta in Supreme Court Jurisprudence' in D B Magraw, A Martinez and R E Brownell II (eds) *Magna Carta and the Rule of Law* (ABA Publishing, 2014).

Index